MILLER'S

pottery & porcelain marks

including a comprehensive guide to artists, makers, factories and forms

Gordon Lang

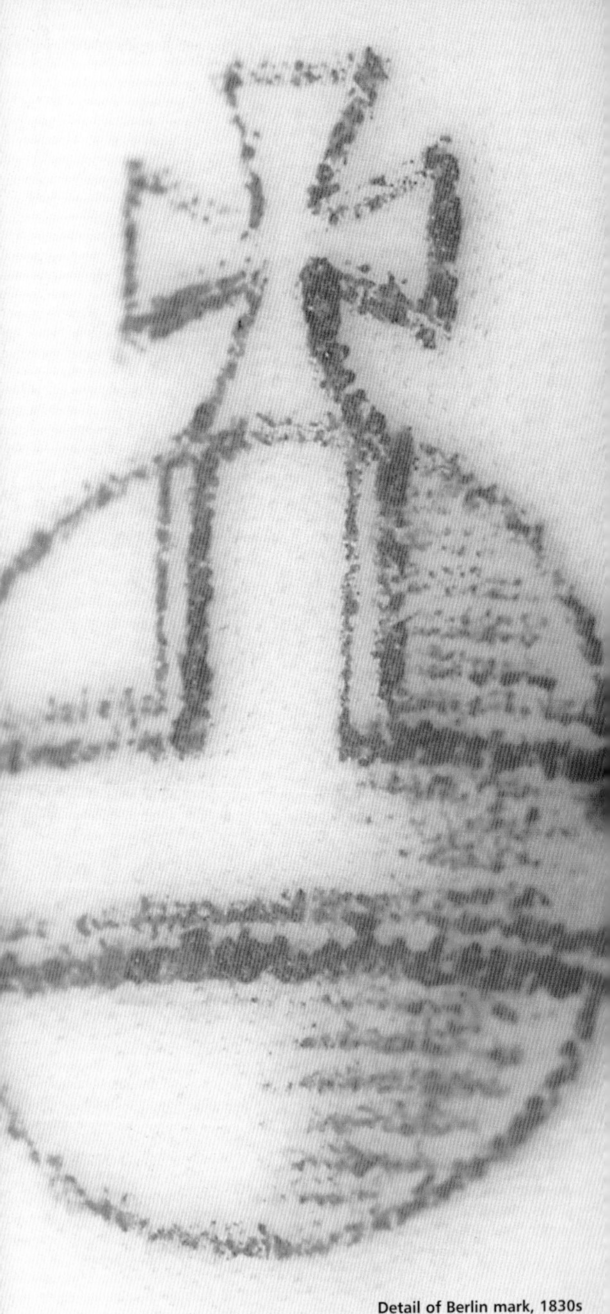

Detail of Berlin mark, 1830s

Miller's Pottery & Porcelain Marks

Gordon Lang

First published in Great Britain in 1995 by Miller's, a division of Mitchell Beazley, both imprints of Octopus Publishing Group Ltd, 2–4 Heron Quays, London E14 4JP
Miller's is a registered trademark of Octopus Publishing Group Ltd, an Hachette Livre UK company.

Reprinted 1996, 1997, 1998 (twice), reissued 2000, reprinted 2003 (twice), 2004, 2005, revised and updated 2007.

A CIP catalogue record for this book is available from the British Library.

ISBN 9781 84533 347 8

Set in ITC Galliard & News Gothic
Colour origination in China by Sang Choy
Printed and bound in China by Toppan

Managing Editor Valerie Lewis
Project Editor Caroline Bugeja
Copy Editor Jo Thom
Designers Mark Winwood, Angel Design & Print
Editorial Assistants MiniMel Smith, Ethne Tragett, Alexandra Lewis-Wortley
Proofreader Clare Hacking
Illustrator Amanda Patton
Indexer Hilary Bird
Production Lucy Carter
Photography Robin Saker, Paul Harding, Jonill Mayer
American Consultant Ellen Paul Denker

Contents

Detail of Worcester mark, 19thC

HOW TO USE THIS BOOK

This new colour edition is divided into a number of sections. Within each section, each entry includes the dates when the factory or potter was in production, the types of wares produced and details of different marks used. Where the same maker is featured more than once, cross references indicate where the main entry can be found. The name of the firm or producer is given first; additions or changes to the style of the manufacturer appear in brackets. The location of the manufacturer appears next, including the county, state or region, followed by the country of origin. The sections are as follows:

Maps

This section shows the main pottery and porcelain-producing centres in China, Japan, Italy, France, Northern Europe, Britain and the USA.

Graphic Marks

This section illustrates different types of marks which can stand alone as a guide to the origin of a piece. These are based on written letters or words, and on symbols or devices.

Single Letters lists marks featuring one letter or multiples of the same letter in alphabetical order.
Initials lists marks featuring initials in alphabetical order.
Monograms lists monogram marks used by makers alphabetically, according to the most dominant letter in the design. If the monogram does not appear to have one dominant letter, it is advisable to check this section under each letter visible within the monogram.
Written Name & Signature Marks lists alphabetically marks that are, or appear to have been, handwritten, according to the surname of the individual potter or the title of the firm. Where the firm or potter's name is unclear, the entry has been placed under the first letter that appears.
Letters & Devices lists marks comprising devices or symbols that appear with the initial or initials of a factory or potter. The initials appear in alphabetical order. The devices appear in the order detailed on the contents page.
Devices lists marks comprising devices or symbols that appear either on their own, or with the name of a factory or potter. The devices appear in the order detailed on the contents page. To aid identification, devices that have a similar form or style appear together so that subtle differences can be detected.
Staffordshire-type Marks include the Royal Arms, the Garter mark, and the Staffordshire knot mark. While these types of marks usually appear on British pottery and

porcelain, they were also used by manufacturers in the USA and Europe. For each type, there is an alphabetical list of the factory name or initials that appear with the device. Many factories used these marks; those featured here used them as one of their principal marks.

Name & Initial Marks

The marks of many factories are characterized by distinguishing name or initial marks. These may appear on their own or in combination with graphic marks. They may be stencilled, incised, impressed, painted or transfer-printed. Several manufacturers detailed in this section used a large number of marks, many of which were characterized by the same name or initials. The name and initial marks in this section appear alphabetically, according to the form in which the name appears in the mark; variations of the names used by the same potter or factory may appear in brackets, or on a new line.

Chinese & Japanese Marks

The Chinese Ming Dynasty (1368–1643) represents the first systematic marking of ceramics. This section illustrates the marks used during the reigns of the emperors of the Ming and Qing (1644–1916) Dynasties, together with information on the types and styles of wares produced during each period, and details of any other marks that may appear on Chinese ceramics.

Marks on Japanese ceramics are often more problematical than those on Chinese porcelain. Japanese dynastic or reign marks were not used before the 19thC. From about 1640 potters often borrowed Chinese Ming reign marks, particularly those of Chenghua and Xuande.

Additional Information

This section includes the following:

Fakes & Copies details of fakes and copies of ceramics from China, Italy, France, Germany, Holland, Britain and the USA.
Appendices contains information on British Patent Office Registration Marks, and details of the year marks and cyphers used by Derby, Minton, Sèvres, Wedgwood and Worcester. A list of important painters', gilders', sculptors' and potters' monograms and symbols found on pieces made at Sèvres is also included.
Glossary a detailed list of terms used in ceramics.

INTRODUCTION

Gordon Lang

The production of ceramics is one of the world's oldest crafts, together with the making of flint tools, basketry and textile weaving. Archaeological evidence of these skills provides us with the basis of our social history. It is the durability of ceramics that sets them apart, however, and they play a vital role in helping us to understand the history on which our cultures rely. Decoration found on pottery and porcelain can tell us a great deal about earlier times. For instance, very many pieces of Italian *istoriato* maiolica show scenes from the history of Greece and Rome or from mythology. There are very few examples of early 16th-century maiolica painted with biblical or religious subjects, suggesting that the influence of the Church was relatively weak at this time and that the Classical world was an area of great interest.

In the 17th century, the vast output of blue and white, rather than polychrome, tin-glazed earthenware in Delft, Holland, is visible proof of the extensive trading links with the Far East, in particular the porcelain of China. In the following century, the delicate porcelain tea and coffee services made at Meissen and Sèvres tell us of sophisticated people with time to dawdle and converse over a cup of a fashionable drink. In the 19th century, the Industrial Revolution is evident not only in the mechanized methods of production, but also in the decorative motifs, such as railways, ships and bridges, that were used on many pieces. Therefore, the collecting and studying of ceramics gives us at least a glimpse of life at other times and places.

Unless one concentrates on early pottery such as Greek or Roman or pre-Tang Chinese ware when pieces were rarely marked in any way, marks are very important in helping to establish the date and place of manufacture. The word 'helping' is a deliberate choice: unfortunately marks are not sacrosanct, and one soon learns, for example, that the crescent mark based on the arms of the city of Worcester was also used by the factories at Bow and Lowestoft, and there are many similar examples. Anyone venturing into the study of Chinese ceramics will soon find that very few reign marks are contemporary with the date of manufacture. Thus, one should not get too excited upon the discovery of the reign mark of the Emperor Chenghua (1465–87): as the porcelains of this period were among the finest ever made, the mark was frequently added by later potters to humbler porcelains. The fact that later potters in China practised this type of 'forgery' almost as a matter of course, is widely understood today, and most people seeking advice on pieces with important reign marks do so with a healthy amount of scepticism.

Japanese ceramics are more problematic than Chinese because many marks were borrowed from China and individual potters were numerous and rarely encountered.

During his or her professional life, a dealer or specialist will acquire a knowledge of those marks that are most commonly faked, as well as some of the more obscure forgeries. Within a relatively short period of time, most people can learn important examples of the former: Emile Samson's 19th-century copies of Worcester, Meissen or Chelsea; Paris hard-paste fakes of early Sèvres soft-paste; and the Dresden pastiches of early Meissen. Almost all of these are inscribed, often with marks deliberately designed to resemble the original. However, the material and the quality of the painted decoration should not fool anyone with even a little experience. For example, while Samson copies of Worcester feature the Worcester crescent, or square flag-shaped seal mark, the greyish, glittery, hard-paste porcelain of the Samson version is quite unlike the irregular, speckled surface and softer appearance of the Worcester original. Likewise, a Samson copy of a Meissen figure will have a very smooth, slightly brushed, pure white surface, which contrasts with the grey-white, flecked, textured Meissen body. Note too, that what looks like the crossed swords of Meissen may simply be the crossed batons of Samson. Therefore it is essential to study the different pastes and colours of each factory in order to be more certain of making a correct attribution.

In order to gain a fuller understanding of ceramics, as well as looking at the mark a piece should be studied from the base upwards, taking into consideration the type and colour of the material used, the appearance and tone of the glaze, how the piece has been made and the colours used in the decoration. Remember, also, that there may be variations in colour or glaze on pieces made in the same region, or even at the same kilns, due to the temperature of the part of the kiln at which a particular piece was fired.

Using a book such as this, together with a close examination of a piece, should make this area of collecting a fascinating and rewarding one.

About this Book

There are a good number of books covering the subject of marks on ceramics; while many are excellent in their way, covering British, European, American and Oriental pottery and porcelain, few of them cover the number of areas included here, and certainly not in such a portable form. This book will be a handy companion when looking around antique shops, auction rooms and car-boot sales.

The range of material covered in this book includes factory marks and other marks commonly used by individual potters or manufacturers which may help to identify the origin of a particular piece. Also included are date marks, such as Chinese reign marks, details of the design registration marks used on British ceramics, and a number of examples of dated inscriptions that may be typical of a group or period. Specialist year marks (numbers, letters or cyphers) used by certain major manufacturers are also included.

The marking of pottery and porcelain is an erratic and often inexact science. The marks included in this book have been arranged in the most logical order possible, but this has not always proved to be the most straightforward exercise. When looking up a particular mark in this book, it is always worth a closer look at the mark on the piece to see whether the main factory name is present, however small, as the index will then refer you to all the different entries for that particular manufacturer. If the factory name does not appear on the mark, but it does feature a symbol or a device (such as a crown, anchor, crescent, triangle, or bird), the mark may be included within the two sections on devices. Where the device appears with the initials of the maker, you should refer to Letters & Devices; where no initials are present then go to Devices. Sometimes, where a manufacturer uses a large number of different devices, or no device at all, the name or initials used by the firm may be located in Name & Initial Marks.

Marks that have been omitted include those that may hinder or confuse the collector, such as the majority of individual workman's or decorator's marks, which may appear as monograms on pieces by particular factories. Important marks that appear on wares decorated at Sèvres have been included however, and appear in the Appendices on p360.

With few exceptions the marks illustrated are representative of a factory, pottery or an individual. With early, handwritten marks there is inevitably some variation on each piece, and it is not unusual to see abbreviations or omissions of secondary names on some pieces. For example, Francesco Xanto Avelli da Rovigo, a leading painter of Italian maiolica in the second quarter of the 16th century, sometimes signed his name in full or simply used initials or one of several other combinations. Where variations exist, we have tried to include as many as possible.

Chinese reign marks from the Ming and Qing Dynasties have been included in this book. It is worth noting that these have been copied extensively both by later Chinese potters, and by manufacturers in Japan. Factory marks were not used on early Japanese pottery and porcelain. Those that do appear are numerous and confusing: as well as marks copied from Chinese ceramics, a large number of artists' signatures and other marks were used, often a seal, or written characters. The fine Japanese porcelains of the 18th century (Kakiemon, Nabeshima and Hirado), rarely feature marks.

Marks on Islamic and other south-east Asian pottery and porcelain, such as Korean, Cambodian and Thai, are not included in this book as there is no consistency in their marks. Factory marks are virtually unknown in these areas, although individual inscriptions are quite often found on examples of Islamic pottery.

The proliferation of factories in the 19th and 20th centuries renders it impossible to include them all, as many of these concerns were either short-lived or relatively unimportant. Furthermore, well-established manufacturers often made regular changes to their trademarks, and to include all the variations of the marks of factories with a high output would occupy more space than is available here.

Pattern numbers began to appear at the end of the 18th century and can be extremely useful when making attributions: the larger factories often used distinctive forms, such as Ridgways in Staffordshire, and Coalport in Shropshire, who have both used fractional numbers. In the second quarter of the 19th century, pattern names began to appear on mass produced transfer-printed wares, and these can help to identify pieces in the absence of the main factory mark. There are, however, so many of them that it is beyond the scope of this book to include them all, and it may be necessary to consult specialist texts for a more comprehensive list.

The intention of this book is to give a concise history of the main pottery and porcelain factories in Europe and the USA, together with a general overview of the most important factory, name and trademarks used, and their different variations. Cross references indicate where the main entry for a particular maker can be found, and the index lists all the entries for that factory that appear in the book.

A Brief History of Pottery & Porcelain Marks

Marks on ceramics fall into several categories that may determine one or more of the following: where a piece was made; who made it (the potter, decorator, factory or factory owner); and when and for whom it was made.

Types of Pottery & Porcelain marks

Incised (or scratched): where a mark is cut into the body of an unfired piece with a sharp tool, leaving a thin line. Until the late 18th century, most marks were done by hand.
Carved: where a mark is cut into soft clay leaving conspicuous trenches with sloping sides.
Impressed: where marks are inscribed by pressing a mould, stamp or stencil, made from metal or wood, into the surface of unfired clay.
Painted: where marks are painted onto the surface of pottery or porcelain. This may be under the glaze or over the glaze. Painted (and printed) marks most often appear in cobalt blue – other common colours are manganese-brown and iron-red.
Printed: where marks are created by covering a copper engraving with coloured pigment, transferring the image to thin paper, and from there onto the ceramic surface, either before or after glazing.

China

It is not until the Chinese Ming Dynasty (1368–1643) that we see the first systematic marking of ceramics. Reign marks were chosen after a new emperor ascended the throne and date from the beginning of the first new year after his accession. This system remained in use for 500 years. Early marks are either incised into the clay or painted in slip or pigment. By the Song Dynasty (960–1278) some pieces are stamped or impressed. In the early 18th century seal marks were introduced which were used concurrently with conventional script.

Japan

Japanese ceramics are rarely marked before 1700 and those that are marked 'borrow' from China otherwise they depend on simple square seal marks of an auspicious nature. The majority of Japanese marks are made within the past 150 years, especially production from Satsuma-type and Arita and Kutani porcelains.

Europe & the USA

Pottery: The earliest devices and marks are found on Italian maiolica. In northern Europe, the date 1559 is the earliest encountered in German ceramics.

The first marks used on Dutch Delftware appear around the mid-17th century; in the British Isles the 16th- and 17th-century delftware potteries never marked their wares, and it was not until the late 18th century that Josiah Wedgwood used proper factory marks. The practice was adopted by most ceramics factories in Europe and the USA.
Porcelain: The first porcelain factories began to mark their wares from the start. These marks could be based on the area, the patron or the proprietor of the factory – Meissen used the crossed swords, derived from the arms of Saxony. These hand-painted symbols or initials are typical of almost all major European porcelain factories until the early 19th century, when printed or impressed marks became the standard. Some factories such as Derby, Spode and Meissen, continued to use handwritten methods.

Patent Office Registration Marks:
By the mid-19th century, plagiarism forced British ceramic manufacturers to adopt a registration system to protect their designs and forms which safeguarded its copyright for a period of three (or after 1883 five) years, after which it was no longer protected unless the patent was renewed.

Dating pottery & porcelain marks:
There are a number of general rules for dating ceramic marks (this list primarily concerns marks used by British manufacturers). These include the following:

- Printed marks that include the Royal Arms date from the 19th or 20th century.
- Printed marks that incorporate the name of the pattern of a particular piece were made after 1810.
- Any English mark that includes 'Ltd' after the firm's title or initials must have a date later than 1855.
- The words 'Trade Mark' indicate a date subsequent to the Act of 1862.
- The inclusion of the word 'Royal' in a firm's title or trade name suggests a date in the second half of the 19th or 20th century.
- In 1891 the US introduced the McKinley Tariff Acts, whereby any exported pottery or porcelain should be marked with the country of origin. Later, probably to avoid confusion, the words 'Made in' were also added.
- The inclusion of the words 'Bone China', 'English Bone China' and other similar styles indicates a 20th-century date.

Porcelain & Pottery Forms

The following four pages feature illustrations of typical forms found in both porcelain and pottery. These can help a collector to identify the country of origin and the date of production of a particular piece.

PORCELAIN FORMS

Arita chrysanthemum dish
Japan, 19thC

Meiping
China, 18thC

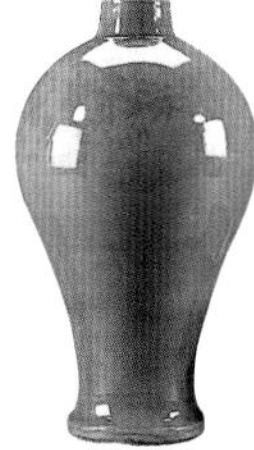

Baluster vase
China, early Ming Dynasty

Hexagonal lidded vase
China, 1680–90

Kendi
China, early 17thC

Ewer
China, early Ming Dynasty

Spode porcelain plate
Britain, c1830

Meissen coffee pot
Germany, 1765

Meissen teapot
Germany, 1740

Meissen tureen
Germany, 1725–30

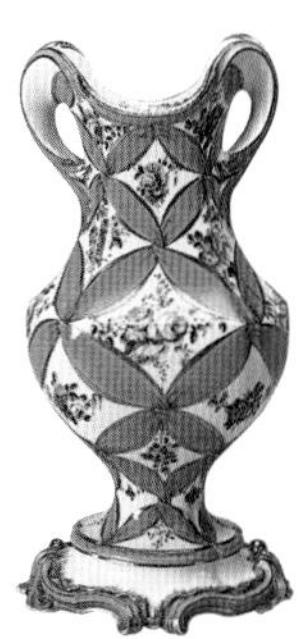

Sèvres vase
France, 1760

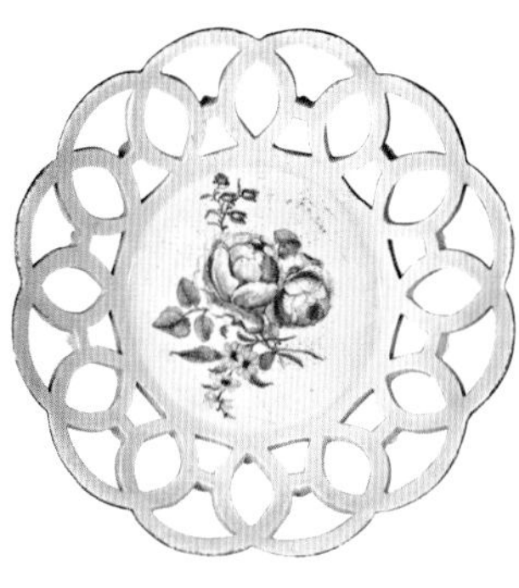

Chelsea basket
Britain, c1755

POTTERY FORMS

Wet drug jar
Italy, early 16thC

Drug jar
Italy, 16thC

Syrup jar
Italy, 16thC

Drug jar
Italy, late 16thC

Wet drug
Italy, 16th

Stoneware tankard
Germany, 17thC

Rookwood vase
America, c1900

Rookwood vessel
America, c1882

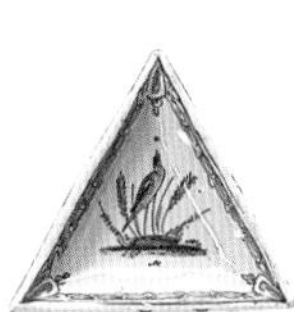

Delft dish
Britain, 18thC

Bristol delft posset pot
Britain, c1720

Dutch Delft vase
Holland, c1700

Delft wine jug
Britain, 1650

Britain & Ireland

It is not certain where the first characteristic British pottery was produced but it is likely that many of the finer examples from the 14thC were made at monasteries. In the 16th and 17thC glazed, relief-moulded slipwares were produced in Staffordshire (especially in the areas around Burslem), and at Wrotham in Kent.

Tin-glazed earthenware first appeared in Britain in the mid-16thC, in London and Norwich. London potters were responsible for the spread of English delftware to many other parts of the country, including Bristol, Wincanton, Liverpool, Glasgow and Dublin.

The production of refined pottery and porcelain was a relatively late development in the British Isles, largely advanced by European immigrants in the 17thC. Until the 18thC no British pottery bore factory marks. Tin-glazed earthenware was made at about half-a-dozen centres scattered about the British Isles; none feature factory marks in the way that Dutch Delftware pieces do. Attributions are made by excavation or by documentary inscriptions on pieces made for individuals or institutes such as the Livery Companies of London. Other types of pottery – redware, basaltes, jasper-type wares, creamware or Prattware – made in Staffordshire, Lancashire, Yorkshire or elsewhere, were rarely, if ever, marked before about 1770. Josiah Wedgwood and his contemporaries then began to impress their products with their initials or full names, and later with a number of different symbols or devices.

The early English porcelain factories were, with the odd exception, based in the great seaports of their day: London (Chelsea, Bow, Limehouse and Vauxhall), Bristol, Plymouth and Liverpool. Oddly enough, the manufacture of porcelain was an unusual activity in Staffordshire, traditionally the home of British ceramics, until the 19thC. By the middle of the 19thC Staffordshire potters were producing millions of pieces of transfer-printed earthenware for the domestic and colonial markets. Many of these pieces were marked not only with factory marks, but also with the title of the pattern.

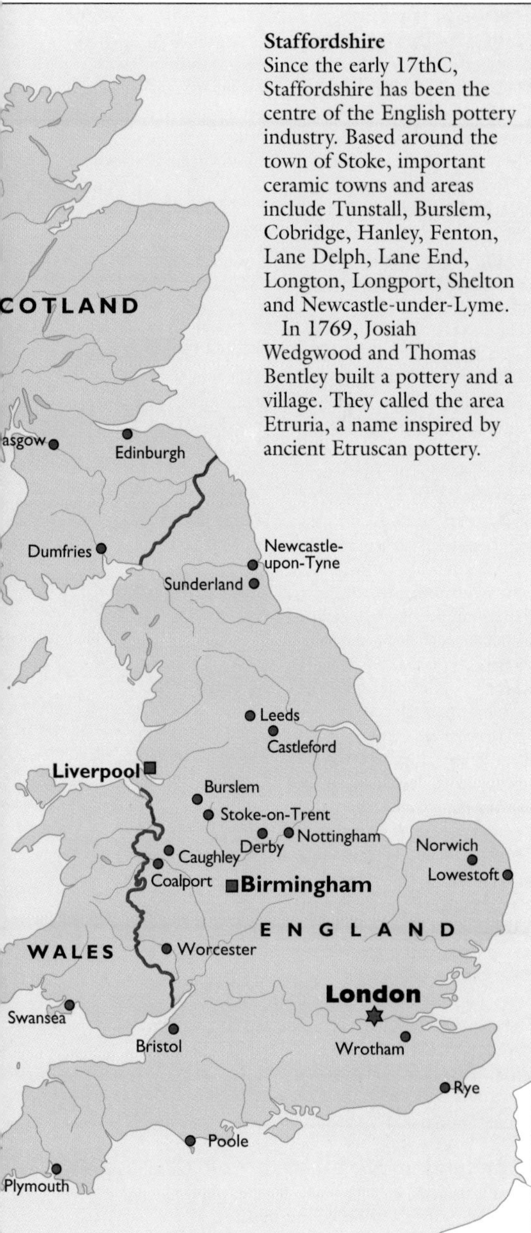

Staffordshire
Since the early 17thC, Staffordshire has been the centre of the English pottery industry. Based around the town of Stoke, important ceramic towns and areas include Tunstall, Burslem, Cobridge, Hanley, Fenton, Lane Delph, Lane End, Longton, Longport, Shelton and Newcastle-under-Lyme.

In 1769, Josiah Wedgwood and Thomas Bentley built a pottery and a village. They called the area Etruria, a name inspired by ancient Etruscan pottery.

France

Among the earliest characteristic French pottery is Bernard Palissy's 16thC relief-moulded wares that feature fish, reptiles, insects, snakes and other naturalistic objects.

Italian maiolica had a great influence on French pottery in the 16thC and faïence, as it was to be called in France, was produced in Rouen, Nîmes, Lyon and Nevers, the most important early factory.

A native French style of faïence began to develop. Rouen became the most important centre by the end of the 17thC, producing faïence that influenced potters in Paris, St Cloud, Lille, Saint-Amand-les-Eaux, Marseilles and Strasburg. Moustiers became important in the late 17thC, making pictorial panels and other wares in styles that were widely imitated.

The earliest reference to the manufacture of porcelain in France is in the patent granted to Louis Poterat of Rouen in 1673. It is not certain, however, whether porcelain was actually made in Rouen – the pieces that have been attributed to the town may have been produced at Saint Cloud. These, together with Chantilly and Mennecy, were the foremost makers in France before the establishment of Vincennes (Sèvres) in 1738. Under the royal control of Louis XV, Sèvres enjoyed a virtual monopoly in elaborately ornamented porcelains.

In the 18thC, enamel-painted earthenwares made in the style of contemporary porcelain were first produced at the factory of Paul Hannong in Strasburg. This style was also adopted at Niderviller, Marseilles, Rouen and Moustiers.

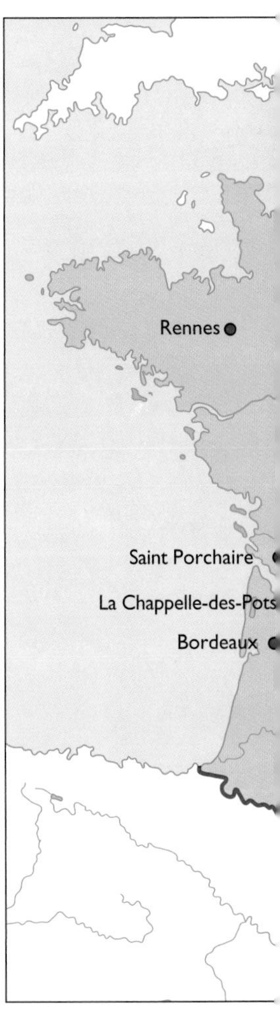

In the early 19thC, a large number of factories were set up in Paris to produce the characteristic glassy, hard-paste porcelain. In the late 19thC, the large deposits of fine porcelain clay near Limoges persuaded manufacturers to establish potteries there. In the late 18th and early 19thC, potteries began to imitate the cream-coloured earthenware made at Staffordshire in England, called *faïence fine* in France. This was made at Lunéville, Bellevue, Saint Clément, Paris and Orléans.

Northern Europe

The main ceramic-producing centres in northern Europe are based in an area now occupied by present-day Holland and Germany. There is a large, complex network of centres situated in Germany, and as a result they are illustrated here.

Some of the earliest German pottery was produced around Cologne in the Rhineland. Salt-glazed stonewares were produced at least from the 14thC in the Rhineland, and during the 16thC in Cologne, Siegburg, Raeren in Westerwald. A number of places in Saxony were important in the 17thC, including Freiburg and Altenburg. Faïence was first produced in Hanau and Frankfurt-am-Main, and later at Nuremberg, Bayreuth and in Thuringia. Enamel decoration on German porcelain and French faïence influenced wares made at Fulda and Künersberg from c1740.

The Royal porcelain factory at Meissen was established in 1710, and was the only factory in Germany producing true porcelain until the mid-18thC. After this date, however, other factories were set up in Höchst, Frankenthal, Nymphenhurg, Ludwigsburg, Fürstenburg and Berlin. The work of the independent decorator, or *Hausmaler*, who worked on both pottery and porcelain, is also important c1720–50.

The main centres in Holland are fewer and better known than those in Germany. They include Rotterdam, Amsterdam, Middleburg, Weesp and Delft. Blue and white tin-glazed earthenwares were produced at Delft in the 17th and 18thC.

Other important centres in northern Europe include the Royal factory at Copenhagen, Denmark, the Imperial factory at St Petersburg, Russia and Rörstrand in Sweden.

Italy

The first important maiolica-producing centres in Italy in the 15thC were Orvieto (possibly the oldest), Viterbo, Florence, Siena and Faenza.

The production of maiolica was well-established by the beginning of the 15thC, and output included large dishes and sets of drug jars. An important centre was Deruta where polychrome and lustre maiolica was produced. Lustreing was later taken up by potters in Gubbio.

One of the most characteristic decorative styles, *istoriato* or pictorial painting, was perfected in Castel Durante and Urbino during the first quarter of the 16thC. The style was quickly taken up by pottery painters in other areas and continued to be popular until the end of the 18thC. These areas include Siena, Castelli, Naples, Castel Durante, Pesaro, Forli, Rimini and Verona.

In the 17th and 18thC the maiolica tradition continued at Venice and Castelli, and also at centres in Sicily, such as Palermo and Caltagirone.

Efforts to make Oriental-style porcelain in Italy probably began in the 16thC. Of several recorded attempts, the only surviving examples are those pieces produced by Bernardo Buontalenti for Francesco Maria de' Medici in Florence 1575–87.

For the further production of porcelain in Italy we have to wait until c1720, when the Vezzi brothers of Venice acquired the arcanum, or secret recipe,

for hard-paste porcelain, probably from Christoph Conrad Hunger formerly of Dresden and Vienna.

In the 18thC there were two other factories in Venice (Hewelcke and Cozzi) as well as the important porcelain concerns at Capodimonte in Naples, and Doccia, near Florence.

The United States

Aside from Native American pottery, the first pottery was produced in the United States in the 17thC. One of the first makers was Philip Drinker of Charlestown, Massachusetts, active from 1635. Early ware comprised simply-decorated redwares in traditional northern European forms. By the second half of the 18thC, a distinctive style of slip-decorated redware was being made in New England, particularly Connecticut. American-style stonewares also developed during the 18thC. Porcelain experiments first began in Georgia in the mid-18thC,

but the production of porcelain started in earnest in Philadelphia c1770.

Commercial potting began in the 19thC, with important centres located in Ohio, Pennsylvania, Maryland and New Jersey by the 1880s. Most of these manufacturers produced a kind of ironstone ware that evolved from early American stoneware. The late 19thC saw the establishment of an art pottery industry in North America. Works were founded as far afield as New Orleans, California and New Hampshire. The best-known and most influential art pottery was the Rookwood factory, founded in Cincinnati, Ohio in 1880.

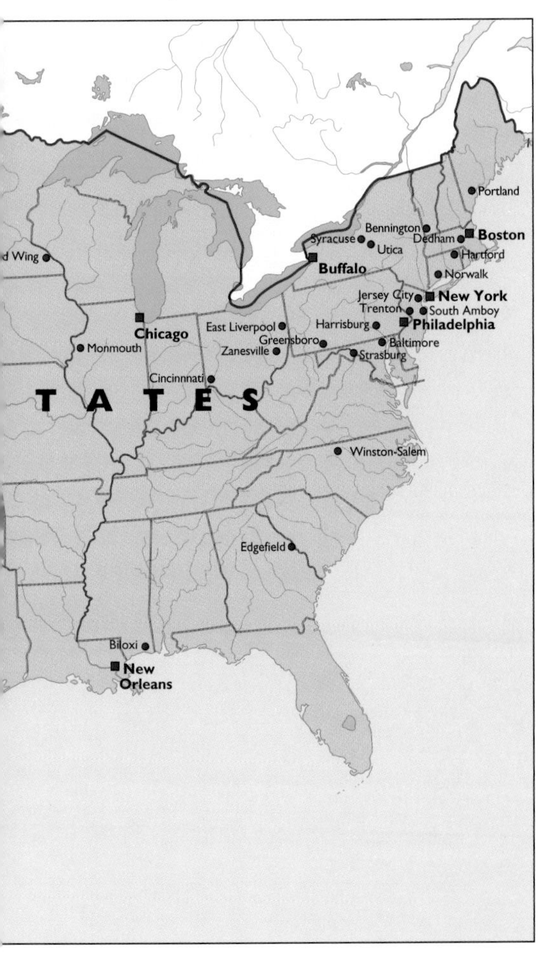

Graphic Marks

The marks shown here have an illustrated form, which can stand alone as a guide to a piece's origin. First are those that are (or appear to have been) written, incised or painted by hand (Single Letters, Initials, Monograms, Written Name & Signature Marks). Second are those that feature devices or symbols, with initials (Letters & Devices), or on their own or with the name of the factory or potter (Devices). The third category is Staffordshire-type Marks (Royal Arms, Garter Marks, and Staffordshire Knot Marks).

Detail of Wedgwood mark, 19thC

Single Letters

Detail of Caughley mark, 1775–95

SINGLE LETTERS

Ansbach *Bavaria, Germany*
Hard-paste porcelain was produced 1758–1860; the factory was transferred to Bruckberg (Bavaria) in 1762. Best pieces made c1767–85. This mark is late and appears in blue. This mark may also appear with a shield or an eagle.

Rue Thiroux *Paris, France*
Hard-paste porcelain made by Leboeuf c1775 to the 19thC, initially under the protection of Queen Marie Antoinette (1755–93). The mark registered in 1776 was 'A' stencilled in red. 'A' with a crown in underglaze blue is also used.

Bow China Works *Stratford, London, UK*
Porcelain was made c1747–76. Forms of functional wares imitate Chinese, Japanese and Meissen pieces, rococo-style decoration, figures copied from Meissen. Before 1760 the palette was delicate and original: opaque light blue, emerald-green, and crimson-purple; a soft shade of yellow was added later. The quality of the painting decreased towards the end of the period. This mark appeared on figures and late pieces in underglaze blue.

Alcora *Valencia, Spain*
This factory made faïence c1727–85, and later hard-paste porcelain and cream-coloured wares. The factory mark of a letter 'A' was used only from 1784 when rival establishments were set up in the area. The mark above is incised; the mark below appears in gold.

Alderney Pottery *Channel Islands, UK*
Studio-type pottery by Peter G. Arnold was first made at Leatherhead in Surrey 1958–62, and the Alderney Pottery, Channel Islands from 1962. Painted mark used from 1958.

Avoncroft Pottery *Hampton Lovett, Nr Droitwich, Hereford and Worcester, UK*
Established by Geoffrey Whiting, Studio-type earthenwares were made from 1952. This impressed seal mark appears within a circular outline.

'Amphora' Porzellanfabrik, *Turn, Bohemia, Czech Republic*
General pottery was made by Riessner & Kessel from 1894. This is one of many marks used.

St Agnes Pottery *Cornwall, UK*
Earthenwares made by A. and N. Homer 1953–57. This seal mark was used by A. Homer.

François-Antoine Anstett
Baden-Baden, Germany
A faïence and porcelain factory was founded here in 1770 by Zacharias Pfalzer, but was abandoned in 1778. In 1793 a new factory was established by Lorenz Müller, who made English-style earthenware. In 1795 he was succeeded by François-Antoine Anstett who became sole proprietor in 1800. His glazed earthenware featured this mark.

Jacques Vermonet
Boissette, Seine-et-Marne, France
Faïence was made in Boisette from 1732. Hard-paste porcelain was later produced by Jacques Vermonet and son 1778–92. This mark on porcelain appears in underglaze blue.

Jacques Féburier and Jean Bossu
Lille, France
Faïence was made here 1696–1802, in a factory founded by Jacques Féburier (d1729) and Jean Bossu, a painter. This mark was used.

Boscean Pottery
St Just-in-Penwith, Cornwall, UK
Studio-type stonewares made by Scott Marshall and Richard Jenkins (both had worked at the Leach Pottery) from 1962. Impressed seal mark.

Antoine Bonnefoy
Marseilles, Bouches-du-Rhône, France
Antoine Bonnefoy (d1793) ran a faïence factory in Marseilles in the late 17th and early 18thC. Bonnefoy's factory operated between 1762 and c1827 and his son Augustin took over after his death. Porcelain was made after 1803.

Johann Valentin Bontemps
Nuremberg, Bavaria, Germany
This is believed to be the mark of faïence painter Johann Valentin Bontemps (1698–1775), whose work is recorded at Nuremberg in 1729, and who also worked at Ansbach and Bayreuth.

Bow China Works *Stratford, London, UK*
See p31. This mark is a rough, incised workman's mark, c1750–60.

Worcester Porcelains
Hereford and Worcester, UK
This the main factory at Worcester produced porcelains from c1751. The history of the factory is classified by periods – the first or 'Dr. Wall' period c1751–83 is named after one of the founders, Dr. John Wall, who worked closely with the first manager William Davis. The second or 'Flight' period, 1783–92 is named after Thomas Flight, the firm's London agent who bought the factory for his sons. The third period, 'Barr and Flight & Barr' (c1792–1807) occurs after the Flight brothers went into partnership with Martin Barr, and the fourth and fifth periods were named 'Barr, Flight & Barr' (c1807–13), and 'Flight, Barr & Barr' (c1813–40). The Kerr and Binns period is c1852–62. It was known as the Worcester Royal Porcelain Company Ltd (Royal Worcester) from 1862. Output includes decorative and tablewares; figures were rare before the late 19thC. The incised 'B' mark on tea wares was used c1792.

Belvedere factory *Warsaw, Poland*
Faïence was made from 1774. Chinese, and Japanese Imari-style items, imitating German pieces, especially Meissen, were made.

Basing Farm Pottery
Ashington, West Sussex, UK
Studio-type pottery by John N. S. Green from 1962. This is an impressed pottery seal mark.

Booths (Limited) *Tunstall, Staffordshire, UK*
Earthenwares were made at the Church Bank Pottery in Tunstall 1891–1948. The company incorporated the Swan and Soho Potteries from c1912. This painted or printed mark appeared on reproductions of antique Worcester porcelains made from opaque earthenware.

Cafaggiolo *Nr Florence, Italy*
Maiolica made from late 15th to mid-18thC. The palette includes a dark red, a strong dark blue, orange and lemon-yellows, and a strong, transparent green. This mark appears on a piece dated 1506, painted with gothic foliage.

Moscow *Russia*
Porcelain factory run by Safronoff from c1820. The Cyrillic 'C' (for 'S') of this mark can be mistaken for the'G' of Gardner (see p37).

Capel Ceramics *London, UK*
Established by Anthony and Elizabeth Lane in 1962, this workshop produced Studio-type pottery, jewellery, dishes etc. They used this impressed seal or painted initial mark.

Caughley Porcelain Works
Nr Brosely, Shropshire, UK
Good porcelain made in the Worcester style c1775–99. In 1799 the works were taken over by the Coalport factory. These printed and painted 'C' marks were used 1775–95, and are sometimes mistaken for the Worcester crescent mark (see p240).

Münden *Hanover, Germany*
A faïence factory was established here c1737 by Carl Friedrich von Hanstein, which remained in operation until 1854. This mark based on the arms of von Hanstein was used 1737–93. May appear in conjunction with a painter's mark.

Höchst *Nr Mainz, Germany*
The Höchst factory was established when Adam Friedrich von Löwenfinck, with the financial backing of two Frankfurt merchants, Johann Christoph Göltz and Johann Felician Clarus, obtained permission from Elector Emmerrich Joseph von Breidenbach to begin production. Löwenfinck was a porcelain painter, who had previously worked in Meissen, Bayreuth, Ansbach and Fulda. Löwenfinck left in 1749 after Göltz had become sole proprietor. After Göltz's death the factory was taken over by the elector until the stock was sold in 1796. Plates, dishes, jugs, tureens, vases and figures were made in faïence and porcelain. The distinctive wheel mark was used with painters' marks. The letter 'C' with the Höchst wheel (see also p235) is the mark of painter Lothar Charlot, c1748. This mark appears in crimson.

Flörsheim *Nr Frankfurt-am-Main, Germany*
A faïence factory was founded here in 1765 by Georg Ludwig Müller and was sold in 1763 to the Carthusian Monks of Mainz, who leased the premises until they were sold in 1797. The factory still exists today. Made functional wares in blue or high-fired colours. Cream-coloured earthenware was made in the later period. The mark seen here is a painter's mark found on faïence made at Flörsheim.

Derby Porcelain Works *Derbyshire, UK*
The original factory at Derby was founded c1750 by William Duesbury and closed in 1848. A new company was formed in 1878 and is still in existence. Periods of production are broken down into the Duesbury period (1750–c1820) and the Bloor period (c1820–48). The Crown Derby Porcelain Co was formed in 1878 and the prefix 'Royal' was added after 1890. Although most pieces made c1750–80 were unmarked, this incised mark was used.

Hamburg *Germany*
One of the earliest German faïence factories existed here for around 50 years from c1625. Much of the output consisted of large jugs and dishes, painted in blue with yellow, and more rarely green and brownish-red. Painters' marks, such as this one from c1625–30, are found.

Barthélémy Dorez *Lille, France*
This mark is found on faïence and soft-paste porcelain made at the factory from 1711 to c1820.

Damm *Nr Aschaffenburg, Germany*
White and cream-coloured earthenware was made in a factory founded by Anna Maria Müllerand and continued by her son, from 1827. It is chiefly known for its reproductions of Höchst figures (see p34) that featured the Höchst wheel together with the letter 'D'.

Hubert Letellier *Rouen, Seine-Inférieure, France*
Mark used by potter Hubert Letellier from 1781. After 1805, he made cream-coloured earthenware and other imitations of English wares.

Ginori Factory *Doccia, Nr Florence, Italy*
The potteries at Doccia were founded in 1735 by the Marquis Carlo Ginori and remains in the hands of the Ginori family. All types of pottery and porcelain were made in the 19thC. These incised marks appear on porcelain from c1810.

Fürstenberg *Brunswick, Germany*
A porcelain factory was founded here in 1747 by Duke Carl I of Brunswick; its principal period was 1770–1814, but it is still in operation today. The mark above is an example of an early mark, and appears in blue. A further mark was used by the factory in the late 18th and early 19thC, and appears in blue.

Kastrup Factory *Copenhagen, Denmark*
The Kastrup factory, situated on the island of Amager to the east of Copenhagen, was started by the Danish Court Architect Jacob Fortling. The factory produced faïence, initially under the guidance of J. A. Hannong of Strasbourg. The mark of a letter 'F' in manganese was used by Fording, and subsequently by his widow after his death in 1761.

Cornelius Funcke *Berlin, Germany*
The factory of Dutchman Cornelius Funcke (d1733), was founded in Berlin in 1699. He made faïence wares in a distinctive style, especially vases with scrolls or baroque panels on coloured grounds. Otherwise decoration is similar to Delft wares in the Chinese style. The factory closed c1760. This mark was one of those used.

Joseph Fauchier
Marseilles, Bouches-du-Rhône, France
Joseph Fauchier I established a factory in Marseilles in 1711 making faïence painted in blue in similar style to Rouen wares. After his death in 1751, his son Joseph Fauchier II took over the factory.

Doccia *Nr Florence, Italy*
See p35. These incised marks are found on fine-paste porcelain, 1792–1815.

Count Ferniani *Faenza, Emilia, Italy*
The factory of Count Ferniani and his descendants, 1693–1900, made maiolica decorated with Chinese and French-style designs. This mark was used in the 18thC.

Joseph Fouque *Moustiers, Basse-Alpes, France*
Joseph Fouque (1714–1800) founded a factory in partnership with Jean François Pelloquin (1715–75). Fouque also acquired the Clérissy factory in 1783, and the operation continued until 1852. This mark is attributed to the factory.

F.F.

Giuseppe and Andrea Fontebasso
Treviso, Venezia, Italy
From the late 17th to the early 18thC soft-paste porcelain was made at Treviso by brothers Giuseppe and Andrea Fontebasso, who later produced cream-coloured earthenware. This mark has been found with the date 1779.

·F·F·

Flaminio Fontana *Urbino, Italy*
Maiolica was made in Urbino c1520–18thC. The area is known for its narrative *istoriato* wares, which are characterized by a rich amber yellow. This mark is attributed to painter Flaminio Fontana, dated 1583.

STAFFORDSHIRE F. F. ENGLAND

Fancies Fayre Pottery *Staffordshire, UK*
This Staffordshire pottery made earthenwares, figures and 'fancies' at Hanley (c1946–51), and Shelton (from c1951). This impressed or printed mark was used from 1950.

G.

Berlin *Prussia, Germany*
In 1761 the porcelain factory in Berlin begun by Wilhelm Wegely in 1752 with the backing of Frederick the Great (1712–86), was taken over by financier Johann Ernst Gotzkowsky. In 1763 he sold the undertaking to the King, together with a large stock of unglazed wares. It is therefore not certain that all the marked pieces (figures and tablewares) with the Gotzkowsky mark seen here were painted in this period. The factory has remained state property to the present day.

G

Moscow *Russia*
The main porcelain factory in Moscow was established c1765 by an Englishman, Francis Gardner. High quality porcelain was made, and figures were modelled in a characteristic, vigorous style. The factory remained in the Gardner family until 1891. This mark was used, together with the Cyrillic letter 'G' in the Russian alphabet.

G

Gera *Thuringia, Germany*
A porcelain factory was founded in Gera in 1779 by Johann Gottlob Ehwaldt and Johann Gottlob Gottbrecht, but was taken over by the Greiner family. Thuringian porcelain is generally greyish in tone, and most was intended for the mass market. Hard-paste porcelain tablewares and figures were made. This mark appears.

G.

Countess Anna Barbara von Gaschin
Glienitz, Silesia, Germany
Faïence production began in 1753 in a factory owned by Countess Anna Barbara von Gaschin. This mark was used 1767–c1780. A double 'G' was also used representing 'Gaschin-Glienitz'.

Gotha *Thuringia, Germany*
Hard-paste porcelain was first produced here in 1757 by Wilhelm von Rotherg, and run by a succession of proprietors. From c1805 the 'G' mark appears in blue or enamel colour.

Tavernes *Nr Moustiers, Var, France*
A faïence factory existed here between 1760 and 1780. This mark was used.

Gera *Thuringia, Germany*
A great deal of faïence, and later porcelain, was made in towns in Thuringia. Faïence is characterized by strong, high-temperature colours; tankards are the most common form. Faïence was made here c1752–80 by Matthias Eichelroth, and then by Johann Gottlieb Gottbrecht. This mark was used.

Louis H. H. Glover
Barnsley, South Yorkshire, UK
Studio-type pottery made from 1930. This impressed or painted initial mark from 1946.

Doccia *Nr Florence, Italy*
See p35. This mark was used on general pottery made at the Ginori factory 1874–88.

Three G's Pottery *Worthing, West Sussex, UK*
First established c1953 in Rowland's Castle, Hampshire, this pottery, run by Mrs Lloyd, made earthenwares. This incised mark was used.

Holitsch *Hungary*
A faïence factory was established here in 1743 by Francis of Lorraine, the consort of the Empress Maria Theresa (1717–80). Wares were made in the style of French faïence. Pieces were marked with an 'H' or a double 'H'. White and cream-coloured earthenware was made after 1786.

Pierre Heugue
Rouen, Seine-Inférieure, France
Pierre Heugue and his family of potters based in Rouen from 1698 to the 19thC used this mark.

Pierre-Antoine Hannong
Faubourg Saint-Denis, Paris, France
A porcelain factory was founded here in 1771 by Pierre-Antoine Hannong who registered this letter mark, as well as a capital 'H'. He left in 1776 and the factory, owned by the Marquis d'Usson, operated under a number of directors.

Benedict Hasslacher
Alt-Rohlau, Bohemia, Czech Republic
From 1813, this factory made cream-coloured earthenware and hard-paste porcelain. Proprietor from 1813–23 was Benedict Hasslacher, whose mark appears here.

St Petersburg *Russia*
After her accession in 1762, Empress Catherine II (1729–96) revived the porcelain factory that was originally established in St Petersburg by her predecessor, Empress Elizabeth (1709–62) in 1744. The Imperial factory then began to flourish. This mark was used by Nicholas II 1894–1917.

Harborne Pottery
Birmingham, West Midlands, UK
Established by E. M. and B. Bloomer in 1956 to produce pottery and tiles. This impressed seal mark was used from 1956.

Thelma P. Hanan *London, UK*
This potter worked in London in 1947, and moved to the Island Pottery, Portsmouth, in 1951. This incised or painted mark was used c1947–53.

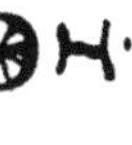

Henry F. Hammond *Farnham, Surrey, UK*
Produced Studio pottery and stonewares at the Oast Pottery and the Farnham School of Art. This incised or impressed mark was used from 1934.

Höchst *Nr Mainz, Germany*
See p34. This 'H' denotes Georg Frederich Hess, 'arcanist' and painter at the Höchst factory, 1746–50 (or his son Ignatz, c1750).

Kelsterbach *Hesse Darmstadt, Germany*
A faïence factory was founded in Königstädten, near Kelsterbach, in 1758 by Wilhelm Cron and Johann Christian Frede who went into partnership with Caspar Mainz in 1759 when Cron withdrew, and the factory moved in 1760 to Kelsterbach. This mark was used on early faïence, denoting 'Kelsterbach' or 'Königstädten'.

Klosterle *Bohemia, Czech Republic*
In 1794 a porcelain factory was founded here on the orders of Count F. J. Thun, the forestry superintendent. From 1797 to 1803 the factory was leased to Christian Nonne. This mark was used 1794–1803. Production continues today.

Edwin M. Knowles China Company
East Liverpool, Ohio, USA
This pottery produced high quality table and toilet wares in semi-porcelain and ironstone with good printed or decal decorations. The first pottery plant was in Chester, West Virginia. Offices remained in East Liverpool until 1931. Knowles was the son of Isaac M. Knowles of Knowles, Taylor & Knowles. This mark should not be mistaken for one used by them.

Langenthal *Switzerland*
Porcelain was made at Langenthal from 1906. This 'L' mark appears on hand-decorated wares.

Langewiesen *Thuringia, Germany*
Hard-paste porcelain was made here in the 19thC. This mark appears.

M Landais *Tours, Indre-et-Loire, France*
Faïence was made at Tours from c1750, and later porcelain and earthenware. This mark was used by M. Landais who made copies of Palissy and 'Henri II' wares in the 19thC.

Jean-Joseph Lassia
Rue de Reuilly, Paris, France
Hard-paste porcelain was made at this factory at the end of the 18thC, c1774–87, by Jean-Joseph Lassia who registered the 'L' mark in 1774. This mark appeared in gold or colour.

Andreas Dolder *Beromünster, Switzerland*
Andreas Dolder ran a faïence factory here 1769–80, which subsequently moved to Lucerne. The factory produced faïence decorated in the Strasbourg style. This mark denotes Münster.

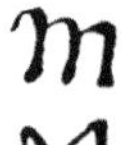

Magdeburg *Hanover, Germany*
A faïence factory was founded in Magdeburg by Philipp Guichard in 1784. Early wares were made from faïence, and included characteristic open basketwork (also made at Münden); later wares were made from glazed earthenware in the English style. These marks were used on faïence 1754–86. The letter 'M' also appears on cream-coloured earthenware 1786–1839.

Patrick McCloskey *Hove, East Sussex, UK*
Studio-type pottery, slip-decorated wares and figures were made from 1948 with this impressed seal-type mark.

William S. Murray *London, UK*
Made Studio pottery in London and at various addresses in England; lived in Southern Rhodesia from 1940. This impressed seal mark was used 1919–40 in England.

Theophilus Brouwer
Middle Lane Pottery, Long Island, New York, USA
Brouwer (active 1894–1932) made earthenware art vases with a variety of lustre and metallic effects first in East Hampton and later in Westhampton. His output was steadier during the earlier years, but as time went on he developed additional interests, particularly to do with cast concrete. The mark mimics the jawbone of a whale that was part of the gate to his studio in Westhampton.

Niderviller *Lorraine, France*
The original faïence factory in Niderviller, founded in 1735, was bought by Baron Jean-Louis de Beyerlé in 1742. By c1765 production almost exclusively comprised porcelain. The factory was bought in 1770 by Adam Philibert, Comte de Custine. François-Antoine Anstett, a former pupil of Paul Hannong, managed the factory 1754–79. Later it was directed by Claude François Lanfrey 1802–27. Faïence wares were strongly influenced by Strasburg, but the palette was softer. Tureens and figures were made in both faïence and porcelain. Porcelain was not produced after 1827. This black 'N' mark has been used on pieces from the start of production. The town name also appears impressed in full and as an abbreviation 'Nider' in black.

Bonnin and Morris
Philadelphia, Pennsylvania, USA
Although the making of porcelain had been attempted previously several times, this pottery is the first for which any ware survives. Gousse Bonnin and George Morris hired potters from the English Bow factory to make porcelain in Philadelphia, 1769–72. Although the ware was a reasonably good copy of the English original, the cost for making it in America was prohibitive and the venture failed within a few years of opening.

Sargadelos *Spain*
White and cream-coloured earthenware was made in Sargadelos between 1804 and 1875. This 'P' mark was used 1835–42.

Prague, *Czech Republic*
A factory producing English-style lead-glazed earthenware was set up in 1795. This mark was used 1795–1810.

Count Leopold von Proskau
Silesia, Germany
A faïence factory was founded in Proskau in 1763 by Count Leopold von Proskau who was killed in a duel in 1769. Following a short period of closure, the factory was taken over in 1770 by Johann Carl von Dietrichstein who owned the premises until 1783 when they were sold to Frederick the Great of Prussia. The factory was managed and then leased by Johann Gottlieb Leopold 1783–93. In 1788, the factory began producing earthenware and the manufacture of faïence was discontinued after 1793. The factory continued until c1850. The mark above was used 1763–69 and the mark below during the Leopold period 1783–93.

Deruta *Umbria, Italy*
Maiolica was produced at potteries in Deruta from c1490. This mark has been found on pieces from a group of wares known as the 'petal back' class: plates and dishes with a distinctive type of floral pattern on the reverse. Other initials also appear in this style.

Cafaggiolo *Nr Florence, Italy*
See p33. This mark was found on a plate made c1513 depicting a procession that included the Medici Pope Leo X.

Tuscany *Italy*
Maiolica was made in Tuscany from the 15thC onwards, especially around Florence and Siena. The double 'P' mark (above) was found on an armorial vase with Spanish-style flower decoration. The single 'P' mark (below) has been found on pieces that feature characteristic 'Hispano-Moresque' and 'Gothic' foliage.

Palgrave Pottery *Broome, Suffolk, UK*
Run by Mr and Mrs J. Colliers, this pottery made Studio-type wares from 1953. This 'P. P.' initial mark was used from 1953.

Miragaya *Nr Oporto, Portugal*
A faïence factory existed here in the late 18thC. This mark has been found.

Robert's Factory

Marseilles, Bouches-du-Rhône, France

Joseph-Gaspard Robert founded a faïence factory in Marseilles c1750. He produced hard-paste porcelain from 1773. The factory operated until at least 1793. Many variations of this factory mark were used on both faïence and porcelain.

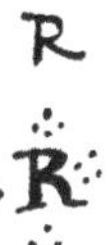

De Roos *Delft, Holland*

This factory (The Rose) operated from 1662 to 1755 under various proprietors. The mark above was principally used in the early 18thC on Chinese-style blue and white wares. The mark below was also used in the 18thC.

Pierre-Joseph Prudhomme

Aire, Pas-de-Calais, France

Faïence was made in Aire c1730–90, in a factory founded by Pierre-Joseph Prudhomme. This mark was used by Prudhomme c1730–55. After 1755 the factory was taken over by his son-in-law, François Dumetz, who continued the concern until c1790.

Roseville Pottery Company

Roseville and Zanesville, Ohio, USA

During its earliest years the company produced utilitarian stoneware at two potteries in Roseville and within a few years painted ware in Zanesville. In 1900, their famous Rozane glazed ware was begun in Zanesville, and by 1910 all pottery production was moved to that city. The firm was active 1892–1954. A variety of glaze effects was made under the Rozane name. In 1918, the trademark 'Roseville U.S.A.' was adopted and the moulded floral wares, such as Pine Cone, Wisteria, Dahlros etc, were added. F. H. Rhead produced an elaborate art line called Della Robbia during the early 1900s.

Roeginga Pottery

Rainham, Kent, UK

This pottery operated 1938–39 producing earthenwares. It was reopened in 1948 by Alfred Wilson Ltd. This incised mark was used 1938–39.

Bow China Works *Stratford, London, UK*

See p31. This is a rough, incised workman's mark, c1750–60.

Nuremberg *Bavaria, Germany*
Evidence suggests that maiolica was made in Nuremberg during the l6thC by Augustin Hirschvogel. Records show that in 1531 he worked in partnership with Hans Nickel and Oswald Reinhard (who had worked in Venice). This mark attributed to Reinhard was found on a dish painted with Samson and Delilah, with the date 1526.

Sargadelos *Spain*
See p41. This mark is found on white and cream coloured earthenware 1804–29.

Sipiagin *Moscow, Russia*
Vsevolojsky and Polivanoff operated a porcelain factory in Moscow from 1813 to 1855. This is the mark of Sipiagin, proprietor from 1820.

Georg Matthäus Schmidt
Erfurt, Thuringia, Germany
Faïence was made in Erfurt c1717–92. Privileges were granted, notably to J. D. Fleischhauer, in 1717, which were then taken over by Laurentius Silberschlag in 1718. Silberschlag's factory was bought in the same year by Johann Paul Stieglitz (also a pewter manufacturer) who obtained another privilege in 1734. Stieglitz's son and grandson continued the factory until it closed in 1792. Tankards, dishes, jugs and, more rarely, figures, all painted in the Thuringian palette, were made. Painters' marks appear, such as this one by Georg Matthäus Schmidt.

Souroux *Rue de la Roquette, Paris, France*
Hard-paste porcelain was made here by Souroux who registered this mark in 1773.

Sinceny *Aisne, France*
A faïence factory was established in Sinceny in 1733 by J. B. de Fayard, and was managed by Denis-Pierre Pellevé of Rouen. Fine quality faïence, including *grand-feu* Chinoiserie was produced which is very similar to wares from Rouen. The factory operated until 1864. This mark was used in the first period, 1733–75.

Cafaggiolo *Nr Florence, Italy*
See p33. This mark appears c1480 on a jug in the Ashmolean Museum, Oxford, painted with the arms of Alessandro dei Alessandri, on a ground that imitates Hispano-Moresque ware.

Schlaggenwald *Bohemia, Czech Republic*
A porcelain factory existed here c1793–1866. This mark was used in the early 19thC.

Caughley Porcelain Works
Nr Brosely, Shropshire, UK
See p34. Blue painted or printed 'S' marks, often appearing with a small cross or circle, are found on underglaze blue decorated wares, c1775–95.

Guiseppe Sinibaldi and Lodovico Santini
Trieste, Italy
From 1783 to the early 19thC creamware was made by Guiseppe Sinibaldi and Lodovico Santini, who used this double 'S' mark.

Stockhardt and Schmidt-Eckert
Kronach, Bavaria, Germany
This mark was used on hard-paste porcelain made by Stockhardt and Schmidt-Eckert from 1897.

Tettau *Franconia, Germany*
A porcelain factory was founded here in 1794 by Georg Christian Friedmann Greiner from Kloster Veilsdorf. Early utility wares were then joined by coffee, tea, chocolate and table services, many with floral decoration. From 1915 the factory was known as Porzellan-fabrik Tettau AG. This 19thC mark and other variations appear in blue.

Johann Samuel Friedrich Tännich *Mosbach, Baden, Germany*
The faïence and creamware manufactory at Mosbach was established in 1770 by Pierre Berthevin under the protection of the Elector Palatine Carl Theodor. Between 1774 and 1781 the factory was run by Johann Samuel Friedrich Tännich, and he was succeeded by Johann Georg Friedrich List who formed a company to take over the factory. From 1787 to 1836 the proprietors were Roemer and Co, and thereafter it was owned by Heinrich Stadler. The early, mainly tableware or other domestic ware was based loosely on the Strasburg style with scattered flowers or landscape vignettes in a polychrome palette. Towards the end of the 18thC the factory switched to the production of cream-coloured earthenware which continued until the closure of the factory in 1836. This 'T' mark stands for Tännich.

Vianna do Castello *Portugal*
This 'V' mark appears in blue on faïence produced here from 1774.

Nathaniel Friedrich Hewelcke *Venice, Italy*
From 1758 to 1763 hard-paste porcelain in the style of Meissen was produced by Dresden dealers Nathaniel Friedrich Hewelcke and his wife Maria Dorothea. The privilege was granted on condition that they mark their pieces with the letter 'V'. This mark was either incised or painted red.

Nicholas Vergette *London, UK*
Working at the Camberwell School of Art and other posts 1946–58, Vergette used this incised mark.

Varages *Vars, France*
Faïence was made here in the 18thC in the Moustiers and Marseilles style. This mark was used.

Villegoureix Noël & Co
Limoges, Haute-Vienne, France
Founded in 1922, this firm became Villegoureix & Cie (1924–26) and S. A. Porcelaine Villegoureix (1928–29).

Pierre Verneuilh *Bordeaux, Gironde, France*
Porcelain was made in Bordeaux from 1781, when a manufactory was established by Pierre Verneuilh and his nephew Jean, until 1787 when it was taken over by Michel Vanier in partnership with Allaud of Limoges. They continued until 1790 and made porcelain similar to wares from Paris. This double 'V' mark was used.

Wiersbie *Silesia, Germany*
A small faïence factory existed in the neighbourhood of Ghenitz with a painter named Fialla 1775–83, making pieces similar to those from Proskau. This mark was used.

Würzburg *Lower Franconia, Germany*
A porcelain factory was established c1775 by Johann Caspar Geyer, and seems to have lasted until 1780. This mark appears in black.

Johann Jacob Wunderlich
Erfurt, Thuringia, Germany
This mark was used by Wunderlich (d1751), a painter at Erfurt, from 1730.

Anne Wedd *Brixton, London, UK*
Studio-type pottery made from 1955. This impressed seal-type mark was used from 1961.

Worcester Porcelains
Hereford and Worcester, UK
See p33. The painted mark above is rare, and was used c1870–85. Several variations of the 'W' mark below appear c1755–70, painted or printed in underglaze blue.

Michael Leach
Yelland Manor Pottery, Devon, UK
Trained by his father Bernard Leach, Michael made Studio-type pottery from 1956. This impressed seal mark was used.

William Absolon *Great Yarmouth, Norfolk, UK*
Absolon worked at The Ovens and 25 Market Row in Yarmouth 1784–1815, decorating earthenwares and glass. He used this painted Yarmouth mark.

Zürich *Switzerland*
A porcelain and faïence factory was established at Schoren near Zürich by a company in 1763. After 1790, faïence and lead-glazed earthenware were the principal output. Both faïence and porcelain were made in the 18thC marked with a 'Z' with or without dots, as seen here.

Zerbst *Anhalt, Germany*
A faïence factory here was one of those founded by Johann Caspar Ripp of Hanau. A factory operated under various owners until 1861. This factory mark was used.

Leipzig *Saxony, Germany*
A hard-paste porcelain decorator, Oscar Zenari, worked out of Leipzig from 1901 and used this mark.

Initials

Detail of decorator's mark, Poole Pottery, 1950s

INITIALS

A. C. W.

Adam Clemens Wanderer *Bayreuth, Germany*
Brown and yellow wares are typically decorated with fired-on gold and silver, with high quality painting. Motifs include scrollwork and monograms.

Bow China Works *Stratford, London, UK*
See p31. This is a rough, incised workman's mark c1750–60.

A. P.

Johann Georg Christoph Popp
Ansbach, Bavaria, Germany
Johann Georg Christoph Popp (1696–1791) was proprietor of the faïence factory at Ansbach (established 1708–10) in 1769. He had been a painter at the factory since 1715, and was manager from 1737 to 1769 (with Köhnlein 1737–47). In 1770, his son Johann Gottfried Popp became his partner. The factory remained in the hands of the Popp family until 1807. This mark, which denotes 'Ansbach-Popp', was used after 1769.

AP.

Aprey *Haute-Marne, France*
See p78. The initials 'A P' were not always used. This mark and the monogram are common on modern copies.

AR

Arras *Pas-de-Calais, France*
A soft-paste porcelain factory was founded here in 1770 by Joseph-François Boussemaert of Lille (see p80). The factory was taken over in 1771 by four female faïence dealers called Delemer. The factory closed in 1790. Only tablewares were made, and are painted in blue or crimson monochrome with flowers, coats-of-arms and festoons. The mark appears in crimson or purple.

ARF

Annette Fuchs *London, UK*
Studio-type pottery from 1961 with painted mark.

AvE

Albrecht von Erberfeld
Aumund, Hanover, Germany
A faïence factory existed here 1751–61. The third owner was Albrecht von Erberfeld (from 1757), whose mark appears here. Output included rococo tureens and cylindrical tankards, painted in blue or *grand-feu* colours.

AW

Alan Wallwork *London, UK*
Based at the Alan Gallery, Wallwork's workshop produced Studio-type pottery and architectural

ceramics from 1959. This incised initial mark appeared on his individual pieces. The letter 'W' was also used, and appears as an incised, impressed or painted mark.

B. C

Duke Karl of Brunswick *Brunswick, Germany*
See p93. In 1756 the Brunswick faïence factory was purchased by Duke Karl who retained it until 1773. This second ducal 'B' mark was used at this time and later as one of the conditions of the privilege granted to Johann Benjamin Heinrich Rabe (who ran the factory from 1773) in 1781.

B &C

Bougon and Chalon *Chantilly, Oise, France*
M. Pigorry founded a factory in 1803, and produced utility ware and tea services. From c1818, Jacques Louis Chalot and Pierre-Louis-Toussaint continued the concern; their pieces feature this mark.

B.F.S.

Adolf Fränkel and Johann Veit Schreck
Bayreuth, Bavaria, Germany
The factory at Bayreuth produced some of the most important German faïence during the early 18thC. It was established with the help of potter Johann Kaspar Ripp (who also worked at Hanau, Ansbach and Nuremberg) and possibly a merchant called Johann Georg Knöller in c1713. Kaspar Ernst Hild was named as manager in 1723. In 1724 the firm was taken over by the Margrave of Brandenburg-Kulmbach, who appointed Johann Nicolaus Grüner as manager. The Margrave died in 1726, and two years later Knöller once again took over the factory, and it became a profitable concern, supplying a large amount of high quality brown-glazed ware to the Court. Knöller died in 1744, and between 1745 and 1747 the factory was run by Adolf Fränkel (d1747) and Johann Veit Schreck, who used this mark.

B&G

Bing & Grøndhal *Copenhagen, Denmark*
Founded in 1853, this factory produced artistic and domestic porcelain and earthenwares. A successful factory, this business still exists today. This mark appears.

·B·K·

Adolf Fränkel and Johann Veit Schreck
Bayreuth, Bavaria, Germany
See above. This mark is one of those used during the Knöller period, 1728–44. The initials 'B. K.' often appear in conjunction with painter's marks.

Bernberg *Thuringia, Germany*
A faïence factory existed c1725–75, with the patronage of Prince Victor Friedrich of Anhalt-Bernberg. There is no written record of the factory, but a set of Chinese Delft-style vases have been found with this mark.

Bernard Leach *St Ives, Cornwall, UK*
Active 1921–79, Bernard Leach was one of the most famous English Studio potters. He also trained a large number of potters at his studio in St Ives. He made pieces with a strong Oriental feel, with simple painted, sgraffito or trailed decoration. These personal marks were used by Leach 1921–79.

Bernard Moore *Stoke, Staffordshire, UK*
Formerly Moore Bros (c1872–1905), a company that made decorative porcelain at Longton, the firm was continued by Bernard Moore, c1905–15, who produced fine glaze effects on porcelain and earthenwares. This painted initial mark was used in several forms 1905–15.

Baldassare Manara *Faenza, Emilia, Italy*
A member of a well known family of Faentine potters, Baldassare Manara decorated a number of pieces of maiolica dated between 1530 and 1536. His initials appear on some of the pieces.

De vergulde Blompot *Delft, Holland*
Founded in 1654 by J. G. van der Houve, De vergulde Blompot (The Golden Flowerpot) operated until c1778. Successive owners included van der Houve's widow, Jacob Pijnacker (see p101), and M. van den Bogaert. This factory mark is one of several used.

Johann Georg Pfeiffer
Bayreuth, Bavaria, Germany
See p50. In 1747, the faïence factory in Bayreuth was taken over by Johann Georg Pfeiffer, who worked in conjunction with Adolf Fränkel's widow until 1760 ('Pfeiffer & Fränkel' period, see mark below), and on his own 1760–67 (see mark above). During the 'Pfeiffer' period the factory was very prosperous, and after his death in 1767 Pfeiffer's widow and children remained as owners until 1783, when the financially-troubled business was taken over by State officials. In 1788 C. A. Wetzel bought it and produced cream-coloured earthenware, as well as faïence, until 1806.

B & R

Johann Heinrich Reichard and Johann Erich Behling *Brunswick, Germany*
See p93. From 1749 to 1756, the proprietors of the factory at Brunswick were Johann Heinrich Reichard and Johann Erich Behling, and the mark used was 'B & R' or 'R & B'.

B.S.

Bartholomäus Seuter
Augsburg, Swabia, Germany
Independent faïence and porcelain painting was one of many crafts practiced by Bartholomäus Seuter (1678–1754). His work is found on faïence jugs and tankards, and features flowers and figures arranged in panels or cartouches, executed on manganese purple or brown and yellow. Other characteristic colours include crimson, egg-yolk yellow and blue. His later work on porcelain includes figure subjects in black, red and especially gilding.

BX

Bayeux *Calvados, Normandy, France*
First established at Valognes in 1793 by Le Tellier de la Bertinière, this hard-paste porcelain factory was transferred to Bayeux in 1810 by Joachim Langlois, and continued by his family after his death in 1830. Owned by François Gosse from 1849, the factory was then taken over by Jules Morlent in 1878, who, together with his descendants, continued until 1951. This Morlent period mark appears sometimes within a circle.

Eckernförde *Schleswig, Germany*
Founded first at Criseby in 1759 by Johann Nicolaus Otte and his brother Friedrich Wilhelm, a faïence factory operated at Eckernförde 1765–85. This mark has been attributed to the early period 1759–64.

CA

Arzberg *Bavaria, Germany*
A hard-paste porcelain factory was founded at Arzberg by Carl Auvera from 1884. Pipe bowls were made with this mark.

Cincinnati Art Pottery *Cincinnati, Ohio, USA*
A variety of art wares was produced at this pottery (active 1879–91) on various earthenware bodies, including 'Hungarian Faïence' with an elaborate overall polychrome pattern or 'Kezonta', the Indian name for turtle, that was an ivory-colored faïence with hand-painted polychrome flowers or gilt scrolls. Some of their ware was supplied in the white to decorators.

C·B

Coburg *Thuringia, Germany*
A small faïence factory was established here in 1738 by Johann Georg Dümmler of Bayreuth under privilege from the Duke of Saxa-Coburg-Gotha, who took over the factory himself in 1760. The concern continued until 1786. This mark appears on general Thuringian-style faïence, and has been ascribed to Coburg.

C B

Clive Brooker *Stanmore and Enfield, London, UK*
From 1956, Clive Brooker has produced Studio-type pottery that features an incised or impressed signature mark (1956–60), or this impressed seal mark (from 1960).

C:BM

Cornelius Boumeester *Rotterdam, Holland*
Tiles and faïence were made at Rotterdam in the 17th and 18thC. Faïence manufacturing in the town dates from 1612, when the son of a Haarlem potter, Pieter Herman Valckenhoff, started a factory. By 1642 there were 11 factories in Rotterdam. This mark belongs to a tile painter called Cornelius Boumeester who was active c1675–1700.

CD

Limoges *Haute-Vienne, France*
Hard-paste porcelain was made at Limoges from 1771 when a factory was established by the brothers Grellet, under the protection of the Comte d'Artois. In 1784 it was acquired by the King to make blanks for decoration at Sèvres. The factory closed in 1796. The usual mark 'CD' which stands for 'Comte d'Artois' is most often incised, but sometimes appears in red or underglaze blue.

C · G
W

Johann Caspar Geyer
Würzburg, Lower Franconia, Germany
See p46. This mark includes the initials of the founder of the porcelain factory at Würzburg, Johann Caspar Geyer (d1780).

C:H

Henri-Florentin Chanou
Barrière de Reuilly, Paris
A hard-paste porcelain factory was run here by Henri-Florentin Chanou of Sèvres, 1779–85. This mark appears in red.

C··K.

G. Frederick Cook *Ambleside, Cumbria, UK*
Studio-type pottery and stonewares were made at the Potter's Wheel Studio in Ambleside from 1948. Cook used this personal mark on individual pieces.

Chelsea Keramic Art Works/Dedham Pottery *Chelsea and Dedham, Massachusetts, USA*
Robertson brothers Alexander, Hugh and George had been making redware flowerpots in Chelsea since the late 1860s, but changed the company's name and improved their product line in the late 1870s to include fine terracotta in Grecian shapes and art wares with faïence glazes. Decorative tiles were also made, designed by John G. Low who later established the Low Art Tile Works in Chelsea. The firm was active in Chelsea 1875–95 and in Dedham 1895–1943. Hugh's experiments to revive ancient Chinese glazes led to the creation of a white crackle glaze that was hand-painted with charming animal and plant figures in cobalt blue. This was the primary product line of the pottery after it was moved to Dedham in 1895; the climate in Chelsea proved too damp to make this type of ware.

C. Newbold *Skipton-on-Swale, North Yorkshire, UK*
Studio-type stonewares produced at Arncliffe from 1961, with this incised or painted mark.

Denver China and Pottery Company *Denver, Colorado, USA*
William Long started this pottery (active 1900–05) with many of the decorators who had been with him at Lonhuda in Steubenville (see p97), and at Weller. They made the original Lonhuda ware, and a line called 'Denaura', that was modelled with relief designs of Colorado flowers and covered with matt green glaze. They also produced flint blue tableware.

Kloster-Veilsdorf *Thuringia, Germany*
See p84. This initial mark is less common than the 'CV' monogram.

Cornelia van Schoonhoven (or Cornelius van Schagen) *Delft, Holland*
This mark appears on pieces from De porceleyn Klaeuw (The Porcelain Claw). It is not clear whether the initials seen here stand for Cornelia van Schoonhoven (proprietor 1668–71) or Cornelius van Schagen (proprietor 1695–c1702).

D
C

Delan Cookson
West Bridgford, Nottinghamshire, UK
From 1958 Studio-type pottery was produced; this impressed seal mark appears on wares after 1961 (marks are rare before this date).

Christiane Hörisch *Dresden, Saxony, Germany*
A faïence factory was first established here in 1708 by Johann Friedrich Böttger (who later established the porcelain manufactory at Meissen). Between 1710 and 1718, the factory was run by Peter Eggebrecht (who held the lease after 1712). After his death in 1738 the factory was continued by his widow and from 1756 by his daughter. In 1768 it passed into the hands of Christiane Hörisch, who was succeeded by her son Karl Gottlieb Hörisch in 1782. The factory closed in 1784. This mark was used (during the Hörisch period (1708–84).

Denis K. Wren *Oxshott, Surrey, UK*
Studio-type ceramics were produced at the Oxshott Pottery from 1919.

Don Pino Bettisii *Faenza, Emilia, Italy*
This mark is thought to belong to Don Pino Bettisii, a potter in Faenza who died c1589.

Proskau *Silesia, Germany*
See p42. This mark was used during the period when Johann Carl von Dietrichstein was proprietor, 1770–83.

Daniel and James Franklin Seagle
Vale, North Carolina, USA
Daniel Seagle worked first as a redware potter in Vale, Lincoln County, North Carolina, and about 1840 began producing ash or alkaline-glazed stonewares. When Daniel died in 1867 his son, James Franklin Seagle, maintained his own pottery on the site. They were active 1828–c1888.

De dobbelde Schenckan *Delft, Holland*
Founded in 1659, this mark for De dobbelde Schenckan (The Double Tankard) was registered in 1764.

Mennecy-Villeroy *Ile-de-France, France*
This porcelain and faïence concern protected by Louis-François de Neufville, Duc de Villeroy, was established first in Paris in 1734. It was transferred to Mennecy in 1748, and then in 1773 to Bourg-la-Reine. The first manager was François Barbin who, with his son (from 1751), ran the factory until 1765. The factory was bought in 1766 by Joseph Jullien and Symphorien Jacques, who had also taken a lease on the concern at Sceaux in 1763.

They ran both factories until 1772 when they sold the Sceaux factory, and in 1773 transferred the factory at Mennecy to Bourg-la-Reine. The factory continued until 1806. Early porcelain is milky-white with a brilliant, clear glaze. Later porcelain has a yellow tone, and is often painted with Japanese-style decoration; others feature floral designs. Distinctive colours are rose pink and bright blue. This mark, and many variations of the initials 'DV' (which stand for 'de Villeroy') were used.

D & W

Deiderich & Wilhelm Terhellen
Aumund, Hanover, Germany
Two brothers named Deiderich and Wilhelm Terhellen (together with Johann Christoph Mülhausen), were the owners of the faïence factory at Aumund between 1751 and 1757. They used this mark. See also p49.

E.L

Eileen Lewenstein *London, UK*
Studio-type pottery was produced from 1959 with this seal-type mark or painted initials. She was previously in partnership with Donald Mills at the Briglin Pottery from 1948 to 1959.

E.S

Eileen Stevens *Crawley, West Sussex, UK*
From 1952, Studio-type ceramics were made, first with this incised or painted mark (1952–55), and with a revised version after 1955.

F.A°

Aveiro *Portugal*
A faïence factory was established here c1785. It used this mark which denotes 'Fabrica Aveiro'. Tablewares and figures were produced.

F B

Frauenberg *Nr Sarreguemines, France*
In 1760 a factory producing faïence and glazed earthenware was established; this mark appears in blue.

F·B

Franz Bustelli *Nymphenburg, Bavaria, Germany*
See p81. Franz Anton Bustelli (1723–63) was appointed to the position of master-modeller at the Nymphenburg factory in 1754, and remained there until his death in 1763.
He produced a wide variety of figures which were made in an essentially rococo style. The models are frequently left uncoloured, but where colours have been used they include tomato-red, yellow, brown, strong green and deep pink.
His figures are impressed with this mark.

Worcester Porcelains *Hereford and Worcester, UK*
See p33. Used during the third historical period of Worcester Porcelains (c1792–1807), this incised initial mark only rarely appears.

Francis Glanville
Cooper Sheffield, South Yorkshire, UK
Studio-type pottery was produced from 1945, with this painted, incised or impressed seal-type mark.

Walter J. Fletcher
Evesham, Hereford and Worcester, UK
These impressed seal marks appear on Studio-type pottery from 1960, and stand for 'Frogland Cottage Pottery' and 'Frogland Pottery'.

Fulda *Hesse, Germany*
Two factories were established here with the patronage of the Prince-Bishops of Fulda. The faïence concern ran from c1741–58, while hard-paste porcelain was produced between 1764 and 1789. The faïence factory was set up with the help of Adam Friedrich von Löwenfinck of Bayreuth, and his brother Karl Heinrich. 'FD' for 'Fulda' was the usual factory mark, perhaps also with a painter's mark or date. Chinese-style, *famille verte* and blue and manganese designs were also used. Output includes figures and tablewares.

Jean-Gaspard Féraud
Moustiers, Basse-Alpes, France
Dating from the late 18thC, some wares were made at Moustiers featuring high-temperature painted subjects that are associated with Jean-Gaspard Féraud (1779–92), who was part of a family of potters and painters. Subjects include figures, mythological and pastoral scenes, and realistic floral designs. Colours are smooth and glossy. The style was continued by his descendants until 1874. This mark appears, with either an upper-case or a lower-case 'F'.

Fr. Erlemann *Wiesbaden, Nassau, Germany*
Erlemann made earthenware at Wiesbaden from 1893 which featured this mark.

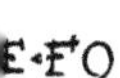

Flaminio Fontano *Faenza, Italy*
This mark, attributed to Flaminio Fontano, also of Urbino (see p37), has been found on maiolica with blue decoration on the reverse, a style that is characteristic of Faentine maiolica.

F
H

Karl Heinrich
Frankfurt-an-der-Oder, Brandenburg, Germany
In 1763 a faïence factory was established here by Karl Heinrich. After his death the factory was continued by his widow and children until the l8thC. Tankards comprised the main portion of the output, decorated in the style of Berlin or Thuringia. Heinrich's wares feature this mark.

F. M
Bäyreith
1744

Johann Friedrich Metzsch *Bayreuth, Germany*
A *Hausmaler* in Bayreuth c1735–51, Metzsch ran a painting school where painters worked on undecorated pieces from Bayreuth or Meissen. Painted subjects include continuous landscapes, figures, ships and obelisks set within baroque cartouches surrounded by garlands of small flowers. This mark appears in gold.

F·R·

Rato *Nr Lisbon, Portgual*
See p80. This mark denoting 'Fabrica Rato', appeared while the Royal factory was directed by Thomaz Brunetto (1767–71).

FSH

Frederick Harrop *Finchley, London, UK*
From 1952, Studio-type pottery and stonewares were produced with these incised or painted initials, often with the date of potting.

·f·X·A·R·
·Urbino·

Francesco Xanto Avelli di Rovigo
Urbino, Italy
This potter is known to have signed and dated works between 1529 and 1542. His signatures range from his full name, these initials, and the letter 'X'. His *istoriato* wares are characterized by emphatic outlines and strong figures; his palette usually includes a bright orange-yellow, brown and azure blue. Lustre was sometimes added to his work by craftsmen at Gubbio.

G:3

Jean-Baptiste Guillibaud
Rouen, Seine-Inférieure, France
Associated with the decorative period of Rouen where the output featured Chinese and baroque-influenced designs, Jean-Baptiste Guillibaud (d1739) and his widow operated c1720–50. The palette was derived from Chinese *famille verte*; flowers and landscapes were popular. A service was made for François II, Duke of Montmorency-Luxembourg, with borders in red and green, or red and black, and Chinese-style figures, plants and birds in the middle panels. This mark and also the name 'Guillibaud' are found.

Widow Van der Strale *Delft, Holland*
This mark was registered by widow Van der Strale for 't Jonge Moriaenshooft (The Young Moor's Head) in 1764.

Johann Georg Christoph Popp
Ansbach, Bavaria, Germany
See p49. This is one of the marks used by Popp while he was a painter at this faïence factory.

Georg Friedrich Kordenbusch
Nuremberg, Germany
Kordenbusch (d1763) worked as a faïence painter (and possibly a potter) in Nuremberg. The best work by Kordenbusch includes figures on tankards, and floral and landscape decoration. He signed his pieces 'GK' with three dots.

G. M. Creyke & Sons *Hanley, Staffordshire, UK*
See p89. This initial mark was used by this firm from 1930 to 1948.

Göggingen *Nr Augsburg, Germany*
Prince-Bishop Joseph, Landgrave of Hesse-Darmstadt, granted a privilege to Georg Michael Hofmann of Oettingen to set up a faïence factory here in 1748. It was continued by a modeller, Joseph Hackl, from 1749 to 1752. Faïence was marked with the name of the town in full or abbreviated as seen here. Wares include figures, stove tiles, narrow-necked jugs and plates. Painting was in European or Chinese style.

Hans Coper *Welwyn Garden City, Hertfordshire, UK*
A respected Studio-potter who worked for a time with Lucy Rie at her studio in London, Coper (1920–81) produced wares in characteristic machine-age forms, with textured surfaces and monochrome colour schemes. He used this impressed or incised seal mark from 1947.

Hilary Carruther
Malvern, Hereford and Worcester, UK
Studio-type pottery was produced from 1960, with this incised or painted initial mark.

Cassel *Hesse-Nassau, Germany*
A branch of the faïence factory sponsored by Landgrave Friedrich II, this concern began producing porcelain in 1766. Production mainly comprised blue and white wares, but some

Japanese Kakiemon-style wares were also made. The factory continued until 1788. This mark denoting 'Hesse-Cassel' was used.

H. S. B. 1732

Hans Gottlieb von Bressler *Breslau, Germany*
A *Hausmaler* in Breslau 1732–40, Bressler signed and dated a number of pieces with marks similar to the one shown here. His work is characterized by delicately-painted flowers and figures with decorative panels.

HM

Heber Mathews *Woolwich, London, UK*
Studio-type stonewares and porcelains were produced 1931–58 by Mathews (d1959), who also held a number of teaching posts. This incised mark was used.

HT

Linthorpe Pottery *Middlesbrough, Cleveland, UK*
See p93. This initial mark was used by Henry Tooth, manager up to 1883.

HVH 2

Hendrik van Hoorn *Delft, Holland*
This mark was used by Hendrik van Hoorn, manager of De 3 vergulde Astonne (The Three Golden Ash Barrels), from 1759 until at least 1764, when he is known to have registered another factory mark. The factory was established c1655 by J. P. van Kessel.

HVMD

Hendrick van Middeldijk *Delft, Holland*
Proprietor of 't Hart (The Heart, established in 1661 by Joris Mes) from 1760, Hendrick van Middeldijk registered this mark in 1764.

HW

Henry Wren *Oxshott, Surrey, UK*
See p55. These initials, in upper or lower case, belong to Henry Wren, and appear with and without the name 'Oxshott' c1919–47.

HW 63.

Helen Walters *Hornsey, London, UK*
Working from Stroud Green, Helen Walters produced Studio-type wares from 1953 (and also Doulton wares 1945–53). They feature this painted or incised initial mark.

·I·P·

Siena *Tuscany, Italy*
The best maiolica made at Siena is characterized by fine, intricate work produced from c1500, such as small, geometric, repeating patterns, and figures enclosed within scrolling borders. This mark appears on two plates painted with religious subjects.

J. van Putten *Delft, Holland*
Potters at De porceleyn Klaeuw (The Porcelain Claw), J. van Putten and Co (also of De 3 Klokken) worked here 1830–50, and registered this mark.

Johann Andreas Fiechthorn *Bayreuth, Germany*
See p50. This mark belongs to Johann Andreas Fiechthorn, a chief painter at Bayreuth c1745.

Joan A. Biggs *London, UK*
Previously based at the Princedale Pottery, Joan Biggs worked in London from 1961 and her Studio-type wares featured this painted or incised initial mark.

Johannes den Appel *Delft, Holland*
Owner of De vergulde Boot (The Golden Boat, founded in 1634) in the mid-18thC, den Appel registered this mark in 1764.

Jacobus de Milde *Delft, Holland*
See p85. This mark was registered in 1764 by Jacobus de Milde while he was owner of De Paauw (The Peacock) c1740–64 or later.

Daniel and James Franklin Seagle
Vale, North Carolina, USA
See p55. This mark was used by James Franklin Seagle.

Johann Julius Popp *Ansbach, Bavaria, Germany*
See p49. Johann Julius Popp (d1792) and his brother Georg Ludwig became proprietors of the factory at Ansbach after the death of their father Johann Georg Christoph in 1791. Prior to this date, Johann Julius was a painter at the factory, and this mark appears with the date 1749.

Joachim Langlois *Bayeux, Calvados, France*
See p52. This mark together with the word 'Bayeux' was used on hard-paste porcelain by Joachim Langlois (d1830).

Jacob Petit *Fontainebleau, Seine-et-Marne, France*
A porcelain factory was founded here in 1795 by Benjamin Jacob and Aaron Smoll. They were succeeded by Baruch Weil in 1830, who sold an offshoot of his factory to Jacob and Mardochée Petit in that year. They produced decorative pieces and their concern was commercially successful. This mark was used by Jacob Petit.

jR

Jacques Jarry *Aprey, Haute-Marne, France*
A well-known painter at Aprey (1772–81) and later at Sceaux, Jarry was famous for designs featuring flowers and birds. This mark appears in black or other enamel colours.

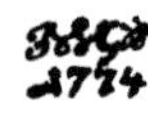

J. W. G. Wanderer *Bayreuth, Germany*
A member of a family of painters that included Adam Clemens Wanderer (see p49), who worked on brown and yellow wares made at Bayreuth in the 18thC. This mark appears with the date 1774.

J.S.T. & CO.
KEENE.NH.

Hampshire Pottery Company/James S. Taft & Company *Keene, New Hampshire, USA*
Active 1871–1923, the original redware flowerpots and stoneware vessels made by this firm were supplanted by the early 1880s by white earthenware art lines decorated with bright majolica and dark matt glazes. All types of jugs, jars, baskets, candlesticks, rose bowls, cuspidors, tea sets, dressing table accessories and souvenir items were made. This mark appears impressed.

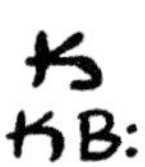

Künersberg *Nr Memmingen, Bavaria, Germany*
Faïence was made in Künersberg from 1745 when a factory was built by Jakob Küner (1692–1764), a banker and merchant from Memmingen, who had founded a new town named after himself. In 1752 his son Johann Jakob Küner and his brother-in-law Sigmund Friedrich Wogau became partners. Künersberg is renowned for faïence painted in muffle colours with a palette that includes greens tinted with yellow and black, and a nut brown. Gilding was also common. These factory marks were sometimes used, and may be accompanied by the initials of the painter. The name of the town also appears in full. A small amount of porcelain was also made at Künersberg, either by Johann Benckgraff, or by C. D. Busch. Two pieces exist, one featuring the arms of the city, and the other marked 'Künersberg'.

KB

Katharine Pleydell-Bouverie
Kilmington Manor, Wiltshire, UK
Based at various addresses between 1925 and 1985, Katharine Pleydell-Bouverie worked from Kilmington Manor from 1946. She was one of Bernard Leach's first pupils at his St Ives Pottery in 1924. She made Studio-type pottery and stonewares with this incised initial mark and also a 'KB' monogram.

K
B
K

K
B
IL

Buchwald and Koch, Buchwald and Leihamer *Kiel, Holstein, Germany*
J. S. F. Tännich (b1728) of Strasburg was the first person successfully to establish a faïence factory in Kiel in 1763, following three failed attempts (in 1758, 1759–60 and 1762–63). The factory was first owned by the Duke of Holstein, but was sold to a company in 1766. Tännich left c1768–69 and was replaced by Johann Buchwald of Eckernförde who was accompanied by painter Abraham Leihamer. Fine wares were made during this time painted in clean, strong muffle colours (such as copper-green and a crimson red), and include decorative bowls, pierced plates, flowerpots and vases. The mark above denotes 'Kiel Buchwald and Koch' (a painter), while the 'JL' within the mark below refers to Johann Leihamer, the father of Abraham Leihamer who joined Tännich before his son arrived in Keil with Buchwald.

KH
B
E

Carsten Behren *Kellinghusen, Holstein, Germany*
Several faïence factories were established here in the 18thC. Carsten Behren's factory operated between 1763 and c1830. After his death in 1782 it passed to his heirs, and then to different owners until production ended. This was the mark while under Behren's ownership.

KH
M

Joachim Moeller *Kellinghusen, Holstein, Germany*
In 1785, the Kellinghusen faïence factory founded by Carsten Behren (see above), was sold to Joachim Moeller who owned it until 1795. He used this mark.

.P.F

Meissen *Nr Dresden, Saxony, Germany*
Johann Friedrich Böttger (1682–1719) experimented with the hard-paste porcelain in Saxony in the early 18thC, the first hard-paste to be made on the Continent. Progress was made, and in 1710 a porcelain manufactory was officially established by the King at the Albrechtsburg Fortress in Meissen. Porcelain and red stonewares were made during this early period. After Böttger's death in 1719, Johann Gregor Herold succeeded him as manager, and techniques of production and decoration developed significantly over the next 25 years. Johann Gottlob Kirchner, a sculptor, was engaged in 1727, and was joined by Johann Joachim Kändler in 1731. After Kirchner was discharged in 1733, Kändler worked with a number of assistants to model the porcelain

figures for which Meissen is renowned. In c1723 the first factory mark was used to act as a guarantee of origin. This mark denoting 'Königliche Pozellan Fabrik' was used around this time.

K/T/C

Tännich and Christopherson
Kiel, Holstein, Germany
See p63. This is the mark of Johann Samuel Tännich, who ran the faïence factory at Kiel between 1763 and c1768, together with the initial of the painter Christoph Christopherson.

L. B.

Jacques-Louis Broillet
Gros Caillou, Paris, France
A hard-paste porcelain factory was set up at this address (also known as Vaugirard-Lès-Paris) in 1765, and this mark was registered in 1762.

L F. M.

Leonhard Friedrich Marx
Nuremberg, Bavaria, Germany
The 18thC faïence factory in Nuremberg produced pieces in a baroque style, owing little to contemporary Delft and Chinese-style decoration. The concern was founded in 1712 by two merchants, Christoph Marx and Heinrich Gottfried Hemmon, in association with the guardians of Johann Conrad Romedi. Johann Caspar Ripp (also of Hanau, Ansbach, Bayreuth, Brunswick and Zerbst), was the first manager, but he left in 1713. In 1715, Hemmon sold his share to his partner's son Johann Andreas Marx (a painter). Romedi's share was sold on his death to Johann Jakob Mayer. Christoph Marx died in 1731, but his widow took over until 1751 when her son and Mayer operated the factory. In 1760 Mayer died, and Marx died in 1770. This mark belongs to Leonhard Friedrich Marx, a partner of the factory after 1770 when it was in decline.

·LFM·

Leo F. Matthews *Walford Heath, Shropshire, UK*
Studio-type pottery was produced from 1954 with this painted or incised initial mark.

L:m·

Leopold Malériat *Sinceny, Aisne, France*
See p44. Malériat succeeded the previous manager Pellevé in 1737, and continued the Rouen styles produced by Pellevé until 1775.

L P K

De Lampetkan *Delft, Holland*
Established in 1637 by Cornelius Harmansz Valckenhoven, De Lampetkan (The Ewer) used this factory mark. The factory closed c1806–10.

Lorenz Speckner
Kreussen, Nr Bayreuth, Germany
An important stoneware-producing area, Kreussen is noted for its brown-glazed wares, often detailed in enamel colours. The best known figures are a family of modellers called Vest from Austria. They were succeeded by Lorenz Speckner (1598–c1669) who married the widow of Georg Vest the Elder. He introduced the production of faïence to the Vest's pottery. This mark appears on a piece dated 1618.

La Seinie *Saint-Yrieux, Haute-Vienne, France*
See p105. This initial mark also appears on porcelain made at La Seinie.

Vendrenne *Vendée, France*
Marc-Lozelet founded a hard-paste porcelain factory here c1800. The mark is the same as La Seinie (see above).

Meissen *Nr Dresden, Saxony, Germany*
See p63. Gilding found on wares produced at Meissen during the early Herold period is now known to have been carried out at Augsburg by Bartholomäus Seuter (see p52) and his associates. Designs in gilt with black and red monochrome include Chinoiseries and European figure subjects often in Watteau's style. This mark (and other types) appears on Augsburg-decorated pieces c1730–35.

Mayer & Elliot *Longport, Staffordshire, UK*
Based at Fountain Place and Dale Hall, and formerly known as Mayer Bros & Elliot (1855–58), this company produced earthenwares 1858–61 with this initial mark, and other marks that incorporate these distinguishing initials. Impressed month and year numbers also occur. Subsequently, the name of the firm changed to Liddle, Elliot & Son, which continued at the Dale Hall Pottery 1862–71.

Buckfast Abbey Pottery *Devon, UK*
Operated by Miss M. Gibson-Horrocks from 1952, this pottery produced Studio-type wares. These were her incised or impressed personal marks, and appear from 1952.

Mervyn Jude *Glyn Ceiriog, Clwyd, Wales, UK*
See p99. This is Mervyn Jude's intial mark, and was used from c1948.

M·J·T

Johann Christoph Mülhausen, Wilhelm and Diederich Terhellen
Aumund, Hanover, Germany
A faïence factory existed here between 1751 and 1761. The Terhellens, together with Johann Christoph Mülhausen, used this mark while they owned the concern 1751–57. See also p56.

M:OL.

Oude Loosdrecht *Holland*
The Weesp porcelain factory was transferred here in 1771 when it was purchased by a pastor called Johannes de Mol. It flourished until 1782 when it was taken over and moved to Amstel. Wares include openwork vases, and egg-shaped tea and coffee pots. Variations of this mark appear during de Mol's ownership, incised or in enamel colours.

M.P.M

Meissen *Nr Dresden, Saxony, Germany*
See p63. Also an early factory mark standing for 'Meissner Porzellan Manufaktur', this example is relatively rare and was used 1723–24.

M·V

Rouen *Seine-Inférieure, France*
The second phase of faïence production began in Rouen in 1644 when a privilege was obtained by Nicolas Poirel, and then transferred to Edmé Poterat who actually started the concern in 1647. Together with his son and heir, Poterat ran the factory until 1720. This is a painter's mark that has been found on pieces made at Rouen in the late 17thC.

Mv

Michel-Mathieu and Michel Vallet
Rouen, Seine-Inférieure, France
General potters in Rouen from 1757; pieces are found with this mark.

NJ

Nerys Jude *Glyn Ceiriog, Clwyd, Wales, UK*
See p99. Nerys Jude used this initial mark c1948.

.N S.

Ottweiler *Rhineland, Germany*
A faïence and porcelain factory was established at Ottweiler in 1763, with the patronage of Prince Wilhelm Heinrich of Nassau, by Etienne-Dominique Pellevé of Sinceny and others. Hard-paste porcelain and faïence were made 1763–94, and glazed earthenware 1784–94. Porcelain wares include tablewares in a rococo style with high quality painting. Porcelain made at the factory features this mark which represents 'Nassau-Sarrbrucken'.

nx

Hirschvogel-Nickel-Reinhard Factory
Nuremberg, Bavaria, Germany
See p44. This mark appears on an armorial dish made at Nuremberg and probably represents the Hirschvogel-Nickel-Reinhard Factory in the second quarter of the 16thC.

OF

Offenbach *Nr Frankfurt-am-Main, Germany*
In 1739, a faïence factory was established in Offenbach by Philipp Friedrich Lay in 1739, who transferred it to his son Georg Heinrich in 1762, who sold it in 1765 to Johann Christoph Puschel. Under various owners the factory continued until the early 19thC. Output comprised mainly tablewares decorated with flowers, birds and figures in high-temperature colours. The factory probably ceased in the l9thC. This factory mark was used.

OP

Sceaux *Seine, France*
Faïence was first produced at Sceaux c1735 by de Bey and Jacques Chapelle; the latter became sole proprietor in 1759. The material was fine quality with good quality painting in muffle colours. Decorative items, tablewares and figures were made. This mark appears on faïence.

O.V.

Ohio Valley China Company
Wheeling, West Virginia, USA
The pottery (active 1887–93) produced good quality hard-paste porcelain tableware as well as some remarkable art wares with figures and elaborate piercing. A shield mark was used on heavy goods, while a 'leafy' mark appears on artistic wares.

PA

Rouen *Seine-Inférieure, France*
See p66. This is a painter's mark found on pieces made at Rouen in the late l7thC.

P

Peggy Cherniavsky *London, UK*
Pottery figures were produced from 1951. This impressed or printed mark was used 1951–54.

PC

Paul Caussy *Rouen, Seine-Inférieure, France*
Paul Caussy (d1731), together with his son Pierre-Paul (d1759) and grandson Pierre-Clement, were potters at Rouen from 1707. This mark appears.

P.F.

Joseph Fouque *Moustiers, Basse-Alpes, France*
See p36. This mark, together with a number of others, was used by Fouque.

P&H
CHOISY

V. Paillart and N. Hautin
Choisy-le-Roi, Seine, France
A factory producing white earthenware and porcelain was established here by the brothers Paillart in 1804, and from 1824 to 1836 the firm was V. Paillart and N. Hautin (Hautin and Boulenger from 1936). This mark was used 1824–36.

PH

PH
F

Paul Hannong *Frankenthal, Palatinate, Germany*
In 1755 Paul-Antoine Hannong of Strasburg was forced to give up porcelain production by the Vincennes authorities. He moved to Frankenthal where he obtained a privilege from the Elector Karl (or Carl) Theodor to begin a factory. His son Charles-François-Paul was manager until Paul Antoine's death in 1757 when another son, Charles-Adam, took over as manager and then owner from 1759. Financial problems led to the factory being purchased by Karl Theodor in 1762. Production in this period was similar to the style used at Strasburg, with rococo forms and distinctive red-toned decoration. These marks denoting 'Paul Hannong' (above) and 'Paul Hannong Frankenthal' (below) were used 1755–59. 'PH' had been previously used at Strasburg 1753–54.

PK

Philip Knight *Lancing, West Sussex, UK*
Studio-type wares, animals and portrait busts were produced from 1950. This impressed seal-type mark with initials in relief was used from 1962.

Po

Count Leopold von Proskau *Silesia, Germany*
See p42. This mark was used 1763–69.

PO:

Johann Georg Christoph Popp
Ansbach, Bavaria, Germany
See p49. This mark was used from 1715.

PP

Joan A. Biggs *London, UK*
See p61. This painted or incised Princedale Pottery mark was used 1958–61.

P.R.P

Paul Revere Pottery/Saturday Evening Girls *Boston and Brighton, Massachusetts, USA*
Daughters of immigrant families, who were members of a club that met weekly in the local public library, decided to take the librarian's advice to make and decorate pottery in order to occupy themselves, earn some money and learn a

trade. Books were read to them as they decorated children's dishes and vases in charming conventional flowers, fauna and landscape patterns. They employed a professional potter and kilnman.

Francisco de Aponte and Pickman & Co
Seville, Andalusia, Spain
Porcelain was produced by this firm at the La Cartuja factory in 1867. This is one of the marks used.

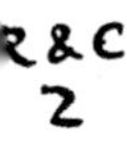

Rabe & Co *Brunswick, Germany*
See p93. In 1773, Johann Benjamin Heinrich Rabe and partner Johann Heinrich Christoph Hillecke leased the faïence factory in Brunswick. Rabe bought the factory in 1776 and ran it until his death in 1803. Rabe was ordered to use the ducal mark 'B' after being granted a privilege in 1781 (see p50). This mark also appears.

Rudolstadt *Thuringia, Germany*
A faïence factory was established here in 1720 by Johann Philipp Frantz and D. C. Freischhauer of Dorotheenthal. The factory continued until c1791. This mark appears; the letter 'C' is probably a painter's initial.

Richard Freeman *Bath, Avon, UK*
From 1956, Richard Freeman produced Studio-type wares at the Bath Pottery with this impressed seal mark.

François Dumetz *Aire, Pas-de-Calais, France*
See p43. This mark was used on faïence made at Aire under the direction of François Dumetz, from 1755 to c1790.

Robert's Factory
Marseilles, Bouches-du-Rhône, France
See p43. This mark was also used by this factory which operated from c1750 until at least 1793. Marks appear in a number of different forms.

Robinson & Leadbeater (Ltd)
Stoke, Staffordshire, UK
Between 1864 and 1924 this factory produced parian figures. This impressed initial mark was found on the back of parian and bone china figures and groups from c1885. The firm was taken over by J. A. Robinson & Sons Ltd and then by Cauldon Potteries Ltd.

R · n

Rauenstein *Thuringia, Germany*
In 1783, Duke Georg von Saxony-Meiningen granted a licence for porcelain production to Johann Georg, Johann Friedrich and Christian Daniel Greiner who founded a factory. To begin with, services were made in the Meissen style. Underglaze designs in blue and purple are characteristic of the concern; rustic overglaze decoration was also used. The factory continued until the late 19thC. This mark appears.

RS

Raymon Silverman *Dulwich, London, UK*
This impressed seal mark appears on Studio-type ceramics from 1962.

R W D

Ruth Duckworth *Kew, London, UK*
Studio-type pottery and sculpture were produced with this painted or incised mark from 1956.

R·X·

Robert's Factory
Marseilles, Bouches-du-Rhône, France
See p43. This mark was also used. Marks appear in a number of different forms.

+ S.t C. T

Saint-Cloud *Seine-et-Oise, France*
Porcelain was made in Saint-Cloud from 1693 by the family of Pierre Chicaneau, who had earlier discovered the process. After his death in 1678, Chicaneau's widow married Henri-Charles Trou, who obtained for the factory the protection of the Duke of Orleans, and letters patent were awarded to the Chicaneau family in 1702. Porcelain production remained their exclusive right until c1722, when the patent was renewed by Henri and Gabriel Trou. The factory was run by the Trou family until it closed in 1766. Saint Cloud porcelain has a creamy or ivory tone, and early pieces are often decorated with lambrequins based on textile ornament. Variations of this mark are found in underglaze blue, red enamel or as an incised mark. The 'T' denotes Henri Trou, who was able to produce porcelain after 1722.

S·c·ÿ

Sinceny *Aisne, France*
See p44. These marks were used during the 'second period' of the factory 1775–95.

S / L

Johann Leihamer *Schleswig, Germany*
A faïence factory was established in Schleswig by Johann Christoph Ludwig Lücke in 1755. From 1756 Adriani, Schmattau and two brothers called Otte were proprietors, and in 1758 Johann

Ramsbusch bought the factory. His son was forced to sell in 1801 and the factory was finally closed in 1841. This mark belongs to painter Johann Leihamer (b1721) from c1758.

·S·P

Sceaux *Seine, France*
See p67. In 1753 the Due de Penthièvre succeeded his aunt, the Duchesse de Maine, as patron of the factory at Sceaux. This painted mark appears on faïence and stands for 'Sceaux Penthièvre'.

SR

Stanislas Reychan *London, UK*
Based at the Garden Studio, Stanilas Reychan produced pottery sculpture and ornaments from 1950 with this impressed seal mark.

S·X

Sceaux *Seine, France*
See p67. The first attempt to produce porcelain at Sceaux 1749–52 was suppressed in the interest of the concern at Vincennes (Sèvres), and little was produced before 1763 when Joseph Jullien and Charles-Symphorien Jacques took over the factory, and the Sèvres monopoly had become more relaxed. The Duc de Penthièvre (see above) gave powerful support for the factory at Sceaux. In 1772 the factory was sold to Richard Glot. This incised mark appears on soft-paste porcelain from c1763, and in 1773 Glot submitted it to the police authorities.

hart

't Hart *Delft, Holland*
This factory (The Heart) was established in 1661 by Joris Mes. This mark appears.

THOM PSON

C. C. Thompson Pottery Company
East Liverpool, Ohio, USA
Created originally to make Rockingham and yellow ware, the company (1868–1938) continued to produce these products until 1917. In 1883, they expanded their product line to include decorated earthenware in miscellaneous table and toilet forms, such as diapers, pitchers, teapots, covered dishes, cuspidors, bedpans and toilet sets. In about 1890, they added white ironstone toilet and dinner ware to the line, and by 1917 semi-vitreous products were made.

TO

Bristol *Avon, UK*
Sophisticated tin-glazed earthenwares were made in Bristol from c1660. In 1748 Lund's factory in Bristol began to make soft-paste porcelain. In 1751 this concern was relocated to Worcester.

Hard-paste porcelain was made from c1770 when a Plymouth porcelain manufacture was taken over by Richard Champion and moved to Bristol in 1774. This impressed or moulded 'repairer's' mark appears on some pieces of hard-paste. This mark also appears on some pieces made at Bow and Worcester (c1760–69).

T°

Plymouth Porcelain Works *Devon, UK*
A porcelain factory was established here by William Cookworthy, and operated between 1768 and 1770. He discovered the porcelain production process independently, and found the materials necessary to begin production in Cornwall after a search that took many years. He took out a patent in 1768, and began a factory with the help of Thomas Pitt and a group of Quakers from the Plymouth and Bristol areas. The usual mark was the alchemist's sign for tin, and this may appear in underglaze blue, blue enamel, red or gold. Painting in underglaze blue has a blackish tone. His pieces feature Oriental designs and occasionally bird designs. In 1770, Cookworthy transferred to Bristol and in 1774 the factory was taken over by Richard Champion. This 'repairer's' mark appears on Plymouth porcelain, as well as pieces made at Bow, Worcester (c1760–69) and Bristol (see p71).

T°

'Tebo' Toulouse *Location unknown, UK*
Believed to he the mark of a ceramic modeller or 'repairer', this impressed or relief-moulded mark appears on porcelain from Bow (c1750–60), Worcester (c1760–69), Bristol (c1770–74) and Plymouth (c1769–70). The letter 'T' was very occasionally used by the same craftsman.

T P

Thomas Plant *Lane End, Staffordshire, UK*
This painted mark was used on earthenware figures made 1825–50.

T. P. Co.
CHINA

Trenton Potteries Company
Trenton, New Jersey, USA
This company (1892–1960) was created out of five potteries that specialized in sanitary ware, although artistic pieces were sometimes produced like the four mammoth urns elaborately decorated in the style of Sèvres for the company's display at the St Louis world's fair of 1904. During the 1930s, when construction had come to a virtual halt in the US, the company made florists' crockery to fill the kilns and keep

the workers busy. These wares with their bright monochromatic glazes are very collectable today. They made hotel ware at the turn of the century.

Turner & Tomkinson *Tunstall, Staffordshire*
Earthenwares were made by this firm 1860–72; it subsequently became G. W. Turner & Sons. The initials 'T. T.' were used in a variety of marks, and also in a fancy form as seen here.

United States Encaustic Tile Company
Indianapolis, Indiana, USA
Colourful floor tiles and standard glossy wall and fireplace tiles decorated with heads and conventional ornaments were made in large quantities by this company (1877–1939), which became the US Tile Corporation in 1932. This incised mark appears.

Vista Alegre *Nr Oporto, Portugal*
A porcelain factory was founded here in 1824 by José Ferreira Pinto Basso, with Royal patronage until 1840. This mark was used after 1840, before which the initials appear beneath a crown. High quality services and luxury porcelain are made at this factory, which is the only one in Portugal to produce these types of wares. The concern is still operated by the family of the founder.

Veuve Langlois *Bayeux, Calvados, France*
See p52. After the death of Joachim Langlois in 1830, the porcelain factory at Bayeux was continued by his daughters until 1849. This mark appears. The letter 'G' was added after the factory was bought by François Gosse who owned it until 1878.

Veuve Arnoux *Apt, Vaucluse, France*
The widow of Apt potter, Antoine Arnoux, who was also a sister of Joseph-Jacques Fouque, continued production of faïence and English-style earthenware in the late 18thC until 1802. This impressed mark appears.

Friedrich Thomin
Würzburg, Lower Franconia, Germany
In the 19thC, a *Hausmaler* at Würzburg, Friedrich Thomin decorated porcelain from Nymphenburg and Thuringia with views of Würzburg. The pieces date from the early 19thC and bear this mark in black.

Derby Porcelain Works
Derbyshire, UK
See p35. This early incised mark used from c1750 to 1755 is rare.

Wrisbergholzen *Hanover, Germany*
A faïence factory was founded 1735–37 by Baron von Wrisberg, and was run by a number of managers until 1804. Production was influenced by Dutch Delft wares. This factory mark appears, often with a painter's mark.

W.E.P.CO.
CHINA

West End Pottery Company
East Liverpool, Ohio, USA
This pottery (active 1893–1938) made ironstone (or white granite) dinner, toilet and hotel wares and some speciality items. Semi-vitreous dinner, hotel, tea and toilet wares were offered by 1927, along with premium assortments and hospital and druggists' ware.

William Moorcroft *Burslem, Staffordshire, UK*
After working as Art Director at Macintyre and Co, William Moorcroft (1872–1945) set up his own factory in 1913. As well as his famous Florian wares designed for Macintyre, Moorcroft produced a wide range of richly-glazed, floral-decorated earthenwares. Moorcroft signed all Florian wares with 'W. M. des.' or 'W. Moorcroft des.'. Sometimes pieces were marked 'Florian Ware Jas. Macintyre & Co. Ltd. Burslem, England'. Florian wares were sold at Liberty's in London, and Tiffany's in New York. These painted initials are found.

WN
53

William Newland
Prestwood, Buckinghamshire, UK
Studio-type pottery, ceramic sculpture and architectural wares were produced by Newland from 1948. This painted or incised initial mark appears with year numbers.

H. M. Williamson & Sons
Longton, Staffordshire, UK
Based at the Bridge Pottery, this firm produced porcelain c1879–1941. Many variations of this mark appear; this example was used from c1903; a plainer version of the same mark was used from c1879.

:V:B

Willem van Beck *Delft, Holland*
Founded 1661–62 by Sebastian M. van Kuyck, and others, De twee Wildemannen (The Two Wild Men) was owned by Willem van Beck between 1760 and 1780. He used this mark.

Reginald Wells *Storrington, West Sussex, UK*
Previously based at Wrotham, Kent (c1909) and Chelsea in London (c1910–24), Reginald Wells (1877–1951) worked from Storrington from c1925. He produced Studio-type pottery, stonewares and figures. This incised or impressed initial mark was used from 1910.

· DEX

Zacharias Dextra *Delft, Holland*
See p60. This mark was used by Zacharias Dextra while he was manager of De 3 vergulde Astonne (The Three Golden Ash Barrels) from 1712 to c1759.

Monograms

Detail of Dresden mark, 19thC

MONOGRAMS

Akron China Company *Akron, Ohio, USA*
This large pottery (1894–1908) made decorated dinner and toilet wares in white granite (ironstone), and hotel ware called 'Revere'.

Elgersburg *Thuringia, Germany*
C. E. & F. Arnoldi produced hard-paste porcelain from 1808. This mark was used together with a circular stamp with the words 'Fabrik Arnoldi Elgersburg'.

Alan Caiger-Smith *Berkshire, UK*
Alan Caiger-Smith established the Aldermaston Pottery in 1955. He is known internationally as one of the most influential potters of his day and a leading authority on tin-glazed and lustred earthenwares. His published works are essential reading to both potters and ceramic historians. His own output is of Studio ceramics. While Alan Caiger-Smith's mark is a combination of his initials, this example is that of A. Partridge who worked with him at the Aldermaston Pottery. Marks on his pottery are incised or painted. Other potters working at Aldermaston also used monograms, each featuring the letter 'A'.

Arthur J. Griffiths
Long Whatton, Leicestershire, UK
This impressed mark was used on Studio-type wares from 1948. Griffiths also worked at the Crowan and Leach Potteries.

Anna Hagen *London, UK*
Anna Hagen produced hand-thrown, moulded and pressed wares from 1956. The mark above was incised, and appeared on hand-thrown pots, and the mark below, an impressed seal mark, appears on moulded and pressed wares.

Adriaenus Koeks *Delft, Holland*
This mark was used by Adriaenus Koeks (also known as Kocks), while he was at De Griekschc A (The Greek A) factory in Delft (1687–1701). Some of Koeks' accounts are preserved at Hampton Court Palace. The mark appears on all types of Dutch Delft wares, and has been extensively faked.

Andreas Kordenbusch *Nuremberg, Germany*
Kordenbusch (d1754) was a faïence painter in Nuremberg from c1726, producing high quality work, including an armorial tankard painted in blue with a figure, dated 1738.

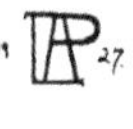

Alfred Pocock *Slinfold, West Sussex, UK*
A. L. Pocock made Studio-type pottery c1920–35, and used an incised or painted monogram mark with the year of production.

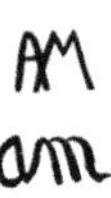

Tenby Pottery *Tenby, Dyfed, Wales, UK*
Owned by Anthony Markes, the Tenby Pottery produced Studio-type wares from 1959. Pieces made and decorated by Anthony himself bore these marks with these initials.

Alfred and Louise Powell
Staffordshire and London, UK
Alfred and Louise Powell worked as pottery designers and decorators for Wedgwood who supplied them with earthenware blanks. Their painted earthenwares usually bear impressed Wedgwood marks. They also worked independently in London. This personal painted mark was used by Alfred Powell (d1960) c1904–39. Louise Powell used a similar mark with the initials 'LP'.

Albert Potteries Ltd
Burslem, Staffordshire, UK
The Albert Potteries produced earthenwares 1946–54. This mark was either printed or impressed. Also used was a printed mark, 'Albert Potteries Ltd, Burslem, Made in England'.

Aylesford Priory Pottery
Aylesford, Kent, UK
This impressed seal mark was used on stonewares from 1955. It also appears with the word 'Aylesford' written underneath.

Aprey *Haute-Marne, France*
A faïence factory was established in Aprey c1744 by Jacques Lallemant, Baron d'Aprey, and his brother Joseph Lallemant de Villehaut. After the former retired, Joseph engaged François Ollivier, a potter from Nevers, and fine wares were made at the factory. Ollivier was director until 1792. The monogram 'APR' was not always used; where it does appear it is often accompanied by the initial of the painter.

Anne H. Thalmessinger *Camberley, Surrey, UK*
From 1961 Thalmessinger made Studio-type pottery using this mark or variations.

American Encaustic Tiling Company
Zanesville, Ohio, USA
The American businessmen who founded the company brought English tile-maker Gilbert Elliott to Zanesville in 1876 to supervize production. Encaustic, relief, glazed, plastic sketches, imitation mosaic, damask, portrait, unglazed floor, and faïence tiles were all made 1875–1935. Plaques, plates, figurines, vases, fountains and bathroom fixtures were also produced. The company was very successful and had a second plant in California by 1920. Half the tiles in New York's Holland Tunnel were made by this company.

Antoine Bonnefoy
Marseilles, Bouches-du-Rhône, France
Personal mark of Antoine Bonnefoy (d1793), who ran a successful factory in Marseilles from 1762 (see p32).

Britannia China Co *Longton, Staffordshire, UK*
The factory produced porcelain 1895–1906. This printed or impressed mark was used 1904–06. The impressed initial mark 'BC Co' was used 1895–1906.

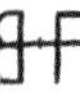

Burmantofts *Leeds, West Yorkshire, UK*
Owned by Messrs Wilcox & Co Ltd, this firm produced Art Pottery 1882–1904. This impressed mark was used, sometimes with the words 'Burmantofts Faïence' also impressed.

Hugo Brouwer *Delft, Holland*
Mark of potter Hugo Brouwer registered in 1764, at De 3 porceleyne Flessies (The Three Porcelain Scent Bottles), where he worked 1748–77. Brouwer also worked at Het Bijltje (The Hatchet).

C. J. C. Bailey (or Bailey & Co) *London, UK*
Operating between 1864 and 1889, this pottery produced stonewares, terracotta and porcelain (from c1873). The name subsequently changed to Fulham Pottery & Cheavin Filter Co Ltd. This incised monogram mark comprising the initials 'CJCB' often appears with the words 'Fulham Pottery' and the date.

Jean Bertin *Rouen, Seine-Inférieure, France*
Between c1700 and 1750, Jean Bertin, his father Henri and his family made faïence in Rouen. This mark appears.

Joseph-François Boussemaert *Lille, France*
Joseph-François Boussemaert took over the factory established by his father-in-law, Jacques Féburier (see p32), after the death of the latter in 1729. Boussemaert remained as proprietor until his death in 1773.

Hamburg *Germany*
See p35. This mark is one of those probably used by a painter, c1625–30.

Baron Jean-Louis de Beyerlé
Niderviller, Lorraine, France
See p41. Although pieces were often unmarked during the ownership of Baron de Beyerlé, this mark occasionally appears on faïence and porcelain (which was made from 1765).

Burgess & Leigh (Ltd)
Burslem, Staffordshire, UK
Active from 1862 and based at the Hill Pottery c1867–89, and Middleport Pottery from c1889, this firm produced earthenwares. Pieces made from 1862 feature this monogram mark.

Thomaz Brunetto *Rato, Portugal*
A royal faïence factory was established in 1767, directed by Thomaz Brunetto from Turin until 1771. This mark was used during Brunetto's period, with the initials 'FR'.

Faenza *Emilia, Italy*
Maiolica was made in Faenza (the origin of the term faïence) from the l4thC, and some of the finest Italian tin-glazed earthenware was made there 1500–30. This 'BT' or 'TB' monogram appears on a number of different pieces that also feature painters' marks, and probably was used by a particular workshop.

Vodrey Pottery Company
East Liverpool, Ohio, USA
Created by three brothers after their father had disastrous results with earlier partnerships in several cities, Vodrey and Brother Pottery Company produced Rockingham and yellow ware in its Palissy Works beginning in 1858.

Following the Civil War, the company prospered and added white ironstone as a product from 1876. Semi-porcelain was added to the ironstone line in 1896, and the company continued to produce dinner, toilet and hotel wares until it closed in 1928.

J. B. Owens Pottery Company
Zanesville, Ohio, USA
Owens built and operated several potteries during his life, but this one featured art wares that were designed, made and decorated by leading potters, chemists and decorators during the brief time that the pottery was in production (1896–1907). Overall the work was derivative, with many references to the pottery produced at Rookwood (see p102) but Owens' ware won gold medals in at least one international fair.

Joseph Clérissy *Saint-Jean-du-Désert, France*
In 1679 Joseph Clérissy, the son of the elder Antoine Clérissy of Moustiers, took over an existing faïence factory located at Saint-Jean-du-Désert (a suburb of Marseilles). Clérissy died in poverty in 1685 and the factory was subsequently managed by his widow, Anne Roux, and her new husband, a faïence painter at the factory. Joseph Clérissy's son Antoine took over the factory on his mother's death in 1694 and conducted the factory successfully until 1733 when it was moved to Marseilles itself. This mark was used by Joseph Clérissy.

Nymphenburg *Bavaria, Germany*
One of the main German porcelain-producing centres of the 18thC, Ignaz Niedermeyer founded the factory at Nymphenburg with the sponsorship of Elector Max III Joseph of Bavaria, and the help of porcelain painter and arcanist Joseph Jakob Ringler. Pieces were high in quality and artistic value, but the concern ran into financial difficulties and the Elector was forced to increase his subsidy. He died in 1770, and the factory passed into the hands of Karl Theodor of the Palatinate, who already had interests in the factory at Frankenthal. The Nymphenburg factory took second place until the Frankenthal works closed in 1799. In the mid-l8thC the factory at Nymphenhurg employed some talented painters and modellers such as Franz Anton Bustelli (active 1754–63), and J. P. Melchior (from 1797). The factory

remained a State possession until 1862, and was then leased into private ownership. It still exists today. Output includes figures and tablewares in the rococo style. This mark appears on a group of coffee cups made for the Turkish market.

Coalport Porcelain Works
Coalport, Shropshire, UK
This factory was established by John Rose in the late 18thC making table and decorative wares. Now at Stoke-on-Trent, the factory is still in production. Early pre-1805 porcelains were unmarked, and marks were rarely used before 1820. The painted or gilt monogram (above) was used c1851–61. The mark below was one of those used on Coalport's decorative floral-encrusted porcelains made during the 1810–25 period. It appears painted in underglaze blue.

Ludwigsburg *Württemberg, Germany*
Faïence was made in Ludwigsburg from 1757 by Häckher, but in 1758 his privilege was transferred by Duke Charles Eugene to Johann Jakob Mergenthaler and Anton Joachim. (Porcelain was also made, see p153) The Duke took over the factory himself in 1763, and it was managed by Frau de Becke (Maria Löwenfinck). Cream-coloured earthenware was made by Gottfried Markt after 1776. Charles Eugene died in 1793, and production went into decline until there was a revival under King Friedrich. Cream-coloured earthenware was the main product. Pieces feature flower decoration on a white ground and also moulded decoration similar to Niderviller. The mark above appears on faïence 1757–1824; the centre mark was used on cream-coloured earthenware 1776–1824; the mark below appears on porcelain during the time of Duke Charles Eugene, 1758–93. The factory closed in 1824.

Sèvres *France*
This porcelain factory moved from Vincennes to Sèvres in 1756, owned by a joint stock company (25% Royal shares) founded in 1753. The eight leaseholders received a Royal privilege for 30 years, but disagreements led to the King taking control of the factory in 1759. Soft-paste porcelain was made up to c1800, hard-paste after c1770. The factory became an Imperial establishment in 1804. Particular marks were used during the tie of each reigning monarch.

This mark was used during the time of Charles X (1824–30) and appears in blue. The number 25 refers to 1825. The mark may also appear beneath a crown.

Daphne Corke *Colchester, Essex, UK*
Daphne Corke worked at the Chelsea pottery 1951–56, and later independently. This incised or painted monogram mark was used from 1951 on Studio-type wares; name and initial marks appear after 1959.

Charles Ford *Hanley, Staffordshire, UK*
Based in Cannon Street 1874–1904 (previously C. & T. Ford and Thomas Ford), this factory produced porcelain. The works were sold to J. A. Robinson & Sons Ltd in 1904. This impressed or printed monogram mark was used, and also appears on a swan.

Christine Hall
Henley-on-Thames, Oxfordshire, UK
This painted mark was used on porcelain and pottery figures and groups from 1960.

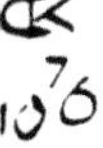

Cornelius Keiser *Delft, Holland*
The son of Aelbrecht Cornelisz Keiser who established De twee Scheepjes (The Two Little Ships) in 1642, Cornelius Keiser worked at the factory from 1668. This is believed to be his mark.

Coldstone Kiln
Ascott-under-Wychwood, Oxfordshire, UK
Run by Chris Harries, this pottery produced slip-decorated earthenwares from 1953. This impressed seal mark was used.

Lambertus Cleffius *Delft, Holland*
Proprietor of De metale Pot (The Metal Pot) (established 1638 by Dirck Hieronymusz van Kessel) 1666–91, Cleffius was also proprietor of De witte Starre (The White Star) from 1687–89. He used this mark.

Michael Cardew *Cornwall, UK*
Cardew (1901–82), a Studio potter, was based at Winchcombe c1926–39, and at Wenford Bridge 1939–42; he then moved to Africa. An early pupil of Bernard Leach, Cardew began potting in 1923 making slip-decorated earthenwares. This impressed seal mark was used by him from c1926.

Carlo Manzoni
Ashby-de-la-Zouch, Leicestershire, UK
Studio ceramics were produced at the Granville Pottery, Hanley, Staffordshire (1895–98), and then at the Coleorton Pottery, Ashby-de-la-Zouch. This incised monogram was used, accompanied by numerals indicating the year of manufacture.

Caen *Calvados, France*
A factory producing hard-paste porcelain existed here 1793–1806, managed by d'Aigmont-Desmares and then Ducheval. Resembling Paris porcelain, pieces were sometimes sent to be decorated by Parisian enamellers Helley and Dastin. This mark appears in red-brown on wares made after 1799.

Newcomb Pottery *New Orleans, Louisiana, USA*
Founded to employ women who had been trained in the art program of H. Sophie Newcomb Memorial College, this pottery (1895–1940) developed a signature style that presented southern flora conventionally in a palette limited to green, blue, yellow and black. Matt glazes were used exclusively after 1911.

Crowan Pottery *Praze, Cornwall, UK*
Harry and May Davis, the owners of the Crowan Pottery, operated in Cornwall producing Studio-type pottery from 1946. In July 1962 they emigrated to New Zealand. This mark was used 1946–62.

Carter, Stabler & Adams (Ltd)
Poole Pottery, Dorset, UK
Formerly Carter & Co, this pottery was established in 1921 and continues to the present day. This impressed 'CSA' monogram mark is rare.

Kloster-Veilsdorf *Thuringia, Germany*
The most important Thuringian porcelain factory was established here in 1760 by Prince Friedrich Wilhelm Eugen von Hildburghausen. After his death in 1795, it was sold to the sons of Gotthel Greiner of Limbach, and Friedrich Greiner of Rauenstein, and remained in their family until 1822. This mark, which stands for 'Closter-Veilsdorf' and appears more rarely as individual letters, appears in underglaze blue. Another 'CV' monogram used at Kloster-Veilsdorf was drawn to imitate the crossed swords of Meissen.

Vera Cheeseman *Marlow, Buckinghamshire, UK*
From 1947, Vera Cheeseman produced Studio-type pottery figures in media such as terracotta. Her monogram mark, which on her pieces appears with the year of production, is similar to one used by Studio potter Charles Vyse (see below), but Vyse did not produce figures during the same period as Mrs Cheeseman.

Charles Vyse *Chelsea, London, UK*
Charles Vyse produced earthenware figures and groups in the 1920s and 1930s, and Chinese glaze-effect stonewares to 1963. This painted mark was used and features the year of production and name 'Chelsea'. He also used incised or impressed initial marks from 1919.

Dorothy Annan *London, UK*
From 1949, Dorothy Annan produced Studio-type pottery, murals and mosaics. She used this incised or painted mark.

De Paauw (The Peacock) *Delft, Holland*
Established in 1652 by Dirck Hieronymusz van Kessel (also of De metale Pot, De Romein and De porceleyn Schotel), De Paauw used this factory mark (and other variations) in the late 17th and early 18thC.

Dora Barrett *Harpenden, Hertfordshire, UK*
This incised mark was used on Dora Barrett's terracotta and stoneware models of animals from 1938.

Derek Clarkson *Bacup, Lancashire, UK*
This impressed seal-type mark was used on Studio-type wares from January 1961.

Derek Emms *Longton, Staffordshire, UK*
Studio-type wares had this impressed seal mark (some were unmarked) from 1955.

Roegina Pottery *Rainham, Kent, UK*
Owned by O. C. Davies, this pottery produced earthenwares and operated between 1938 and 1939. It was reopened in 1948 by Alfred Wilson Ltd. This monogram 'GBD' was used on wares decorated by Mrs Davies c1938–39.

Daphne Henson *Whitton, Middlesex, UK*
This incised mark, often with the date, appears on Studio-type pottery from 1951.

Dorothy Kemp *Felixstowe, Suffolk, UK*
Trained by Bernard Leach, Dorothy Kemp made Studio pottery, slipwares and stonewares from 1939. She used this incised or impressed mark from c1939.

Newlyn Harbour Pottery *Cornwall, UK*
Run by Dennis Lane, this pottery produced Studio-type wares from 1956. Pieces made by Lane feature this incised or impressed mark. The standard impressed mark is 'Newlyn Harbour Pottery'.

N. Dickinson *Worthing, West Sussex, UK*
Dickinson made Studio-type pottery from 1948, and used this initial mark.

Deacon Pottery *London, UK*
Studio-type pottery was made here 1952–58. This impressed, circular seal mark was used.

Sally Dawson *London, UK*
Having previously potted in Canada, Sally Dawson worked at the Canonbury Studio in north London from 1962. She used this impressed seal-type mark from 1963, that may also feature the name 'Canonbury Studio'.

Dirck van der Does *Delft, Holland*
Proprietor of De Roos (The Rose) 1755–79 (see p43), van der Does registered this mark in 1764.

Eric Barber *Newcastle-upon-Tyne and Sunderland, Tyne and Wear, UK*
From 1951, this company produced non-commercial, Studio-type earthenwares. This incised or painted initial mark appeared with the year of production.

E. J. D. Bodley *Burslem, Staffordshire, UK*
Based at the Hill Pottery and then Crown Works from 1882, the firm (formerly Bodley & Son) operated between 1875 and 1892, producing general ceramics. The distinguishing initials are found on several printed or impressed marks of differing design. The initials 'J' and 'B' are often joined.

E. Duncombe *Wimbledon, London, UK*
Miss E. Duncombe made Studio-type pottery from 1953, with stonewares from 1962. This incised or painted mark was used.

Eila Henderson *Eastbourne, East Sussex, UK*
Based in London before 1954, Eila Henderson was at the Theda Pottery c1948–54. She produced Studio-type pottery, and one of her marks was this painted or incised mark.

Lambertus van Eenhorn *Delft, Holland*
Proprietor of De metale Pot (The Metal Pot) (see p83) 1691–1721, Lambertus van Eenhorn used this monogram mark. The initials below possibly belonged to the painter.

East Liverpool Pottery Company
East Liverpool, Ohio, USA
Organized by John and Robert Hall and Monroe Patterson, this company (1894–1901) made plain and decorated ironstone until 1896 and then semi-vitreous porcelain tableware, toilet ware and souvenir pieces. In 1901, it was one of six firms that merged as the East Liverpool Potteries Company, but two years later the Halls left to form Hall China Company (see p127). In addition to the company initials, the firm also designated its ware as 'Waco China'. Other marks featuring these initials were also used.

Raymond Everett *Rye, East Sussex, UK*
Studio ceramics were produced by this potter from 1963, with this painted monogram appearing on selected pieces.

Samuel van Eenhorn *Delft, Holland*
Manager of the De Grieksche A (The Greek A) factory (established by his father, Wouter van Eenhorn (also of De 3 vergulde Astonne, De porceleyn Schotel and Het hooge Huys) and Q. A. van Cleynoven in 1658) from 1674–78, then proprietor from 1678–87. Various combinations of the 'SVE' monogram painted in blue on blue and white Delftware. His pieces are generally of high quality, with particular emphasis on Chinese Transitional style wares.

Arnoux Fouque & Cie
Valentine, Haute-Garonne, France
Between 1832 and 1860, Joseph-Jacques and Arnoux Fouque produced white earthenware and hard-paste porcelain. This mark appears in red. The Fouques also made creamwares at Toulouse from 1797; a similar mark to this one was used by Antoine and François Fouque with Arnoux from 1829.

H. M. French *Peckham, London, UK*
An assistant to Charles Vyse (see p85) before World War II, Miss French produced Studio-type pottery from 1945. This incised initial mark appears on some pieces made at Vyse's Chelsea pottery in the 1930s.

Faïence Manufacturing Company
Brooklyn, New York, USA
The company (1880–92) made a variety of highly decorative earthenware vases, jardinières and baskets, including lines with faïence glazes and modelled and applied flowers, as well as a fine creamware with elaborate piercing and gilding. English decorator Edward Lycett directed the factory from 1884 and developed deep cobalt blue and iridescent Persian glazes.

F. S. Robinson *Thundridge, Hertfordshire, UK*
Based at the Duckett Wood Pottery from 1959, F. S. Robinson first worked with A. G. Shelley, but produced Studio-type wares featuring this impressed seal mark, independently from 1961.

Sybil Finnemore *Bembridge, Isle of Wight, UK*
Sybil Finnemore and her husband T. R. Parsons owned the Bembridge pottery producing Studio-type wares 1949–61. This is her personal mark which she also used during her time at the Yellowsands Pottery, Bembridge c1927–39.

Anne Gordon
Quick's Green, Pangbourne, Berkshire, UK
Producing Studio-type pottery, figures and bird models, Mrs Gordon used this incised or painted mark, often with the year added from 1958.

Gater, Hall & Co *Burslem, Staffordshire, UK*
Formerly Thomas Gater & Co (established 1895), the firm was based at New Gordon Pottery, Tunstall c1899–1907, and subsequently at the Royal Overhouse Pottery 1907–43. This mark was used 1914–43. The company became Barratt's of Staffordshire Ltd in 1943.

Griffen, Smith & Hill
Phoenixville, Pennsylvania, USA
This company (1879–94) was one of a succession of several companies making many different products in the same pottery under different names. During the Griffen, Smith & Hill period the product was majolica, that is cream-coloured

earthenware in naturalistic shapes covered with brightly-coloured glossy glazes. Uncoloured ware was called 'Ivory'. Marks featured the impressed words 'Etruscan Majolica', or sometimes just the word 'Etruscan'.

Isabel Goudie *Edinburgh, Scotland, UK*
Potting between 1920 and 1930 producing Studio-type wares, Isabel Goudie used this monogram mark.

Margaret J. Galbraith *Sydenham, London, UK*
From 1961, Studio-type wares were produced with this impressed seal-type mark.

Agnes Benson *Ruislip, London, UK*
Based at King's College Road from 1951, Agnes Benson produced Studio-type pottery with this monogram mark from 1959.

Gerald Makin *Bilston, Staffordshire, UK*
This impressed, incised or painted monogram mark appears on Studio-type pottery from 1958.

Geoffrey Maund *Croydon, Surrey, UK*
Hand-made earthenwares were produced at Geoffrey Maund Pottery Ltd from 1952. This impressed mark was used from c1953.

G. M. Creyke & Sons *Hanley, Staffordshire, UK*
Between 1920 and 1948 earthenwares were produced by this firm at Bell Works. Pieces are found bearing the initials 'GMC'.

Grove & Stark *Longton, Staffordshire, UK*
Previously called R. H. Grove, this firm was based at the Palissy Works 1871–85, making earthenwares. This monogram appears within a circle on plates in the early 1880s.

Avoncroft Pottery *Hampton Lovett, Droitwich, Hereford and Worcester, UK*
See p31. This mark is the personal seal mark of owner Geoffrey Whiting used from 1952.

Oldswinford Pottery
Oldswinford, Stourbridge, West Midlands, UK
Operating between 1955 and 1960, this mark comprising the initials of owner Howard Bissell appears on Studio-type wares. The name of the firm was changed to Swincraft Productions c1960. This impressed seal-type mark was used

up to 1962. Incised initials in a flowing style were used after 1962. The basic mark 'Oldswinford Pottery' was also used with the name of the individual potter.

Antoine de la Hubaudière
Quimper, Finistère, France
In c1690 a faïence factory was founded near Quimper by Jean-Baptiste Bousquet. In 1743 it was taken over by Pierre-Paul Caussy of Rouen, and similar wares to those made at Rouen were produced. In 1782 the factory was taken over by Antoine de la Hubaudière (d1794), the husband of Pierre-Paul Caussy's granddaughter. In 1872 the factory's director, Fougeray, began to make imitations of 18thC faïence with this mark.

Kelsterbach *Hesse Darmstadt, Germany*
Originally a faïence-producing factory (see p39), in 1761 it was taken over by the Landgrave Ludwig VIII and hard-paste porcelain began to be made under the direction of C. D. Busch of Meissen, who stayed there until 1764. Porcelain continued to be made until the death of Ludwig VIII in 1768 and was not resumed until 1789 with help from J. M. Höckel of Höchst while Johann Jakob Lay was director. Lay bought the factory from the Landgrave in 1799, and in 1802 the Landgrave withdrew his support and the production of porcelain was discontinued. The factory continued, and cream-coloured earthenware was made until c1823. This mark appears on faïence in manganese (more rarely in blue), and on porcelain (during the two periods of production) in underglaze blue usually below a crown from 1766–1802.

Joseph Hannong
Strasburg, France and Frankenthal, Germany
Joseph Hannong (b1734) was the son of Paul Hannong (d1760), who had been the proprietor of the factory at Strasburg. Joseph was forced to sell his porcelain manufactory at Frankenthal in 1760. He returned to Strasburg two years later to run the factory. In an attempt to make porcelain as well as faïence he speculated rashly and as a result bankrupted the concern in 1780. His mark can appear confusing as it appears as an 'H' with a dot over the first upright. This is in fact a combination of 'J' and 'H'. In the 18thC the letter 'I' was often used as a 'J'. His mark appears on wares produced at both Strasburg

(above), and Frankenthal (below), but the mark used at Frankenthal may be incised, as well as written in blue.

T. S. Haile *Shinners Bridge, Darlington, Devon (and other locations), UK*
Samuel Haile was active from c1936 until his death in 1948 (apart from a two-year gap during WWII, from 1943–45). He produced Studio ceramics using this impressed monogram.

Joseph Holdcroft
Sutherland Pottery, Longton, Staffordshire, UK
From 1865–1940 Holdcroft produced general ceramics as well as more decorative wares, including parian and lead-glazed majolica.

Joyce Haynes *Tuxford, Nr Newark-on-Trent, Nottinghamshire, UK*
Studio pottery, including stoneware and wood-ash glazed wares, was produced c1940–60. This impressed monogram was used from c1947.

Johann Heinrich Koch
Cassel, Hesse-Nassau, Germany
A faïence factory was founded here c1680 by the Landgrave of Hesse-Cassel, run by a succession of managers. Johann Heinrich Koch was the manager 1719–24 and the mark above was probably used by him. From 1924 the factory was bought by Johann Christoph Gilze of Brunswick and his son Ludwig. It became a successful concern, producing mainly blue and white faïence. The 'HL' in the monogram below stands for 'Hessen-Land'; this mark may appear with the letter 'G' for 'Gilze'.

Homer Laughlin China Co *East Liverpool, Ohio and Newell, West Virginia, USA*
Prior to 1877, Homer Laughlin was in business with his brother Shakespeare, first in the distribution of pottery made in East Liverpool and then, from 1874, in the production of whiteware. Semi-vitreous porcelain was added during the 1890s. The company, which is still in operation, has made a wide variety of dinner, hotel and toilet wares over the years, although it may be most famous for its Fiesta line, which has been made periodically since 1936. The company expanded to Newell by 1914 and moved its entire operation there in 1929. Today, it is one of the largest potteries in the world.

Paul Hannong *Strasburg, France*
From the second generation of the Hannong family who ran the faïence factory during its greatest period from 1739–60, Paul introduced the full *petit-feu* palette into France and used some of the finest and most experienced decorators, modellers and arcanists. For example, he employed Adam von Löwenfinck, the Meissen porcelain painter, Johann-Wilhelm Lanz, the modeller who later worked at Frankenthal, and Joseph-Jacob Ringler, the arcanist from Vienna who had gained the secrets of hard-paste porcelain by using his charms on the daughter of the director of the State factory. The marks are generally painted in blue, brown or black, although a few are incised or impressed.

Pierre-Antoine Hannong *Strasburg, France*
Son of Paul Hannong, Pierre-Antoine (1739–94) was manager of the factory at Strasburg and Haguenau (1760–62), founder of porcelain factories at Vincennes (1765), Paris (1771) and Vinovo (1776). He revived the production of porcelain at Haguenau 1783–84 using this mark.

Haverfordwest Pottery *T. & A. Whalley, Haverfordwest, Dyfed, Wales, UK*
From 1962 producers of Studio-type ceramics, including low-fired earthenwares and stonewares. Marks are all impressed.

Seth (or James) Pennington
Liverpool, Mersey, UK
A potter and painter at Liverpool, c1760–80. Liverpool porcelains made with this mark probably relate to the Penningtons, rather than the Herculaneum Pottery of Liverpool (c1793–1841). This mark is painted.

Helen Pincombe *Oxshott, Surrey, UK*
Operating at The Forge in Oxshott from 1950, using this impressed mark on Studio-type pottery.

Lorenz Hutschenreuther
Selb, Bavaria, Germany
This hard-paste porcelain factory was founded in 1856 and production began in 1859. Both utility and artistic wares were made. The company expanded taking over other premises and became one of Germany's leading porcelain manufacturers, producing tea and coffee services, household, hotel and restaurant ware, oven-proof

pieces and gift items. This monogram mark was used, sometimes together with the words 'Hutschenreuther, Selb'.

Linthorpe Pottery *Middlesbrough, Cleveland, UK*
Founded in 1879 by John Harrison and Henry Tooth, one of the foremost late Victorian potters (from 1882 proprietor of the Bretby pottery where a similar monogram was used). Especially noted for its somewhat unusual forms designed by Christopher Dresser after pre-Columbian and Japanese types. The factory closed in 1889.

Tooth & Co *Woodville, Derbyshire, UK*
The Bretby Art Pottery was established in 1883 by Henry Tooth and William Ault (who later ran his own concern from 1887). Production was similar to the Linthorpe Pottery (see above) with coloured, lead-glazed and ornamental earthenwares as well as everyday wares, some after designs by Christopher Dresser. Large pieces, such as jardinières with plinths and umbrella stands, are characteristic of Bretby. Marks were printed.

Brunswick *Germany*
Although established as a small concern in 1707 by Duke Anton Ulrich, this mark refers to the period between 1710 and 1749 when the factory at Brunswick was leased to Heinrich Christoph von Horn and Werner von Hantelmann (although the substance of the partnership changed many times). At first production followed Dutch Delftware but towards the end of this period more sophisticated and innovative wares appeared. Production included everyday wares such as dishes and cylindrical tankards but somewhat unusually for a faïence factory a relatively wide range of figures and animals in the rococo style. Marks were painted.

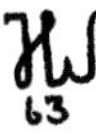

Helen Walters
Stroud Green, Hornsey, London, UK
Studio pottery was produced from 1945. Painted or incised monograms appear, usually with the last two numbers denoting the year of manufacture.

Hawley, Webberley & Co
Garfield Works, Longton, Staffordshire, UK
Operated 1895–1902 producing general earthenwares, including majolica. This printed mark was used.

Ian Auld *Wimbish, Saffron Walden, Essex, UK*
From 1959 Studio ceramics, stoneware and earthenware were produced. Marks are either impressed or painted.

Odney Pottery
Grove Farm, Cookham, Berkshire, UK
John Bew of the Odney Pottery (1937–56), used these painted initials on earthenwares between 1950 and 1954.

Joanna Connell
Great Baddow, Chelmsford, Essex, UK
Joanna Connell produced Studio ceramics, mainly high-fired wares including stoneware and porcelain with impressed seal marks.

George Jones & Sons *Burslem, Staffordshire, UK*
Based at the Trent Pottery (c1864–1907) and then the Crescent Pottery (1907–57), producing high quality wares for the domestic market and especially for export to North and South America, Africa and the Colonies. While a wide range of wares (including porcelain after 1872) was produced, the factory is probably best known for its decorative majolica lead-glazed earthenwares such as centrepieces, vases and baskets. The mark originally 'GJ' (1861–73) has '& Sons' added after this date together with a crescent. The mark is usually printed or impressed, but some of the early monograms appear in slight relief.

Joan Crawford
Isle of Mull and Dalkeith, Lothian, Scotland, UK
Studio-type ceramics made from 1951. Marks may be painted or incised with the initials 'JC'. 'Mull' appears on specimens made in the Isle of Mull. After her marriage in 1958 the initials change to a combined 'JF' (Mrs J. Faithfull).

John Fisher *Rowlands Gill, Tyne and Wear, UK*
From 1950 John Fisher produced Studio ceramics in association with Denis Rock. As well as his monogram, which may be either painted or incised, John Fisher also used the kingfisher as his rebus.

Christopher D. Warham
New Malden, Surrey, UK
Studio pottery was produced from 1949. The mark 'JG' is impressed from 1959. Warham's incised initial mark was also used 1949–56.

James Hadley & Sons
Worcester, Hereford and Worcester, UK
Operated 1895–1905. Employed as a modeller (later chief modeller) during the proprietorship of Kerr and Binns at Worcester (c1852–62), James Hadley continued to produce models for Royal Worcester even after he became independent in 1875. He established his own company in 1895, and produced a wide range of porcelain and pottery. The mark is either printed or impressed.

Judith Partridge *Lewes, East Sussex, UK*
From 1954 this potter produced Studio pottery and majolica wares. Her monogram appears painted, with or without the word 'Lewes'.

June Sarene *Pinner, London, UK*
From 1954, Studio-type ceramics were produced. An incised or painted monogram may appear, or simply the initials 'JS'.

John Shelly *Bath, Avon, UK*
The Bath Pottery also operated in Dorset and Devon from 1949 to c1960, producing Studio pottery. The marks are for 1949–56, and at Littlehempston from 1957.

Kenneth Clark Pottery *London, UK*
Tiles and Studio ceramics were produced from 1952, with painted marks.

De Porceleyn Schotel *Delft, Holland*
According to some authorities. there was a factory of this name (The Porcelain Dish) in Delft from 1612 until 1777. Over this period it passed through a considerable number of owners including Ghisbrecht Cruyck (or Kruyck) who ran it from 1663 to 1671. Cruyck was also involved with De witte Starre, (The White Star), De Paauw (The Peacock) and De Dissel (The Pole). This and most of the 30 or so Delft factories produced blue and white tin-glazed pottery (Delftware) in the 17thC. This monogram mark is written in cobalt blue.

Kenneth Quick *St Ives, Cornwall, UK*
Apart from the five years from 1955 to 1960, Kenneth Quick spent all his working life as a potter at the Bernard Leach Pottery making Studio ceramics. Marks are incised. He also worked at the Tregenna Hill Pottery.

Looe Pottery (K. and M. Webb)
Barbican, Looe, Cornwall, UK
Stonewares were produced 1932–62 by K. and M. Webb. Initials appear impressed, printed or incised.

Amédée Lambert *Rouen, Seine-Inférieure, France*
Faïence was produced by from c1827 with this impressed mark.

Laszlo Bruckner *London, UK*
From 1949, Bruckner produced pottery animals and ceramic jewellery. The mark is an impressed monogram but Roman-type initials are also used.

Bernard Leach *St Ives, Cornwall, UK*
See p51. This personal mark was used by Bernard Leach from 1921 to 1979.

David Leach *Bovey Tracey, Devon, UK*
Between 1932 and 1956, David Leach worked with his father, Bernard, at the St Ives Pottery. Pieces made by David at the St Ives Pottery feature his initials 'DAL' as an incised or seal mark. After 1956, David Leach was based at the Lowerdowne Pottery at Bovey Tracey in Devon. He used this impressed seal mark from 1956.

Eileen Stevens *Ifield, Crawley, West Sussex, UK*
Studio ceramics with incised or painted marks were made from 1952 onwards. This monogram was used from 1955 to 1960, and a similar mark after 1960.

Louis H. H. Glover
Barnsley, South Yorkshire, UK
From 1930. Glover made Studio-type ceramics. Incised or painted marks appear, sometimes with the year of manufacture.

John Leach *Muchelny Pottery, Somerset, UK*
Grandson of Bernard Leach (see p51), John Leach worked at the St Ives Pottery between 1950 and 1963 and his pots bore the Leach Pottery mark. His individual pieces made before 1958 bear this mark.

Lawrence Keen
Moat House, Stanmore, London, UK
From 1953, Lawrence Keen produced Studio-type ceramics, with these impressed seal marks o painted initials.

Michael Leach
Yelland Manor Pottery, Fremington, Devon, UK
See p47. Michael Leach trained at his father's St Ives Pottery in Cornwall, but from 1956 worked at the Yelland Manor Pottery. This is his personal seal mark.

Max Läuger *Baden, Germany*
This architect, engineer, sculptor and Art Nouveau ceramicist (1864–1952) is known for pieces with French-style floral or organic forms.

Lahens and Rateau *Bordeaux, Gironde, France*
Lahens and Rateau conducted a short-lived porcelain factory here in 1819, using this mark.

Lonhuda Pottery Co *Steubenville, Ohio, USA*
William Long formed a pottery company with W. H. Hunter and Alfred Day, which they named by using the first two or three letters of each name. The earthenware art vases were covered with a mahogany-coloured slip ground and slip-decorated with flowers. The company operated from 1892–94. Long went to work for Weller (see p236) in 1895 and moved to Denver, Colorado in 1900 where he founded the Denver China and Pottery Company (see p54).

Masseot Abaquesne *Rouen, France*
Active 1526–57, Abaquesne was the director of an important faïence pottery supplying drug pots, tile pavements and interiors for grand chateaux. His work is distinctive, employing the style of decoration associated with the Fontainebleau School of Mannerist ornament. This monogram appears to combine the letters 'MAB'.

Molly Coryn *Gomshall, Surrey, UK*
From c1939 Studio pottery was produced and was marked with this monogram. In 1953 she opened the Gomshall Pottery.

Dorothy B. Martin *Brighton, East Sussex, UK*
Studio ceramics were produced c1920–35. This 'DBM' monogram is incised or painted.

Green Dene Pottery *East Horsley, Surrey, UK*
Studio ceramics made at the Green Dene Pottery from 1953 feature the impressed monogram (above) of the proprietor Denis Moore. The 'MB' monogram (below) was used by Moore's associate Michael Buckland.

Erna Manners *Ealing, London, UK*
From c1920 to 1935, Studio ceramics were produced with either the initials 'EM', or a painted or incised signature.

M. E. Bulmer *Burrill, Yorkshire, UK*
Studio ceramics and figurines were produced c1956–60 with this incised or painted monogram.

Joris Mes (or Mesch) *Delft, Holland*
Mes (d1691) potted at 't Fortuyn (The Fortune) and also at 't Hart (The Hart) factories in Delft. This mark is from 1661.

Fortuné de Monestrol *Rungis, Nr Paris, France*
Historismus pieces, ie historical revivals of classic wares, mainly Italian maiolica, especially Gubbio lustreware, were made in the second half of the 19thC. This painted monogram appears in black.

Maureen Cooper
Roehampton Village, London, UK
From 1955 Studio ceramics and panels were made with this incised signature, or incised or painted monogram.

Muriel Harris *Washington, Tyne and Wear, UK*
Operating from Old Hall Smithy, Muriel Harris produced Studio-type pottery 1953–59. From 1961 she worked from St Margarets-at-Cliffe, Dover and used this monogram mark.

Milton Head Pottery *Brixham, Devon, UK*
From 1951 the Milton Head Pottery produced earthenware marked with an incised or painted 'MHP' monogram.

Cricklade Pottery *Cricklade, Wiltshire, UK*
This pottery was established 1951 to produce Studio pottery. Impressed seal marks were used comprising the initials of the proprietors Ivan and Kay Martin.

James Macintyre & Co
Washington Works, Burslem, Staffordshire, UK
Manufacturers of earthenwares from 1860 to 1928 (after this date only electrical wares were produced). Of especial note are the black-glazed wares, including door furniture and the fine, cream-coloured body sold under the name 'Ivory China'. This impressed or printed monogram appears in a number of forms.

M. J. Lamb *Kensington, London, UK*
Studio ceramics were made from 1951 with this impressed or printed monogram which appears within a circle.

Joan Motley *Much Wenlock, Shropshire, UK*
Based in Chelsea, London (1946–57), Joan Motley moved to Shropshire in 1957. She made Studio pottery and figures, with her incised or painted monogram.

Mervyn Jude *Glyn Ceiriog, Clwyd, Wales, UK*
Previously based in Oxshott, Surrey (1948–54), and Cranleigh, Surrey (1954–63), Mervyn and Nerys Jude moved to North Wales in 1963. Studio ceramics are produced. Mervyn Jude used this individual monogram.

Ray Marshall
Stedham, Nr Midhurst, West Sussex, UK
Based at the Milland Pottery at Liphook, Hampshire prior to establishing his own pottery at Bridgefoot Cottages in 1957, from 1945 Marshall produced Studio-type stonewares. This impressed seal mark was used during this period.

Mildred Lockyer *Various locations, UK*
Based at a number of addresses in England during her career, Mildred Lockyer produced Studio ceramics between 1928 and 1939, with this incised or painted mark.

Maestro Giorgio Andreoli *Gubbio, Italy*
Born at Intra in Lombardy, Giorgio Andreoli established a pottery in Gubbio with his brother Salimbene (d1523) in 1492. In 1498, Giorgio became a citizen of Gubbio. From surviving documents it is apparent that he was making lustreware before 1500, although no piece from this date can he attributed to him. His marked specimens, which bear similar devices to the one illustrated here, date from 1518 to 1541. Maestro Giorgio's workshop not only produced both plain and lustred pottery but also lustred pieces made by other Urbino potters. Pieces signed by him are among the most sought-after by modern collectors.

Pierre Mouchard & Family *Rouen, France*
These Rouen-based potters operated from c1740 onwards. Pieces are marked with this painted 'MP' monogram.

Reginald Marlow *Various locations, UK*
Working at a number of addresses in England, and also holding a number of teaching posts, Marlow produced Studio-type pottery from c1930. His pieces are marked with this impressed or relief monogram.

Marjorie Scott-Pitcher *Rye, East Sussex, UK*
Studio ceramics and figurines were produced in Rye from 1954 onwards. They feature this painted or incised monogram.

Mosbach *Baden, Germany*
See p45. The 'MB' monogram under the Palatinate crown is generally accepted as Mosbach. The monogram 'MT' probably stands for 'Mosbach-Tännich', used while Tännich was the manager and proprietor of the factory.

Morris and Willmore
Columbian Art Pottery, Trenton, New Jersey, USA
English potters founded this pottery (1893–1905) making decorated ironstone table and toilet wares as well as Belleek art wares.

Norah Braden *Coleshill, Wiltshire, UK*
Based at The Leach Pottery at St Ives, Cornwall from c1924, Nora Braden moved to Wiltshire in 1928. She produced Studio pottery until 1936 with this impressed and incised monogram.

Nuremberg *Bavaria, Germany*
See p44. This factory mark was used on faïence made at Nuremberg after 1750.

Nicola da Urbino *Urbino, Italy*
Full name was probably Nicola di Gabriele Sbraga (or Sbraghe)and arguably the most accomplished painter in the *istoriato* or narrative style of maiolica painting. He was active in Urbino from c1520 until his death in c1537, and his work has been identified, starting with five pieces bearing signatures or monograms such as the present mark. Among his greatest work are the two services commissioned firstly by Isabella d'Este of Mantua and secondly by the Calini family of Brescia.

St Agnes Pottery (A. & N. Homer)
St Agnes, Cornwall, UK
See p32. This impressed monogram and seal mark was used.

Nerys Jude *Glyn Ceiriog, Clwyd, Wales, UK*
See p99. Nerys Jude used this monogram mark from 1948.

Nora Kay *Gerrards Cross, Buckinghamshire, UK*
Studio ceramics were made by Nora Kay from 1951 with this impressed monogram.

Nicholas Vergette *London, UK*
Also working from other addresses around England, Vergette produced tiles and Studio ceramics from 1946 to 1958. This incised or painted monogram was used.

Joseph Olerys *Moustiers, Basse-Alpes, France*
Established in 1738–39 by Joseph Olerys and his brother-in-law Joseph Laugier, this pottery was one of several in Moustiers. After spending over ten years with the Alcora factory in Spain, Olerys introduced polychrome decoration to Moustiers using the *style Berain* at first, but this was soon replaced by medallions and festoons, and also with a fantasy style of exotic vegetation and strange creatures. Although Moustiers is associated with the *grand-feu* palette, *petit-feu* was used to a limited extent after c1770.

Orchard Pottery *Addiscombe, Surrey, UK*
The workshop of B. J. Cotes (later with the Hastings Pottery), the Orchard Pottery produced Studio ceramics 1954–56 with this mark.

Peter Ainslie *Leicestershire and Chester, UK*
Studio ceramics with impressed seal marks as initials or in the form of a monogram were produced from 1948.

Percy Brown *Twickenham, London, UK*
Percy Brown made Studio-type pottery from 1930 to 1947, featuring either initials or the monogram seen here.

Pijnacker and Keiser *Delft, Holland*
This monogram incorporates the initials of Adriaen and Jacobus Pijnacker with Albrecht Keiser. These three potters were involved with several potteries in Delft from c1680 including De vergulde Blompot, De porceleyn Schotel, De twee Scheepes and De twee Wildemannen. These factories produced mainly blue and white tin-glazed ware. This monogram appears painted in cobalt blue.

Patty Elwood
Meon Pottery, West Meon, Hampshire, UK
Initially based in Newlyn, Cornwall from 1953 , Patty Elwood operated from Meon Pottery from 1962, producing Studio ceramics and tablewares This impressed monogram was used.

Gordon Plahn
Langton Pottery, Nr Langton Green, Kent, UK
Potter Gordon Plahn made Studio-type pottery at Langton Green from 1961 with this impressed seal comprising his monogram. The mark was previously used by Plahn at the Sevenoaks Pottery, Kent, 1988–61.

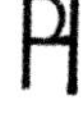

Peter Holdsworth *Ramsbury, Wiltshire, UK*
Earthenwares and stonewares were made at the Holdsworth Potteries from 1945. This is one of the marks used.

Peter Lane *Andover, Hampshire, UK*
Peter Lane made Studio ceramics at The Pottery from 1961. He used this impressed monogram, and also painted and incised marks.

Rookwood Pottery *Cincinnati, Ohio, USA*
Founded by Cincinnati socialite and ceramics decorator, Maria Longworth Nichols, this factory (1880–1967) was considered the quintessential art pottery c1900. Trained decorators painted a variety of subjects in naturally coloured slips on damp earthenware forms that were bisque fired and then glazed. Hand-decorated pieces were made well into the 20thC, but the company's later work was largely moulded and covered with a monochromatic glaze. Pieces can be dated by the number of flames and the Roman numerals that appear in the mark. Many pieces are artist-signed, and contemporary collecting is largely focused on individual artists' work.

Robineau Pottery *Syracuse, New York, USA*
Adelaide Alsop Robineau was a ceramics painter when she began publication of *Keramic Studio*, a monthly magazine from New York City and Syracuse. During the early 1900s, she studied pottery-making with Charles Fergus Binns (see p176), and by 1905 was producing her own work regularly. From 1909 to 1911 she worked at the University City Pottery (see p177), returning to Syracuse after it closed. By 1920, she was on the faculty at Syracuse University. Her work, almost

all ornamental, is characterized by exquisite detail in form, surface modelling and glazing. The company was active c1905–28.

Pierre Roussencq
Marans-la-Rochelle, Charente-Inférieure, France
Founded in 1740, this factory was one of several large concerns operating in the general area around La Rochelle. These factories being at a cultural crossroads absorbed influences from Moustiers and Marseilles in the south and from Nevers and Rouen in the north, making certain attribution difficult in most cases. This factory may have ceased production in the early to mid-1750s when Henri Brevet, one of the partners, opened a new factory at La Rochelle. The monogram of Pierre Roussencq is painted.

Paula Schneider *London, UK*
Based in London, Paula Schneider produced Studio pottery, marked with her incised or painted monogram, from 1956.

Bryan Rochford
Willowdene, Cheshunt, Hertfordshire, UK
Studio ceramics were produced from 1960. This personal seal mark was used by Bryan Rochford.

Robert and Sheila Fournier
Greenwich Studios, London, UK
Previously based at Ducketts Wood in Hertfordshire c1946–61, and London from 1962, Robert and Sheila Fournier produced Studio ceramics. This 'RF' impressed monogram was used by Robert Fournier.

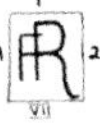

Frances E. Richards *Highgate, London, UK*
Studio ceramics were made from 1922 to 1931, marked with an incised monogram and the date. Examples of this potter's work exist in the Victoria & Albert Museum, London.

Richard Franz Bayer
Shipley, West Yorkshire, UK
Bayer's Studio ceramics from 1959 to c1960 were marked with impressed or painted initials.

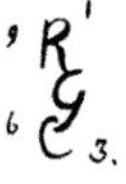

Ronald G. Cooper *London, UK*
Working from Hornsey College of Art and other addresses in England, Cooper made Studio ceramics from 1946. His mark consists of his painted or incised initials (sometimes with date).

Lucie Rie *London, UK*
Active 1938–95, Lucie Rie was one of the most important and influential Studio potters of the 20thC. Her work was executed mainly in stoneware and porcelain, classic in their simplicity, and included some highly abstracted Chinese forms. She used this impressed monogram.

Lowe, Ratcliffe & Co *Longton, Staffordshire, UK*
General earthenwares were made at the Gold Street Works 1882–92. The mark was impressed or printed.

Renée Mendel *London, UK*
Studio ceramics and terracotta figures were produced from 1942 onwards with this incised or painted initial mark.

R. M. Greenwood *London, UK*
A ceramic decorator from 1948 onwards, Miss Greenwood used this painted monogram.

Bryan Rochford
Willowdene, Cheshunt, Hertfordshire, UK
See p103. This is the Rochford Pottery monogram, which was used from July 1960 on Studio-type wares.

Eric & Meira Stockl *Stroud Green, London, UK*
Studio-type pottery and stoneware were made from 1956. Initially the couple used a joint initial mark 'MES' but after 1961 they used this painted, incised or impressed mark.

Samuel E. Saunders
East Cowes, Isle of Wight, UK
The monogram of Samuel E. Saunders was first registered as a trademark in 1927. Saunders was at the Isle of Wight Pottery (1930–40) and the Carisbrooke Pottery (1930–32). Both potteries used printed or impressed marks which comprised his initials.

Robert and Sheila Fournier
Greenwich Studios, London, UK
See p103. This 'SF' impressed seal mark was used by Sheila Fournier.

Hilda M. Snowden
Thackley, Bradford, West Yorkshire, UK
Studio ceramics were produced from 1950, some featuring this incised or impressed monogram.

La Seinie *Saint-Yrieix, Haute-Vienne, France*
Hard-paste porcelain was made here between 1774 and 1856, with the monogram 'LS' in red enamel. St Yrieix is where the first deposits of clay suitable for producing hard-paste were discovered in France in 1768.

Mildred Slatter
High Wycombe, Buckinghamshire, UK
Studio ceramics produced from 1956 onwards. Her monogram is painted, incised or impressed.

Cafaggiolo *Nr Florence, Tuscany, Italy*
One of the foremost maiolica potteries in Renaissance Italy. In 1498 the Medici drafted in two potters, Stefano and Piero di Filippo, from Montelupo to oversee production in an outhouse of the Medici villa. From this date pottery was produced here until well into the 18thC. However, it is the output of brilliant wares from the first 30 or 40 years of the 16thC that guarantees its place in the front rank of Renaissance maiolica. The mark of Cafaggiolo is 'SPR' or 'SF', as well as a trident and occasionally the place name. There are a considerable number of fakes bearing the marks of this pottery.

Taylor, Smith & Taylor *East Liverpool, Ohio (with a plant in Chester, West Virginia), USA*
Originally Taylor, Lee & Smith in 1899, the firm was reconfigured in 1901 when Lee withdrew and continued until 1972. After several poor years at the beginning, the firm was reorganized in 1906 and production commenced in earnest. Although a wide range of semi-vitreous dinner and toilet wares as well as products for hotels and restaurants were produced, the pottery's most popular lines were Lu-Ray and Vistosa, both solid-colour dinner wares. Another type of ware was 'Pebbleford', which was plain coloured with speckles in light and dark blue-green, yellow, grey and tan. Anchor Hocking Corporation's ceramic products division operated the factory from its purchase in 1972 until its closure in 1981.

Mosbach *Baden, Germany*
See p45. Also thought to be the mark of Frankenthal, this 'CT' monogram was derived from the initials of the Elector Palatine Carl Theodor, who was patron or protector of the ceramics concerns in Mosbach and also in Frankenthal.

Thomas Cone Ltd *Longton, Staffordshire, UK*
From 1892 to c1935, Thomas Cone Ltd were makers of general earthenwares. This printed monogram was used 1912–35.

C. C. Thompson Pottery Company
East Liverpool, Ohio, USA
See p71. This monogram mark also appears on earthenwares, stonewares and other wares made by this firm 1868–1938.

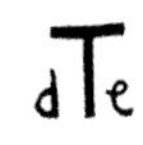

Marianne de Trey
Shinner's Bridge, Dartington, Devon, UK
Formerly a potter in the United States, de Trey produced Studio ceramics in Devon from 1947. This painted or incised mark was used.

Tiffany Studios *Corona, New York, USA*
Although Louis Comfort Tiffany, famous for glass and metal work, began experimenting with pottery as early as 1898, the official introduction of the ware was at the St Louis Exposition in 1904. Vases and lamp bases made to hold his famous leaded-glass shades were the principal products, many formed by making the master models from natural plant materials such as ferns, Queen Anne's lace, jack-in-the-pulpits, etc. Green, brown, ivory and blue glazes predominate, although crystalline and iridescent effects are known. The Studios operated 1902–19.

Tregenna Hill Pottery *Cornwall, UK*
Studio pottery was made here by Kenneth Quick c1955–60 (see p95). The 'TH' monogram is incised or impressed.

Ruskin Pottery
Smethwick, Nr Birmingham, West Midlands, UK
Highly refined earthenwares with innovative monochromatic glazes (eg copper-red flambé, orange or mottled) were produced in this pottery owned by W. Howson Taylor. The forms are often derived from classic Chinese ceramics. The factory was established in 1898 and closed in 1935. This painted or incised monogram was used from c1898.

MADE IN ENGLAND

Thomas Mayer (Elton Pottery) Ltd
Hanley, Staffordshire, UK
General earthenwares were produced from 1956. This monogram mark was used 1956–60. An Elton Pottery name mark was also used.

Mosaic Tile Company *Zanesville, Ohio, USA*
Karl Langenbeck, a chemist, and Herman Mueller, a modeller, had worked together for American Encaustic Tiling Company (see p79), before establishing Mosaic Tile Company (1894–1967) which they operated until 1903. Many different kinds of plain and ornamental tiles were made for floors, walls and fireplaces. Faïence tiles were added in 1918. The firm's tiles were used in a number of important buildings in the US, including some New York subway stations. A variety of miscellaneous forms was made when the Depression slowed the construction business, including boxes, bookends, souvenirs, hot-plates and the like.

T. Ristori *Marzy, Nièvre, France*
From 1854, tin-glazed reproductions of classic French faïence including Nevers and Rouen were made by this firm.

William Tudor
High Wycombe, Buckinghamshire, UK
Studio ceramics made from 1947 feature this impressed monogram seal mark.

Union Co-operative Pottery Company/Union Potteries Company
East Liverpool, Ohio, USA
Organized by a group of potters during a general strike, the pottery (1894–1905) produced ironstone and semi-porcelain table and toilet wares and railroad sanitary ware.

Veuve Perrin *Marseilles, France*
Operating between c1740 and c1795, the Veuve Perrin factory was one of the leading Marseilles faïence makers, noted for painterly use of the *petit-feu* enamels. Chinoiserie subjects, fish and landscapes were typical. The painted 'VP' monogram has been faked extensively within the past hundred years.

Anne Wedd *Brixton, London*
See p47. Anne Wedd used this incised monogram, which may feature the year numbers 1955–57.

William Barnes
Swinton, Greater Manchester, UK
Studio-type pottery was produced both before and after World War II, featuring this incised or painted initial mark. Between 1948 and 1957,

Barnes worked at the Royal Lancastrian Pottery, (Pilkington's), whose pieces are marked with a 'P'.

William B. Dalton *London, UK*
Studio-type stonewares and porcelain were produced from 1900 with this incised or painted monogram mark. Dalton emigrated to the United States in 1941.

Wiesbaden *Nassau, Germany*
A small faïence concern was established here in 1770, under the patronage of Prince Karl of Nassau-Usingen, by Johann Jacob Kaisin of Poppelsdorf. Kaisin's work was deemed to be unsatisfactory and the work was taken over by Strupler and Hagemann but poor quality faïence was still made. In 1774 Caspar Dreste of Flörsheim was employed to improve the production. The factory was continued by his widow after his death in 1787 until its closure in 1795. Output includes figures, stoves, mirror frames etc. Wares are characterized by a strong, copper-green enamel. This mark stands for 'Wiesbaden-Dreste'.

Edward R. Wilkes
Various locations, Staffordshire, UK
A decorator of earthenwares 1900–30, Edward Wilkes' signature mark has been found on vases made by A. G. Richardson of Cobridge. This monogram can be seen on pieces decorated for Bernard Moore. Wilkes also decorated for other Staffordshire manufacturers.

William Gill & Son(s)
Castleford, West Yorkshire, UK
Formerly G. Gill, this company worked from the Providence Pottery from 1880 to 1932. This printed 'WGS' mark was used from 1880, with 'England' added from 1891.

Willets Manufacturing Company
Trenton, New Jersey, USA
The factory purchased by the Willets brothers in 1879 was one of the largest in the United States. The pottery (1879–1908) produced large quantities of decorated ironstone table and sanitary wares. Beginning in 1886, they also made Belleek porcelain having hired the Bromley potters and Walter Lenox from Ott and Brewer (see p159). Their early Belleek ware is often

factory decorated, but by the mid-1890s they were selling much of their Belleek in the white for independent decorators.

Helen Wickham *London, UK*
Earthenware figures were made from 1920–35. This painted mark appears and an incised or painted signature mark is also used.

Tom W. Howard *Loughton, Essex, UK*
From 1956, Tom Howard produced a variety of Studio-type pottery and earthenware, and 'Semi-Stoneware' from 1960. This incised mark was used, with the number relating to the year of production.

Monkton Combe Pottery *Bath, Avon, UK*
Studio ceramics were produced at the Monkton Combe Pottery by Rachael Warner between 1946 and 1953; she used this incised monogram. The pottery was subsequently operated by Peter Wright, who used a painted or incised 'PW' mark, and also a written name mark.

Winifred Rawsthorne
Bramcote, Nottinghamshire, UK
Studio-type pottery was produced by Winifred Rawsthorne at the Winthorn Pottery from 1958. Some pieces feature this incised or painted monogram mark.

William Ruscoe *Exeter, Devon, UK*
Ceramic sculptures and figures were made at Stoke, Staffordshire from c1920–44 and subsequently at Exeter, with this incised or painted monogram, sometimes accompanied by the year of manufacture.

Peters and Reed/Zane Pottery Company
Zanesville, Ohio, USA
Founded by John D. Peters and Adam Reed, who had been working at Weller (see p236), the pottery (1898–1941) started with flowerpots, added cuspidors and jardinières, and by 1903 was making cookware. In 1905, Frank Ferrel designed several ornamental lines, including Moss Aztec, for florists' crockery and garden wares. Like the utilitarian pieces, these latter wares were made of red clay. From 1921 to 1941, the firm was called Zane Pottery Company, and after 1926 white clay was used rather than red.

Written Name & Signature Marks

Detail of Gouda mark, Holland, 1930s

WRITTEN NAME & SIGNATURE MARKS

This section has been ordered alphabetically according to the surname of the individual potter or the title of the company. Where the firm's or potter's name is unclear, the entry has been placed under the first letter that appears.

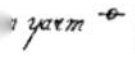

William Absolon *Great Yarmouth, Norfolk, UK*
See p47. This painted name mark was used 1784–1815. 'N 25' was added to some pieces made after 1790 and refers to the address, 25 Market Row.

Alpha Potteries *Sidcup, Kent, UK*
This pottery made individually-designed studio wares 1954–58. This written mark was used. The Greek symbol for 'alpha' appears as an incised mark.

D. & J. Henderson/American Pottery Company *Jersey City, New Jersey, USA*
This is the earliest of the large production potteries to be successful in the United States, and was active from 1828 to c1850. Methods, moulds and skills brought from England and Scotland were translated into an array of high quality brown-glazed, Rockingham and yellow ware products for kitchens, tables and taverns. The pottery was incorporated as the American Pottery Company in 1833, but the corporate structure changed several times after the death of David Henderson in 1845. By 1855, English potters John O. Rouse and Nathaniel Turner owned the company and the Jersey City Pottery (see p178).

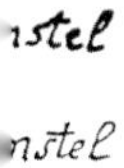

Amstel *Nr Amsterdam, Holland*
This concern was transferred here from Oude Loosdrecht in 1784. The wares are conventional and in keeping with contemporary neo-classical or a somewhat old-fashioned rococo style, echoing Meissen and Sèvres. The decoration is generally of high quality, in which a mid-brown is used extensively in landscapes or natural settings. The script mark is rendered in various colours sometimes incorporating the letters 'MOL' which denote 'Mol Oude Loosdrecht', Johannes de Mol (d1782) being the name of the proprietor.

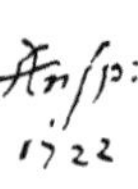

Ansbach *Bavaria, Germany*
One of the most important faïence factories in Germany which made some of the finest wares, especially in the first half of the 18thC. The earlier wares copy Delft, Rouen and Strasburg but the factory is noted more for the brilliant 'green-family' of enamelled wares loosely based on Chinese export ware and a curious group of Imari-type wares in which fired cobalt blue is employed together with unfired red and gold. Factory marks are rare and are mostly initials, bu a few marks include an abbreviated town mark.

aprey

Aprey *Haute Marne, France*
See p78. This rare mark sometimes appears.

Ashby Potters' Guild
Burton-on-Trent, Staffordshire, UK
Based at Woodville near Burton-on-Trent, this firm produced earthenwares 1909–22. The company became Ault & Tunnicliffe Ltd. This mark appears.

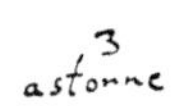

De 3 Astonne *Delft, Holland*
See p60. This mark was registered by the proprietors in 1764.

Avon Art Pottery Ltd *Longton, Staffordshire, UK*
Earthenwares were made by this firm from 1930 first at the Jubilee Works (to 1961), and then at Edensor Road. The printed mark above was use 1939–47 and the mark below, also printed, from 1947 onwards.

Aylesford Priory Pottery *Aylesford, Kent, UK*
See p78. This impressed mark was used from 195

I·E·BARON·1752

I. E. Baron *Moustiers, Basses Alpes, France*
The painted mark, I. E. Baron, is that of a decorator apparently employed at the Olerys factory in Moustiers c1750.

Jean Baron *Rennes, France*
Jean Baron was faïence decorator in Rennes in the second half of the 18thC. He used this mark

Bar: Terchi Roma

Bartolomeo Terchi *Rome, Italy*
Bartolomeo Terchi, probably born in Rome, was active as a maiolica decorator from c1714 until

the 1730s. In terms of palette, the sombre, brown-dominated tones resemble Castelli maiolica but his subjects, which include large-scale biblical and classical figures, are perhaps more vigorously treated. A small number of pieces signed by Terchi (and in some cases dated) are extant. He worked at San Quirico, Siena and Bassano in the first half of the 18thC.

Bassano *Nr Venice, Italy*
Maiolica was produced in this area from the 16thC but such early pieces have never been clearly identified. As well as drug jars and other utilitarian vessels, output included dishes painted with architectural ruins. A number of different potters are known to have worked in this area including Antonio and Bartolomeo Terchi.

Bayeux *Calvados, Normandy, France*
See p52. The mark above was used during the time of Joachim Langlois (d1830). The mark below was used by Jules Morlent in the 19thC.

Bayreuth *Bavaria, Germany*
See p50. This town mark appears on faïence from c1713.

D. Beckley *Seaview, Isle of Wight, UK*
Formerly the Island Pottery Studio Ltd (1956–58), this printed or impressed mark appears on earthenwares from 1959.

Edwin Bennett Pottery *Baltimore, Maryland, USA*
Bennett of Derbyshire, England worked first in Jersey City, New Jersey in 1834, and later founded potteries in East Liverpool, Ohio and Pittsburgh, Pennsylvania before settling permanently in Baltimore. His pottery in Baltimore (1845–1936) made a variety of popular wares including Rockingham, majolica, parian, porcelain, and white ware. The company was incorporated in 1890. Bennett died in 1908.

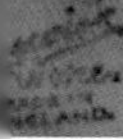

John Beswick (Ltd) *Longton, Staffordshire, UK*
Earthenwares were made by this firm (formerly called J. W. Beswick) at Gold Street, Longton from 1936 and this mark was used from that time.

Biltons (1912) Ltd *Stoke, Staffordshire, UK*
Known as Biltons Ltd c1900–12, this firm produced earthenwares. This mark is the standard post-war mark; pattern names may also appear.

De vergulde Blompot *Delft, Holland*
See p51. The mark above appeared from 1654; the mark below was registered by the proprietor in 1764.

Blue John Pottery Ltd *Hanley, Staffordshire, UK*
From 1939 the Blue John Pottery in Hanley produced earthenwares. This mark was used from 1939.

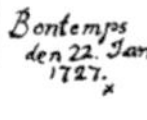

Johann Valentin Bontemps
Ansbach, Bavaria, Germany
See p32. This is the full signature of Johann Valentin Bontemps, a faïence painter at Ansbach from c1716 to 1729.

Giacomo Boselli (or Boselly) *Savona, Italy*
A potter and painter in Savona in the last quarter of the 18thC, this is the painted signature of Giacomo Boselli.

Ignaz Bottengruber *Breslau, Silesia, Germany*
An independent decorator or *Hausmaler*, Ignaz Bottengruber was active in the 1720s and 1730s. He painted mainly on Meissen blanks and occasionally Chinese export ware, and after c1730 on Vienna porcelain. One of the most accomplished *Hausmalerei*, Bottengruber painted battle and hunting scenes, putti and bacchic subjects, flowers and ornate strapwork. He sometimes worked in monochrome, especially purple and black.

Lester & Barbara Breininger
Robesonia, Pennsylvania, USA
Perhaps the finest of the contemporary American colonial revival potteries is that established by Lester and Barbara Breininger in 1965. While production is limited by the labour-intensive process of reproducing or adapting early Pennsylvania German red-ware, many signed examples may be found. They have collected fine early local wares for inspiration, as well as old

potters' tools that they then use to produce their new examples. All wares are clearly marked with incised inscriptions and dates in order to discourage confusion with antique pieces.

Pountney & Co (Ltd) *Bristol, Avon, UK*
Formerly Carter & Pountney, Pountney & Allies (c1816–35) and Pountney & Goldney (1836–49), this pottery produced earthenwares from 1849 to 1969. It is now Cauldon Bristol Potteries Ltd. The mark above appeared c1816–35. The words 'Pountney' and 'Bristol' appear as distinguishing details on a variety of marks used from 1889.

John Burger *Rochester, New York, USA*
In 1839 John (or Jean) Burger, from Alsace-Lorraine operated a stoneware factory with partners that included Nathan Clark of Lyons, New York. By 1854, Burger owned and operated the pottery himself and moved to a Mount Hope Avenue site in Rochester in 1860. The usual wide variety of forms were made that included beer bottles, preserve jars, jugs, water fountains, butter pots, pitchers, and churns. Other members of the family joined Burger after 1861 and the pottery maintained production until 1890.

Caen *Calvados, Normandy, France*
See p84. These written marks appear in the early 19thC.

Sterling China Company *East Liverpool, Ohio, USA*
Although the firm has always used East Liverpool as its address, the pottery is actually located in Wellsville, Ohio. Founded by a group of investors that refitted an old yellowware factory in 1917, the pottery has long produced vitreous hotel china. Indeed, by 1949 the company was one of the three largest hotel ware producers in the world, although it is probably best known among collectors for its line designed by Russel Wright in about 1945. Caribe China was produced by Sterling at a plant in Vega Baja, Puerto Rico, established to manufacture hotel ware, between 1951 and 1976. In 1954, the firm absorbed Scammell China Company, Trenton, and continues to produce its Lamberton China.

Carlton Ware Ltd *Stoke, Staffordshire*
Previously Wiltshaw & Robinson (Ltd) (1890–1957), the firm was retitled Carlton Ware Ltd from 1958. This style of mark was used by both companies.

Carter Poole 1906

Carter & Co (Ltd) *Poole, Dorset*
This company produced earthenwares, art pottery and tiles 1873–1921 and later became Carter, Stabler & Adams. This mark was used 1873–1921.

C Cazin

Charles Cazin *Fulham, London*
Cazin, a Frenchman, worked in England at C. J. C. Bailey's works in Fulham designing stonewares 1871–74. He returned to France c1874. Pieces bearing his signature are rare.

Chantilly

Chantilly *Oise, France*
See p200. This written mark featuring the full town name is rare.

C Clar.

Christian Friedrich Clar
Rendsburg, Holstein, Germany
Clar established a factory in Holstein in c1765, producing tin-glazed earthenware, lead-glazed pottery, creamware, redware and a type of black basalte. The concern survived under different proprietors until 1818. Initials 'CR' are also used.

N. CLARK JR.
ATHENS, N.Y.

Nathan Clark Pottery *Athens, New York, USA*
Nathan Clark Senior founded the stoneware and redware pottery at Athens, New York with Captain Thomas Howe, an Englishman, in 1805 and it was operated by the family and employees including his son until c1899. Branches of the pottery were also operated at Lyons, Mt Morris, and Rochester, New York.

Clement-Massier
Golfe-Juan AM

Clement & Jerome Massier *Vallauris, France*
Clement and Jerome Massier produced high quality Studio-type pottery from c1870 in Art Nouveau style. This mark is one of those used.

Clermont fd
M

Clermond-Ferrand *Puy-de-Dôme, France*
A small number of factories were established here in the 18thC making, with a few notable exceptions, mostly mundane faïence in the manner of Moustiers. In the late 18thC robust and somewhat crude '*faïence patriotiques*'

was made here. The full town mark is generally associated with the early factory of Perrot and Sèves, active from 1730 to 1743.

Clarice Cliff *Burslem, UK*
Clarice Cliff (1899–1972) joined A. J. Wilkinson's Royal Staffordshire Pottery in 1916 where she was taught modelling, firing, gilding and pottery design. After 1927, with a group of assistants, she began hand-decorating whitewares (mainly tablewares) with bold, geometric designs in vivid colours. Most of her pieces are marked with this signature.

Clinton Pottery Company *Clinton, Missouri, USA*
The Clinton Pottery Company opened in 1889, and quickly became a dominant force in the stoneware industry of the Midwest. In 1891, one million gallons of pottery were shipped, which amounted to one-third of all Missouri pottery manufactures in that calendar year. A large, steam-operated pottery, the firm made mainly utilitarian brown-wares with a slip glaze, such as crocks and jugs. By 1906, the Clinton Stoneware Company (as it had been reorganized) merged into the Western Stoneware Company (see p262).

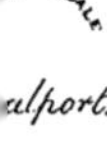

Coalport Porcelain Works
Coalport, Shropshire, UK
See p82. The mark above is a rare early mark from c1805–15. The mark below is from another early period 1810–29, and appears painted in underglaze blue, usually on colourful, encrusted floral wares.

Colclough China Ltd *Longton, Staffordshire, UK*
Formerly H. J. Colclough (1897–1937), and subsequently Booths & Colcloughs Ltd (1948–54), this firm produced porcelain 1937–48. This style of mark was used in a number of forms from 1939, and was also used by Booths & Colcloughs Ltd. The company now forms part of the Ridgway group of potteries.

Morris and Willmore
Columbian Art Pottery Trenton, New Jersey, USA
See p100. This mark also appears on wares produced by this firm.

COMMERAW:S STONEWARE NEW YORK

Thomas H. Commereau
Manhattan, New York, USA
Near Corlear's Hook on the East River in Manhattan, Thomas H. Commereau established a stoneware pottery in 1797, which operated sporadically (1797–98, 1802–19), sometimes with David Morgan, until 1819. A number of salt-glazed stoneware vessels survive and the best of them feature impressed swags and tassels highlighted in cobalt blue.

Susie Cooper *Burslem, Staffordshire, UK*
Susie Cooper worked for A. E. Gray & Co. c1922–29, decorating a variety of wares in floral, abstract or, more rarely, geometric designs. From 1929 she decorated blanks bought in from other manufacturers, and in 1931 she set up her own pottery producing vases, jugs, tea and dinner sets. The company became Susie Cooper Ltd from c1961 and from 1966 formed part of the Wedgwood group. This signature appears in many forms and was used from c1922–80; 'Crown Works' does not appear before 1932. She also used a leaping deer mark 1932–64.

Agostino Corado a Nevers

Agostino Corrado *Nevers, France*
The Corrado or Conrade family emigrated to France and helped establish the faïence factory at Nevers under the patronage of Lodovico Gonzaga. At first the Italian style predominated, but by the second quarter of the 17thC the influence of Chinese porcelain is evident. From about 1650 the native baroque style, following Poussin and Vouet, emerged. Nevers was the foremost faïence factory in France until it was superseded by Rouen at the end of the 17thC. The full signature marks appear mainly in the late 16th and early 17thC.

COWAN

Cowan Pottery *Cleveland and Rocky River, Ohio, USA*
Begun as a backyard studio pottery by R. Guy Cowan in Cleveland in 1913, the firm expanded and moved in 1920 to nearby Rocky River. The product also changed from a lead-glazed redware to a high-fired porcelain body that was covered with brilliant coloured faïence glazes. Although Cowan created most of the designs for the vases and figures that were made, several artists provided models for limited editions, including

Waylande Gregory, Viktor Schreckengost, Paul Bogatay, Alexander Blazys and others. The firm continued until 1931.

Jacob Dorris Craven
Randolph and Moore Counties, North Carolina, USA
Many members of the Craven family were active as potters in North Carolina during the 18th and 19thC. Jacob Dorris Craven worked in Randolph and then in the Browers Mill vicinity of neighbouring Moore County. In 1860 he was manufacturing over 60,000 gallons of alkaline-glazed stoneware annually, and continued until 1890. Some other Craven potters remained in business in Randolph County until 1917.

Crailsheim *Wurtemberg, Germany*
A faïence factory was established here in c1714 and continued in production until the early 19thC. A considerable portion of the output consisted of tankards painted in manganese and blue with detailing in green and yellow. The subject matter includes figures, animals, heraldic devices and flowers.

Crépy-en-Valois *Oise, France*
Louis-François Gaignepain, a former employee of the Mennecy factory, established a soft-paste porcelain manufactory here in 1762 which closed in 1770. Production appears to have been snuff boxes and figures in the manner of Mennecy. It is most likely that a considerable number of such items have been mistakenly attributed to Mennecy. This rare name mark, or the initials 'C. P.' have so far only been found on porcelain figures.

Clarkson Crolius *Manhattan, New York, USA*
Clarkson Crolius was born into a family of New York potters in 1773 and took over his father John Crolius Junior's stoneware pottery in 1800 and continued until 1838. His extensive production was marketed as far as New England and the Carolinas and, for advertising purposes, he marked a large number of pieces. An early price list dated 28 March 1809 includes jugs, jars, pots, pitchers, mugs, oyster pots, chamber pots, inkstands and churns. Most wares were plain, although fine cobalt-blue decorated

incised examples may be found. Crolius' son, Clarkson Junior, operated the pottery until 1849. A number of different marks in this style were used, all featuring the name 'C. Crolius'.

3: Custode ff

Pierre Custode *Nevers, France*
Pierre Custode is recorded as a master potter in 1632, and as a merchant dealing in faïence in 1652. His family remained in the business until the late 18thC.

DARTE FRERES A PARIS

Darte Frères *Paris, France*
Prominent manufacturers and decorators of hard-paste porcelain from 1795 until c1840. The mark is usually stencilled in red.

DASTIN
Dastin

Dastin *Rue de Bondy, Paris, France*
A decorator and retailer of hard-paste porcelain, these marks appear in red and gold.

TH. DECK

T. H. Deck *Various locations, France*
Théodore Deck (1823–91) was one of the foremost ceramicists in 19thC France. Writer, historian, designer and potter, he was one of the earliest Studio potters producing pieces with Islamic or Oriental influence from c1860.

delemer l'an 1771 AR

Dlles Delemer *Arras, Pas-de-Calais, France*
See p49. This mark was used by the Dlles Delemer 1771–90.

W. DE MORGAN

William De Morgan *London, UK*
From 1863 William De Morgan (1839–1917) designed tiles and glass for the William Morris workshops. He decorated pottery with Islamic-style designs from 1869 and set up his own kiln. In 1873 he established a workshop in Chelsea but was later based at Merton Abbey (1882–88) and Sand's End in Fulham (1888–1907). This name mark appears after 1882 in various forms. '& Co' was added to most marks after 1888.

de Villeroy

De Villeroy *Mennecy, Ile-de-France, France*
See p55. This is the incised mark of the Duc de Villeroy, patron of the Mennecy factory.

Dihl

Dihl *Rue de Bondy, Paris, France*
Dihl made hard-paste porcelain from 1780 to 1829, with this mark in red or underglaze blue.

A. P. Donaghho *Parkersburg, West Virginia, USA*
The most prolific stoneware production in the state of West Virginia was that of Pennsylvania-born A. P. Donaghho, active 1874–1900. Most common salt-glazed stoneware forms were made, and preserve jars and pans are frequently found with stenciled cobalt blue geometric designs.

Doulton & Co (Ltd) *Lambeth, London, UK*
A stoneware works was established at Vauxhall in 1815 by John Doulton. John Watts became his partner and c1826 the works moved to Lambeth. Watts died in 1858 but the factory was continued by Doulton in partnership with his sons and was retitled Henry Doulton & Co. The company produced decorative, domestic, architectural and industrial wares in stoneware and terracotta. Another works was opened at Burslem in 1882 and has continued to the present day. Production ceased at the Lambeth factory in 1956. A large number of marks were used, characterized by the words 'Doulton Lambeth' or 'Doulton Burslem'. This impressed mark was used c1869–77; the year of production was used in the centre from 1872.

Duban *Rue Coquillière, Paris, France*
A potter active c1800; this script mark appears in red.

Duhamel *Quai de la Cité, Paris, France*
A dealer and perhaps manufacturer of hard-paste porcelain 1790–1827. This script mark appears in gold.

Edmands & Co *Charlestown, Massachusetts, USA*
Barnabas Edmands was a well-to-do brass founder in Charlestown, Massachusetts who owned a pottery run first by Frederick Carpenter (see p300), but later wares were marked with Edmands' name. In 1852 he passed ownership of the stoneware pottery (1827–1905) to his two sons, Thomas and Edward. They ran the factory until 1868, when a third generation, John B. Edmands, took over and managed the company into the 20thC. This is an example of one of the signatures that appear; another mark features just the name 'Edmands & Co' (spellings vary.)

Sir Edmund Elton *Clevedon, Somerset, UK*
Earthenwares were made by Elton (d1930) from 1879 and by 1882 his Sunflower Pottery was in production. Decoration on pieces of Elton Ware, as it became known, was created using coloured slips covered with transparent glaze. This painted or incised mark was used 1879–1920, sometimes with the date.

Etiolle x bre 1770 Pellevé

Etoilles *Seine-et-Oise, France*
From c1768 Jean Baptiste Monier and Dominique Pellevé were manufacturers of hard-paste porcelain. The name of the town appears in script, together with initials 'P' and 'M. P.' and the name 'Pellevé'.

Fait a Rennes Rue Rue 1771

Michel Derrennes *Rennes, Ille-et-Vilaine, France*
Michel Derrennes was faïence decorator at Tutrel's factory (est 1748). This mark appears.

W.H. FARRAR & CO. GEDDES, N.Y.

William H. Farrar *Geddes, New York, USA*
William H. Farrar of Vermont established a redware pottery at Geddes (later part of Syracuse, New York) c1840 and later produced stoneware and Rockingham ware, including spaniel and lion figures based upon Staffordshire prototypes until 1872. William Farrar also appears to have been an investor in the United States Pottery Company (see p145) in Bennington, Vermont, and by 1856 had established a pottery in Kaolin, South Carolina where Rockingham and fine whitewares, including porcelain, were manufactured.

Fauchier

Joseph Fauchier
Marseilles, Bouches-du-Rhône, France
See p36. This rare script mark is sometimes found.

Fayence d'Auxerre

Auxerre *Yonne, France*
Claude Boutet established a pottery here in 1799 apparently concentrating on popular wares including '*faïences patriotiques*' in the manner of Nevers, mainly employing cobalt and manganese colours. This mark appears.

Ferrat moustier

Jean-Baptiste Ferrat
Moustiers, Basses Alpes, France
Jean-Baptiste Ferrat established a factory here in 1718 and until about 1770, or slightly later, most of its production is similar to other

Moustiers wares. After this date, and to the end of production in 1791, the most notable products are those painted in *petit-feu* enamels (developed at Strasburg) in the Aprey or Marseilles style with birds and flowers, landscapes or chinoiserie subjects. The relatively rare marks are either handwritten or stencilled in overglaze enamels.

Feuillet *Paris, France*
A decorator of hard-paste neo-rococo porcelain from about 1820 to 1850. The full and the single 'F' marks are generally written in gilding or green enamel. This workshop also used a mark that imitated the interlaced 'LL' of Sèvres (see p173).

Homer Laughlin China Company
East Liverpool, Ohio and Newell, West Virginia, USA
See p91. This tradename was used.

Fleury *Rue de Faubourg Saint Denis, Paris, France*
From 1803 until c1835, this factory made good hard-paste porcelain.

Worcester Porcelains *Hereford and Worcester, UK*
See p33. Used during the Flight Period, 1783–92, the painted 'Flight' mark appears in various forms, with a crescent c1783–88 and with a crown c1788–92. This mark was used c1788–92.

Johann Leonhard Forster
Ansbach, Bavaria, Germany
Johann Leonhard Forster (1714–44) was a faïence painter at Ansbach and used this mark.

Fossé (or Fossey) *Rouen, Seine-Inférieure, France*
Gabriel Fosse and widow were potters from c1740 to c1760. This script mark was used.

Joseph Fouque *Moustiers, Basses Alpes, France*
In 1774, Joseph Fouque and Jean-François Pelloquin took over the factory established by Pierre Clerissy. It remained in production until 1852. The wares are barely to be distinguished from the other Moustiers factories. On the later wares the hand-written mark is abandoned in favour of a stencilled mark. A number of different marks incorporating this name are found.

Fownhope Pottery
Fownhope, Hereford and Worcester, UK
Dennis Lacey produced Studio-type wares at the Fownhope Pottery from 1956. This painted mark appears from 1958. The impressed name 'Herefordshire' was used 1956–58.

Fulper Pottery *Flemington, New Jersey, USA*
A pottery for making utilitarian stoneware and drainage tiles was begun in Flemington about 1815 by Samuel Hill and taken over in 1858 by Abraham Fulper, who had been a potter for Hill during the 1820s and continued to make stoneware and tiles. In 1909 the firm replaced its utilitarian product with Vasekraft, an art pottery line that featured elaborate crystalline and flambé glazes over the traditional stoneware body. J. Martin Stangl acquired the company in 1929 and eventually changed the name and product.

G.A.F.F
Treviso

Treviso *Venetia, Italy*
Guiseppe and Andrea Fratelli, Fontebasso, manufacturers of soft-paste porcelain probably from c1790 to 1840. 'G. A. F. F. Treviso' is the full factory mark.

Gailliard
passage de
l'opera.

Gailliard *Passage de l'Opéra, Paris, France*
This decorator of hard-paste porcelain, who operated in Paris c1840, used this script mark that appears in gold.

GALLE
NANCY

Gallé *Nancy, Meuthe-et-Moselle, France*
Emile Gallé (1846–1904) was an artist potter who is better known for his acid-etched Studio glass, but was also a manufacturer of contemporary style faïence including the celebrated glass-eyed cats. This is his handwritten mark.

Gardiner Stoneware Manufactory
Gardiner, Maine, USA
Several substantial stoneware potteries were located during the 19thC in Gardiner, Maine, north-east of Portland. One of the more successful ones was owned by Charles Swift and William M. Wood. Often decorated with cobalt blue impressed or stamped motifs of eagles, cows or swans, their work was attractive and competitive with the more commonly employed blue brushed or trailed designs. The firm was active 1876–92.

George Fishley Holland *Dunster, Somerset, UK*
Previously based at The Pottery, Clevedon (1955–59), Holland moved to Dunster in 1959. His earthenwares bear this printed, painted or impressed mark, with 'Dunster' added after 1959.

Agnes Benson *Ruislip, London, UK*
See p89. This painted or incised mark was used from 1951.

Michele Giordano *Naples, Italy*
Michele Giordano and his son Guiseppe were modellers at Naples in the late 18th and early 19thC. They used this incised mark.

Giovine *Naples, Italy*
A decorator of imported ceramics 1826–30, Giovine's wares feature this mark inscribed in red enamel.

Justus Alex Ernst Glüer
Nuremberg, Bavaria, Germany
Justus Alex Ernst Glüer was a faïence decorator at Nuremberg and at Oettingen-Schrattenhofen between 1719 and 1740). He specialized in biblical subjects rendered in polychrome. His signature is very small and is invariably incorporated into the design rather than inscribed on the base.

Goldscheider (Staffordshire) Pottery Ltd
Hanley, Staffordshire, UK
Formerly Goldscheider Art Pottery, this firm produced earthenware and porcelain figures 1946–59. This printed signature of Marcel Goldscheider was used.

G. F. Grebner *Nuremberg, Bavaria, Germany*
Georg Friedrich Grebner (active 1717–41) was a faïence painter at Nuremberg, Bayreuth, Oettingen-Schrattenhofen and Donauworth. He was a versatile painter, capable of working in many styles including landscape, biblical and floral subjects. A considerable number of his signed and dated pieces exist. As well as his signature, Grebner also added the day, month and year to many of his possibly independently-decorated (*Hausmaler*) pieces.

V: H:
Groß-Stitten
Chely
9

Gross-Stieten *Mecklenburg, Germany*
Christoph Rudolph Chely and other members of his family were faïence potters at Brunswick as well as Gross-Stieten from c1753.

Groves

Lavender Groves *Chelsea, London*
From 1952 Studio-type pottery was produced here. This incised or painted mark appears.

GRUEBY POTTERY
BOSTON.U.S.A.

Grueby Faïence Company/Grueby Pottery/ Grueby Faïence and Tile Company
Boston, Massachusetts, USA
Founded to make glazed bricks and architectural tiles in 1894, the company added an art pottery line during the late 1890s, producing vases with low relief floral decoration made with rolled fillets of clay and covered with a green flowing matt glaze that was sometimes accented with yellow, ochre, rose or white. The art pottery was discontinued in 1910, but tiles were made until 1920 when the firm was purchased by the C. Pardee Works of Perth Amboy, New Jersey.

F. Guignet

F. Guignet *Giey-sur-Aujon, Haute Marne, France*
F. Guignet, manufacturer of hard-paste porcelain 1809–40, used this mark.

Guillibaud

Jean-Baptiste Guillibaud
Rouen, Seine-Inférieure, France
Jean-Baptiste Guillibaud (d1739) and his widow succeeded Edmé Poterat at Rouen. They were active 1720–40 making good quality blue and white and polychrome faïence, often using a combination of formalized Chinese motifs and indigenous 'textile' or embroidery designs within trellis diaper borders.

gun

Rouen *Seine-Inférieure, France*
Inscribed script mark 'gun' associated with the second (Poirel-Poterat) phase of faïence production at Rouen from the mid-17thC until c1720 or beyond.

Hadley

James Hadley & Sons (Ltd)
Worcester, Hereford and Worcester, UK
See p95. This incised or impressed signature appears on figures, groups, vases and other decorative pieces made by James Hadley for the Worcester Royal Porcelain Company c1875–94.

Haeger Potteries Inc *Dundee, Illinois, USA*
In 1912, flowerpots were added to bricks and tiles, which had been the primary products of this pottery since 1871. In 1914, they started glazing the pots and what started as florists' crockery expanded to include ornamental, garden and table wares in a variety of solid glossy glazes. This firm is still in operation.

Hall China Company *East Liverpool, Ohio, USA*
Robert Hall created this firm in 1903 from his portion of the East Liverpool Potteries Company's assets, at first making bed pans, cuspidors and some dinnerware. In 1911, the company developed the first successful leadless glaze which allowed them to produce ware in a single fire. This breakthrough, coming just before US markets were closed to foreign products used in food preparation and service during World War I, gave the firm a decided advantage with its institutional line. The firm also became famous for its range of gold-decorated teapots which were produced from 1919. Speciality items for domestic kitchens, refrigerators and tea services as well as some dinnerware have also been made. These marks are among those used.

Pierre or Philippe Haly *Nevers, France*
Pierre or Philippe Haly came from a family of potters active in Nevers in the 18thC. Recorded as painters, they produced a number of signed pieces dated in the 1760s and 1770s. This family is associated with figures and trompe l'oeil dishes of fruit.

Hampshire Pottery Company/James S. Taft & Co
Keene, New Hampshire, USA
See p62. This mark was used.

Hanau *Nr Frankfurt-am-Main, Germany*
See p180. The two marks above appear during the Hieronymus von Alphen period (1740–86); the mark below is a later mark. Hieronymus von Alphen became the owner of the faïence factory in Hanau on the death of his father, Heinrich Simons von Alphen, in 1740. Hieronymus von Alphen died in 1775, and his daughters continued the factory until 1787.

R. Hancock fecit

Robert Hancock *Various locations, UK*
Hancock was an engraver who worked at a number of factories c1755–65 (Battersea, Bow, Worcester, Caughley). He is best known for his work on First Period Worcester porcelains (see p33). This signature mark in various forms occurs on pieces with fine quality printed patterns.

W.M. HARE WILMINGTON, DEL.

William Hare Pottery *Wilmington, Delaware, USA*
The most productive pottery in the state of Delaware, established by Pennsylvania-born William Hare in Wilmington on French Street, c1838. In the earliest years, redware and stoneware were made but, later, stoneware utilitarian forms were made exclusively. 'Air-Tight Stone Jars' were featured from the mid-1850s on for their superior (to glass) strength and cheapness. Virtually all stoneware was plain and salt-glazed; blue decoration is infrequently found. The firm continued until 1882.

Harker Pottery Company *East Liverpool, Ohio and Chester, West Virginia, USA*
Founded by Benjamin Harker Senior in 1840 and operated by his sons, Benjamin and George, the Harkers joined with James Taylor in 1847 and after 1851 continued as George S. Harker and Company until 1890 through several changes in management. Before 1879, the pottery made yellow ware and Rockingham kitchenware and jugs, after which time it specialized in white granite table and toilet ware Incorporated in 1890 as the Harker Pottery Company, the firm soon changed its products tc semi-porcelain dinner, kitchen, toilet and hotel ware and advertising novelties. In 1931, the pottery moved into the old Edwin M. Knowles factory in Chester, West Virginia. The firm continued until 1972.

C. HART & SON
SHERBURNE

James and Charles Hart
Sherburne, New York, USA
James Hart and his brother, Samuel, were potte trained by their father in High Halden, Kent, England, before settling in New York State in th 1820s. By 1841, James and his son Charles established a stoneware pottery at Sherburne, New York, that remained in operation until 1885; after 1866, Charles was in partnership

with his son, Nahum. The Hart family also maintained extremely successful potteries in Fulton and Ogdensburgh.

Hastings Pottery *Sussex, UK*
Studio-type pottery was produced by Bernard J. Cotes at the Hastings Pottery 1956–59. This incised mark was used.

William Ellis Tucker/Tucker and Hulme/Tucker and Hemphill *Philadelphia, Pennsylvania, USA*
Tucker started his career in ceramics by decorating French blanks for his father's ceramics and glass store. By 1825, his experiments to make hard-paste porcelain were successful. Thomas Hulme was a partner briefly in 1828; Joseph Hemphill joined the firm c1832 and continued operating the pottery after Tucker's death in 1838. Tucker's brother, Thomas, managed the workers. Sometimes known as the American China Manufactory, they made porcelain table and ornamental wares in the style of French porcelain painted mostly with flowers and landscapes. This is Hemphill's mark.

D. & J. Henderson/American Pottery Company *Jersey City, New Jersey, USA*
See p111. This mark was used. Other marks in a similar style appear featuring the company name and 'Jersey City'.

William Fishley Holland *Clevedon, Somerset, UK*
Formerly at Fremington, W. F. Holland produced earthenwares from c1921. He used this incised signature mark as well as an initial mark.

Nathan Clark Pottery *Athens, New York, USA*
See p116. This mark was used by this company.

Christoph Conrad Hunger *Various locations, Europe*
One of the most important German enamellers and gilders in the first half of the 18thC. He worked at Meissen c1715–17 and later at Du Paquier's factory in Vienna (1717–19), Vezzi's factory in Venice (1719–24), Rørstrand (1729), Copenhagen (1730 and 1737), Stockholm (1741) and St Petersburg (1744–48).

Ignatz Hess *Hochst, Mainz, Germany*
Ignaz Hess, faïence painter c1750, specialized in landscape and flower subjects often enclosed in elaborate rococo cartouches. He was the son of Georg Friedrich Hess, also a notable faïence painter. This mark appears c1750.

Faenza *Emilia, Italy*
Faenza was one of the most important maiolica centres in Renaissance and post-Renaissance Ital A large quantity of wares were exported, and thi probably gave the name 'faïence' to tin-glazed wares later produced in other European centres. Noted for very high quality wares, especially the blue-ground *berettino* type and the celebrated and influential *bianco-di-Faenza* of the Manneris period at the end of the 16thC. The word 'Faenza' rarely, if ever, appears alone, but is generally used with initials such as these examples, which are probably those of the workshop of Maestro Virgiliotto Calamelli (died c1570). Faenza is still active as a centre for tin-glazed ware.

Frederic Langlois *Calvados, Normandy, France*
Frederic Langlois was a manufacturer of hard-paste porcelain in Isigny 1839–45.

Isis Pottery *Oxford, Oxfordshire, UK*
Studio-type pottery bearing this mark was produced at the Isis Pottery c1947–53.

Jeanne *Paris, France*
This decorator of hard-paste porcelain from 1827 used this gold mark.

Jever *Oldenburg, Germany*
A faïence factory was established here in 1760 by Johann Friedrich Tännich (later to move to Kiel in 1763). Barely viable for most of its short life, the factory closed in 1776 but did make some fine quality faïence, especially in the first few years. The full or abbreviated place name rarely occurs alone and is usually accompanied by one of the following letters or initials: 'K', 'J. C. K.', 'K. O.', or 'R'.

Jill Salaman *Selsey, Sussex, UK*
Jill Salaman's signature mark appears on Studio-type pottery and tiles made 1929–50.

Kiel *Holstein, Germany*
A number of mainly short-lived faïence factories were active here 1758–88 employing craftsmen such as Johann Tännich (of Jever) and Abraham Leihamer (also of Eckernförde and Stockelsdorf). Johann Tobias Kleffel was the proprietor of one factory that survived only a year in 1762–63. The other mark shown is the town mark.

Halley-Lebon *Paris, France*
A decorator of hard-paste porcelain 1800–12, Halley-Lebon used this script mark in gold.

Lagrenée le jeune *Paris, France*
Decorator of Paris porcelain 1793–1800. This script mark appears in russet.

Peter Lane *Andover, Hampshire, UK*
Studio-type ceramics were produced at The Pottery in Andover from 1961. Important pieces bear this signature mark.

Leplé *Rue de Bacq, Paris, France*
Leplé directed a porcelain-decorating studio in Paris c1808. Pieces signed by his son (Leplé jeune) are also found.

Jean-Marie Levavasseur
Rouen, Seine-Inférieure, France
Jean-Marie Levavasseur and family were potters in Rouen in the 18thC. A group of polychrome *petit-feu* enamelled wares was made at this factory from c1770 onwards. This script mark appears.

Leveille *Rue Thiroux, Paris, France*
Manufacturers of hard-paste porcelain in Paris 1832–50. This mark was used.

L. Levy *Vallauris, France*
Lucien Levy was an artist and designer at Clément & Jérome Massier in the late 19thC.

Lille *France*
Lille was an important ceramics centre producing common pottery, faïence and both hard- and soft-paste porcelain in the 18thC. The faïence was strongly influenced by Rouen and Delft in the first half of the 18thC and by Strasburg in the latter half. The mark illustrated appears

on an original piece but is one of the most faked marks in French ceramics. It is frequently found on small metal-mounted snuff boxes painted in *petit-feu* colours with Watteauesque figure subjects, landscapes or flowers. This mark appears in blue.

·Limoges· ·1741·

Limoges *Haute-Vienne, France*
Although faïence was produced here in the 18thC, Limoges is probably best known for its later hard-paste porcelain of which there were (and still are) a considerable number of factories in the area. Mostly the word 'Limoges' appears on porcelain from the second half of the 19thC. While the majority of the marks are stencilled or printed, earlier wares tend to be hand-written. This mark appears on faïence.

L M Jan 29 1859 Dave

Lewis Miles *Horse Creek, South Carolina, USA*
John Landrum established a pottery at Horse Creek, about 15 miles (24km) south east of Edgefield, South Carolina in 1817. In 1847 his son, Benjamin F. Landrum, and his son-in-law, Lewis Miles, took over the management of this pottery. The 'L. M.' seen in the mark here, is for Lewis Miles. Dave (died c1863), an African-American slave potter, worked for Landrum and Miles, and his large alkaline-glazed storage jars, sometimes inscribed with poems, dates and his name, are among the most sought-after pieces of American southern pottery The firm continued until c1865.

LOU IS

Jean Louis *Orléans, Loiret, France*
Jean Louis was a modeller employed from 1756 to 1760 by the factory established by Jacques-Etienne Dessaux de Romilly in 1753. As well as faïence, the factory produced a soft-paste porcelain of Mennecy type. The factory probably closed in 1812. This mark appears on a figure.

Lpkan

De Lampetkan *Delft, Holland*
Over 30 tin-glazed (delftware) factories were active in Delft in the 17thC onwards. De Lampetkan (The Jug or Ewer) appears to have had a large output judging by the number of marked specimens extant. Most bearing the script marks date from the middle of the 18thC. This mark was registered in 1764.

Lyman Fenton & Co *Bennington, Vermont, USA*
Although a short-lived partnership (1848–52), the principals, Christopher Webber Fenton and Alanson Potter Lyman, working with Calvin Park in 1848 and 1849, and Oliver Gager after 1852, produced a wonderful assortment of parian, Rockingham and porcelain. Coloured metal oxides were frequently used to decorate the fine Rockingham pitchers and wash basins, picture frames, animal figurines, etc and the impressed oval '1849' mark is probably the most frequently encountered on all American Rockingham ware. This firm evolved into the United States Pottery Company.

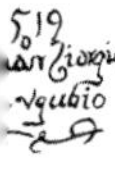

Maestro Giorgio Andreoli *Gubbio, Urbino, Italy*
Gubbio has been a pottery centre since the 14thC but its fame rests with the lustred wares decorated by Maestro Giorgio Andreoli in the first half of the 16thC. While painted maiolica was probably first made towards the end of the 15thC, it is difficult to say when lustre appears. The Maestro's script marks and monograms bear dates ranging from 1519 until 1541 on wares which, in many cases, were painted in polychrome elsewhere, prior to their arrival at Gubbio for the final addition of lustre decoration.

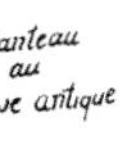

Manteau *Paris, France*
Manteau was a decorator of hard-paste porcelain 1807–11. This mark appears.

Martin Brothers *Fulham and Southall, London, UK*
The four Martin brothers (Robert Wallace, Walter, Edwin and Charles) designed, made and decorated individual stoneware c1873–1914. They are regarded by many as the first of the Studio potters, and notable wares include their models of birds with human-type expressions, decorated with cream and brown salt-glaze. Their incised signature mark with the address 'Fulham' was used 1873–74; 'London' 1874–78; 'Southall' c1878–79; 'London & Southall' from 1879. 'Bros' or 'Brothers' was added from 1882. Most pieces feature a date near the signature mark.

Clement & Jerome Massier *Vallauris, France*
See p116. This mark appears on Studio-type wares produced by these potters.

William Moorcroft *Burslem, Staffordshire, UK*
See p74. William Moorcroft's signature was registered as a trade mark in 1919, but it was previously used on pieces decorated by Moorcroft while at Macintyre & Co.

Matt Morgan Art Pottery *Cincinnati, Ohio, USA*
An English cartoonist, Morgan settled in Cincinnati in the 1870s, where he worked for a lithography company and briefly operated a pottery as a sideline in partnership with George Ligowsky, the inventor of the clay pigeon, 1883–84. The art wares have a Moorish look that combined low relief, moulded decoration with gold or painted coloured slip.

McNicol, Burton and Company/D. E. McNicol Pottery Company *East Liverpool, Ohio and Clarksburg, West Virginia, USA*
This pottery (active 1869–1954) produced good quality Rockingham and yellow ware. White ironstone table and toilet wares were added some time in the 1880s. In 1892, the firm was incorporated as D. E. McNicol and Co and continued to make the same products. Indeed, yellow ware was produced as late as 1927, although the firm was most famous for its calendar and souvenir plates. The company built a large additional plant in Clarksburg in 1914, which specialized in hotel ware for a wide variety of institutions, and concentrated production there after 1927. Marks usually appear on dinner and oven wares, and on food dishes.

C. H. Menard *Rue de Popincourt, Paris, France*
C. H. Menard was a manufacturer of hard-paste porcelain in the mid-19thC.

Johann Friedrich Metzsch
Various locations, Germany
Johann Friedrich Metzsch (d1766) was a leading independent decorator or *Hausmaler* and arcanist (active 1731–51 in Bayreuth, Dresden and Fürstenberg). His work which employs a sophisticated colour scheme includes landscapes and shipping scenes after engravings by Melchior Kysell, as well as birds on table tops. All his signed pieces date from 1744–48. He decorated Chinese, Meissen and other German porcelains.

Donald Mills *London*
Studio-type pottery and stonewares were produced 1946–55. This signature was registered as a trademark in 1948 and was used until c1955, often with the year added. A painted initial mark was also used.

Minton *Stoke, Staffordshire*
Thomas Minton (1765–1836), who trained as an engraver at the Caughley China Works, established his own pottery in 1793 that has continued under various titles and ownership until the present day. The company produced tiles, porcelain (some in the Sèvres style), stoneware (domestic and decorative wares), china (services and ornaments), earthenware, parian and majolica. A large number of marks were used including year marks; this painted mark appeared on earthenwares c1900–08. (For further details of year marks, see p363 in Additional Information.)

Bernard Moore *Stoke, Staffordshire, UK*
See p51. This painted or impressed mark appears 1905–15; the year may be added to these marks.

Morley & Company *Wellsville, Ohio, USA*
This is one of the few American potteries that made majolica, and its wares were of very high quality. It operated 1879–85. The pottery also produced good white ironstone tableware.

Moulins *Allier, France*
Faïence has been produced here probably from the early 18thC until the beginning of the 19thC. Although rarely marked, several types can be attributed to this town. The best wares date from the third quarter of the 18thC.

Keith Murray *Staffordshire, UK*
A New Zealander, Murray (1892–1981) produced modernist ceramic wares in the 1930s and 1940s. From 1933, Murray worked part-time for Wedgwood, designing tablewares and other functional but ornamental items. His initials also appear within a Wedgwood mark.

Nast *Rue Popincourt, Paris, France*
Manufacturers of porcelain 1793 to mid-19thC. The mark is usually stencilled in red.

New York Stoneware Company
Fort Edward, New York, USA
George A. Satterlee and Michael Mory operated a successful stoneware and Rockingham manufactory, the New York Stoneware Company at Fort Edward, New York on the upper Hudson River. Even before their partnership, this enterprise (known as the Fort Edward Pottery Company and so marked) was a thriving one, producing 75,000 pieces in 1860. The New York Stoneware Company was active 1861–91.

Nicola da Urbino *Urbino, Italy*
See p100. These marks have also been attributed to Nicola di Gabriele Sbraga (or Sbraghe), a pottery decorator in Urbino from c1520 until his death in 1537–38.

Niloak Pottery *Benton, Arkansas, USA*
Various naturally-coloured clays were combined, but not mixed, to make the variegated agate ware in simple wheel-thrown forms of bowls, vases, smoking sets, candlesticks, punch sets, fern dishes, clock cases and other items that were produced by this firm 1909–46. The basic line was called 'Mission Ware', a swirled, hand-thrown type of art pottery.

Niderviller *Lorraine, France*
See p41. The town name can be impressed or written in script, either in full or abbreviated.

Nove *Venezia, Italy*
An important faïence and porcelain centre in the 18thC. A number of painted, impressed and incised name marks appear.

Østerbro *Copenhagen, Denmark*
A faïence factory was established here in 1763 by Peter Hoffnagel but was forced out of business after a law-suit in 1769. Østerbro wares are usually lower quality than the fine faïence made at Store Kongensgade, but their wares are sometimes confused.

Offenbach *Nr Frankfurt-am-Main, Germany*
A factory was set up here by Philipp Friedrich Lay in 1739 and passed through several owners; the last recorded owner was Johannes

Klepper (1775–79) although a number of dated pieces with the town marks indicate that production continued into the early 19thC. 'Offenbach', 'Offenbak' and simply 'Off' are all recorded marks of this town.

E. OHR,
BILOXI.

George E. Ohr's Biloxi Art Pottery
Biloxi, Mississippi, USA
Ohr described himself as the 'Greatest Art Potter on Earth' because of his ability to wheel-turn red earthenware into exquisitely thin vase and teapot forms and then alter them with twists and pinches to resemble ornamental art glass and frilly Belleek china. The murky, pitted glazes that are highly prized today were secondary to the forms, many of which were left unglazed. He was active 1883–1906.

LLIVIER
A PARIS

Ollivier *Rue de la Roquette, Paris, France*
One of a number of Paris faïenciers, the Ollivier factory specialized in the manufacture of stoves of which a number of dated and documentary specimens survive. These marks, both impressed and painted, are typical.

WENS

J. B. Owens Pottery Company
Zanesville, Ohio, USA
See p81. This mark was used.

1740

De Paauw *Delft, Holland*
See p85. This mark appears. The proprietor of this factory 1729–40 was Jan Verhagen. He was succeeded by Jacobus de Milde.

Padua *Italy*
A centre for maiolica and sgraffiato earthenware from the late 15th to the 18thC. As well as maiolica, Padua is noted for Isnik (Turkish) influenced designs. This script mark is known.

ENT
ILE WORKS
HELSEA
MASS. USA

Low Art Tile Works *Chelsea, Massachusetts, USA*
Although a factory was started in 1877 by John Gardner Low and his father, John, production did not begin until 1879 under the direction of George W. Robertson from Chelsea Keramic Art Works (see p54), and continued until 1902. Tiles were made by the pressed dust, and plastic or wet process, both covered with glossy, coloured glazes. Subjects included heads, ornamental

patterns, realistic and conventional flowers, figures and scenes. English artist Arthur Osborne produced a large series of 'plastic sketches', hand-worked low-relief pictures in clay.

Potsdam *Nr Berlin, Germany*
The principal factory in Potsdam was started by Christian Friedrich Rewend in 1739, producing conventional Delft style faïence as well as unglazed and lacquered pottery (probably similar to the chinoiserie lacquered vases of Berlin).

Pewabic Pottery *Detroit, Michigan, USA*
Ceramic painter Mary Chase Perry joined up with her neighbour Horace Caulkins, who was in the dental supply business, to make vases and tiles with a variety of decorative glazes, including flambé, crystalline, volcanic and lustre from 1903. The pottery was most famous for its iridescent lustre effects. Many important churches in the United States are paved with tiles from this pottery. From 1966 to 1981, Michigan State University operated the pottery as a ceramic centre, museum and studio. Since 1981, the non-profit making Pewabic Society has been making tiles and continuing the educational programme.

Pierre Renault (or Renard)
Orléans, Loiret, France
Repairer and modeller, Renault was engaged at the faïence manufactory at Orléans c1760. He used this incised mark.

Pinxton Works *Derbyshire, UK*
The Pinxton Works was established by John Coke c1796. He employed William Billingsley of the Derby China Works, who produced high quality porcelain, and a famous group of wares painted with views of Derbyshire. Billingsley left in 1799 and landscape painter John Cutts was then appointed manager. He became a partner, and in the final years of the works ran the concern alone. Cutts left to work for Wedgwood in 1813, and Pinxton closed.

De Rosly *Pontenx-les-Forges, Landes, France*
De Rosly was a small-scale manufacturer of hard-paste porcelain from 1779 to 1790, and used this script mark.

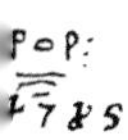

Johann Georg Christoph Popp
Ansbach, Bavaria, Germany
See p49. This mark was one of those used by Johann Georg Christoph Popp (1697–1786), faïence painter, manager and latterly proprietor of the Ansbach factory.

N. Possinger *Nuremberg, Bavaria, Germany*
N. Possinger was a faïence painter of bibical subjects in strong high-fired colours. He is recorded at Nuremberg between 1725 and 1730.

Christopher Potter
Rue de Crussol, Paris, and Chantilly, France
Christopher Potter was an Englishman who established a hard-paste factory in 1789 which continued in production in the early 19thC. He used this painted mark in underglaze blue.

Providential Tile Works *Trenton, New Jersey, USA*
The company made plain or relief glazed tiles using glossy coloured glazes, underglaze decoration, gilding and cloisonné-like effects 1885–1913. Isaac Broome was the company's first designer and modeller.

Pruden Pottery *Elizabeth, New Jersey, USA*
Keen Pruden bought an existing pottery and made brown glazed redware and blue-decorated stoneware. His son, John Mills Pruden, continued the business beginning about 1835. He made utilitarian stoneware, Rockingham and yellow ware for domestic use as well as drainage tiles and other industrial stoneware products, c1820–79.

Red Wing Stoneware *Red Wing, Minnesota, USA*
In the southwestern corner of Minnesota, below Minneapolis, a number of stoneware potteries were established at or near Red Wing, Goodhue County. The Red Wing Stoneware Company was organized in 1877 and prospered, in spite of competition from the Minnesota Stoneware Company (1883–94), North Star Stoneware Company (1892–97), and Union Stoneware Company (1894–1906). Eventually, in 1906, the Red Wing Union Stoneware Company was formed from the remaining potters and they continued to 1930, when the name was changed to Red Wing

Potteries Inc. A variety of different names and tradenames were used; most incorporate 'Red Wing'.

Rennes ce 12 8bre 1763

Rennes *Ille-et-Vilaine, Brittany, France*
A number of minor potteries have existed here from the 16thC on, and apart from a small handful of documentary pieces little can be readily ascribed to Rennes. Apart from conventional northern French faïence, the output included figures of saints. Marks are rare but this example is characteristic of Rennes.

REVIL Rue Neuve des Capucines

Renou *Paris, France*
Decorator of hard-paste porcelain from late 18thC to 1820. This mark was gilded.

Bursley Ware Charlotte Rhead England

H. J. Wood (Ltd) *Burslem, Staffordshire, UK*
Now part of Wood & Sons Ltd, H. J. Wood (Ltd) produced earthenwares from 1884. During the 1920s Charlotte Rhead produced wares for the company which bear this mark.

RH Worcester

Worcester Porcelains *Hereford and Worcester, UK*
See p33. Signature marks sometimes appear in the design of some printed wares. The initials 'R. H' are those of Robert Hancock, an engraver at Worcester c1756–65 (see p128). This mark appears in various forms.

Rihouet

J. Rihouet *Paris, France*
J. Rihouet was a decorator of Paris hard-paste porcelain from 1820. This mark appears.

J&R.Riley

John & Richard Riley *Burslem, Staffordshire, UK*
Based first at Nile Street (c1802–14) and later at the Hill Works (c1814–28), this factory produced general ceramics. Several different painted, printed or impressed marks appear featuring the name 'Riley' 1802–28. The works were later taken over by Samuel Alcock.

R.F Sevres

Sèvres *France*
See p82. This mark in blue was used at Sèvres during the First Republic (1793–1804).

ROOKWOOD 1882

Rookwood Pottery *Cincinnati, Ohio, USA*
See p102. This impressed mark was used, and may appear with the monogram mark.

De Roos *Delft, Holland*
See p43. This mark was used during the late 17thC and early 18thC.

Rossi *Coimbra, Portugal*
A faïence factory was established here by Rossi in the late 18thC, and survived into the 19thC. This mark appears.

Rousseau *Rue Coquillere, Paris, France*
F. Rousseau manufactured and decorated hard-paste porcelain in Paris from 1837 to 1870. Pieces bear this mark.

Salamander Works *Woodbridge, New Jersey, USA*
Operated by Michel Lefoulon and Henry DeCasse 1836–42, this pottery made high-quality, brown-glazed yellow wares for domestic and public use, especially as pitchers and coolers. Some designs were patterned after the successful ware made by the American Pottery Company. While some pieces identify Woodbridge as the location of manufacture, others mention New York. The firm had a shop in nearby New York City and it is thought that this site was also a second pottery works. Fire-brick and drainage tiles were made in the same Woodbridge pottery both before and after the operation of Lefoulon and DeCasse.

Samadet *Landes, France*
In 1732 a faïence factory was founded here by the Abbé de Roquepine. The factory passed through several hands, finally closing in 1836. The pre-Revolutionary wares are an eclectic borrowing from Rouen, Moustiers and nearby Bordeaux with whom it was in competition. This mark was used.

Sargadelos *Spain*
See p44. This mark appears during the mid-19thC. There are a number of variations of this mark.

Sarreguemines *Lorraine, France*
In 1770 Paul Utzschneider established a faïence and pottery factory which remained in production throughout the 19thC making a variety of fine wares including *faïence fine*, Wedgwood-style stonewares, and lead-glazed

pottery such as majolica. This mark was used together with a straightforward mark 'Majolica Sarreguemines'.

Sceaux *Seine, France*
See p226. This late stencilled mark appears on faïence made at Sceaux.

Schleswig *Germany*
A faïence factory was founded here in 1755 by arcanist Johann Christoph Ludwig Lücke (Ludwig von Lück). Between 1756 and 1758 the factory was owned by Adriani, Schmattau and the Otte Brothers, before it was bought by Johann Rambusch in 1758. The factory produced typical Danish type wares including tabletops, centrepieces, baskets and punchbowls in the form of a bishop's mitre. The factory passed through a number of different owners before closing in 1814, unable to keep pace with competition from British cream-coloured earthenware. The script marks (seen here) are relatively rare; various letter and initial marks are more frequently found.

Oettingen-Schrattenhofen *Bavaria, Germany*
A faïence factory was established here in 1735 on the initative of Jeremias Pitsch from Ansbach. It was taken over in 1748 by Albrecht Kohler and Johann Sperl. Output in the earlier years seems to have included tankards of standard German form and decoration in high-fired colours. During the 19thC, the factory concentrated on the production of cream-coloured earthenware. This mark was used.

Marc Schoelcher *Paris, France*
Marc Schoelcher was a hard-paste porcelain decorator in Paris from c1800 to 1810. This script mark appears in red and occasionally in other colours.

Seligmann *Nuremberg, Bavaria, Germany*
This faïence painter worked at Nuremberg from c1760 to 1780. He used this script mark.

Sèvres *France*
See p82. This impressed mark was used c1810–20 on cameo-relief wares made in Wedgwood style.

Sinceny *Aisne, France*
See p44. The mark (top) was used at Sinceny during the early period 1733–75. The mark (centre) appears during the 'second period', 1775–95. The mark (below) was used by Denis-Pierre Pellevé, director of the factory 1733–37.

Joseph Clérissy *Saint-Jean-du-Desert, Marseilles, Bouches-du-Rhône, France*
In 1679 Joseph Clérissy, son of Antoine Clérissy of Moustiers, took over an existing factory in this suburb of Marseilles. The factory was continued by his family after his death in 1685, and was relocated to Marseilles in 1743. The best period was probably from about 1700 to 1720 when blue and white with purple manganese detailing was chiefly used. Subjects were typical baroque with classical figures, hunting scenes or biblical themes. This factory has been much faked. A number of other minor factories also operated in this area at the time. This script mark appears.

Johann Heinrich Steinbach
Bayreuth, Bavaria, Germany
Steinbach (d176l) was a painter of faïence at Bayreuth. This name mark was used.

Stockelsdorff *Nr Lübeck, Germany*
A faïence factory was started here in 1771, principally making stoves and tablewares, cisterns, jardinières and vases painted in *petit-feu* enamels in rococo, Chinoiserie or Neo-classical style. The factory closed in 1811. Abraham Leihamer formerly from Kiel was a decorator here for a brief period. This mark appears.

William Sipe & Sons
Williamsport, Pennsylvania, USA
William Sipe was born in 1826, the son of the potter Phillip Sipe, and he built his first pottery in 1869 at Williamsport. He worked in partnerships – Sipe, Nichols & Co 1875–77, and Moore, Nichols & Co 1877–79 and later worked with his sons Luther and Oscar until 1893. Their blue-decorated stonewares were thrown by male potters but were decorated on the second floor of the pottery by women. Wares were shipped all over Pennsylvania and Maryland.

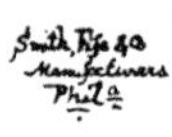

Asa E. Smith Pottery *Norwalk, Connecticut, USA*
On 31 October 1825, Asa E. Smith established a stoneware factory 'at the foot of Mill Hill a few rods east of the Bridge' in Norwalk, Connecticut. In 1843, Asa's cousin Noah S. Day joined the firm and they remained together until 1849. Smith's several sons also joined the company and ran it after the father's retirement in the early 1860s until 1887.

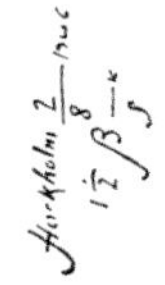

Smith, Fife and Company
Philadelphia, Pennsylvania, USA
Little is known about this short-lived company, active 1830, since few pieces survive, and all of them are flower-painted Grecian pitchers like those produced by William Ellis Tucker (see p129), at the same time.

Rörstrand *Nr Stockholm, Sweden*
Founded in 1752, this faïence factory produced wares similar to Copenhagen, Rouen and Delft with table-tops, dinner wares and stoves similar to other Scandinavian and north German factories. Wares were decorated in high-fired and low-fired colours. A novelty of this factory was the use of *bianco-sopra-bianco* decoration similar to that on Bristol delftware. In 1773 the factory began to make English style creamware, and in the middle of the 19thC bone-china. The factory still exists, producing high-quality ceramics. Many marks exist, such as the example seen here.

C. Tharaud *Limoges, Limousin, France*
C. Tharaud established a hard-paste porcelain factory in 1919. The monogram 'CT' together with the name Limoges, was also used by Tharaud.

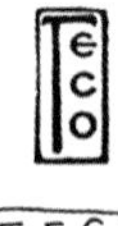

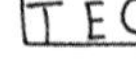

Teco Gates *Terra Cotta, Illinois, USA*
William Gates, a maker of tiles since 1881, officially introduced the art pottery line TECO in 1902, although experimental pieces had been made since 1895. Many modellers, designers and architects furnished designs for the ornamental ware decorated almost entirely in a matt green crystalline glaze, including Fernand Moreau, Kristian Schneider, Hugh Garden, William Le Baron Jenney, Howard Van Doren Shaw and Frank Lloyd Wright. The company closed in 1929. These impressed marks were used.

Tomaszów *Poland*
Michael Mezer produced hard-paste porcelain here between 1805 and 1810. This script mark appears in black and other colours.

Trenton Potteries Company
Trenton, New Jersey, USA
See p72. This mark also appears.

William Ellis Tucker/Tucker and Hulme/ Tucker and Hemphill
Philadelphia, Pennsylvania, USA
See p129. This mark was used by William Ellis Tucker.

United States Pottery Company
Bennington, Vermont, USA
After the firm of Lyman, Fenton & Co disbanded (see p133) the financial backer, Oliver A. Gager, reopened the factory as the United States Pottery Company in 1852. Daniel Greatbach of England modelled a number of new shapes for the company, including a fine hound-handled pitcher, and John Harrison, a modeller from Copeland's works in Stoke-on-Trent, England, assisted C. W. Fenton with developing new shapes in parian. The pottery was one of only seven American potteries to exhibit at the New York Crystal Palace Exhibition in 1853. In 1858, the factory shut down but was vainly reopened for one additional year. Porcelain, parian, and Rockingham were the principal lines.

Varsovie *Warsaw, Poland*
Seen here is the written mark of the Belvedere factory established in 1774 by Elector King Stanislas Poniatowski. Wares including the famous Poniatowski service intended for the Sultan of Turkey were based on Japanese Imari porcelain or more commonly on Chinese export ware. Single letters 'B' or 'W' are also used. Some fakes of the Turkish service are known.

Valognes *Manche, France*
A factory was founded here in 1793 by Le Tellier de la Bertinière. By 1795 it belonged to Le Masson. In 1802 it was taken over by Joachim Langlois who transferred the concern to Bayeux in 1812. A number of marks occur, including those seen here.

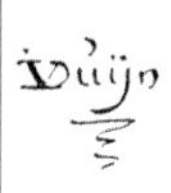

Johannes Van Duyn *Delft, Holland*
Johannes Van Duyn was proprietor of De porceleyn Schotel (The Porcelain Dish) factory in Delft 1763–77, making mainly black and white wares. This mark was registered in 1764.

Venezia.
VEN:
Ven·

Venezia *Veneto, Italy*
Various tin-glazed and porcelain factories were established here from the 16thC. These marks belong the Vezzi factory which produced hard-paste porcelain c1719–40. The full town name may appear in blue, with abbreviations in red, green or blue.

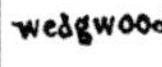

Wedgwood & Bentley.

Josiah Wedgwood (& Sons Ltd)
Various locations, Staffordshire, UK
From c1759 to the present day, this celebrated company has produced earthenwares and porcelain at Burslem, Etruria and Barlaston. Founded in 1759 by Josiah Wedgwood (d1795) Wares include creamware, jasper, basalts, majolica, lustre, agate, red and other wares. This basic impressed name mark appears on earthenwares from c1759. Early examples have individually impressed upper and lower case letters. A 'Wedgwood & Bentley' circular mark was used c1769–80 on ornamental basalt, jasper and marbled wares. (For further details of year marks, see p374 in Additional Information.)

Noah, Nicholas A and Charles N. White
Utica, New York, USA
Noah White of Vermont began one of the most successful family dynasties of potters in the United States. Born in 1793, he was working as a potter by 1831 and owned his own stoneware manufactory in 1838 at Utica, New York with his son Nicholas. Through time there were many changes as family came and went. When Noah died in 1865, Nicholas and his son controlled the firm as N. A. White and Son (later the Central New York Pottery). Nicholas died in 1886, and his son Charles N. White ran the pottery until 1910. Under the direction of Hugo Bilhardt, a German designer, moulded stoneware pitchers, mugs, water coolers, steins and other wares were introduced in 1894, and these proved to be as profitable then as they are popular now with collectors.

Willoughby Smith *Womelsdorf, Pennsylvania, USA*
Although most American redware potters did not sign their products, one exception stands out – Willoughby Smith of Womelsdorf, Pennsylvania. Traditional wares included milk pots, pitchers, jugs, jars, dishes, pie plates, spitoons, and chamber pots, made for a local, rural eastern Pennsylvania clientele. The quality of the work is excellent, and a good many slip-decorated pie plates survive to tempt collectors. He was active from 1864 to 1905.

Sterling China Company
East Liverpool, Ohio, USA
See p115. This company is probably best known among collectors for its line designed by Russel Wright shortly after World War II. This mark was used.

Zeschinger *Höchst, Mainz, Germany*
Johannes Zeschinger (b1723) was employed as a painter of faïence from c1750, Furstenberg (1753) and Poppelsdorf (1756). He appears to have specialized in fine quality bird painting.

Letters & Devices

Detail of Royal Doulton mark, 1949–83

LETTERS & DEVICES

n this section, devices are featured in the order listed on 1e contents page, together with one or more initial (in phabetical order), that may refer to an individual potter, rm, centre of production or patron of a factory.

Crowns

St Petersburg *Russia*

See p39. The marks used on porcelain made at the Imperial factory in St Petersburg during the reigns of Alexander I (above) 1801–25, II (below left) 1855–81, and III (below right) 1881–94; all three emperors used the letter 'A' together with a crown.

Rue Thiroux *Paris, France*

See p31. This mark appears on porcelain by André Marie Leboeuf in gold. The 'A' mark was originally registered in 1776.

Fulda *Hesse, Germany*

The Fürstlich Fuldaische Feine porcelain factory was founded in 1764 by the Prince Bishop of Fulda, Heinrich von Bibra (1759–88). The factory produced figures (similar in style to those made at Frankenthal) and other wares, characterized by a pure white body and a shiny glaze. This mark was used on porcelain made at Fulda. The mark represents Adalbert III von Harstall, Prince Bishop 1788–1803. Production ended in 1789.

Wagner & Apel *Lippelsdorf, Thuringia, Germany*

A porcelain factory was founded here in 1877, producing figures of animals and children, boxes, vases, ornaments and technical porcelain.

Beyer & Bock

Rudolstadt Volkstedt, Thuringia, Germany

Utility porcelain was produced at this factory from 1890, but it is thought that it existed as a decorating workshop from 1853. These marks appear; the mark below often includes the date 1853 as the year of foundation. The factory became known as VEB (K) Porzellanfabrik Rudolstadt-Volkstedt.

J. S. Vaume *Schaerbeek, Brussels, Belgium*

A porcelain factory was founded at Schaerbeek near Brussels in 1786 by J. S. Vaume. Dominant colours include sepia and green.

Bremer & Schmidt *Eisenberg, Thuringia, Germany*
Founded in 1895, this porcelain factory produced household wares, mocha services and mocha cups for export to the Balkans and for China and the Far East. The company still exists under the name VEB Spezialporzellan Eisenberg. This mark was used.

Worcester Porcelains *Hereford and Worcester, UK*
See p33. This standard impressed mark was used on all wares during the Barr, Flight & Barr period c1807–13. Many written marks featuring the full name of this period in various forms, appear beneath a crown.

Naples/Savona *Italy*
Large maiolica vases with this mark and dated 1684 were recorded at Naples. It is possible that they were made locally, but it is more likely that they were made in Savona.

Burroughs & Mountford *Trenton, New Jersey, USA*
Although this pottery made the general line of decorated hotel ware and domestic table and toilet ware characteristic of late 19thC American potteries, the quality of their decal work and printed and filled decorations was exceptional. They also produced an art ware having raised gold decorations on a royal blue ground, and some tiles. They were active 1879–c1900.

Schomberg & Söhne *Teltow, Prussia, Germany*
Founded in 1853, this factory produced good utilitarian porcelain wares. It became a subsidiary of the royal factory in Berlin from 1866, but was independent by 1904. At different periods the factory produced ordinary and art porcelain, and technical wares. Marks of this form were registered in the early 20thC, denoting 'Berliner Porzellan-Manufaktur'.

Robert Wilson *Hanley, Staffordshire, UK*
Originally Neale & Wilson (c1784–95), and subsequently called David Wilson (c1802–18), this firm based at the Church Works in Hanley produced Wedgwood-style earthenwares and creamwares. Robert Wilson died in 1801; his sons Daniel and then David continued the Church Works to c1815; the firm was David Wilson & Sons to 1818. This mark was one of those used by Robert Wilson 1795–c1802.

Pauline Pottery
Chicago, Illinois, and Edgerton, Wisconsin, USA
Pauline Jacobus started as a ceramic painter, and became interested in making pottery during the early 1800s. In 1883 she established her first small pottery in Chicago, but expanded in 1888 to Edgerton. Art wares were decorated by a small group of artists. A battery cup factory on the first floor made the art pottery viable, but the operation failed in 1902.

Carl Alberti *Uhlstädt, Thuringia, Germany*
Utility porcelain was produced at this factory from 1837. Various forms of this mark were used.

Charles Amison & Co Ltd
Longton, Stafforshire, UK
Porcelains were made at the Stanley China Works by this firm 1889–1962. These impressed initials were used from 1889 (the 'L' stands for Longton). This printed mark was used 1906–30.

Cartwright & Edwards (Ltd)
Fenton, Staffordshire, UK
See p177. This mark was used on wares made at the Victoria Works from c1912. Most other marks include the initials 'C. & E.'

Limoges *Haute-Vienne, France*
See p53. Wares made at Limoges for decoration at Sèvres sometimes feature the Sèvres mark and a painter's mark together with the mark of the Comte d'Artois, as seen here. This mark appears incised and in blue enamel.

Collingwood & Greatbatch
Longton, Staffordshire, UK
Based at the Crown Works, this pottery produced porcelain 1870–87. The mark used was the crown (above) with or without the initials 'C. & G.' The company subsequently became known as Collingwood Bros (Ltd) and operated 1887–1957. The Crown Works were then taken over by Clayton Bone China Co. The printed mark (below) was used 1900–12; a crown mark was also used up to 1930.

C.P.

Fauborg Saint-Denis (or Saint-Lazare)
Paris, France
See p38. This factory was taken over by Stahn, who registered the mark 'CP' in 1779,

indicating the protection of Charles-Philippe, Comte d'Artois. Various forms of this mark appear in red, underglaze blue and gold.

Carl Theodor *Frankenthal, Palatinate, Germany*
See p68. Elector Karl Theodor owned the porcelain factory at Frankenthal between 1762 and 1795, when successive military occupations forced the factory to change hands a number of times. It was closed in 1800. During the 'Carl Theodor' period this mark appears in blue in various forms. From 1762–70 the crowned monogram occasionally appears with the initials of Adam Bergdoll, the manager. The mark appears 1770–88 with the last two digits of the year of production. The late mark (below) (c1780–93) features a row of dots under the monogram. This mark has also been recorded on some Derby pieces that were probably made as replacements for Frankenthal services.

Charles Waine (& Co) (Ltd)
Longton, Staffordshire, UK
Formerly Waine & Bates, this company produced porcelain 1891–1920. This printed mark appeared c1913–20.

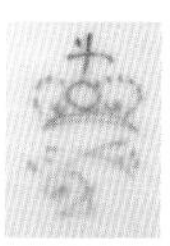

Derby Porcelain Works *Derbyshire, UK*
See p35. This painted Derby porcelain mark was used c1770–82. This mark appeared with dotted crossed swords c1782–1825 (puce, blue and black c1782–1800; red c1800–25).

Thomas Dimmock (Junr) & Co
Shelton, Staffordshire, UK
Based at Albion Street (c1828–59) and Tontine Street (c1830–50), this pottery produced earthenware 1828–59. The distinguishing initial 'D' appears in many marks including this crown. Marks such as this may also be dated.

Helena Wolfsohn *Dresden, Germany*
Helena Wolfsohn ran a studio for porcelain decoration in Dresden from 1843, decorating pieces in the Meissen style. The studio was taken over by Leopold Elb and W. E. Stephan. This mark appears.

Dahl-Jensens *Copenhagen, Denmark*
Founded in 1925, this factory produced Art Nouveau and other porcelain bearing this mark.

Mennecy-Villeroy *Ile-de-France, France*
See p55. This crowned mark appears in red on early wares in Japanese style.

B. Bloch *Eichwald, Bohemia, Czech Republic*
This factory was founded in 1871, was granted a licence to produce porcelain by Meissen, and pieces were made with the onion pattern. This mark was used.

Edwin Bennett Pottery *Baltimore, Maryland, USA*
See p113. The mark shown (above) appears on cream-coloured earthenware in 1897; the mark (below) was used in 1896. Many different marks were used by this company: most incorporate the name mark 'Bennett', or the initials 'E. B. P. Co.' Decorators' marks, usually in the form of a monogram, may also appear.

Ackermann & Fritze
Rudolstadt Volkstedt, Thuringia, Germany
Fine porcelain figures and luxury goods were produced here from 1908. This is one of the factory marks.

Ludwigsburg *Württemberg, Germany*
The porcelain works at Ludwigsburg was founded by decree of Duke Charles Eugene von Württemberg (1737–93) in 1758; Johann Gottlieb Trothe was appointed the first director, and was succeeded by Joseph Jakob Ringler in 1759. The palace at Ludwigsburg housed the court between 1762 and 1775, and this period represents some of the best production. The court returned to Stuttgart in 1775. King Friedrich of Württemberg assumed the administration of the factory in 1802, and there was a period of revival 1806–16. The factory closed in 1824 following an order by King Wilhelm I. Fine figures were made, with quality declining after 1793. This 'F' mark representing King Friedrich was used 1806–16.

Fürstenberg *Brunswick, Germany*
See p35. This mark used on 19th and 20thC wares, and appears in underglaze blue.

Worcester Porcelains *Hereford and Worcester, UK*
See p43. This standard impressed mark which may appear with or without the crown, was used at Worcester during the Flight, Barr & Barr period, c1813–40.

Emil Fischer *Budapest, Hungary*
Hard-paste porcelain items such as utility wares, vases and bonbonnières were produced at this factory founded in 1866. This is one of the marks used.

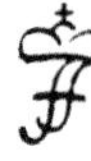

Fulda *Hesse, Germany*
See p149. This mark found on porcelain appears 1780–88, and denotes 'Fürstlich-Fuldaisch'.

Fraureuth *Saxony, Germany*
Utility porcelain was produced in Fraureuth from 1866, with a branch factory at Wallendorf from 1919–26. This mark appears on wares from both factories; the monogram stands for 'Porzellanfabrik Fraureuth'. The factory closed in 1935.

Ludwigsburg *Württemberg, Germany*
See p153. This mark appears 1806–16; the monogram denotes 'Friedrich Rex'.

Royal Factory *Naples, Italy*
Ferdinand IV of Naples established a porcelain factory in 1771, which was moved to the Royal palace in 1773. From 1806 to 1834 the factory operated under various owners. Copies of antique marble and bronze were made in biscuit, and also figures in the Empire and neo-classical style. This monogram stands for 'Fabbrica Reale Ferdinandea', and appears 1773–87 in purple, red or blue.

(James) Neale & Co *Hanley, Staffordshire, UK*
This firm produced Wedgwood-type earthenwares c1776-84. The partnership was previously called Neale & Palmer (c1709–76. This impressed mark comprising a crown and the letter 'G' or 'C' was used c1776–86

Greiner & Herda *Oberkotzau, Bavaria, Germany*
Founded in 1898, this porcelain factory produced utility wares. It became the 'Neuerer porcelain factory KG' in 1943. This mark was used.

Metzel Brothers *Könitz, Thuringia, Germany*
A porcelain factory was founded here in 1909, and was taken over by a company based at Hermsdorf in 1950. Items produced include porcelain services with the onion pattern. Various forms of this mark appear.

George Procter & Co Ltd
Longton, Staffordshire, UK
Operating from the Gladstone Pottery, and formerly known as Procter, Mayer & Woolley, this firm made porcelain 1891–1940. This printed mark was used 1924–40.

George Warrilow (& Sons) (Ltd)
Longton, Staffordshire, UK
Based at the Queen's Pottery, this firm (formerly Warrilow & Cope) made porcelain 1887–1940. The initials 'G. W.' were included in many marks used by this company. '& S' or '& Sons' was added after 1892, and 'Ltd.' after 1928. The company later became Rosina China Co Ltd.

Harvey Adams & Co *Longton, Staffordshire, UK*
This company made porcelain and earthenwares 1870–85. Many pieces feature floral relief patterns in the style of Dresden. Formerly Adams & Scrivener and then Hammersley & Co (see below), the firm used this printed mark.

Hibbert & Boughley *Longton, Staffordshire, UK*
This printed mark was registered by a firm operating under this name in 1889 producing earthenware and porcelain.

Hammersley & Co *Longton, Staffordshire, UK*
Based at the Alsager Pottery in Longton, this firm produced porcelain 1887–1932. It continued as Hammersley & Co (Longton) Ltd from 1932. This crown mark appears with various marks, including the initials 'H. & Co.'

Heber & Co *Neustadt, Gotha, Germany*
A porcelain factory producing utility items, figures and other wares, was established in 1900. This mark was used.

Kelsterbach *Hesse Darmstadt, Germany*
See p90. This mark is rare on porcelain before 1789 and appears in blue; it is impressed on cream-coloured earthenware.

Hilditch & Son *Lane End, Staffordshire, UK*
Formerly Hilditch & Martin (and subsequently Hilditch & Hopwood), this pottery produced porcelain and earthenwares 1822–30. The initials 'H. & S.' appear in a variety of marks, including this crowned version.

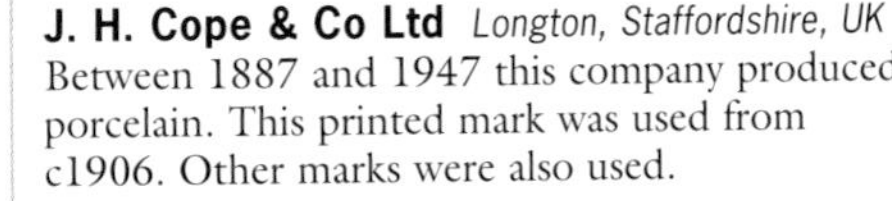

J. H. Cope & Co Ltd *Longton, Staffordshire, UK*
Between 1887 and 1947 this company produced porcelain. This printed mark was used from c1906. Other marks were also used.

J. H. Walton *Longton, Staffordshire, UK*
Formerly Walton & Co, this firm based at the Albino China Works produced porcelain 1912–21. These initials appear on their marks.

J. H. Weatherby & Sons (Ltd)
Hanley, Staffordshire, UK
From 1891 this pottery made earthenwares at the Falcon Pottery. Many marks were used; this printed example was used from 1928.

J. Wilson & Sons *Fenton, Staffordshire, UK*
Operating at the Park Works 1898–1926, this company (formerly Wilson & Co) used this printed mark.

Carl Knoll *Karlsbad, Bohemia, Czech Republic*
Pottery was made by Knoll from 1844. One of his marks is this 'KC' monogram with a crown.

Keller & Guérin *Lunéville, Meuthe-et-Moselle, France*
In 1731 a faïence factory was established at two premises by Jacques Chambrette. The factories were conducted by his heirs after his death in 1758, but by 1788 had run into financial problems and were sold to Keller & Cuny, later Keller & Guérin (from 1788). Characteristic wares are models of lions and dogs. This mark was used from 1788 into the 19thC.

Carl Krister *Waldenburg, Silesia, Germany*
Krister (1802–67) came to Waldenburg from Thuringia, initially working as a decorator for Rausch. He founded a porcelain factory in 1829 and in 1833 he purchased Rausch's factory. Afte his death the factory changed hands. This mark denotes 'Krister Porzellan Manufaktur'.

Philipp Dietrich *Passau, Bavaria, Germany*
Founded in 1840, and formerly known as Dressel, Kister & Co, this factory belonged to the Lenck family until 1937 when it was taken over by the Philipp Dietrich porcelain factory of Passau. At some point the factory began to call itself Aelteste (the oldest) Volkstedter Porzellan-Fabrik AG. It closed

in 1942. Wares include artistic porcelain and pieces made from Höchst moulds. This is one of the marks known, 1937–42.

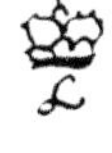

Ludwigsburg *Württemberg, Germany*
See p153. This mark appears in blue and appears on porcelain made at the time of Duke Ludwig of Württemberg, 1793–95.

Rue Amelot *Paris, France*
Porcelain was made from 1784 by Louis Honoré de la Marre de Villiers and Montarcy, at rue Amelot, and later at rue Pont-aux-Choux. In 1786 Montarcy, together with Outrequin and Edmé-Alexis Toulouse, secured the protection of Louis-Philippe-Joseph, duc d'Orléans, and registered this mark. Wares are painted in monochrome with no gilded decoration which, at this time, were exclusive to Sèvres. This mark appears in underglaze blue.

Maddock Pottery Company
Trenton, New Jersey, USA
There were three potteries in Trenton operated by Maddock family members. In this pottery (1893–1923) they made vitreous hotel ware with and without decoration under the name Lamberton China (Lamberton is the section of Trenton in which the pottery stands).

Sèvres *France*
See p82. This 'LP' monogram beneath a crown was one of the marks used at Sèvres (during the reign of Louis-Philippe (1830–48) and appears in blue or gold. This particular mark is frequently faked.

Moore (Bros) *Longton, Staffordshire, UK*
Samuel Moore's porcelain-producing business, established 1859, was continued by his sons Bernard and Samuel from 1870, and became Moore (Bros) in 1872. Good quality porcelain services and ornamental pieces were produced. The firm also developed some new glazes and produced some original gilded and enamelled designs. Notable are richly decorated 'pilgrim's' bottles. Painted decoration was also high quality. Majolica, *pâte-sur-pâte* wares and mirror frames were also made. After 1905 Bernard Moore moved to Stoke and ran his own business (see p51). This printed mark was used 1902–05.

Marieberg *Nr Stockholm, Sweden*
The founder of the faïence factory at Marieberg in 1760 was Johann Eberhard Ludwig Ehrenreich, who engaged Johann Buchwald as his manager in 1758. Porcelain was produced at the factory from 1766 when Pierre Berthevin of Mennecy and Copenhagen succeeded Ehrenreich as manager. Wares include modelled pieces, figures, and items featuring delicate flower painting. This mark comprising three crowns appeared with the initials denoting the respective managers: 'MB-E' (for Ehrenreich) 1760–66, 'MB-B' (for Berthevin) 1766–69 (Heinrich Sten was manager 1769–88). Painters' marks sometimes also appear.

Buen Retiro *Madrid, Spain*
Carlos III of Spain (previously Karl IV of the two Sicilies) moved his porcelain and maiolica factory to Buen Retiro from Capodimonte (Naples) in 1759, when he inherited the Spanish throne. Soft-paste porcelain was made 1760–1804. Hard-paste porcelain was made after 1804 under the direction of Bartolome Sureda who had studied at Sèvres. This mark was used during the 'Sureda period' at Buen Retiro, 1804–08, and afterwards at La Moncloa 1817–50.

Metzler Brothers & Ortloff
Ilmenau, Thuringia, Germany
Founded in 1875, this porcelain factory produced artistic porcelain, ornaments and small useful wares. This crowned monogram is one of the marks used.

Myott, Son & Co (Ltd) *Hanley, Staffordshire, UK*
Based first in Stoke (1898–1902), and then at Cobridge (1902–46), this firm moved to Hanley in c1947. Earthenwares were produced with various marks including this one used from c1900. The word 'Stoke' indicates a date prior to 1903.

Mayer & Sherratt *Longton, Staffordshire, UK*
Porcelain was produced by this firm at the Clifton Works 1906–41. This printed mark was one of those used. The firm also used the trade name 'Melba'.

Müller & Co *Rudolstadt Volkatedt, Thuringia, Germany*
This factory, founded in 1907, produced all kinds of luxury wares. Destroyed during WWII, it was in operation again by 1949. This mark was used.

Ernst Bohne & Söhne
Rudolstadt Volkstedt, Thuringia, Germany
See p170. This was another mark used by this factory.

Royal Factory *Naples, Italy*
See p144. In 1806 production came to a halt owing to French occupation, and in 1807 the factory was taken over by the French firm Giovanni Poulard Prad in Doccia who sold the concern in two halves. After changing hands again, the factory closed in 1834. Various forms of this mark were used in the 19thC, and appear incised or in underglaze blue.

Sèvres *France*
See p82. This mark was used during the Second Empire (1852–70) under Napoleon III, a period in which the production of soft-paste was revived. This mark appears in red, and may feature numerals that denote the date of decoration.

Ginori Factory *Doccia, Nr Florence, Italy*
See p35. General pottery and porcelain was produced from 1848. This mark appears on pieces made using moulds and models bought from Capodimonte and Naples. In the late 19thC the Ginori family went into partnership with Giulio Richard of the Milan factory.

Ott & Brewer/Etruria Pottery
Trenton, New Jersey, USA
The Etruria Pottery was operated by changing partnerships from 1865 until John Hart Brewer and Joseph Ott offered a stable combination (1871–93). This large pottery produced a wide variety of ironstone wares as well as the earliest ornamental eggshell-thin Belleek wares made in America. English potters of the Bromley family that had worked for Goss and Belleek developed the body in Trenton using American materials. Walter Scott Lenox was their designer 1881–84.

Krummennaab *Bavaria, Germany*
A porcelain factory was founded in 1897 making coffee and table services, gifts and useful wares. Known under a number of different names, including W. Mannl (from 1892), Illinger & Co (from 1931) and Hermann Lange (1934–39), this is one of the marks used.

Lubau *Bohemia, Czech Republic*
A porcelain factory was first founded in by the Martin brothers in 1874. It became known as 'Porzellan Fabrik and Kaolinschämmerei Alp GmbH'. This mark was one of those used.

Pfeiffer & Löwenstein
Schlaggenwald, Bohemia, Czech Republic
See p168. This mark was used on wares.

J. & H. Procter (& Co) *Longton, Staffordshire, UK*
Based at a number of potteries (Heathcote Pottery c1887–59, New Town Pottery c1859–75, Heathcore Road Pottery c1876–84), this firm made earthenwares 1857–84. This printed or impressed mark was used.

Winterling Brothers *Röslau, Bavaria, Germany*
A hard-paste porcelain factory was founded by the Winterling Brothers in Röslau in 1906. This mark is found on their wares.

Joseph Rieber & Co *Mitterleich, Bavaria, Germany*
From 1868 this firm produced hard-paste porcelain, and has operated under a number of different names. Output includes utility wares and tea and coffee services. This mark appears.

Scäfer & Vater
Rudolstadt Volkstedt, Thuringia, Germany
This porcelain factory and decorating studio was established in 1890, producing utility and luxury articles and dolls' heads with this mark.

C. & E. Carstens *Reichenbach, Thuringia, Germany*
Founded in 1900, producing good quality utility porcelain, this company was still operating in 1977. This mark is currently used. Older pieces do not include the words 'Carstens Porzellan' that appear on the example seen here.

Grünlas *Bohemia, Czech Republic*
A porcelain factory was founded here 1908–11 and produced tableware. This mark is one of those used.

Roper & Meredith *Longton, Staffordshire, UK*
Earthenwares were produced by this firm at the Garfield Pottery 1913–24. This mark appears. A crown device which appears with the pattern name was also used.

Richard Vernon Wildblood
Longton, Staffordshire, UK
Operating from the Peel Works, this firm produced porcelain 1887–88. Also working from the Peel Works at this time was Massey & Wildblood, which operated 1887–89.

P. Donath *Tiefenfurt, Silesia, Germany*
This mark was one of those used by this factory on table services made here from 1883.

Carl Hans Tuppack *Tiefenfurt, Silesia, Germany*
Founded 1808 and now closed, this factory produced porcelain household services. This was one of the marks used.

Alfred Voigt *Sitzendorf, Thuringia, Germany*
Good quality copies of Meissen porcelain were made at the factory owned by the Voigt brothers, founded in 1850 and still in operation in 1977.

Christian Seltmann *Weiden, Palatinate, Germany*
From 1911 this factory made utility porcelain, gift items, ovenproof cooking vessels and hotel porcelain. This is one of the marks used.

Shore, Coggins & Holt *Longton, Staffordshire, UK*
Based at the Edensor Works, this pottery produced porcelain and earthenware 1905–10. It was formerly known as J. Shore & Co 1887–1905, and then Shore & Coggins (1911–66). This printed mark was used c1905–10.

Fielding & Co (Ltd) *Stoke, Staffordshire, UK*
Operating from the Railway Pottery and the Devon Pottery from 1911, this firm produced earthenwares, majolica and other wares from c1879. The mark (above) was used c1891–1913, and also appears with a lion above the crown. The mark (below) was used from c1913. Other crown marks appear with the Fielding's.

Derby Porcelain Works *Derbyshire, UK*
See p35. Following the closure of the original Derby factory in 1848, a group of former employees started a new works at King Street in Derby. This mark (the old basic Derby mark with the initials 'S' and 'H' added for Stevenson & Hancock) was used 1861–1935, when the King Street factory was taken over by the Royal Crown Derby Co Ltd.

Paul Meyer *Bayreuth, Bavaria, Germany*
Founded at the turn of the century, this porcelain factory produced household, hotel and restaurant ware. Various forms of this mark appear.

Samuel Radford (Ltd) *Fenton, Staffordshire, UK*
Originally based in Longton (1879–85), Samuel Radford established a pottery in Fenton that produced good quality china under the trade name 'Radfordian'. The concern continued until 1957. Marks in the style of the one above were used c1880–c1913. A monogram such as the one seen in the mark below was used after c1924.

E. & A. Müller
Schwarza-Saalbahn, Thuringia, Germany
Luxury hard-paste porcelain wares were produced at this factory from 1890. Some pieces bear this mark; other marks were used.

Thomas Bevington *Hanley, Staffordshire, UK*
The Bevington family ran a pottery at the Burton Place Works from 1862, making useful and ornamental wares, ivory earthenware, gold thread ware and 'Victorian Ware' which was designed to resemble quartz. This is the usual factory mark used by the firm.

Thomas C. Wild & Co *Longton, Staffordshire, UK*
Porcelain was produced by this firm at the Albert Works 1896–1904; marks such as this one with these initials were used. The business continued as Thomas C. Wild at St Mary's Works in Longton (1905–17).

Klosterle *Bohemia, Czech Republic*
See p39. This mark, painted in chrome-green underglaze, was used from 1895. A variety of other marks appear.

Taylor & Kent (Ltd) *Longton, Staffordshire, UK*
From 1867, this pottery produced a wide range of porcelain and majolica ware at the Florence Works. Printed marks with the initials 'T. K. L.' appear, such as this one used from 1880.

Taylor, Tunnicliffe & Co *Hanley, Staffordshire, UK*
Earthenwares and porcelain were made by this firm from 1868, with useful wares only made after c1898. Marks with a monogram beneath a crown were used c1875–98.

Vista Alegre *Nr Oporto, Portugal*
See p73. This mark was used on porcelain made here 1824–40.

William Lowe *Longton, Staffordshire, UK*
See p176. This mark was used from c1912. Other marks featuring crown devices were used featuring the name 'W. Lowe' or the initials 'W. L. L.' (the final 'L' stands for Longton).

Ludwigsburg *Württemberg, Germany*
See p153. This mark which comprises two interlaced 'Cs' under a ducal coronet for Charles Eugene, Duke of Württemberg, was used in various forms 1758–93, and also appears without the crown during this period. The modern factory at Ludwigsburg also used a similar mark (among others) from 1948.

Wildblood & Heath *Longton, Staffordshire, UK*
See p161. Based at the Peel Works from 1889, this firm produced porcelain until 1899, when it became known as Wildblood, Heath & Sons (Ltd) (1899–1927). The mark (above) was used by Wildblood & Heath c1889–99; the mark (below) was one of those used by Wildblood, Heath & Sons (Ltd) from 1899.

Fasolt & Staunch
Bock-Wallendorf, Thuringia, Germany
From 1903 ornamental porcelain was produced by this firm. This mark was one of those used.

Comte de Custine *Niderviller, Lorraine, France*
See p41. These marks were used during the time of Comte Philibert de Custine 1770–93. Painter and chemist François-Antoine Anstett was director until 1779.

Rome *Italy*
Filippo Cuccumos and Samuel Hirtz founded a porcelain factory in 1761 that continued until 1784. This mark has been attributed to this factory. A piece inscribed 'Roma 1° Maggio 1769' bears this mark.

M. Bauer & Pfeiffer
Schorndort, Württemburg, Germany
Now closed, this factory founded in 1904 produced household porcelain. This mark was one of those used; the letters 'WPM' that

appear beneath the mark stand for the factory name Württembergische Porzellan-Manufaktur. Other marks used by this factory are based on those used on 19thC porcelain made at Ludwigsburg.

Royal Devices

Agostino Levantino *Savona, Liguria, Italy*
See p165. Possibly the son of another known Italian potter, Luigi Levantino, to whom the orb mark seen here is attributed, Agostino Levantino worked in Savona in the late 17th and early 18thC.

Luigi Levantino *Savona, Liguria, Italy*
This mark is found on late 17th and early 18thC faïence from Savona.

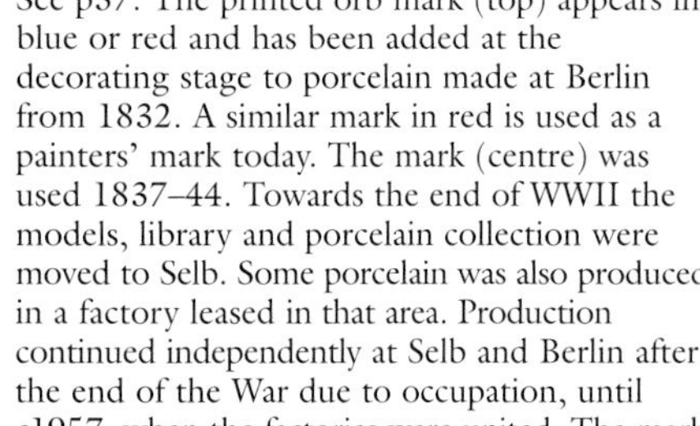

Berlin *Prussia, Germany*
See p37. The printed orb mark (top) appears in blue or red and has been added at the decorating stage to porcelain made at Berlin from 1832. A similar mark in red is used as a painters' mark today. The mark (centre) was used 1837–44. Towards the end of WWII the models, library and porcelain collection were moved to Selb. Some porcelain was also produced in a factory leased in that area. Production continued independently at Selb and Berlin after the end of the War due to occupation, until c1957, when the factories were united. The mark (bottom) was used on pieces made at Selb.

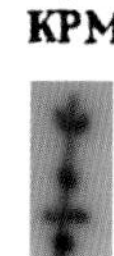

C. Tielsch & Co *Altwasser, Silesia, Germany*
See p185. This is one of a number of different marks used by this firm. After Tielsch's death, the factory was taken over by his son, Egmont, in 1882.

Joseph Schachtel
Charlottenbrunn, Silesia, Germany
See p186. This mark was used. A cross may also appear beneath the mark

Shields

Ansbach *Bavaria, Germany*
See p31. This mark on Ansbach porcelain appears in underglaze blue.

A. B. Jones & Sons (Ltd)
Longton, Staffordshire, UK
Formerly A. B. Jones, this company based at the Grafton Works and other addresses in Longton, produced porcelain and earthenwares 1900–72. In its latter years the firm became known as Royal Grafton Bone China Ltd. Many different marks were used, including several in the style of this example used 1900–13. The same mark appears with the word 'England' after 1930.

Savona *Liguria, Italy*
Faïence was made in and around Savona, Albissola and Genoa in the 17th and 18thC. This mark features the arms of Savona.

Benedict Hasslacher
Alt-Rohlau, Bohemia, Czech Republic
See p39. This mark was one used 1813–23.

Brown-Westhead Moore & Co
Hanley, Staffordshire, UK
This firm was based at Cauldon Place, originally established in c1802 by Job Ridgway and then run by his sons, John and William, together with various partners. It became Brown-Westhead, Moore & Co in 1862. All types of ceramics were made, including services and ornamental articles with high quality decoration. Also notable are the firm's floral-encrusted wares. This printed mark was one of those used from c1895 until 1904, when the company became Cauldon Ltd (1905–20).

Kloster-Veilsdorf *Thuringia, Germany*
See p84. This rare and early mark, which incorporates the arms of Saxony, was used before 1765. Many other forms of these initials were used.

McNicol, Burton and Company/D.E. McNicol Pottery Company
East Liverpool, Ohio, and Clarksburg, West Virginia, USA
See p134. Different marks were used by this firm. Most feature the name 'Mc.Nicol'.

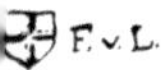

Fulda *Hesse, Germany*
See p57. This mark used on faïence features the arms of the city, and the signature of Adam Friedrich von Löwenfinck of Bayreuth.

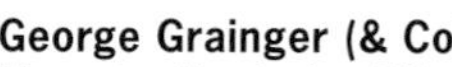

George Grainger (& Co)

Worcester, Hereford and Worcester, UK

These works were established in 1801 by Thomas Grainger, who worked with different partners (Grainger & Wood, Grainger & Lee) until his death in 1839, when the business was run by his son, George. Up to 1848 only porcelain was made, but after this date hardwearing 'semi-porcelain' was invented and produced at the works. Parian vases, figures and ornaments were also made. In 1889 the company was taken over by the Worcester Royal Porcelain Co Ltd, and production continued until 1902. The mark (above) was used c1870–89. The mark (below) was used 1889–1902; the letter that appears under the word 'England' represents the year of production: A (1891) – L (1902).

Godwin & Hewitt

Hereford, Hereford and Worcester, UK

Tiles were produced by this firm at the Victoria Tile Works (subsequently known as Godwin & Thynne) 1889–1910. This impressed or printed mark was registered in 1889 and used in 1910.

Gareis, Kühnl & Cie

Walssassen, Bavaria, Germany

This porcelain factory was founded in 1889, and made household porcelain, vases and other basic wares. The company became a joint stock concern in 1950. This mark was one of those used.

Savona *Liguria, Italy*

See p165. This mark features the arms of Savona; the initials 'G. S.' may refer to Girolamo Salomini, a potter at Savona in the late 18th and 19thC.

Josef Strnact Jnr *Turn, Bohemia, Czech Republic*

This mark appears on earthenwares made at Turn from 1881.

Worcester Porcelains

Hereford, Hereford and Worcester, UK

See p33. Used during the Kerr & Binns period (c1852–62), this printed shield mark appears on fine quality specimens. The last two numerals of the year of production occur in the central bar. An artist's monogram may also appear. The 'TB' monogram seen here, was used by Thomas Bott, an artist who specialized in painting in enamels.

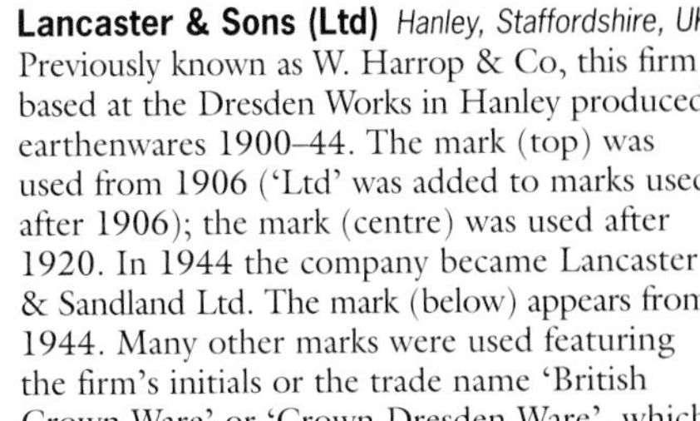

Lancaster & Sons (Ltd) *Hanley, Staffordshire, UK*
Previously known as W. Harrop & Co, this firm based at the Dresden Works in Hanley produced earthenwares 1900–44. The mark (top) was used from 1906 ('Ltd' was added to marks used after 1906); the mark (centre) was used after 1920. In 1944 the company became Lancaster & Sandland Ltd. The mark (below) appears from 1944. Many other marks were used featuring the firm's initials or the trade name 'British Crown Ware' or 'Crown Dresden Ware', which were both continued by Lancaster & Sandland.

Morley & Company *Wellsville, Ohio, USA*
See p135. This mark was also used. A number of different marks appear: most feature the name 'Wellsville'. Some of the marks were also used by the Sterling China Co, which owned this firm 1959–69.

Mueller Mosaic Tile Company
Trenton, New Jersey, USA
Herman Mueller (active 1909–41), from the Mosaic Tile Company (see p107), organized this firm. In Trenton he made matt glazed conventionalized pictorial tiles and mosaics for interior and exterior decoration as well as fountains and architectural ornament.

Zacharias Pfalzer *Baden-Baden, Germany*
See p32. These marks appear on faïence in black or in colour. Pfalzer had worked at Strasburg, and founded this concern with financial help from J. G. Wörscheler and J. G. Geyer.

Ansbach *Bavaria, Germany*
The faïence factory at Ansbach was established 1708–10 with the support of the Margrave Frederick William of Brandenburg by a Nuremberg merchant, Mathias Bauer, and the help of arcanists Johann Bernard Westernacher and Johann Caspar Ripp. Bauer was succeeded after his death in 1725 by his son-in-law Georg Christian Oswald who had worked as a painter in the factory since 1711. Johann Georg Köhnlein became manager in 1734, and remained there until 1747, when the factory came under the management of the Popp family (see p49). The coat-of-arms seen here, appears together with an abbreviation for 'Onolzbach', the 18thC name for Ansbach.

Onondaga Pottery *Syracuse, New York, USA*
The large, long-lived company (1871–1966) was organized to make white granite table and toilet ware. In 1890, they added 'Imperial Geddo', the earliest vitreous ware made by the company. After 1897, this line was called 'Syracuse China'. A cream-coloured earthenware line was added in 1893 and an extensive line of hotel ware was made for many years.

Ollivant Potteries Ltd *Stoke, Staffordshire, UK*
Based at the Etruscan works, Ollivant potteries Ltd (formerly H. J. Ollivant) produced earthenwares 1948–54. This mark appears c1948–54, together with a similar mark that features the initials 'O. P' only.

Ohio Valley China Company
Wheeling, West Virginia, USA
See p67. This mark was also used.

Ferdinand Selle
Burgau-Göachwitz, Thuringia, Germany
Established in 1900 but no longer in operation, this porcelain works produced luxury and Art Nouveau porcelain as well as useful wares. The initials on this mark stand for 'Porzellan-Manufaktur-Burgau'.

Pfeiffer & Löwenstein
Schlaggenwald, Bohemia, Czech Republic
This porcelain factory operated between 1873 and 1945, and produced coffee and tea services, hotel and domestic wares. This mark appears.

Retsch & Co *Wunsiedel, Bavaria, Germany*
Founded in 1885, this factory produced utility and other services, together with vases, bowls and boxes. This was one of the marks used.

Savona *Liguria, Italy*
See p165. This mark is based on the arms of Savona.

Gotha *Thuringia, Germany*
Wilhelm Theodor von Rotberg founded a porcelain factory here in 1757. In 1782 the factory was leased to its workers, and named Schultz & Co. In 1802 von Rotberg's widow sold the factory to Prince August von Sachsen-Gotha, whose heirs sold the concern to the Simson brothers in 1833. Wares were made with Meissen

floral-type decoration in the rococo style, and include dinner, coffee and tea services, memorial cups, solitaires and *tête-à-têtes*. This mark was used from 1883.

Scammell China Company

Trenton, New Jersey, USA

This company was created by five Scammell brothers and occupied the old Lamberton works of the Maddock Pottery Co (see p157). D. William Scammell had been in business with the Maddocks since 1901, and in 1923 bought their remaining stock. They produced high quality vitreous china, lightweight for domestic use and heavier for institutional use 1924–54. The company's railroad memorabilia is probably best known among collectors who treasure the cobalt blue patterns made for the Baltimore and Ohio Railroad. This firm was taken over by the Sterling China Company (see p115) in 1954, who continued to use this mark which appears in a number of different forms: 'Lamberton China' is usually accompanied by 'Scammell', and 'Ivory' occurs in some marks, such as here.

Wardle & Co (Ltd) *Hanley, Staffordshire, UK*

Formerly James Wardle, this firm made earthenware, parian, majolica and other wares 1871–1935. The company went by the name of Wardle Art Pottery Co Ltd after 1910, and was a branch of A. J. Robinson c1910–24, and Cauldon Potteries Ltd 1924–35. This printed mark was one of those used c1890–1935.

Anchors

British Anchor Pottery Co Ltd

Longton, Staffordshire, UK

Earthenwares were produced from 1884 and have been known as Hostess Tableware Ltd from 1971. This printed or impressed mark was used 1884–1913; 'England' was added from 1891.

Coalport Porcelain Works

Coalport, Shropshire, UK

See p182. This anchor mark with the letter 'C' appears in blue on a Coalport copy of a Chelsea vase. Other copies feature a gold anchor which is larger than that on original Chelsea wares, c1845–55.

Chelsea Porcelain Works *London, UK*
This 18thC soft-paste porcelain factory was established c1745 by Nicholas Sprimont, a Huguenot silversmith from Liège. The production of the factory is divided into periods according to the marks used (incised triangle, raised anchor, red anchor, gold anchor). In 1769 the Chelsea works were bought by William Duesbury, the proprietor of the Derby Porcelain Works. Porcelain continued to be made here until 1784; this period of the factories at Chelsea and Derby is known as the 'Chelsea-Derby' period. The Chelsea gold anchor mark was continued, and this new mark incorporating the letter 'D' was introduced, painted in gold.

Ernst Bohne & Söhne
Rudolstadt Volkstedt, Thuringia, Germany
From 1854 Bohne made hard-paste porcelain, marked with an anchor bearing the initials 'E. B.' (as here) or simply 'B'. After 1945, the company became known as Albert Stahl & Co. Luxury and fancy items were produced.

Thomas Fell (& Co) (Ltd) *Newcastle-upon-Tyne, UK*
All the usual earthenwares and creamwares were made by this firm at St. Peter's Pottery c1817–90. This impressed mark occasionally appears 1817–30. Other marks were used incorporating the name 'Fell' or the initials 'T. F. & Co.'

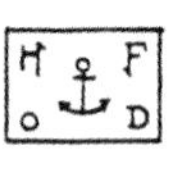

Boulogne *Pas-de-Calais, France*
A porcelain factory was founded here c1817 by Haffringue. In 1857 the owners were Clarté and Dunand and high quality hard-paste was made. Haffringue employed Italian modellers. The factory closed in 1859. This mark appears in red

Britannia Porcelain Works
Meierhöfen, Bohemia, Czech Republic
This works producing luxury and useful wares was founded by the Moser brothers in 1890; it was formerly known as Eberhard & Co. In 188- the factory was acquired by the Benedikt brothers who ran another porcelain firm in the same locality. This mark was used before 1884.

Möller & Dippe *Unterköditz, Thuringia, Germany*
An earthenware and porcelain factory was established in 1846 producing dolls and luxury porcelain figures. The works is now closed.

Middlesbrough Pottery Co *Yorkshire, UK*
Established c1834, this pottery produced creamwares and general earthenwares until 1844 when it became known as the Middlesbrough Earthenware Co (1844–52). This mark was used c1834–44. The anchor device continued to be used 1844–52 with the initials 'M. E. & Co.', and occasionally with the words 'Middlesbro Pottery'. The firm was renamed Isaac Wilson & Co in 1852, and operated until 1857.

Porsgrunn *Norway*
The Porsgrunn porcelain factory was established in 1887, and produced porcelain services. This mark appears, sometimes with the words 'Porsgrunn Norge'.

Andrea Fontebasso *Treviso, Veneto, Italy*
Initially working with his brother Giuseppe producing soft-paste porcelain from the end of the 18thC, Andrea Fontebasso made earthenware from the mid-19thC. This mark with letters denoting 'Royal Fabrique, Fontebasso' was used from 1873.

Sampson Bridgwood & Son (Ltd)
Longton, Staffordshire, UK
Established c1805, this factory was based at the Anchor pottery. Output included services for the home and export markets, particularly Canada and the United States. White graniteware was also made for export to the United States, Australia and Canada. Their speciality was 'Parisian Granite' (stamped 'Limoges') which had a fine durable body and an excellent glaze. Many printed marks were used, including a number featuring anchors. This one was used in 1885. Other 20thC anchor marks feature the name of the company.

Thomas Morris *Longton, Staffordshire, UK*
Based at the anchor works, this pottery produced porcelain c1897–1901, when it became the Anchor Porcelain Co Ltd. This impressed or printed anchor was used as a trademark, often with the letters 'TM'.

Vernon *Fismes, Marnes, France*
English-style, soft-paste porcelain was produced by Vernon at Fismes from 1840. This mark, and a more elaborate version were both used.

Swords

John Bevington *Hanley, Staffordshire, UK*
Operating from the Kensington Works in Hanley, Dresden-style porcelain was made here c1872–92. This blue painted mark was used, often on floral-encrusted porcelains or figures.

Baehr & Proeschild *Ohrdruf, Thuringia, Germany*
This porcelain factory established in 1871 produced utility porcelain, religious pieces, dolls and dolls' heads. This hallmark was used.

Dornheim Koch & Fischer
Gräfenroda, Thuringia, Germany
Founded in 1860, this porcelain factory produced luxury and fancy goods, dolls and dolls' heads. The factory is now closed.

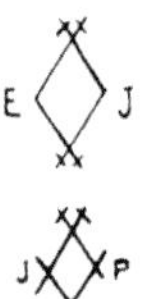

Fontainebleau *Seine-et-Marne, France*
A porcelain factory was founded in 1795 by Benjamin Jacob and Aaron Smoll. In c1830 the factory was sold to Jacob and Mardochée Petit, who used the mark (below) 1830–62. The initials of E. Jacquemin, a decorator, appear within a similar mark (above) in 1863.

Meissen *Nr Dresden, Saxony, Germany*
See p63. Another early Meissen factory mark denoting 'Königliche Porzellan Manufaktur', thi was used on teapots and sugar basins 1723–24. Here it appears in combination with the crossed swords mark which was proposed by manager Steinbruck c1722, but not adopted until 1724.

Rauenstein *Thuringia, Germany*
See p70. This mark was used by the factory at Rauenstein in the 19thC.

Scroll Marks

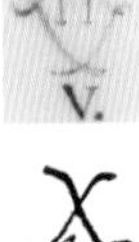

Sèvres *France*
See p82. Scroll marks (in fact crossed 'L's for Louis XV and XVI) were used at Sèvres, from 1749 without date letters, and from 1753 with date letters, used to indicate the year of manufacture, such as these seen here. Any letter that appears below the mark usually denotes the painter. These marks generally appear in blue enamel.

Burford Brothers *East Liverpool, Ohio, USA*
Organized originally by three brothers to make floor and wall tiles, the factory was converted a few years later to make ironstone and earthenware, and was active 1879–1904. They made semi-porcelain table, tea and toilet sets as well as miscellaneous speciality items,such as cuspidors and punch bowls. Hotel ware was also produced here. The factory was sold in 1904 to Standard Pottery Company, which occupied the plant until 1920.

Coalport Porcelain Works
Coalport, Shropshire, UK
See p82. The painted mock Sèvres mark (above) was used on ornate pieces made at Coalport c1845–55. The ampersand mark (below) appeared painted or in gilt c1861–75; the gold anchor mark of Chelsea (which represents the Chelsea period c1756–69) was also copied.

Carl Thieme *Potschappel, Dresden, Germany*
See p191. This mark was one of those used by this firm from 1875.

Sèvres *France*
See p82 and p172. This Sèvres mark which appeared in blue or red enamel bears the date letter for 1781. The crown seen here was usually used on hard-paste porcelain c1770–93.

Derby Porcelain Works *Derbyshire, UK*
See p35. This painted imitation Sèvres mark was one of those used on wares made during the Bloor period, c1825 48.

Rue de la Paix *Paris, France*
Feuillet established a porcelain decorating studio here c1820. His work appears primarily on hard-paste porcelain in the Sèvres style. This mark appears in green or gold.

Ludwig Wessel *Poppelsdorf, Bonn, Germany*
A faïence and general ceramics factory was founded here in 1755, producing utility and luxury porcelain, artistic faïence, services, vases and flowerpots. This mark was one of those used in the late 19thC. A similar mark appears on modern wares. As well as featuring the name of the town in full, this mark also appears with the letter 'P' below the mark.

Minton *Stoke, Staffordshire, UK*
Founded by Thomas Minton in 1793, this factory produced earthenwares, parian, majolica, stoneware, china, *pâte-sur-pâte*. Minton's sons Herbert and Thomas were admitted into the partnership in 1817, but the latter left in 1828. After Thomas Minton's death in 1836, Herbert took over the company, entering into a partnership with John Boyle c1836–41, and subsequently with Michael Hollins and Colin Minton Campbell (a nephew). Hollins and Campbell continued the firm after Herbert's death in 1858. The trading name after 1873 became simply 'Minton'. Up to the end of the 18thC only white, blue and white, and creamwares were made, porcelain was made 1797–1816 and from 1824 onwards. Highly skilled painters were employed. Minton's celebrated majolica was produced from 1850. All types of items were produced, from ornamental vases and ewers to mass-produced tiles after 1844. The first mark shown here (above) appears on early porcelains c1800–30 and may occur with or without the pattern number. The second mark (below), is one of those used c1822–36. A number of different marks in this decorative, scrolling style were used

Pierre-Joseph Fauquez
Saint-Amand-les-Eaux, Nord, France
Fauquez founded a faïence factory here in 1718 as a branch of his works at Tournai. Fauquez's son (Pierre-François-Joseph) and grandson (Jean-Baptiste-Joseph) succeeded him in turn, and the factory was given up by the family following the Revolution c1793. Soft-paste porcelain was made 1771–78, but was stopped due to competition with Tournai. This mark was used on cream-coloured earthenware.

United States Pottery Company
Bennington, Vermont, USA
See p145. This mark was one of those used.

Triangles

Noel Brannan *Burbage, Leicestershire, UK*
From 1947 Studio-type pottery was produced with this incised or painted mark. In some cases 'Noel' replaces the letter 'N' beneath the mark.

Bridge Products Co *Winscombe, Somerset, UK*
Earthenwares were produced by this company, owned by H. C. Swann, between 1954 and 1963. This printed or impressed mark was used.

C. T. Maling *Newcastle-upon-Tyne, Tyne and Wear, UK*
Christopher T. Maling originally worked for his father, William, at the North Hylton Pottery in Sunderland (established 1762) which made patterned earthenwares. This factory continued until 1815 when William Maling's other son Robert founded the Ouseburn Pottery in Newcastle, where he produced other types of pots. Christopher Maling took over in 1859 and built the Ford Potteries. Called C. T. Maling c1859–90, the company became known as C. T. Maling & Sons (Ltd)(1890–1963). Government measure jugs and mugs and a wide range of other wares were made. This impressed or printed mark was used 1875–1908.

Antoine de la Hubaudière
Quimper, Finistère, France
See p90. This mark was also used by Hubaudière in the 19thC.

Schoenau Brothers
Hüttensteinach, Thuringia, Germany
Founded in 1865, this factory made utility ware. This mark was used. The firm was later known as Porzellan-Fabriken Gebr. Schoenau, Swaine & Co.

Janet Leach *St Ives, Cornwall, UK*
The seal mark, found on Studio-type wares made by Janet Leach (wife of Bernard Leach, see p51) at the Leach Pottery, appears from 1956.

J. Tiélès *Paris, France*
Hard-paste porcelain was produced by this factory probably in the 19thC. This mark appears.

Lonhuda Pottery Company
Steubenville, Ohio, USA
See p97. This mark was also used. Pieces made at Lonhuda may also feature the initials and monograms of the decorator.

Diana Myer *London, UK*
This painted mark appears on Diana Myer's Studio-type wares from 1958.

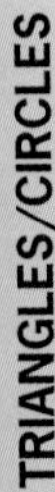

Sèvres *France*
See p82. After the capture of Napoleon III at Sedan in 1870, the Third Republic (1871–1940 was established in France. The mark (above) in chrome-green was used on porcelain from 1900; the mark (below) was used on stoneware.

William Lowe *Longton, Staffordshire, UK*
Previously known as Tams & Lowe, this company operated between 1874 and 1930 producing china. This printed or impressed mar was used 1874–1912; sometimes it appears beneath a crown.

Circles

Adam Ludwig *Höchst, Nr Mainz, Germany*
See p34. Adam Ludwig was a painter at Höchst (c1749–58). This mark is not to be confused with Adam Friedrich von Löwenfinck, founder of the factory.

Charles Fergus Binns *Alfred, New York, USA*
Although born and trained in Worcester, England, where his father was director of the Royal Porcelain Works, Binns made his reputation as the first director of the School of Ceramic Ar at Alfred University from 1900 to 1931, where many important American studio potters were later trained. Binns' mature work in stoneware was characterized by disciplined forms based on classic Asian models and finely textured matt an crystalline glazes developed in his research.

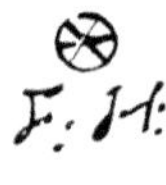

Georg Friedrich Hess *Höchst, Nr. Mainz, Germa*
See p34. Hess was employed at Höchst from th beginning, from 1746 to 1750 as an arcanist and later as a painter and probably a modeller. His son Ignatz also worked at the factory.

Johannes Zeschinger *Höchst, Nr Mainz, Germar*
See p34. Johannes Zeschinger was a painter at the Höchst porcelain factory from 1750; he use this mark.

Casa Pirota *Faenza, Emilia, Italy*
A workshop was believed to have existed in Faenza during the 16thC, the name 'Casa Pirota' is mentioned in a number of inscription found on Faentine maiolica. Two pieces are

known to bear the name of the workshop in full. This device featuring a fire-ball (*pyros rota*) was believed to be associated with the factory. This mark with the date 1525 has been found on a plaque. A number of variations occur.

University City Pottery

University City, Missouri, USA

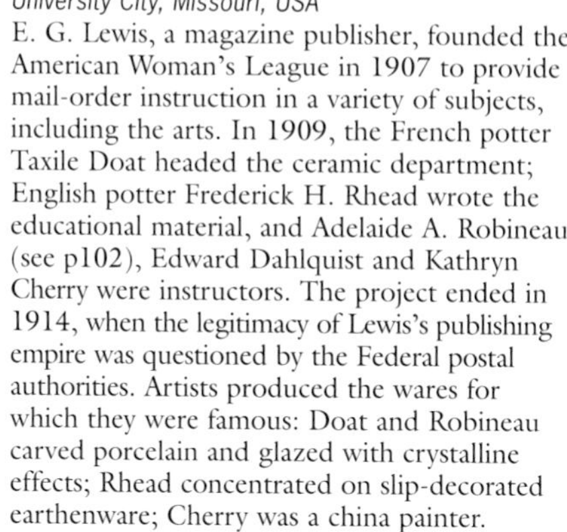

E. G. Lewis, a magazine publisher, founded the American Woman's League in 1907 to provide mail-order instruction in a variety of subjects, including the arts. In 1909, the French potter Taxile Doat headed the ceramic department; English potter Frederick H. Rhead wrote the educational material, and Adelaide A. Robineau (see p102), Edward Dahlquist and Kathryn Cherry were instructors. The project ended in 1914, when the legitimacy of Lewis's publishing empire was questioned by the Federal postal authorities. Artists produced the wares for which they were famous: Doat and Robineau carved porcelain and glazed with crystalline effects; Rhead concentrated on slip-decorated earthenware; Cherry was a china painter.

Maximilien-Joseph Bettignies

Saint-Amand-les-Eaux, Nord, France

Production of porcelain was originally begun by Jean-Baptiste-Joseph Fauquez, but competition from Tournai forced production to stop in 1778. It was resumed c1800 by Maximilien-Joseph Bettignies. Reproductions of Sèvres and other early porcelain were produced with this mark in underglaze blue, c1800–82.

Diamonds

Cartwright & Edwards (Ltd)

Fenton, Staffordshire, UK

Based at Borough Pottery from 1896, Victoria Works from 1912, Longton and Heron Cross from 1916, this firm produced general ceramics from c1857. The initials 'C. & E.' appear in many marks, in this form from c1900.

Heath & Greatbatch *Burslem, Staffordshire, UK*

Based at the Union Pottery 1891–93, this company was previously known as Buckley Heath & Co (1885–90). Earthenwares were produced with this printed or impressed mark.

E. Hughes & Co *Fenton, Staffordshire*
This firm operated 1889–1953 at the Opal China Works in Fenton producing porcelain. This impressed or printed mark was used 1898–1905

Jersey City Pottery *Jersey City, New Jersey, USA*
English potters John Owen Rouse and Nathanie Turner acquired the works of the American Pottery Company about 1850. This firm was active c1850–92. Although they continued to make Rockingham and yellow ware, perhaps until the pottery closed, they also made earthenware blanks for the amateur and professional decorating trade and telegraphic insulators. This printed mark was one of those used.

R. Floyd & Sons *Stoke, Staffordshire*
Earthenwares were produced by this company (formerly R. Floyd & Co) 1907–30. This printed or impressed mark was used.

New England Pottery Company
East Boston, Massachusetts, USA
Founded for making Rockingham and yellow ware, the pottery added white granite and cream-coloured earthenware dinnerware to its repertoire in the early 1870s. In addition, the pottery also made toilet sets and short sets of odd dishes. The firm was active 1854–1914.

Peter Ainslie
Leicester, Leicestershire, and Chester, Cheshire, UK
See p101. Peter Ainslie also used this impressed initial mark.

Hearts

Baehr & Proeschild *Ohrdruf, Thuringia, German*
See p172. This mark was used; the initials may appear within the heart.

Stars

Albertus Kiehl *Delft, Holland*
De witte Starre (The White Star) was founded i 1660 by Wilhelm Cleffius (also proprietor of D Paauw, and Het hooge Huys) and Gisbrecht Cruyck (also of De Dissel and De Paauw) and changed hands a number of times before 1761,

when it was taken over by Albertus Kiehl until 1772. Delft wares produced during the time of Kiehl may bear this or a similar mark.

Deruta *Umbria, Italy*
See p42. This mark appears on a piece in the 'petal-back' class, c1500–10.

A. Farini *Faenza, Emilia, Italy*
Urbino and Patanazzi-style maiolica was made at Faenza in the 19thC. This mark was used from 1878.

Nymphenburg *Bavaria, Germany*
See p81. This hexagram mark in blue underglaze was used 1763–67. The letters and numbers seen here also appear as a mark without the hexagram.

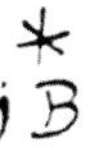

Johannes van den Bergh *Delft, Holland*
Together with his brother Dirk, Johannes van den Bergh ran De witte Starre (The White Star) factory (see p178), 1772–89. This mark has been ascribed to him.

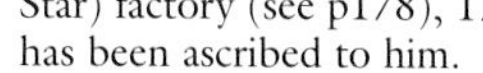

Joseph Hackl *Göggingen, Nr Augsburg, Germany*
See p59. This mark is one of those used probably after the factory was closed in 1752.

Ilmenauer Porzellanfabrik Graf von Henneberg AG *Ilmenau, Thuringia, Germany*
A factory was established in Ilmenau in 1777 by Gräbner. It was taken over by Duke Karl August von Sachsen-Weimer in 1782. In 1784 he appointed Franz Joseph Weber as director. The factory was leased to Gotthelf Greiner in 1786, and to Christian Nonne in 1792. In 1808 Nonne bought the factory together with his son-in-law Roesch. In 1871 it was taken over by a limited liability company, and until 1945 was known as Ilmenauer Porzellanfabrik Graf von Henneberg AG. It is now known as VEB Henneberg Porzellan Ilmenau. Notable wares are Meissen copies, produced during the early years of the factory, and Wedgwood-style jasper wares. These are later marks.

Lettin *Saxony, Germany*
Porcelain was made at this factory from 1858. This is one of the marks used. The letter also appears with a crown device.

Deruta *Umbria, Italy*
See p42. 'M' is the most common letter that appears on pieces in the 'petal-back' class of maiolica made at Deruta in the late 15thC.

Price Brothers *Burslem, Staffordshire, UK*
Based at the Crown Works 1896–1903, this firm produced earthenwares. It continued at other premises after 1903 under different titles. This printed mark was used 1896–1910 and then by successors Price Bros (Burslem) Ltd 1903–61.

Arno Fischer *Ilmenau, Thuringia, Germany*
Fancywares were made at this porcelain factory from 1907. This is one of the marks used.

Rauenstein *Thuringia, Germany*
See p70. This is an early mark used on porcelain made by the Greiner brothers at Rauenstein.

Girolamo Salomini *Savona, Liguria, Italy*
This pentagram or 'Solomon's seal' is found on all classes of faïence from Savona, and was probably used by Salomini, a potter in Savona, together with his family, in the 17th and 18thC. It has also been ascribed to Siccardi who worked in Savona at around the same time.

Seville *Andalusia, Spain*
Faïence was made in Seville in the 19thC. This mark appears.

Schoenau & Hoffmeister
Burggrub, Bavaria, Germany
Porcelain dolls and dolls' heads were made at this factory from 1901 with this mark.

Crescents

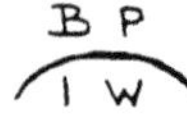

Bembridge Pottery *Bembridge, Isle of Wight, UK*
See p88. This seal or painted mark was used by T. R. Parsons and his wife Sybil Finnemore at their Bembridge Pottery 1949–61.

Hanau *Frankfurt-am-Main, Germany*
Established in 1661 by Dutchmen Daniel Behaghel and Jacobus van de Walle, this faïence factory was one of the earliest and most

productive in Germany. The factory's first manager Johannes Bailly took over in 1671. After his death in 1688 it was continued by his widow, who was joined by Behagel and van de Walle's widow. In 1727 it became the property of Heinrich Simons von Alphen, and then in 1740 that of his son Hieronymus. Early wares are similar to Delft, painted with Chinese-style motifs including 'dotted' grass in the manner of Transitional wares. European motifs are also used. Wares include the characteristic Enghalskrug, inkstands, salt-cellars and pear-shaped jugs. The crescent mark appears on early wares with the incised marks of throwers and painters, such as the 'H' seen here.

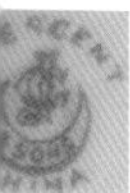

George Jones (& Sons Ltd)
Burslem, Staffordshire, UK
See p94. A crescent appears under the 'GJ' monogram from 1874, and the word 'crescent' was also used c1924–51.

Ott and Brewer/Etruria Pottery
Trenton, New Jersey, USA
See p159. This mark is one of the many used.

William H. Lockitt *Hanley, Staffordshire, UK*
Formerly Bednall & Heath and Wellington Pottery Co, this company produced earthenwares 1901–19. This printed mark was used 1901–13.

Crosses

Carl Schumann *Arzberg, Bavaria, Germany*
Founded in 1881, this factory produced porcelain table and coffee ware, vases, bowls and gifts. These distinguishing initials appear in a number of marks including this one.

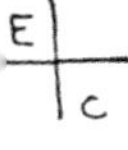

Estella Campavias *London, UK*
While most pieces made by this potter are unmarked, this incised or painted mark is found on pieces 1954–56.

Miss P. Shillinglow *Ringmore, Shaldon, Devon, UK*
Formerly working at the Kenn Pottery near Exeter (1945–59), Miss P. Shillinglow produced hand-made pottery from 1945. This mark appears.

Hanau *Frankfurt-am-Main, Germany*
See p180. Hieronymus von Alphen was proprietor of the faïence factory at Hanau from 1740 until his death in 1775; his daughters carried the factory on in a diminished form until 1787 when it passed into other hands. Marks such as this 'F', with a double cross on one end of the Hanau crescent device, appear 1740–87.

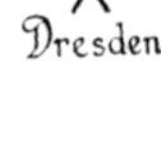

F. Hirsch *Dresden, Germany*
This company painted wares in the Meissen style from the late 19thC until c1930. This mark was used until legal action by Meissen 1896–98 succeeded in it being struck from the register.

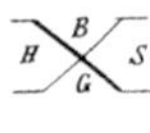

H. Bühl & Söhne
Groszbreitenbach, Thuringia, Germany
This porcelain factory was founded in 1780, and output included pipe bowls, dolls and dolls' heads. This was one of the marks used. The factory is no longer in operation.

Henry Dreydel & Co *London, UK*
Retailers and importers of ceramics in the late 19thC, this company used this mark on the foreign and English wares that it distributed.

Raeren *Rhineland, Germany*
Stonewares were made at Raeren from the 15thC, but the best wares were not produced until the late 16thC. The potteries declined in the late 17thC, and simple tavern wares were then produced until the late 19thC. This is the mark of Jan Emens, active c1566–94).

Hanau *Frankfurt-am-Main, Germany*
See p180. This mark was also used during the Hieronymus von Alphen period.

A. W. F. Kister *Scheibe, Thuringia, Germany*
This award-winning factory produced high quality porcelain figures in the Meissen style, busts, tomb ornaments, dolls and dolls' heads 1836–1914. This is one of the marks used.

Giovanni Brame *Faenza, Emilia, Italy*
This mark appears on a plaque from Faenza dated 1546, and signed by Giovanni Brame 'in Faenza'.

Karl Friedrich Lüdicke
Rheinsberg, Brandenburg, Germany
A faïence factory was founded here in 1762 by Baron von Reisewitz, and continued until 1770 when it was bought by Karl Friedrich Lüdicke of Berlin. The factory flourished, with English-style cream-coloured earthenware as the principal output from 1786. After Lüdicke's death in 1797, the factory was continued by his family until 1866. This 'RL' mark appears on polychrome wares in the Thuringian style, but pierced wares were also made.

F. A. Reinecke *Eisenberg, Thuringia, Germany*
This factory produced porcelain utility ware and pieces decorated with the Meissen onion pattern from 1796. This mark was originally used.

E. Liebmann *Schney, Bavaria, Germany*
This porcelain factory operated from 1780 and produced utility wares bearing this mark. The factory no longer exists.

A. W. F. Kister *Scheibe, Thuringia, Germany*
See p182. Variations of this mark were also used by this firm.

Swaine & Co *Hüttensteinach, Thuringia, Germany*
This mark was used on porcelain from 1854. Swaine & Co merged with Schoenau Bros and luxury and utility porcelain items were made.

Rye Pottery *Rye, Sussex, UK*
Based at the Bellvue Pottery, this firm operated from 1869. The mark (above) denoting 'Sussex Art Ware' was used c1920–39; the mark (below) denoting 'Sussex Rustic Ware' was used c1869–c1920. The factory closed 1939–45, and was reopened by John C. and Water V. Cole in 1947.

Carl Thieme *Potschappel, Dresden, Germany*
See p191. This manufacturer also used this mark on its porcelain.

Vinovo *Nr Turin, Italy*
In 1776 Giovanni Vittorio Brodel founded a porcelain factory at Vische with Paul-Antoine Hannong, but this was forced to close in 1780. A workshop run by Dr. Gionetti moved to Vinovo,

where it flourished and continued until 1820. The owner for the last five years was Lomello. This mark appears in blue, and may also feature the initials of Dr Gionetti. At the time of Lomello, the mark appears along with the letter 'L'.

Arrows

Carl Schneidig *Gräfenthal, Thuringia, Germany*
Decorative and electro-porcelain was produced from 1906. The company is now known as VEB Gräfenthaler Porzellan-Figuren, and is the factory of the ornamental porcelain works, Lichte. This mark appears.

Unger, Schneider & Hutschenreuther
Gräfenthal, Thuringia, Germany
A porcelain factory was founded here in 1861. Schneider was a businessman and Unger was a modeller. After 1885 the firm became Schneider & Hutschenreuther; Hutschenreuther left the firm in 1886. Wares include figures, groups and animals, and some fancy pieces. This mark was used in various forms.

Christian Nonne *Giesshübel, Bohemia, Czech Republic*
Christian Nonne (also of Rudolstadt Volkstedt and Ilmenau) founded a porcelain factory here in 1803 called Nonne & Roesch. It was sold in 1810 to Johann Anton Hladik. Output included figures, vases and export wares. This is an early mark used 1803–28.

Schrezheim *Württemberg, Germany*
A faïence factory was founded here in 1752 by Johann Baptist Bux (or Buchs). When Bux died in 1800 the factory was continued by his heirs until 1862. Modelled wares such as melon, cabbage and boars'-head tureens (as made at Strasburg) are characteristic, as well as traditional items decorated in blue and later in muffle colours. This factory mark appears with additional, unidentified marks.

Harker Pottery Company
East Liverpool, Ohio, and Chester, West Virginia, USA
See p128. This mark was also used by this firm, and appears in a variety of forms.

C. Gebrauer *Bürgel, Thuringia, Germany*
'Majolika' wares were made at this factory with this mark from 1892.

Birds

Charles Ford *Hanley, Staffordshire, UK*
See p83. This impressed or printed swan mark featuring the monogram was used c1900–04.

C. Tielsch & Co *Altwasser, Silesia, Germany*
A porcelain factory was founded in 1845 by C. Tielsch and a partner. The company expanded and continued under different ownership into the 20thC. This mark was one of those used.

Walter Crane *Various locations, UK*
An independent designer, Crane worked for Wedgwood, Mintons and Pilkingtons. This personal mark was used by him c1865–1915.

Erdmann Schlegelmilch *Suhl, Prussia, Germany*
A porcelain factory was founded by Erdmann Schlegelmilch in 1861 producing utility porcelain and luxury wares. These bird marks each with the initials 'E. S.' are both found. Other marks may feature these initials, the name 'Suhl', or the names 'Prussia' or 'Germany'.

Sebastian Folco *Savona, Liguria, Italy*
A potter in Savona named Folco used this mark and variations in the 18th and 19thC.

Count Ferniani *Faenza, Emilia, Italy*
See p36. This mark was used by the descendants of Count Annibale Carlo Ferniani in the 18thC.

Ford & Pointon Ltd *Hanley, Staffordshire, UK*
Based at the Norfolk works, this firm (formerly known as Pointon & Co Ltd 1883–1916) made porcelain 1917–36. It merged with the Cauldon group c1921. This printed mark was used.

Hulme & Christie *Fenton, Staffordshire, UK*
Formerly Forester & Hulme (1887–93), Christie & Beardmore (1902–03) and then Frank Beardmore & Co (1903–14), this firm produced earthenwares 1893–1902. This mark was used

in various forms 1903–14, and appears with the initials of the relevant company. This mark with the initials 'C. p. p. Co.' was also used by the Crystal Porcelain Co Ltd based in Cobridge, Staffordshire 1882–86. This company produced pottery and porcelain tiles and plaques.

New York City Pottery *New York, USA*
First known as Morrison and Carr, this pottery made a variety of bodies from American materials, including Rockingham and yellow ware, majolica, parian, ironstone and porcelain in forms for kitchen and table 1853–88. The parian busts for the 1876 Centennial Exhibition in Philadelphia included George Washington, Jesus Christ and Ulysses S. Grant modelled by W. H. Edge.

Glasgow Pottery *Trenton, New Jersey, USA*
Founded by John Moses, the pottery (1863–1900) produced decorated white granite, hotel and steamboat china in table and toilet sets as well as souvenir wares. They made much institutional ware for various US government agencies. The firm was known as John Moses & Sons 1900–05.

Joseph Schachtel
Charlottenbrunn, Silesia, Germany
Joseph Schachtel bought a porcelain factory in 1859. To begin with only pipe bowls were produced, in an attempt to curb the need to buy supplies of these expensive products from Thuringia. Simple white utility wares were produced after 1866. Painted decoration appears after 1875. The factory closed c1920.

Johann Seltmann *Vohenstrauss, Bavaria, Germany*
Founded 1901, this porcelain factory made table, coffee and mocha services and gift items. This mark appears on some of the pieces produced.

Knowles, Taylor and Knowles
East Liverpool, Ohio, USA
Isaac Knowles began making Rockingham and yellow ware as early as 1853 in East Liverpool, and in 1870 he was joined by his son, Homer, and son-in-law, John N. Taylor. The firm was active 1870–1929. The company began making white ironstone in 1872 and has specialized primarily in tableware for home and hotel use throughout

its history. Lotus ware, a fine white porcelain body cast in elaborate ornamental shapes, was made between 1890 and 1897.

M Z
ALTROHLAU

Moritz Zdekauer

Alt-Rohlau, Bohemia, Czech Republic

See p39. In 1823 the founder of the porcelain factory at Alt-Rohlau sold the concern to August Nowotny who continued until 1884. The factory was bought by banker Moritz Zdekauer. C. M. Hutschenreuther from Hohenberg acquired the business in 1909. The mark above was used c1900; the mark below 1938–45.

New Milford Pottery Company/Wannopee Pottery *New Milford, Connecticut, USA*

Active 1886–1903, during the earliest years of operation the company made white granite, cream-coloured and semi-porcelain table and toilet wares. In 1890, the name was changed to Wannopee and the pottery produced a variety of novelty table wares, such as a luncheon set to look like lettuce leaves, and art wares with muddy brown glazes.

Peter Holdsworth *Ramsbury, Wiltshire, UK*

See p102. This mark appears on wares from 1945.

Shorter & Son (Ltd) *Stoke, Staffordshire, UK*

Formerly Shorter & Boulton, this company produced earthenwares from 1905. This printed mark was used from 1940.

Stiegauer Porzellanfabrik

Stanowitz, Silesia, Germany

Formerly C. Walter & Co, this firm was founded in 1873 and made table, coffee and washing services. This mark appears.

Union Porcelain Works

Greenpoint (Long Island), New York, USA

C. H. L. and Thomas Smith purchased the Boch factory, and continued to make porcelain table and ornamental wares, such as coffee and tea cups, bowls, shaving mugs, oyster plates and miscellaneous serving dishes 1863–c1922. Their work for the 1876 Centennial Exhibition in Philadelphia included important parian exhibition pieces designed by German sculptor Karl Muller.

They also produced decorated house hardware such as door knobs and escutcheons. They later produced electrical porcelain insulators c1900.

Thomas Forrester & Sons (Ltd)
Longton, Staffordshire, UK
Based at the Phoenix Works, this firm (formerly Thomas Forrester) made china and earthenwares 1883–1959. This printed mark was used 1891–1912 ('LD' or 'LTD' did not appear before 1891). 'Phoenix China' is used in later marks.

Touze, Lemaitre Frères & Blancher
Limoges, Haute-Vienne, France
Originally founded by Soudana & Touze in 1863, this porcelain-decorating studio operated under a variety of names including Touze, Lemaitre Frères & Blancher (1920–42). This mark appears.

T. Rathbone & Co *Tunstall, Staffordshire, UK*
Earthenwares were made at the Newfield Pottery 1898–1923. The mark (above) was used from 1912, the one (below) c1919–23. Other marks also appear. The same initials were used by Thomas Rathbone & Co of Portobello, near Edinburgh. This firm made earthenwares c1810–45.

Animals

E. Brain & Co Ltd *Fenton, Staffordshire, UK*
Porcelain was produced by this factory, formerly Robinson & Son (1881–1903), at the Foley China Works, 1903–63. This printed mark was used 1948–63. In 1958 this company took over the business of Coalport China Ltd, and since 1963 it has continued under the Coalport name.

C. C. Thompson Pottery Company
East Liverpool, Ohio, USA
See p71. This mark appears. A variety of marks were used, and may feature the company name or the pattern name.

Hudson & Middleton *Longton, Staffordshire, UK*
Known as Middleton & Hudson and William Hudson c1889–92, and based at the Sutherland Pottery in Longton, this firm produced porcelain from 1941. This printed mark was used from 1947.

Lorenz Hutschenreuther *Selb, Bavaria, Germany*
See p92. This is one of the marks used. The modern mark features the date 1814 (the year Lorenz's father founded his original porcelain factory at Hohenberg-upon-Eger), and the name 'Hutschenreuther'.

Redfern & Drakeford (Ltd)
Longton, Staffordshire, UK
Based at the Chatfield Works (c1892–1902) and the Balmoral Works (c1902–33), this company made porcelain 1892–1933, when it was taken over by the Royal Albion China Co, which continued in Longton until 1948. This printed or impressed mark appears c1892–1909; the same mark appears painted 1909–33 with the trade name 'Balmoral China' and 'England'.

Tettau *Franconia, Germany*
See p45. This 20thC mark appears in a number of variations.

Wood & Clarke *Burslem, Staffordshire, UK*
Formerly E. Clarke, this firm made earthenwares c1871–72. The company became W. E. Withinshaw 1873–78. This printed mark with lion rampant appears c1871–72.

Holinshed & Kirkham (Ltd)
Tunstall, Staffordshire, UK
Based at the Unicorn Pottery in Tunstall from 1876 this company produced earthenwares 1870–1986, when it was bought by Johnson Bros (Hanley) Ltd. Printed marks featuring unicorns such as this one were used 1900–56.

Yvonne Hudson *Chichester, Sussex, UK*
Studio-type pottery and sculpture were made at Earnley near Chichester 1947–48 and from 1957. One of the marks used was this seal mark based on a Greco-Roman intaglio. The numbers are the last two digits of the year of manufacture.

Edge Malkin & Co (Ltd)
Burslem, Staffordshire, UK
This firm produced earthenwares at the Newport and Middleport Potteries in Burslem 1871–1903. The company had a number of different names from 1846, and continued with

more title changes until 1919. This trademark was registered in 1873, but slight variations occur. A variety of name and initial marks were also used.

Thomas Forrester & Co *Longton, Staffordshire, UK*
Based at the Melbourne Works (previously known as Leigh & Forrester), this factory made earthenwares from c1888 with this printed mark.

Knowles, Taylor and Knowles
East Liverpool, Ohio, USA
See p186. This mark was also used. Many different marks appear, most of which incorporate the company initials.

C. K. Weithase
Rudostaldt Volkstedt, Thuringia, Germany
This decorating studio founded in the late 19thC specialized in views, armorials and lettering on individual orders. This was one of the marks.

Forrester & Hulme *Fenton, Staffordshire, UK*
This earthenware factory operated between 1887 and 1893 and used this printed mark, with 'England' added from c1891. The firm subsequently became Hulme & Christie (see p185).

Ford & Riley *Burslem, Staffordshire, UK*
Formerly Whittingham, Ford & Riley (1876–82) and later Ford & Sons (Ltd) (1893–1938) and then Ford & Sons (Crownford) Ltd, this firm made earthenwares 1882–93. Many different designs of mark appear, often with the name of the pattern. This is one example.

Fish

Julius Hering & Söhn
Köppelsdorf, Thuringia, Germany
Founded in 1893, among other items this factory produced coffee and tea services, and figures. Variations of this mark appear.

Pfluger Bros & Co *Nyon, Switzerland*
Originally founded in 1781, this factory was started by Fränkenthal decorator Ferdinand Müller and Johann Jakob of Berlin. Porcelain was produced until 1813, after which general

pottery including pipe-clay was produced. This mark appears on general pottery.

John Dan *Wivenhoe, Essex, UK*
Studio-type pottery was produced from 1953. This factory mark was used.

Peter Wright *Bath, Avon, UK*
See p109. This mark was used on repeat items made at the Monkton Combe pottery after 1953.

Plants, Flowers & Trees

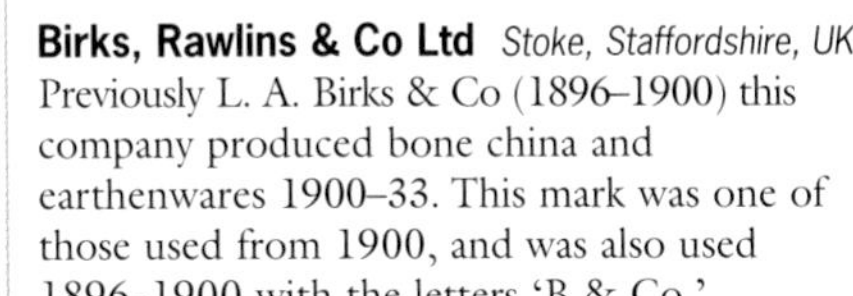

Birks, Rawlins & Co Ltd *Stoke, Staffordshire, UK*
Previously L. A. Birks & Co (1896–1900) this company produced bone china and earthenwares 1900–33. This mark was one of those used from 1900, and was also used 1896–1900 with the letters 'B & Co.'

Burroughs and Mountford
Trenton, New Jersey, USA
Although this pottery (active 1879–c1900) made a general line of decorated hotel ware and domestic table and toilet ware, the quality of their decal work and printed and filled decorations was exceptional. They also produced an art ware having raised gold decorations on a royal blue ground and some tiles. The initials 'B. M.' or 'B. & M. Co.' appear with a variety of different marks.

Carl Thieme *Potschappel, Dresden, Germany*
A porcelain factory was founded here from 1872, making hand-painted fancy wares and luxury porcelain. This mark is one of those used. The factory was still in operation in 1977.

R. F. Dixon & Co *Longton, Staffordshire, UK*
This London firm of importers and retailers used this mark on porcelain and earthenwares made for them at the Ruby Porcelain Works 1916–29.

Dressel Kister & Co *Passau, Bavaria, Germany*
See p157. This mark appears on artistic porcelain wares made at this factory, which was founded in 1840.

William De Morgan *London, UK*
See p120. This impressed or printed mark was used from 1882, the year in which the pottery was relocated to Merton Abbey in south London.

Wade (Ulster) Ltd.
Portadown, Co Armagh, Northern Ireland, UK
From 1953 earthenwares with the trade name 'Irish Porcelain' have been made at the Ulster Pottery in Portadown. This printed or impressed mark was used from 1953; 'Made in Ireland' was added from 1954. Later 'Wade Co. Armagh' was also added. The mark appears with or without a painter's initial, such as the letter 'E' seen here.

New England Pottery Company
East Boston, Massachusetts, USA
Originally founded by Frederick Meagher in 1854 for making Rockingham and yellow ware, by 1875 the plant was owned by Thomas Gray and W. L. Clark and became the New England Pottery Company. The pottery added white granite and cream-coloured earthenware dinnerware to its repertoire in the early 1870s. They made 'Reiti' ware 1886–89, a semi-porcelain decorated ware, and also porcelain with old ivory and mazarine blue finish. Many pieces were decorated with old designs which were engraved and printed by J. W. Phillips. Output included chocolate jugs, vases, jardinières, biscuit jars, rose jars and other items. The firm was active 1854–1914.

Haas & Czjzek *Chodau, Bohemia, Czech Republic*
A porcelain factory was originally opened here in 1811 by coalmine owner, Franz Miessl. The factory changed hands a number of times before it was purchased by Haas & Czjzek of Schlaggenwald in 1872. The business became successful, with output principally consisting of utility porcelain for households, restaurants and hotels. This is one of the marks used.

Jaeger & Co *Marktredwitz, Bavaria, Germany*
This company made porcelain table, coffee and tea services and gift items from 1872. This is one of the marks used, and is also incorporated into other marks.

Lenox China/Ceramic Art Company

Trenton and Lawrenceville, New Jersey, USA

Walter Scott Lenox, who had worked for Ott & Brewer and Willets (see p159), founded the Ceramic Art Company in 1889 to make only ornamental Belleek wares, dainty tea sets and luxury souvenir items. The name changed to Lenox in 1906. Bone china tableware was added about 1905 and Belleek tableware about 1910. The firm made dinner services for the White House from 1918. These marks appear.

Ohio Valley China Company

Wheeling, West Virginia, USA

The pottery (1887–93) produced good quality hard-paste porcelain tableware as well as art wares with figures and elaborate piercing. The shield mark was used on heavy goods, while the other 'leafy' mark appears on artistic wares.

Pilkington's Tile & Pottery Co. Ltd.

Manchester, UK

This factory made tiles and ornamental wares with decorative lustre effects, c1897–1938. Early wares were generally unmarked. The trademark (above) was registered in 1904. This stylized 'P' appeared within a Lancastrian rose c1914–38, with 'England' until c1920, and 'Made in England' c1920–38. The initials or monogram of the designer or artist also appears on most pieces. The mark (below) was used when the factory reopened their pottery department 1948–57.

Portishead Studio Potteries

Portishead, Bristol, UK

Studio-type wares were made here by Gwen Horlick, 1950–61, bearing this mark.

Retsch & Co *Wunsiedel, Bavaria, Germany*

See p168. This mark is one of those used. Other marks may feature a shield or crown device, usually including the initial 'R'.

Rousset & Guillerot

Limoges, Haute-Vienne, France

Founded in 1923 and formerly known as Rousset & Co, this concern was a porcelain-decorating studio. This mark was used.

Reinhold Schlegelmilch *Tillowitz, Silesia, Germany*
Utility and luxury porcelain was produced at this factory from 1869. Various forms of this mark appear, and may also feature the words 'Prussia' or 'Germany'.

Steubenville Pottery Company
Steubenville, Ohio, USA
This pottery (1879–1960) made dinner and toilet sets throughout its history of a variety of bodies, including ironstone, earthenware and semi-porcelain. Russel Wright designed American Modern in 1939. This is one of many marks used.

Sebastian Schmidt
Schmiedefeld, Thuringia, Germany
Founded in 1857, this porcelain factory made luxury porcelain and figures with this mark.

Union Céramique *Limoges, Haute-Viennes, France*
This porcelain factory was founded in 1900. This mark appears, also without the wreath. Other Limoges firms used this style of mark, featuring different initials in the centre of the wreath.

August Schweig *Weisswasser, Silesia, Germany*
Founded in 1895, this factory makes porcelain and still operates today. This mark was used.

Count Wrtby *Teinitz, Bohemia, Czech Republic*
In 1801 a factory producing English-style lead glazed earthenware was founded by Count Wrtby. This impressed mark was used 1801–39.

Buildings

A. Bauer *Magdeburg, Hanover, Germany*
Magdeburg had been a faïence-producing centre since c1754. Bauer ran a pottery manufacturing earthenwares in Magdeburg from 1865. His pieces bear this mark.

Bing & Grøndhal *Copenhagen, Denmark*
See p50. Marks such as this were used by Bing & Grøndhal from 1853. Marks may feature the words 'Danish China Works', 'Made in Denmark' or 'Copenhagen'.

C. T. Maling & Sons (Ltd)
Newcastle-upon-Tyne, Tyne and Wear, UK
See p175. This printed mark was one of those used by this firm, formerly C. T. Maling c1859–90, at the A. & B. Ford Potteries between 1890 and 1963.

Florence *Tuscany, Italy*
A type of soft-paste porcelain was made here during the time of the Medici c1575–87, with the majority being made 1581–86. The slightly yellowish paste was covered in a white tin glaze. This mark in blue appears in a number of different variations.

Josef Kratzer & Son
Haindorf, Bohemia, Czech Republic
A porcelain-decorating workshop using this mark operated here in the late 19th and 20thC. Output included domestic goods, children's and dolls' services. The factory closed c1941.

Joseph Boussemaert *Liège, Belgium*
The first successful faïence factory in Liège was established by Jacques Lefèbvre and Nicolas Gauron of Tournay (a previous venture by Baron von Bülow started in 1752 was unsuccessful). In c1770 Lefèbvre and Gauron sold the factory to Joseph Boussemaert, said to be a son of Joseph-François Boussemaert of Lille. The concern continued until 1811. The mark is taken from the arms of Liège. Wares were painted in the Rouen and Strasburg styles, and with Chinese-style figures.

Pfaltzgraff Pottery *York, Pennsylvania, USA*
Established in 1811 and still in existence today, this firm makes utilitarian redware and stoneware for house and barnyard, kitchenware, stoneware dinnerware and serving dishes and some ornamental wares. A line of bone china was added during the late 1980s.

Porzellanfabrik Königszelt
Königszelt, Silenia, Germany
Founded in 1860, this porcelain factory made tablewares, hotel ware and gift articles and has been known by various titles. This is one of the marks used.

Porzellanfabrik Kloster Vessra
Kioster Vessra, Saxony, Germany
All types of utility porcelain were made at this factory from 1892 with this mark. The factory no longer exists.

Sampson, Bridgwood & Son (Ltd)
Longton, Staffordshire, UK
See p171. This printed mark was used from c1853, and a variation of this crest mark was used from 1884. Other marks feature the name 'Bridgwood & Son' or the initials 'S. B. & Son'.

David Eeles *London and Dorset, UK*
A Studio-potter, first at the Shepherd's Well Pottery, London from 1955, and then at Mosterton in Dorset. This impressed mark of th Shepherd's Well Pottery was used from 1955.

Boats

C. & E. Carstens *Neuhaldensleben, Saxony, Germany*
This company produced earthenware from 1904 with this mark.

Della Robbia Company Ltd
Birkenhead, Mersey, UK
Owned by Harold Rathbone, this firm was established in 1894 and produced earthenwares, tiles and plaques until 1901. Pieces made here were based on Italian maiolica, and were very popular. This incised mark was used during this period. The initials above relate to the decorator

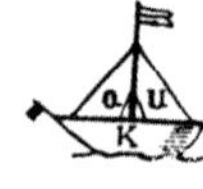

Ohnemüller & Ulrich *Küps, Bavaria, Germany*
From 1890 this factory produced utility porcelain, figures, vases, and watch and clock cases. This mark appears on some pieces.

Marblehead Pottery
Marblehead, Massachusetts, USA
Established originally to benefit patients in the sanatorium of Dr Herbert J. Hall, the pottery (1904–36) was separated from that institution about 1908 and acquired in 1915 by Arthur Baggs, who had been managing the pottery since its inception. The factory specialized in simple forms and stylized decoration with speckled matt glazes.

Wilhelm Dienst *Wiesbaden, Nassau, Germany*
This area was known for its faïence and cream-coloured earthenware. General pottery was produced by Wilhelm Dienst from 1770.

Pots

Johannes and Dirk Harlees *Delft, Holland*
Proprietors of De porceleyn Fles (The Porcelain Bottle) c1795–1800, these marks were used. De porceleyn Fles was founded in 1655 by Wouter van Eenhorn and Quirinus Aldersz van Cleynoven (also of De Grieksche A).

Gibson & Sons (Ltd) *Burslem, Staffordshire, UK*
Formerly Gibson, Sudlow & Co, this firm made earthenwares at the Albany and Harvey Potteries from 1885. A large number of marks were used; this is an early example which appeared c1904–09.

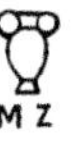

Morley Fox & Co Ltd *Fenton, Staffordshire, UK*
Previously known as William Morley, this company produced earthenwares at the Salopian Works 1906–44. Many different marks were used, many incorporating the initials 'M. F. & Co.' This one appeared c1906. It then became William Morley & Co Ltd (1944–57).

Moritz Zdekauer
Alt-Rohlau, Bohemia, Czech Republic
See p187. This mark was one of those used by this manufacturer c1900.

Paul Revere Pottery/Saturday Evening Girls
Boston and Brighton, Massachusetts, USA
See p68. This mark was one of those used by this firm.

Figures

Abicht & Co *Ilmenau, Thuringia, Germany*
Both faïence and porcelain were produced in Ilmenau. This company produced earthenwares from 1875 with this mark.

Mount Saint Bernard Abbey
Nr Coalville, Leicestershire, UK
Situated in Charnwood Forest, this pottery produced earthenwares from 1949; this trademark was registered in 1951.

J. H. Cope & Co Ltd *Longton, Staffordshire, UK*
See p169. This printed mark appears c1924–47. Other marks also feature 'Wellington China', the initials 'J. H. & Co.' and 'Longton, England'.

W. & J. A. Bailey *Alloa, Scotland, UK*
Formerly Anderson & Gardner, this pottery made earthenwares 1855–1908. This late printed mark was used 1890–1908. Earlier mark feature the name 'Bailey'.

Globes

Barkers & Kent *Fenton, Staffordshire, UK*
Based at the Foley Pottery in Fenton, this firm produced earthenwares 1889–1941. Other marks incorporate the initials 'B. & K.' or 'B. & K. L.'

Globe Pottery Company *East Liverpool, Ohio, USA*
This company (active 1881–1912) started as Frederick, Shenkle, Allen and Co but reorganize in 1888 as Globe. Beginning in 1901, the compan joined East Liverpool Potteries Company and then returned to independent status in 1907. The pottery's business declined steadily and it finally closed due to extensive damage from the flood of 1912. Their early wares were Rockingha and yellow ware. By the 1890s they had added cream-coloured ware, decorated jet ware, teapc and speciality items. During the last phase of operation they made semi-porcelain dinner and toilet wares as well as vases, plaques, tankards, jugs, trays and other speciality items. This is or of the many marks used, although most feature the name 'Globe' or the initials 'G. P. Co.'

Joseph Holdcroft
Sutherland Pottery, Longton, Staffordshire, UK
See p91. This printed mark was used 1890–1939. The company was renamed Holdcrofts Ltd in 1906, and then Cartwright & Edwards who continued the works until 1940.

H. J. Colclough *Longton, Staffordshire, UK*
Based at the Vale Works 1897–1937, this company made general ceramics. It became Colclough China Ltd after 1937. These initials were used with many marks, including this example which appears on ware produced 1908–28.

J. Goodwin Stoddard & Co
Longton, Staffordshire, UK
Based at King Street in Foley, Longton, this company made bone china 1898–1940. This mark was used 1898–1936; the words 'Foley Bone China' and 'England' were added 1936–40.

Green & Clay *Longton, Staffordshire, UK*
This firm (formerly Green, Clark & Clay) made earthenwares at a works in Stafford Street 1888–1991. This printed or impressed mark was used during this period. Another mark incorporating a compass device, was used by the Campbell Tile Co (Ltd) from 1882.

Bells

C. F. Kling & Co *Ohrdruf, Thuringia, Germany*
This porcelain factory operated between 1836 and 1941, making fancy wares, gift articles, dolls and dolls' heads. This mark was used.

Franz Manka *Alt-Rohlau, Bohemia, Czech Republic*
A porcelain factory was originally founded in 1926. In 1936 it was taken over by Franz Manka and expanded into a master workshop. Output consists of utility ware with this mark.

Flags

Harrop & Burgess *Hanley, Staffordshire, UK*
Based at the Mount Pleasant Works, this company produced earthenwares 1894–1903. The firm subsequently became Thomas Burgess and continued until 1917. This mark was used.

Julius Hering & Söhn
Köppelsdorf, Thuringia, Germany
See p190. A number of different marks were used incorporating the initials 'J. H. & S.'

J. H. Weatherby & Sons (Ltd)
Hanley, Staffordshire, UK
See p156. This printed mark was used by this firm from 1892. Other marks feature the initials 'J. H. W.' and the name 'Falcon Ware'.

C. K. Weithase
Rudostaldt Volkstedt, Thuringia, Germany
See p190. This mark was used.

Wings

F. Hirsch *Dresden, Germany*
See p182. This mark was used on pieces painted in the Meissen style from late 19thC until 1930.

Hoffmann Brothers
Erkersreuth, Oberfranken, Germany
This modern factory produces hard-paste porcelain bearing this mark.

Ignaz Bottengruber *Breslau, Silesia, Germany*
A celebrated porcelain *Hausmaler*, Bottengruber (or Pottengruber) worked in Breslau and Vienna 1720–30. This mark appears on a piece decorated at Breslau.

Louis Lourioux *Foecy, Cher, France*
Founded in 1898, this porcelain factory made luxury and utility wares. This is one of the marks.

Miscellaneous

Hilda Burn *Edinburgh, Scotland, UK*
In the 1920s and 1930s earthenwares were made by Hilda Burn with this incised or painted mark.

Chantilly *Oise, France*
A soft-paste porcelain factory was founded here by Louis de Bourbon, Prince de Condé, in 1725, and run by a succession of directors until 1792. The factory was then bought by an Englishman, Christopher Potter, who also owned a factory in Paris. Potter gave up the works c1800. A high quality, smooth white tin glaze was used on early wares; good pieces were also made 1755–80. Notable wares decorated

with Japanese Kakiemon-style designs, and many of the forms are Japanese-inspired. Figures were also produced. The hunting horn of Chantilly appears in many variations, often with incised letters (the marks of throwers and other workmen) such as the ones seen here. The marks are found in red (and sometimes black) in the early period, and blue (and occasionally crimson) during the later period.

Pigory *Chantilly, Oise, France*
The mayor of Chantilly, Pigory, founded a porcelain factory in the town in 1803 which specialized in utility wares and tea services. This mark in underglaze blue was used.

Johann Seltmann *Vohenstrauss, Bavaria, Germany*
See p186. This mark also appears on porcelain made here from 1901.

Samuel Ford & Co *Burslem, Staffordshire, UK*
Based at the Lincoln Pottery and the Crown Pottery (from c1913), this firm produced earthenwares 1898–1939. The company was previously known as Smith & Ford (1895–98). This mark was used 1895–1936. The initials 'F. & Co.' may appear instead of 'S. & F.' 1898–1936.

Jo Lester *Freshwater, Isle of Wight, UK*
Based in London c1951–52, and at Freshwater from 1953, Jo Lester produced Studio-type earthenwares. This printed Isle of Wight outline mark was used from 1953. It was also used by J. H. Manning at Cowes, with the initial 'M' added c1956–61.

William Ratcliffe *Hanley, Staffordshire, UK*
Based at the New Hall Works in Hanley, earthenwares with this printed mark in underglaze blue were produced c1831–40.

New Milford Pottery Company/Wannopee Pottery *New Milford, Connecticut, USA*
See p187. Established 1886, the company made white granite, cream-coloured and semi-porcelain table and toilet wares. In 1890, the name was changed to Wannopee, and continued until 1903.

Devices

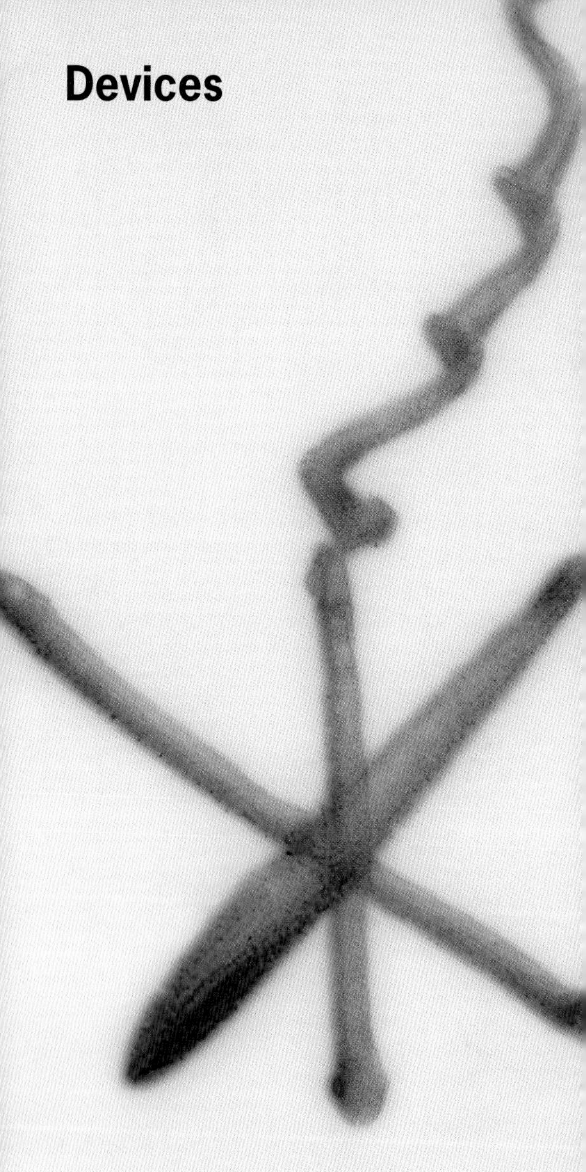

Detail of Nove mark, Italy, 19thC

DEVICES

In this section, devices that appear on their own are featured first, followed by those that appear with the name of the individual potter or firm in alphabetical order. Devices of a similar form or style within each category appear together.

Crowns

Thomas Poole *Longton, Staffordshire, UK*
Based at the Cobden Works 1880–1952, this pottery (formerly Johnson & Poole) produced general ceramics for the domestic and export markets. The firm continued as Thomas Poole until c1925 when it became Thomas Poole (Longton) Ltd. It merged with Gladstone China Ltd in 1948, and after 1952 continued under Royal Staffordshire China. This impressed or printed crown mark was also used by Enoch Plant of the Crown Pottery, Burslem 1898–1905.

Pauline Pottery
Chicago, Illinois and Edgerton, Wisconsin, USA
See p151. As well as using marks featuring a crown device, this firm also used a written name mark which appears in various forms.

Hicks, Meigh & Johnson
Shelton, Staffordshire, UK
Formerly John & Edward Babbeley (1784–1806) and Hicks & Meigh (1806–22), this successful Staffordshire firm (active 1822–35) made earthenwares and high quality ironstone in the tradition of Mason's (see p200). They used the name 'Stone China'. This printed mark appears on wares 1822–30.

Höchst *Nr Mainz, Germany*
See p34. This mark appears on pieces made at Höchst c1765–74.

Worcester Porcelains
Hereford and Worcester, UK
See p33. From 1862 the firm was known as Worcester Royal Porcelain Co Ltd and this standard printed mark was used 1862–75. From c1876–91 the crown was closed in, and a year letter appeared below the mark. From 1891 the mark featured 'Royal Worcester England', with a series of dots. 'Made in England' was added in the 20thC.

W. Adams & Sons
England

William Adams & Sons (Potters) Ltd

Tunstall and Stoke, Staffordshire, UK

Founded in 1769 this family firm, known under a number of different versions of this name, produced earthenwares, basaltes, jasper-type ware, parian etc. Earthenwares were noted for richness of colour and variety of patterns. Output consisted of tea, toilet and table services etc. An impressed mark on earthenwares (above) was used 1810–25. The printed mark (centre) appears 1914–40. The mark (below) was used after 1945.

Adderleys Ltd *Longton, Staffordshire, UK*

Originally known as William Alsager Adderley & Co (1876–1905), from 1906 this company produced good quality general ceramics. The name 'Adderley' was used in many marks. The company was taken over by Ridgway Potteries in 1947 but a similar mark continued to be used.

ALLERTONS
ENGLAND
VERA

Charles Allerton & Sons

Longton, Staffordshire, UK

Based at the Park Works in Longton, this company (1859–1942) produced general ceramics, including lustre wares. It was taken over in 1912 by the Cauldon Potteries Ltd. Various printed marks appear, including the one above from 1890, and the one below c1903–12.

ART POTTERY Co
ENGLAND

Coopers Art Pottery Co

Hanley, Staffordshire, UK

Formerly the Art Pottery Co (1900–11), this company produced earthenwares c1912–58. This printed mark was used by both firms.

G. L. Ashworth & Bros (Ltd)

Hanley, Staffordshire, UK

This company produced earthenwares, ironstone and other wares at the Broad Street Works 1862–1968. This firm produced Mason's 'Patent Ironstone' using the mark originally used by Mason's (see p210). This printed mark was used c1880 onwards with slight variation in the wording.

John Aynsley & Sons (Ltd)

Longton, Staffordshire, UK

Porcelain was made at the Portland Works from 1864. Early wares were unmarked, but printed marks such as this one were used from 1891.

P. E. Bairstow & Co
Shelton and Stoke, Staffordshire, UK
Formerly Fancies Fayre Pottery (see p37) this company used this mark on its earthenware and porcelain from 1954.

Barker Bros *Lane End, Staffordshire, UK*
From 1867, this pottery produced general ceramics. Many marks were used; this one appears in variations from 1937.

Booths (Ltd) *Tunstall, Staffordshire, UK*
See p33. The printed mark (above) was used 1891–1906. The mark (below) appears from c1906, with or without the word 'England'. The company later became Booths & Colcloughs Ltd and became part of the Ridgway group in 1955.

Arthur Bowker *Fenton, Staffordshire, UK*
Porcelain figures and other items were produced by Arthur Bowker at King Street, Fenton, 1948–58 with this printed mark (used 1950–58) with slight variations.

Bradley's (Longton) Ltd
Longton, Staffordshire, UK
Operating 1922–41, this firm made porcelain at the Crown Clarence Works. This printed mark was used 1922–28, with a variation c1928–41.

E. Baggerley Ltd *Bournemouth, Dorset, UK*
Formerly Branksome Ceramics Ltd (1945–56), this firm produced earthenwares from 1957. Both companies used variations of this mark.

British Anchor Pottery Co Ltd
Longton, Staffordshire, UK
See p169. This mark was used from 1954. Many marks appear, usually comprising name marks on their own, or an anchor device.

Lancaster & Sons (Ltd) *Hanley, Staffordshire, UK*
This pottery produced earthenwares at the Dresden Works in Hanley 1900–44. These marks were used from c1935. It became Lancaster & Sandland Ltd after 1944, and these two marks continued to be used. Many other written name marks, and marks featuring devices such as shields, were used by Lancaster & Sandland.

Brown-Westhead, Moore & Co
Hanley, Staffordshire, UK
See p165. This printed or impressed mark was one of those used after 1891. The company became known as Cauldon Ltd 1905–20 and then Cauldon Potteries Ltd 1920–62.

Clementson Bros (Ltd) *Hanley, Staffordshire, UK*
Started by Joseph Clementson c1839, this company was based at the Phoenix Works from 1865 and produced earthenwares until 1916. This printed mark was used 1913–16.

James & Ralph Clews
Cobridge, Staffordshire, UK
Earthenwares were made by this firm 1818–34, and porcelain 1821–25. This impressed mark is found on good quality blue-printed earthenwares. Many other marks were also used.

J. Dimmock & Co *Hanley, Staffordshire, UK*
Formerly Thomas Dimmock (Junr) & Co (see p152), this firm produced earthenwares 1862–1904 From c1878 the firm was owned by W. D. Cliff whose name occurs in most marks c1878–1904.

Coalport Porcelain Works
Coalport, Shropshire, UK
See p82. Printed crown marks were used by Coalport c1881–1939, with 'England' added after 1891, and 'Made in England' from c1920. Crown marks were also used after WWII. Since 1967 this firm has formed part of the Wedgwood Group.

Ridgway Potteries Ltd *Hanley, Staffordshire, UK*
See p212. This mark was one of those used after 1962 by one of Ridgway's associate potteries. This name was formerly used by H. J. Colclough (1897–1937) in a mark that appeared 1935–37.

Collingwood Bros (Ltd)
Longton, Staffordshire, UK
See p151. This printed mark was one of those used 1912–24. Other marks feature a crown device or just the name of the firm.

Alfred Colley & Co Ltd *Tunstall, Staffordshire, UK*
Based at the Gordon Pottery, this firm made earthenwares 1909–14 with this mark.

Barratt's of Staffordshire Ltd

Burslem, Staffordshire, UK

Formerly Gater, Hall & Co (see p88), this company operated from 1943. As well as using marks that featured the new company name, this mark used by the previous company (from 1914) was also continued by Barratt's from 1943.

T. W. Barlow & Son Ltd

Longton, Staffordshire, UK

Established in 1882, this pottery produced all types of earthenwares until 1940. This printed or impressed mark was used 1928–36. A variation of this mark appeared without a surrounding circle 1936–40.

Co-operative Wholesale Society Ltd

Longton, Staffordshire, UK

Based at the Crown Clarence Pottery, this firm produced earthenwares from 1946. Porcelain was also produced by this company at the Windsor Pottery in Longton from 1911. A number of marks were used on earthenwares, including this one from 1950, all featuring 'Crown Clarence'.

S. Fielding & Co (Ltd) *Stoke, Staffordshire, UK*

This company founded the Railway Pottery in 1870, and produced majolica and earthenwares, including 'Majolica argenta'. Hand-modelled flowers and foliage appeared on the finest pieces of majolica. Many different patterns were produced, and ouput included all types of services and ornamental wares. The 20thC trade name is 'Crown Devon' and many marks exist such as the ones shown here: the mark (above) c1917–30, the mark (below) from c1930. Variations occur.

A. G. Richardson & Co Ltd

Cobridge, Staffordshire, UK

Based at Tunstall 1915–24, this pottery then moved to the Britannia Pottery in Cobridge. The firm used the trade name 'Crown Ducal' in many of its marks, such as this one used from 1925.

Crown Staffordshire Porcelain Co Ltd

Fenton, Staffordshire, UK

Based at the Minerva Works from 1889 making porcelain goods. Marks of this type were used from 1906, before which it appears within a wreath.

Davenport *Longport, Staffordshire, UK*
See p226. A crown mark was used on porcelains produced c1870–86. From 1815, printed mark features the words 'Davenport Longport'.

Derby Porcelain Works *Derbyshire, UK*
See p35. Used during the Bloor Period (c1820–48) the mark (top) appeared printed or was transferred by thumb c1820–40. The mark (centre) was printed in red c1830–48. The mark (below) is impressed on 'Crown' earthenware made by Derby Crown Porcelain Company Ltd after 1876. Potting dates may occur under this last mark, and include the month represented by a digit (March=3) and the last two digits of the year (99=1899). 'Derby' on its own appears on porcelains.

Doulton & Co (Ltd) *Burslem, Staffordshire, UK*
See p121. These marks were among those used by the Burslem works c1882–1902. 'England' appears from 1891. A lion was added above the crown from 1902, and many variations occur. Porcelain was made from 1884. 'Made in England' was added from c1930. The names of different effects also appear with the mark.

Dresden

Dresden *Germany*
In 1883 this mark was registered by four decorating studios in Dresden, including Donath & Co (est 1872) and Adolf Hamann (see p256).

A. T. Finney & Sons (Ltd)
Longton, Staffordshire, UK
A. T. Finney took over Blythe Porcelain Co Ltd based at the Duchess China Works in 1935, and the company was renamed in 1947. 'Duchess' was used in many marks c1947–60.

Empire Porcelain Co Ltd
Stoke, Staffordshire, UK
Established c1896 at the Empire Works, this company produced pottery and porcelain. This mark used 1928–39. The company closed in 1967.

Worcester Porcelain Works
Hereford and Worcester, UK
See p33. This mark was used on porcelains made at Worcester during the Barr and Flight & Barr Period c1792–1807 and is rare.

Thomas Forester Son & Co
Fenton, Staffordshire, UK
Operating 1884–88, this firm produced general ceramics at the Sutherland Pottery with this printed mark. The firm subsequently became Forester & Hulme (see p190).

Gibson & Sons (Ltd) *Burslem, Staffordshire, UK*
See p197. The printed mark (above) used from c1930 is one of a wide range of marks that appear c1909–40. The mark (below) was used from c1950. The trade name changed to 'Gibsons' from c1940.

Ginori Factory *Doccia, Nr Florence, Italy*
See p35. Marks such as this were used on general pottery made at the Ginori Factory 1847–1903.

Gladstone China *Longton, Staffordshire, UK*
Formerly Gladstone China (Longton) Ltd 1939–52, this firm made porcelain 1952–70. This printed mark was used in variations by both firms.

Thomas Goode & Co Ltd *London, UK*
A retailing firm since the 19thC, this mark was one of those used. The word 'Ltd' appears after 1918.

W. H. Grindley & Co (Ltd)
Tunstall, Staffordshire, UK
Based at the New Field Pottery c1880–91 and the Woodland Pottery from 1891, this pottery made earthenwares and ironstones. Many marks featuring the name of the factory were used with this one appearing from 1925.

Jackson & Gosling (Ltd)
Longton, Staffordshire, UK
Originally established at Fenton, the firm moved to Longton c1909. Output comprised porcelain tea, breakfast and dessert services until 1961. This mark was one of those used, and appeared from c1912.

Sampson & Hancock (& Sons)
Stoke, Staffordshire, UK
Earthenwares were made by this firm 1858–1937. Many marks were used, with this one appearing 1912–37.

Herculaneum Pottery *Liverpool, Mersey*
This pottery was established in 1796. The first owner was Richard Abbey, and he sold the concern to Humble & Holland. The first articles produced were blue and white printed wares of all types. Cream-coloured wares were made later. Subsequent owners continued the works until 1841. This impressed or printed mark was one of those used c1796–1833.

Carl Magnus Hutschenreuther
Arzberg, Bavaria, Germany
A porcelain factory in Arzberg founded by Äcker in 1839 was incorporated into Hutschenreuther's company in 1918. C. M. Hutschenreuther later merged with Lorenz Hutschenreuther of Selb.

Johnson Bros (Hanley) Ltd
Hanley, Staffordshire, UK
Established in 1883, this pottery produced earthenwares and ironstone. This printed mark appears from c1900. Other marks also appear.

Worcester Porcelains
Hereford and Worcester, UK
See p33. This rare printed mark appears during the Kerr & Binns period (c1852–62), and was used c1856–62.

Hermann Lange *Krummennaab, Bavaria, Germany*
This company made hard-paste porcelain utility ware from 1934. In 1939 the firm was taken over by Christian Seltmann.

John Maddock & Sons (Ltd)
Burslem, Staffordshire, UK
See p263. Many crown marks were used. This example appears c1880–96. Many marks feature the name 'John Maddock & Sons'.

Charles James Mason
Lane Delph, Staffordshire, UK
Charles James Mason invented the famous Mason's Patent Ironstone China, and took out a patent in 1813. The original firm was G. M. & C. J. Mason, 1813–29. It was carried on under many titles until c1845–48, when the name Charles James Mason was used. In 1848 the firm went bankrupt and Francis Morley bought the business. The mark

was continued by him and later by G. L. Ashworth & Bros (Ltd) (see p204).

Alfred Meakin (Ltd) *Tunstall, Staffordshire, UK*
Working from a number of works in Tunstall (Royal Albert, Victoria and Highgate Potteries), this firm produced earthenwares and good ironstone wares from 1875. It was renamed Alfred Meakin (Tunstall) Ltd from c1913. Many marks feature the name of the company, such as this one that was used from c1907, as well as marks used after WWII. Other marks appear.

Mellor, Taylor & Co *Burslem, Staffordshire, UK*
Earthenwares were produced by this firm 1880–1904. This printed or impressed mark was one of those used.

W. R. Midwinter (Ltd) *Burslem, Staffordshire, UK*
Established c1910, this company produced earthenwares. A number of post-WWII marks featured crowns, such as this one used from c1946.

Francis Morley (& Co)
Shelton, Hanley, Staffordshire, UK
Based at the Broad Street Works 1845–58, this company produced earthenwares and Mason's Patent Ironstone China (see p210). This is one of the marks used.

Myott, Son & Co (Ltd) *Hanley, Staffordshire, UK*
See p158. This mark was used from c1936. The firm was renamed Myott-Meakin Ltd from 1977. Many other printed marks were used. Most incorporate the name of the firm or simply 'Myott'.

British Anchor Pottery Co Ltd
Longton, Staffordshire, UK
See p169. This mark was used from 1952. Other trade names were used by this firm, but most marks feature the name of the company.

Reid & Co *Longton, Staffordshire, UK*
Based at the Park Place Works, this pottery made porcelain 1913–46. Pieces made from 1913 feature this mark. The trade name 'Roslyn' was used from c1914. The company became Roslyn China in 1946.

Crown Pottery Company

Evansville, Indiana, USA

This pottery (active 1891–1955) made decorated ironstone and semi-porcelain dinner and toilet ware and sets of odd dishes. In the firm's later years, their ware was sold in the white; their business declined when they could not expand from their original building. This mark was one of those used.

British Anchor Pottery Co Ltd

Longton, Staffordshire, UK

See p169. This mark appears on wares from 1958.

Ridgway Potteries Ltd *Stoke, Staffordshire, UK*

This firm was founded in 1866 at the Bedford Works in Shelton, built by Edward John Ridgway, son of William. In 1870 Ridgway took his sons into the business, and on his retirement they formed a partnership with Joseph Sparks, and the firm continued as Ridgway, Sparks & Ridgway until 1879. The firm produced all types of fine and utility earthenware for the home and export market. This firm continued under various titles into the 20thC (Ridgways 1879–1920, Ridgways (Bedford Works) Ltd 1920–52, Ridgway & Adderley with Booths & Colcloughs 1952–55, Ridgway, Adderley, Booths & Colcloughs Ltd January–February 1955, Ridgway Potteries Ltd February 1955–64). By 1955 the business comprised eight different works in Staffordshire. Many marks include the name of the pottery concerned. The mark (above) is the basic Ridgway mark; several variations occur. The mark (below) is an example of those used by Ridgway Potteries Ltd c1962.

Rosina China Co Ltd *Longton, Staffordshire, UK*

See p155. Various forms of this mark were used from 1941, with those previously used by George Warrilow (& Sons) (Ltd).

Thomas C. Wild & Sons (Ltd)

Longton, Staffordshire, UK

See p162. Previously Thomas C. Wild & Co (1896–1904) and Thomas C. Wild (1905–17), this firm operated from St Mary's Works from 1917. The Royal Albert trade name was incorporated into all printed marks, such as this.

Royal Albion China Co *Longton, Staffordshire, UK*
This company produced china at Albion Street, Longton 1921–48. Marks used include this one that appeared from c1921.

Thomas Cone Ltd *Longton, Staffordshire, UK*
The name 'Alma Ware' was incorporated into many printed marks, such as this from 1946.

Clough's Royal Art Pottery
Longton, Staffordshire, UK
Previously Alfred Clough (Ltd) (c1913–61), the parent company to Barker Bros, Cartwight & Edwards, W. H. Grindley, Royal Art Pottery and Sampson Smith, Clough's Royal Art Pottery made earthenwares from 1961. This mark was also used by Alfred Clough Ltd from 1951.

Cauldon Potteries Ltd *Stoke, Staffordshire, UK*
See p206. Marks such as this one were used 1920–62. In 1962 the firm was taken over by Bristol-based Pountney & Co Ltd.

The Royal Factory *Copenhagen, Denmark*
After attempts to produce porcelain in 1731 and 1754, the first successful factory was established in 1755, directed by Johann Gottlieb Mehlhorn. It merged with the faïence factory of Jakob Fortling at Kastrup in 1760 and was taken over by the state in 1779, becoming the Royal Danish Porcelain Factory. Highly skilled painters were employed and pieces are of good quality. Many marks were used with the original 'wave-mark' from 1775, such as the one (above) used from 1889, and the example (below) from 1884. Many variations exist.

Norfolk Pottery Co Ltd *Shelton, Staffordshire, UK*
From 1958, this pottery made earthenwares with printed marks such as this one. Marks may include 'Staffordshire, England' as seen here, or 'Made in England'.

Royal Stafford China *Longton, Staffordshire, UK*
Formerly Thomas Poole (see p203) and Gladstone China Ltd, this pottery made porcelain from 1952. A number of marks featuring the name Royal Stafford including this one were used, by this firm and previously by Thomas Poole.

Colclough & Co *Longton, Staffordshire, UK*
Based at the Stanley Pottery from 1887, this firm became known as Stanley Pottery Ltd in 1928 and continued until 1931. The trade name Royal Stanley Ware was used during both periods.

William Lowe *Longton, Staffordshire, UK*
See p176. This printed mark featuring the place where the firm was based was used from c1915.

Royal Tara *Galway, Eire*
From 1942 this company, based at Tara Hall in Galway, has produced bone china wares with this mark or others that feature the name 'Royal Tara' or 'Regina'.

James Sadler & Sons (Ltd)
Burslem, Staffordshire, UK
Based at the Wellington and Central Potteries in Burslem, this company (previously Sadler & Co) produced earthenwares (mainly teapots) from c1899. This printed mark was used from c1947.

Salisbury Crown China Co
Longton, Staffordshire, UK
Bone china was made at the Salisbury Works by this firm c1927–61, when it was taken over by Thomas Poole. Many marks featuring the name Salisbury were used, including this one c1927–37.

Soho Pottery (Ltd)
Tunstall and Cobridge, Staffordshire, UK
Based at the Soho Pottery in Tunstall 1901–06, and then at the Elder Works in Cobridge, this firm produced earthenwares 1901–44. Marks before 1906 feature 'Tunstall'; after this date 'Cobridge' appears. This mark was used c1906–22.

The Staffs Teapot Co Ltd
Burslem, Staffordshire, UK
Teapots were made by this firm 1929–48 with this printed mark. The firm became the Hanover Pottery in 1948, continuing until 1956.

Chapmans Longton, Ltd
Longton, Staffordshire, UK
From 1916, this firm produced porcelain with the trade name 'Royal Standard' on some marks. This printed mark was used 1916–30.

Charles Amison & Co Ltd
Longton, Staffordshire, UK
See p151. This printed mark was used 1930–41. A similar mark was used with 'Made in England' added 1946–49.

Andrew Stevenson *Cobridge, Staffodshire, UK*
Formerly known as Bucknall & Stevenson, this firm was founded c1816 and continued to 1830. Earthenwares were produced, some with this impressed mark.

John Steventon & Sons Ltd
Burslem, Staffordshire, UK
Formerly Brown & Steventon (1900–23), this firm produced earthenwares at the Royal Pottery in Burslem from 1923. This printed mark was used c1923–36.

Grimwades Ltd *Stoke, Staffordshire, UK*
Previously known as Grimwade Bros (1886–1900), this firm made a variety of earthenwares at the Winton and Stoke Potteries. This early mark c1900 was one of those used. The trade name Royal Winton appears in many marks after 1930. This mark was also used by J. Plant & Co at the Stoke Pottery (1893–1900) before it was taken over by Grimwade Bros c1900. It may also have been used by previous firms operating at the Stoke Pottery.

William Hudson *Longton, Staffordshire, UK*
Based at the Alma Works (c1889–92) and the Sutherland Pottery (c1892–1941), this concern produced porcelain. This printed mark was used 1912–41. In 1941 the firm became Hudson & Middleton Ltd (see p188). This firm should not be confused with William Hudson & Son of Longton, active c1875–94.

Porzellanfabrik Viktoria
Alt-Rohau, Bohemia, Czech Republic
Formerly Schmidt & Co, this porcelain company was founded in 1883, producing keepsakes and utility ware. Various marks were used.

Chesapeake Pottery/D. F. Haynes & Son
Baltimore, Maryland, USA
Founded by three Englishmen in 1880, the firm flourished after its purchase by noted ceramics

dealer David F. Haynes. The company made ornamental earthenwares, decorated with transfer prints filled with colour and gilded by hand, as well as parian plaques and figures. Many shapes and decorations were designed by Haynes himself, his daughter Fannie or his staff. It closed in 1924.

Wedgwood & Co (Ltd) *Tunstall, Staffordshire, UK*
Headed by Enoch Wedgwood, this firm made earthenware and stone china at the Unicorn Pottery and Pinnox Works. Earthenware items included dinner, breakfast, toilet and other services for the Colonial, Continental and American markets. The main product 'Imperial Ironstone China' was made to a very high standard, and was artistic as well as durable and practical. One of the most successful designs was 'Asiatic Pheasants', which was extensively copied. The marks used by this firm are not to be confused with those of Josiah Wedgwood & Sons Ltd. This mark appears from c1908. A similar crown was used to mark the firm's 'Imperial Porcelain'.

Westminster Pottery Ltd
Hanley, Staffordshire, UK
Earthenwares were produced 1948–56. This printed mark was one of those used. This firm also used the trade name 'Castlecliffe Ware', registered in 1952.

Arthur J. Wilkinson (Ltd)
Burslem, Staffordshire, UK
Based at the Royal Staffordshire Pottery, this firm made earthenwares and ironstones particularly with gold lustres from 1885. Clarice Cliff was based here from 1916 (see p117). This printed mark was among those used from c1930.

Winterton Pottery (Longton) Ltd
Longton, Staffordshire, UK
Earthenwares were made by this firm 1927–54. This mark was used 1927–41. 'Bluestone ware' was a trade name.

Wood & Son(s) (Ltd) *Burslem, Staffordshire, UK*
Based at the Trent and New Wharf Potteries, this firm made earthenwares and ironstones. This printed mark appears 1891–1907. From c1907 '& Sons' appears. 'Ltd' was added from c1910.

Royal Devices

Royal Factory *Berlin, Prussia, Germany*
See p37. After the Berlin porcelain factory became the property of Frederick the Great in 1763, the King took an active role in ensuring its success. The sceptre mark was adopted and appears in many forms, such as those seen here. The mark (above left) was used c1763–65 and later; the mark (above right) c1778–1800. The mark (below) was used from 1870. (See also p164.)

Limoges *Haute-Vienne, France*
See p53. In 1784 the porcelain factory previously owned by the Grellet brothers became the property of the crown. White wares were made here to be painted at Sèvres. This impressed or incised fleur-de-lys was one of the marks used.

Honoré Savy *Marseilles, Bouches-du-Rhône, France*
Formerly a partner of Veuve Perrin, Honoré Savy founded a factory in Marseilles from c1770. This mark has been found.

Buen Retiro *Madrid, Spain*
See p158. The fleur-de-lys was used 1760–1804 in many forms, and may be impressed, or painted in blue, black or gold.

Duc de Penthièvre *Sceaux, Seine, France*
See p226. This painted fleur-de-lys was used.

Pont-aux-Chou *Paris, France*
Mignon owned a factory producing soft-paste porcelain in the English style 1774–84. This mark executed in underglaze blue was registered in 1777.

Saint-Cloud *Seine-et-Oise, France*
See p70. This mark appears on soft-paste porcelain c1700–66, when production ceased.

Capodimonte *Italy*
This factory was founded by King Charles II of the Two Sicilies in 1743. Initially pieces were made for the Court. The factory moved to Spain in 1759. The mark above is impressed, the mark below was used c1745 and appears in gold.

Barker Bros *Lane End, Staffordshire, UK*
See p205. This printed mark was one of those used 1912–30; a variation of this mark was also used 1930–37.

Cook Pottery Company
Trenton, New Jersey, USA
This company (active 1894–1929) succeeded to the business of Ott & Brewer, and continued under the name Etruria as the former owners had done. They made a variety of wares for domestic and institutional consumption, including white granite, semi-porcelain, hotel ware and some Belleek. In order to avoid confusion with Cook & Hancock, a dinnerware company operating at the same time, the designation Mellor & Co frequently appears in their marks as seen here.

Mintons *Stoke, Staffordshire, UK*
See p174. Mintons used this type of mark to commemorate pieces made for special events, and these usually include the date. Others incorporate the name of the retailer Thomas Goode & Co Ltd (see p209).

Hammersley & Asbury
Longton, Staffordshire, UK
This firm was based at the Prince of Wales Pottery in Longton 1870–75, producing earthenware tea, coffee, dessert and trinket services. The pottery was originally established by Benjamin Shirley of Bangor, Wales on the day of the marriage of the Prince of Wales (later King Edward VII) on 10 March 1863. Many of their marks feature the Prince of Wales crest such as this one. A similar mark was also used by the firm's successor, Edward Asbury & Co (1875–1925), which appears with the word 'Trade Mark' above the crest and also features the motto 'Ich Dien'.

John Turner *Longton, Staffordshire, UK*
John Turner began at Lane End in 1762 and successfully produced earthenwares, creamwares and Wedgwood-type wares until his death in 1787. His sons John and William continued until 1806. This printed or impressed mark was used after 1784 when John Turner was appointed potter to the Prince of Wales.

Shields

Vienna *Austria*
The Vienna porcelain factory was founded in 1718 by Claudius du Paquier, the Austrian War Commissioner, assisted by the Meissen enameller and gilder Christoph Konrad Hunger. It was sold to the state in 1744, and du Paquier retired in 1745. Wares followed a baroque style. In the second period of state ownership (1744–85) the influence of rococo and subsequently Sèvres is evident. The discovery of high quality kaolin made the factory independent with regard to raw materials, and pieces were marked with a banded shield in underglaze blue. The mark is based on the State shield, a simple device with one, two or more cross-bars. Various forms appear, and it remained in use until the firm's closure in 1864. Following financial difficulties the factory was taken over by Konrad Sorgenthal in 1784. This third period is characterized by neo-classicism. The factory closed in 1864 and the moulds were sold. The two marks (top) are from the first period; these generally appear irregular because they were incised or impressed by hand. The two next examples are from the second period and appear in blue. The mark (below) is one used during the Sorgenthal period and also appears in blue. A small proportion of Vienna marks are scored through with a shallow groove cut on the wheel which indicates that the piece is flawed in some way and was sold as a second. In addition to the factory marks, throwers' marks (numerals), year numbers (the last two or three numerals of the date from 1783 onwards), modellers' or repairers' marks (initials or signs), signs indicating the type of paste used, and painters' or gilders' marks in colour or gold, may also appear.

Wachtersbach *Schlierbach, Prussia, Germany*
Manufacturer of porcelain, stonewares and pottery from 1832. This mark was registered in 1884. Note the resemblance to the Vienna mark.

Frankenthal *Palatinate, Germany*
A quarter or part shield, painted with a checked pattern in underglaze blue was used, taken from the arms of Karl Theodor, Elector of the Palatinate. It appears on the earliest wares c1756.

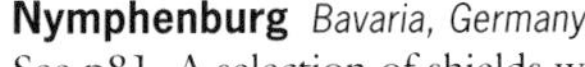

Nymphenburg *Bavaria, Germany*
See p81. A selection of shields were used by potters at Nymphenburg in the 18th and 19thC. While most are impressed using a pre-worked mould, a few were incised *ad hoc*. The marks shown here appear (from the top) 1754–65, c1765–80, c1780–90, c1810–50, mid-19thC. Unlike other factories the mark is often prominently displayed as part of a design or on the upper side of the base. Modern wares made at Nymphenburg can be marked with both an impressed and an underglaze blue printed mark.

Ludwigsburg *Württemberg, Germany*
See p153. The shield mark with antlers was used at the end of the 18th and into the early 19thC.

Muriel Harris *Washington, County Durham, UK*
Studio-type pottery was made at Old Smithy Hall 1953–59 before continuing at St Margaret's-at-Cliffe, Dover from 1961. This impressed or printed shield mark appears 1953–59.

Kieler Kunst-Keramik *Kiel, Holstein, Germany*
Active during the first quarter of the 20thC, this company produced general pottery and porcelain wares featuring this mark.

C. H. Brannam Ltd *Barnstaple, Devon, UK*
Based at the Lichdon Pottery from 1879, this potter made earthenware jugs and vases decorated with coloured slip or incised motifs. This printed or impressed mark was from 1929.

Greenwood Pottery Company
Trenton, New Jersey, USA
This company (active 1868–1933) made a variety of good quality domestic and institutional wares, decorated with prints or decals. From 1883 to 1886 they made a line of art porcelain called Ne Plus Ultra, in imitation of Royal Worcester with a mark that mimicked the original.

William Morley & Co Ltd
Fenton, Staffordshire, UK
See p197. Formerly Morley Fox & Co Ltd, this company operated at the Salopian Works 1944–57. This printed mark was one of those used.

Grossherzogliche Keramische Manufaktur
Karlsruhe, Baden, Germany
This firm made general earthenwares from c1901.

Moritz Fischer *Herend, Budapest, Hungary*
Moritz Fischer manufactured hard-paste porcelain in Chinese export style as well as conventional wares. Still making high quality wares and decorative animals. This mark usually appears in blue enamel applied over the glaze.

Mühlberg *Eisenberg, Thuringia, Germany*
Produced earthenwares during the first half of the 19thC. This mark appears on their wares.

C. G. Schierholz & Sohn
Plaue-on-Havel, Thuringia, Germany
Manufacturers of hard-paste porcelain from 1819 and for most of the 19thC. Mainly decorative wares: candlesticks or flower holders with encrusted flowers. This mark appears.

Rudolf Eugen Haidinger
Elbogen, Bohemia, Czech Republic
See p309. This manufacturer produced hard-paste porcelain and earthenwares. This mark was used in a number of different variations; the example seen here appears coloured, and also as an underglaze mark.

Gibson & Sons (Ltd) *Burslem, Staffordshire, UK*
See p197. This printed shield mark appears on Gibson wares from c1930. Most marks incorporate the name of the firm, and many feature a crown device.

Ernst Wahliss *Turn, Bohemia, Czech Republic*
Ernst Wahliss, a porcelain retailer, took over a porcelain factory in Turn in 1897, bringing with him some original models from the discontinued Vienna factory. He died in 1900 but his sons took over the business, producing artistic porcelain and faïence under the trademark 'Alexandra Porzellan Works'. In 1902–03 high-fire enamelling on white and coloured porcelain was introduced. Porcelain flowers were produced. A number of shield and crown marks in varying sizes were used, including this one.

The Henry Alcock Pottery
Stoke, Staffordshire, UK
Formerly Henry Alcock & Co (Ltd) (1861–1910), this company moved from the Elder Pottery, Cobridge to the Clarence Works in Stoke, and produced earthenwares 1910–35. This printed mark appears 1910–35.

Thomas Dean (& Sons) (Ltd)
Tunstall, Staffordshire, UK
Based at the Black Works, this company made earthenwares 1789–1947. Between 1947 and 1952 the firm operated from the Adderley Teapot Works. This printed mark was used 1896–1947.

Empire Porcelain Co Ltd
Stoke, Staffordshire, UK
See p208. This mark is one of those used on porcelains made in the 1930s. Most marks feature the name of the company, and sometimes a trade name such as 'Shelton Ivory' or 'Empire Ware'.

Phillips *London, UK*
W. P. & G. Phillips (c1858–97), later Phillips & Co (c1897–1906), Phillips Ltd (c1908–29), retailers of porcelain. This mark appears with the address of the firm which gives an approximate guide to dating: c1858–97, Oxford Street; c1859–89, 155 New Bond Street; c1897–1906, Mount Street; c1908–29, 43 Bond Street.

Lorenz Reichel *Schirnding, Bavaria, Germany*
This porcelain factory founded in 1902 producec utility services. This mark is among those used. Marks feature the name 'Schirnding', sometimes together with the name 'Bavaria'.

T. & R. Boote (Ltd) *Burslem, Staffordshire, UK*
T. & R. Boote took over the Waterloo Works in Burslem in 1850. In 1853 the firm took out a patent on a style of pottery which involved coloured relief-moulded designs on different coloured grounds. The company also made vases groups and jugs among other items in parian. After 1865 the firm only made white granite ware for the American market, and pavement tiles. Later the firm made domestic wares in 'Royal Patent Ironstone'. This mark appears 1890–1906. After 1906 only tiles were produced.

International Pottery/Burgess & Campbell

Trenton, New Jersey, USA

Between 1879 and 1936, this pottery made hotel ware, semi-porcelain, and white granite, dinner and toilet sets and novelties. Most of the ware was decorated and included 'Royal Blue' and 'Rugby Flint' ware. For a few years, this pottery shared owners and products with the New York City Pottery (see p186), and the Mercer Pottery Co (see p319) and shared a double shield mark that was differentiated by their names.

Edward Clarke (& Co)

Tunstall and Burslem, Staffordshire, UK

Based at the Phoenix Works, Tunstall c1865–77, and at the Churchyard Works, Burslem c1878–87, this company produced earthenwares. This printed mark was used c1880–87. The firm subsequently became A. J. Wilkinson.

East Liverpool Potteries Company

East Liverpool, Ohio, USA

A merger of six potteries in 1901 was made in an effort to compete with the larger potteries making semi-vitreous table and toilet wares. In 1903, four of the companies abandoned the merger and in 1907 the last two returned to independent operations. The name, however, went on for some time, and pieces with the printed marks that only show the name 'East Liverpool Potteries Co' were actually made by a former member of the cooperative, the United States Pottery Company, after the merger had finally disbanded.

(W.) Baker & Co (Ltd) *Fenton, Staffordshire, UK*

This firm produced the usual types of printed, sponged and pearl-white graniteware, mainly for export to North America, the West Indies, Africa and India 1839–1932. The printed shield mark denotes a date c1930–32.

Burgess & Leigh *Burslem, Staffordshire, UK*

This company made utilitarian and decorative earthenwares at the Hill Pottery (c1867–89) and the Middleport Pottery (from c1889). This printed mark appears 1880–1912. Many marks were used, including a monogram mark from 1862 and marks featuring a globe device from 1906.

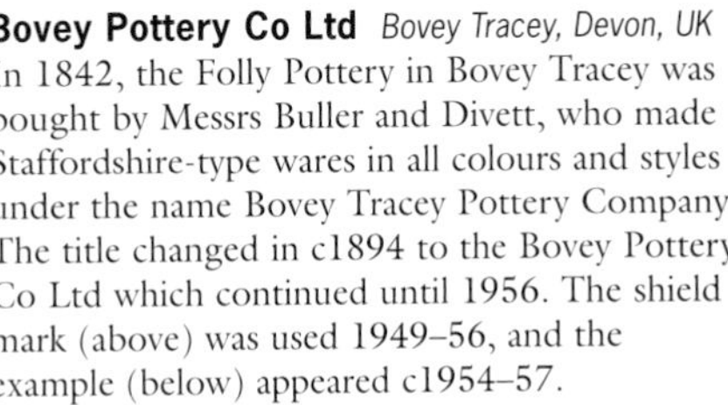

Bovey Pottery Co Ltd *Bovey Tracey, Devon, UK*
In 1842, the Folly Pottery in Bovey Tracey was bought by Messrs Buller and Divett, who made Staffordshire-type wares in all colours and styles under the name Bovey Tracey Pottery Company The title changed in c1894 to the Bovey Pottery Co Ltd which continued until 1956. The shield mark (above) was used 1949–56, and the example (below) appeared c1954–57.

Co-operative Wholesale Society Ltd
Longton, Staffordshire, UK
This manufacturer of bone china was based at the Windsor Pottery from 1911. Many printed marks appear; this was used in the 1950s and 1960s.

Franz Junkersdort *Dresden, Germany*
Founded in 1897, this firm specialized in buttons, belt buckles, hat pins, armorial painting and heraldic articles. This mark was one of those used.

T. G. Green & Co (Ltd)
Church Gresley, Derbyshire, UK
Situated near near Burton-on-Trent, the pottery at Church Gresley were taken over by T. G. Green c1864. The company produced general household earthenwares and stonewares, and wa best known for its 'Cornish Kitchen Ware'. This mark was one of those used during the 1930s.

Leighton Pottery *Burslem, Staffordshire, UK*
Makers of earthenwares at Orme Street, Burslem 1940–54. This printed mark used 1946–54.

Myott, Son & Co (Ltd) *Hanley, Staffordshire, UK*
See p158. The mark (above) appeared from c1930, the mark (below) from c1961. Other marks incorporate a crown device, and either the firm's name or initials. If the place name 'Stoke' appears on a mark, this indicates a date before 1902. The trade name 'China-Lyke Ware' was used from c1959.

Wedgwood & Co (Ltd) *Tunstall, Staffordshire, UK*
See p216. This mark was used from c1957, and gives a date of 1835 for the original foundation of the company. A wide range of other marks were also used.

Rustington Pottery *Rustington, West Sussex, UK*
Studio pottery was produced from 1947. This impressed or printed trademark was used.

Washington Pottery Ltd
Shelton, Staffordshire, UK
Manufacturers of earthenwares 1946–73, this company used this printed mark. Other marks include the name in full.

C. & A. Carstens
Blankenhainer, Thuringia, Germany
Originally founded in 1790 by Christian Andreas Speck, this factory made high quality porcelain. table, coffee, tea and mocha ware with a variety of decoration. This mark was used by various owners.

Anchors

Chelsea Porcelain Works *London, UK*
See p170. Production at Chelsea can be roughly divided into periods according to the mark used. The raised anchor, a small moulded mark (top), was used c1749–52, but rarely appears. The small red anchor mark (centre) was used 1752–56. Chelsea figures made during the raised anchor or red anchor periods are generally held to be the best in England. The gold anchor mark (below) appears c1756–69. This mark is often used on reproductions of Chelsea porcelains; on genuine pieces the mark should never be more than ¼in (0.6cm) in height. The gold anchor may also appear on Derby porcelain decorated at Chelsea c1769–75. The anchor mark was also used during the Chelsea-Derby period 1769 to c1784.

Derby Porcelain Works *Derbyshire, UK*
See p35. A small anchor painted in red, brown or gold (usually a Chelsea mark) sometimes appears on Derby porcelains 1760–80. From c1769 to 1775 William Duesbury was working the Chelsea factory in London, and then at Derby. This is known as the Chelsea-Derby period.

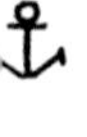

Worcester Porcelains *Hereford and Worcester, UK*
See p33. Rare pieces of Worcester porcelain painted in gilt by independent decorators sometimes bear this Chelsea anchor mark.

Duc de Penthièvre *Sceaux, Seine, France*
See p67. The anchor in these two marks refers to the Duc de Penthièvre, who was the patron and protector of the factory. The painted anchor mark above appears on faïence, and the mark below is found on porcelain made from c1775.

Ludwig Wessel *Poppelsdorf, Rhineland, Germany*
This factory was established in 1755 and made pottery and porcelain of all kinds. This anchor mark is one of those used.

Geminiano Cozzi *Venice, Italy*
A porcelain factory was founded in Venice by Geminiano Cozzi in 1765 with help from the Venetian senate; the concern continued until 1812. The material was a hybrid soft-paste porcelain with a greyish colour. Output primarily comprised tablewares, figures and vases. Good pieces are distinguished by their fine colours (bright emerald green and bluish purple), and gilding was finely executed. An anchor mark in red, or more rarely gold, was used.

James Woodward (Ltd)
Burton-on-Trent, Staffordshire, UK
Based at the Swadlincote Pottery 1859–88, this factory made terracotta and majolica. Output consisted mainly of sanitary wares after c1880. This painted or impressed mark was used.

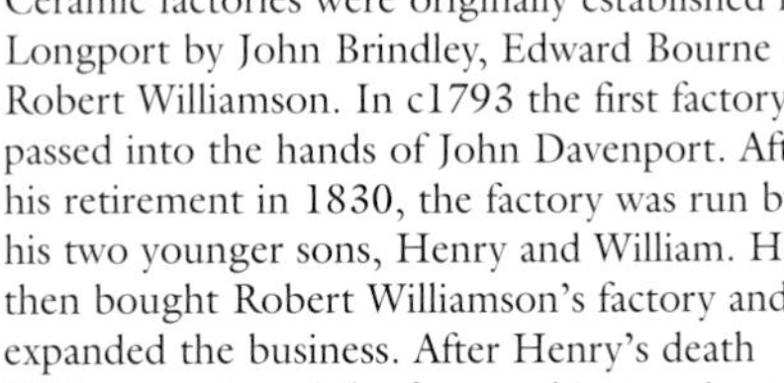

Davenport *Longport, Staffordshire, UK*
Ceramic factories were originally established in Longport by John Brindley, Edward Bourne and Robert Williamson. In c1793 the first factory passed into the hands of John Davenport. After his retirement in 1830, the factory was run by his two younger sons, Henry and William. Henry then bought Robert Williamson's factory and expanded the business. After Henry's death William continued the firm, and in turn it was taken over by his son after his death. In 1881 the business became a private company. Early output comprised white, cream-coloured and blue and white earthenwares. Porcelain was subsequently produced in many forms and styles. The anchor is the distinguishing characteristic of Davenport marks; the anchor alone appears on porcelains and earthenwares made in the 1820s (top).

The anchor frequently appears with the name of the company as in these further examples (from the top: from c1795; on blue porcelains c1850–70; printed mark on wares sold in the Liverpool shop c1860–87).

Anchor Porcelain Co Ltd
Longton, Staffordshire, UK
See p171. This firm produced porcelain at the Anchor Pottery 1901–18. The impressed or printed anchor mark (above) was used 1901–15, and the printed mark (below) appears 1915–18. Another mark comprises the initials 'A. P. Co.' 'Royal Westminster China' was also used.

Bow China Works *Stratford, London, UK*
See p31. The hand-painted anchor and dagger mark was the standard Bow mark from c1760–76, usually found on figures and groups. Pieces with this and other later marks are usually made from less high quality paste (which often features black specks) than earlier wares.

Thomas Furnival & Sons
Cobridge, Staffordshire, UK
Based in Elder Road, this company produced earthenwares 1851–90. Output included white granite, vitrified ironstone and decorated sanitary ware for export to the United States, Canada and Europe. For the domestic market they made 'patent ironstone' services. The crest mark (above) was registered in 1878. The firm later became Furnivals (Ltd) and continued until 1968. The trademark (below) was used 1890–1910.

Gustavsberg *Sweden*
The Odelberg factory existed from the mid-17thC; porcelain was first made here in 1822, and bone china was made from 1866 (the only European factory to produce bone china apart from England). Still in existence today, the factory produces 'Modern Swedish' wares. Some 20thC marks feature an anchor together with 'Gustavsberg'.

Thomas Fell (& Co) (Ltd)
Newcastle-upon-Tyne, Tyne and Wear, UK
See p170. This impressed mark appears 1817–30. Several impressed or printed marks were used by this firm, many with the company name or initials.

Anchor Pottery *Trenton, New Jersey, USA*
This pottery (1893–1926) made decorated semi-porcelain dinner and toilet sets in its early years and later made premiums used by the Grand Union Tea Company in its house-to-house sales programme. The Fulper Pottery (see p124) bought the works in 1926.

Herculaneum Pottery *Liverpool, Mersey, UK*
See p210. This impressed mark appears c1796–1833

Mafra & Son *Caldas da Rainha, Portugal*
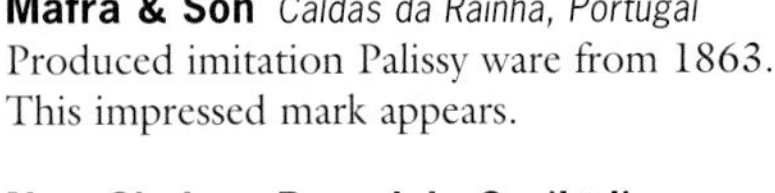
Produced imitation Palissy ware from 1863. This impressed mark appears.

New Chelsea Porcelain Co (Ltd)
Longton, Staffordshire, UK
Porcelain was made by this company c1912–61 (the name changed to the New Chelsea China Co Ltd in 1951). A number of anchor marks were used, often featuring the words 'New Chelsea' (as here) and later 'Royal Chelsea'.

Sampson Bridgwood & Son (Ltd)
Longton, Staffordshire, UK
See p171. Marks such as this were used on wares from 1912.

Duc de Penthièvre *Sceaux, Seine, France*
This late mark is another that refers to the Duc de Penthièvre, patron of the factory at Sceaux.

Swords

Meissen was the first factory to employ crossed swords as a mark, and did so from 1724. As in so many cases, particularly in the German-speaking world, factories used a mark based on either the coat-of-arms of the state or principality, or indeed the initials of the patron or proprietor.

Meissen, the most important porcelain factory in Europe until the 1750s, derived its mark from the crossed swords of Saxony. The success of Meissen encouraged lesser factories not only to emulate its wares and figures, but also to copy its famous mark. This mark, and that of Sèvres, are the most copied marks in European porcelain.

It is fairly safe to assume that the majority of wares bearing either of these marks are reproductions or outright fakes but, if in doubt, always seek expert advice. In Germany the following factories used marks imitating the Meissen crossed swords: Wallendorf, Nymphenburg and Limbach as well as many minor Thuringian firms in the 18th or 19thC. In France, Choisy-le-Roi, Fontainebleau and Montreuil followed suit; in Belgium, Tournai; in Holland, Weesp; and in Britain, Bristol, Coalport, Derby, Longton Hall (and West Pans), Lowestoft and Worcester.

Meissen *Nr Dresden, Saxony, Germany*
See p63. First used in 1724, the earliest version of the crossed swords mark is relatively small with quite open blades, transecting roughly at right-angles. These are usually drawn in overglaze blue or black enamel.

- Prior to c1745 some crossed swords have tiny blobs at the tip of the handle.
- From 1763 to 1774 a dot appears between the hilts of the swords (although the odd piece of c1740 can be marked in a similar way).

- From 1774 until 1814 a star that generally appears above the handle is used to denote the Marcolini period.
- From 1814 to 1818 the Roman numerals I or II accompany the crossed swords, and are known to appear on pieces for which the paste has an individual composition.

- From 1818 until 1924 the swords are long with slightly curved blades. '1710' and '1910' appear on marks of important pieces during 1910.
- From 1924 the crossed swords marks appear with a dot between the points of the blades. Previously, the dot appears between the handles.

Georg Heinrich Macheleid
Rudostaldt Volkstedt, Thuringia, Germany

Founded in 1762, this factory had various owners and the crossed pitchforks can be mistaken for the crossed swords of Meissen. These marks were hand-drawn in the 18th and early 19thC, but later became more formalized. Due to a protest from Meissen, a cross-bar was added at the intersection of the two forks (see mark below) after 1787, but it is not known for how long this was used.

Coalport Porcelain Works
Coalport, Shropshire, UK
See p82. Crossed swords were used by Coalport on some decorative, flower-encrusted, Dresden-style porcelains during the 1820–30 period.

Bristol *Avon, UK*
See p71. Crossed swords marks were used by Richard Champion's hard-paste porcelain factory between 1770 and 1781.

Derby Porcelain Works *Derby, Derbyshire, UK*
See p35. A rather thin and weak-looking crossed swords mark was used here intermittently between c1780 and 1830. It was usually painted in blue enamel.

Lowestoft *Suffolk, UK*
See p241. Crossed swords marks were used at Lowestoft between 1775 and 1790.

Worcester Porcelains *Hereford and Worcester, UK*
See p33. Crossed swords were used on various wares between c1760 and 1770. They are painted in underglaze blue, and may appear with or without numerals.

Longton Hall *Staffordshire, UK*
One of the few Staffordshire factories to produce porcelain in the 18thC, Longton Hall survived only from c1749–60. The factory produced figures, decorative leaf-shaped wares and blue and white wares. This mark, while clearly trying to imitate a Meissen crossed swords mark, is in fact a pair of entwined 'L's, used probably because the owner's name was William Littler.

Wallendorf *Thuringia, Germany*
A small hard-paste factory producing standard, mainly Meissen-inspired wares, and some figures. This hand-drawn mark appears in blue and other colours before 1778. Later marks resemble a 'W'.

Fountainebleau *Seine-et-Marne, France*
See p172. This mark appears c1850–1900.

Ruskin Pottery *Smethwick, West Midlands, UK*
See p86. This painted or incised scissor mark was used on some wares.

Choisy-le-Roi *Seine, France*
A crowned, crossed swords mark appears on some early hard–paste porcelain from c1785.

Tournai *Belgium*
A porcelain factory was founded here in 1751 by F J. Peterinck under the patronage of the Empress Maria Theresa. In 1800 it was taken over by the de Bettignies family who continued it until 1850. Pieces were made in the style of Sèvres and Meissen. This complicated arrangement of crossed swords and tiny crosses was used on porcelain between 1756 and 1781.

Nymphenburg *Bavaria, Germany*
See p81. Crossed swords in various guises (including a straightforward copy of Meissen) was used on porcelain made for the Turkish market in the mid-1760s.

Weesp *Holland*
Established in 1759 by Count Gronsfeldt-Diepenbroek, this short-lived and financially insecure factory produced hard-paste porcelain in the manner of contemporary German porcelain. It was acquired by Johannes de Mol in 1771 who transferred the enterprise to Oude Loosdrecht. The crossed swords mark vaguely resembles Tournai.

Montreuil *Seine, France*
This double crossed swords mark was used on hard-paste porcelain 1815–73.

Pountney & Co (Ltd) *Bristol, Avon, UK*
See p115. Pountney's factory, which made earthenwares, incorporated the crossed swords (they were never used alone) into some of their marks from 1900 until c1960.

Warwick China Company
Wheeling, West Virginia, USA
This large pottery (active 1884–1951) made a tremendous amount of hotel, table and toilet ware over a long period of time in various vitreous and semi-porcelain bodies. Their wares for domestic consumption were decorated with prints, including flow blue, or decals. Umbrella stands, vases, pitchers, tankards etc were also made.

Scroll Marks

Sèvres *France*
See p82 and p172. The royal porcelain factory was first established at Vincennes in 1738 when Louis XV granted a privilege to the brother of his Minister of Finance. Porcelain was successfully produced from 1745. After 1751 the concern was retitled 'Manufacture Royale de la Porcelaine de France', and adopted the royal crest as a mark. The factory was transferred to Sèvres in 1756. The first two marks shown here are examples of those before 1753 in underglaze blue. The third mark is one of those used during the reign of Louis XVIII (1814–24). The number 21 refers to 1821, the date of manufacture. The final mark was used during the reign of Charles X (1824–30), and appears in blue; this mark may feature a cross between the interlinked letter 'C's.

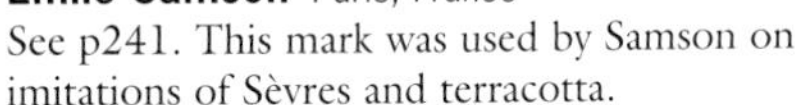

Emile Samson *Paris, France*
See p241. This mark was used by Samson on imitations of Sèvres and terracotta.

Saint-Amand-les-Eaux *Nord, France*
See p174. These marks were used on faïence produced at Saint-Amand-les-Eaux during THE first part of the 18thC.

De porceleyne Klaeuw *Delft, Holland*
Founded in 1662, this factory (The Porcelain Claw), used a number of marks. This example is one of the forms of the mark registered in 1764.

Greenwood Pottery Company
Trenton, New Jersey, USA
See p220. The number '61' in the centre of the mark represents the year in which the pottery was originally organized.

Worcester Porcelains *Hereford and Worcester, UK*
See p33. The standard Royal Worcester has been used in a number of forms to the present day. This version was used c1862–75. A similar mark used c1876–91 differed in two ways: a crescent appeared in the centre rather than the letter 'C', and the crown was filled in and fitted the circle. After 1891 'Royal Worcester England' was added together with year marks. From 1938, 'Bone

China' appear. (For further details of year marks, see p375 in Additional Information.)

W. T. Copeland (& Sons Ltd)
Stoke, Staffordshire, UK
See p255. This printed mark was used by Copeland 1851–85. An earlier, less elaborate version appears c1847–51.

Thomas Dimmock & Co *Hanley, Staffordshire, UK*
This firm was based at a number of works in Hanley 1828–59, producing fine quality earthenwares. This mark appears impressed or in conjuction with other printed marks.

Derby Porcelain Works *Derbyshire, UK*
See p35. This printed mark appears c1878–90; a similar mark was used from c1890. Both feature year cypher marks printed below. 'Bone China' occurs on marks used after WWII.

Lille *France*
This mark commonly found on modern forgeries. When in doubt about the authenticity of a piece, always seek expert advice.

Maddock Pottery Company
Trenton, New Jersey, USA
See p157. This is one of the marks used; most marks incorporate the company name.

Minton *Stoke, Staffordshire, UK*
See p174. This mark is a typical example of a 19thC Minton mark.

Josiah Spode *Stoke, Staffordshire, UK*
The first Josiah Spode was born in 1733 and worked for Thomas Whieldon. His son, also called Josiah, was born in 1754 and took over a works in Stoke in 1784 producing earthenwares to begin with and porcelain after c1790. A new development, 'Stone China', was made in 1805. The third Josiah Spode took over the works after his father's death in 1827, but he died only two years later. The business was then carried on until 1833 when the whole concern was bought by Alderman William Taylor Copeland. This printed mark was one of those used on special earthenware bodies c1805–33.

Triangles

Trevor Logan *Leeds, West Yorkshire, UK*
Studio-type pottery and stonewares with this impressed mark have been made since 1957.

Chelsea Porcelain Works *London, UK*
See p170. This incised triangle mark, sometimes with the addition of 'Chelsea' and the year was used c1745–49. On rare occasions the triangle appears painted in blue.

Pinder, Bourne & Co *Burslem, Staffordshire, UK*
This firm took over the works at Nile Street, Burslem in 1862 and produced a variety of printed, enamelled and gilded earthenwares and redwares. This mark was one of those used by the firm 1862–82.

Iden Pottery *Rye, East Sussex, UK*
From October 1961 Studio-type earthenwares and stonewares were made by D. Townshend (who previously worked at the Rye Pottery) and J. H. Wood. This printed mark was used from 1961. Originally established at Iden, in 1963 it moved to Rye but kept its original name.

Van Briggle Pottery
Colorado Springs, Colorado, USA
Founded by Artus van Briggle, who had been a decorator for the Rookwood Pottery (see p102), the pottery made ornamental wares with matt glazes applied over moulded Art Nouveau forms. Van Briggle died in 1904. Many of the old designs are still made, along with newer forms.

Circles

Colin Pearson *Aylesford, Kent, UK*
Studio-type pottery was produced here from 1962 at the Quay Pottery. Colin Pearson previously worked at the Aylesford Priory Pottery. This impressed seal mark was used.

Derek M. Davis *Arundel, West Sussex, UK*
From 1953 this potter produced Studio-type earthenwares; stonewares and tiles were made c1959–62. This painted or incised mark was introduced early in 1963.

Walton Pottery Co Ltd
Old Whittington, Nr Chesterfield, Derbyshire, UK
William Gordon produced salt-glazed stonewares 1946–56 with this incised or impressed mark.

Höchst *Nr Mainz, Germany*
See p34. This wheel mark was used by the Höchst factory in many variations. This example was used 1762–96 and appears in underglaze blue. A crowned version was used c1765–74.

Philipp Dietrich *Passau, Bavaria, Germany*
See p156. This mark was used on wares made from Höchst moulds.

Josiah Spode *Stoke, Staffordshire, UK*
See p233. This impressed mark was used on early porcelains c1790–1820.

Margaret Leach *Various locations, UK*
Not related to Studio potter Bernard Leach, although she did work at the Leach Pottery in St Ives between 1943 and 1945. Margaret Leach began potting at the Barnhouse Pottery in Brockweir, Monmouth in 1946. This mark was used while she was at the Taena Pottery at Aylburton in Gloucestershire 1951–56.

Humphrey Palmer *Hanley, Staffordshire, UK*
Based at the Church Works in Hanley c1760–78, Palmer made Wedgwood-type earthenwares including basaltes in association with James Neale. The firm (J.) Neale & Co was formed at Church Works from c1776. This mark appears.

Roseville Pottery Company
Roseville and Zanesville, Ohio, USA
See p43. This applied clay mark appears. A foil label with 'Roseville Pottery' was also used.

Wedgwood & Bentley *Etruria, Staffordshire, UK*
Josiah Wedgwood and Thomas Bentley formed a partnership from c1768–80 with the intention of producing ornamental wares in the Classical style. They established a new factory which they named Etruria after a site in Ancient Italy where pottery had been excavated. This impressed or raised mark appears only on ornamental wares c1769–80; the word 'Etruria' is sometimes missing.

Weller Pottery/S. A. Weller Company
Fultonham and Zanesville, Ohio, USA
Active between 1872 and 1948, Weller's earliest potteries made painted flowerpots and stoneware garden ware and umbrella stands. In 1893, the first art wares were produced. During the early years of this century, the pottery produced a wide variety of decorative effects on ornamental wares, including painted underglaze slip in the Rookwood (see p102) style and unique iridescent effects brought from France by Jacques Sicard, a protégé of Clement Massier. While much of this early art ware was artist decorated, the later work depends on moulds and decorative glazes. The name Weller appears in most marks; a large number of decorators' marks (as signatures or monograms) were also used.

Squares & Diamonds

Worcester Porcelains *Hereford and Worcester, UK*
See p33. This square or fret mark was used in many variations, hand-painted in underglaze blue c1755–75. It also appears on hard-paste porcelain and earthenware reproductions.

C. H. Menard *Rue de Popincourt, Paris, France*
See p134. This mark is one of those used by Menard, whose output primarily comprised copies of Chinese porcelain.

Meissen *Nr Dresden, Saxony, Germany*
See p63. Imitation Chinese marks such as this one were sometimes used, mainly on blue and white wares c1720–25.

Mayer China Company/Mayer Potteries Company Ltd *Syracuse, New York, USA*
Although this pottery (1881–present) made high grade hotel ware for some time, over the last century they have included white ironstone with lustre sprig (tea leaf), white granite and decorated semi-porcelain dinner and toilet sets and tableware.

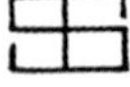

Emile Samson *Paris, France*
See p241. This mark was used by Samson on Japanese and Chinese-style wares.

Doulton & Co (Ltd) *Lambeth, London, UK*
See p121. This impressed mark was used c1912–56 on slip-cast wares and is incorporated into many other Doulton marks down to the present day. It appears with a crown and a lion c1902–22 and c1927–36, and a lion from c1922.

William Marshall *St Ives, Cornwall, UK*
See p242. This impressed seal mark was one of those used from 1956.

William Bloor's East Liverpool Porcelain Works *East Liverpool, Ohio, USA*
Bloor worked alternately in East Liverpool, Ohio, and Trenton, New Jersey, over many years. During this time in Ohio (1861–62), he converted an existing pottery to the production of parian and 'double thick hotel ware.' But the Civil War created financial and labour problems. This raised diamond-shaped mark is similar to a British Patent Office Registration Mark.

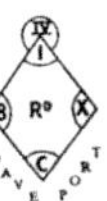

Davenport *Longport, Staffordshire, UK*
See p226. This printed mark was found on Davenport porcelains of registered form or pattern c1842–83.

G. & J. Hobson *Burslem, Staffordshire, UK*
Formerly C. Hobson (1865–80), this firm produced earthenwares 1883–1901. This printed mark occurs on the firm's advertisements in 1884. Other forms of mark may occur.

Thomas Ford *Hanley, Staffordshire, UK*
Originally established in 1854 as T. & C. Ford, this firm operated as Thomas Ford 1871–74. Many marks were used; this example is based on the registration device.

J. E. Jeffords and Company/Philadelphia City Pottery *Philadelphia, Pennsylvania, USA*
Rockingham and yellow ware were Jeffords' stock-in-trade throughout their years of business, 1868–1915. The pottery made cow creamers, teapots, florists' crockery, table and toilet wares (some in white ware) and blue-glazed ware. Much of the company's work is not signed.

Hearts

Benedikt Brothers
Meierhöfen, Bohemia, Czech Republic
The Benedikt Brothers founded a factory here in 1883 and produced white and decorated porcelain Various marks featuring a heart were used.

C. H. Menard *Rue de Popincourt, Paris, France*
See p236. This mark was also used.

Stars

Florence *Tuscany, Italy*
The star (or aterisk) mark seen here can be single or as a group of three, and located below the lower terminal of the strap handle on 'oak-leaf' drug jars made in Tuscany. It is tentatively associated with the workshop of Giunta di Tugio. In 1430–31 a large order for about 1,000 drug jars was placed with this workshop by the hospital of the Santa Maria Nuova whose device or emblem was a crutch. A considerable number of 'oak-leaf' jars bearing both the emblem of the crutch and the asterisk have survived in international collections and these are probably the earliest documentary wares in European ceramics.

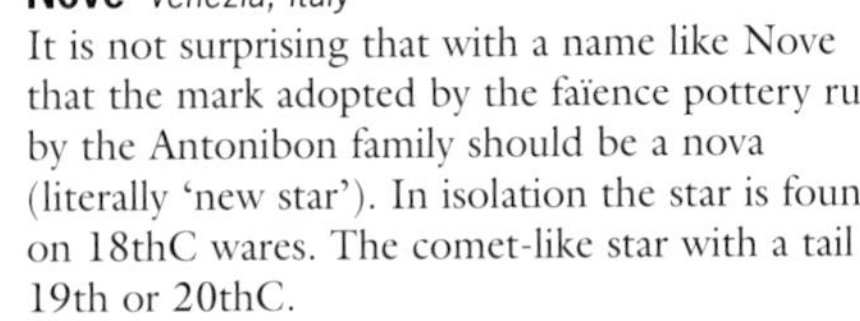

Nove *Venezia, Italy*
It is not surprising that with a name like Nove that the mark adopted by the faïence pottery run by the Antonibon family should be a nova (literally 'new star'). In isolation the star is found on 18thC wares. The comet-like star with a tail is 19th or 20thC.

Ginori Factory *Doccia, Nr Florence, Tuscany, Italy*
See p35. One of the most important Italian porcelain factories established in 1735 by Carlo Ginori and still in production today. The star mark can be impressed or enamelled in blue, red or purple, and dates from late 18thC or early 19thC.

David Hilton
Compton Dundon, Somerton, Somerset, UK
In production from 1956, David Hilton produced Studio pottery. From 1962 he specialized in stonewares. The mark is impressed.

L. B. Beerbower *Elizabeth, New Jersey, USA*
Beerbower, formerly of the Phoenix Pottery in Phoenixville, Pennsylvania, took over the old Pruden pottery in Elizabeth, New Jersey. The new pottery (active 1880–c1905) made ironstone china, semi-granite, cream-coloured and print-decorated goods in druggists' ware, and toilet, table and kitchen sets.

F. Legrand & Cie *Limoges, France*
Known under various names (Betoule & Legrand (1910), Betoule & Cie (1920)), this firm was known under this title 1923–26. This is one of the marks used.

Star China Co *Longton, Staffordshire, UK*
Based at the Atlas Works and other addresses, this porcelain manufacturer operated 1900–19. The firm became the Paragon China Co from 1920. Various printed marks were used including these examples used c1912–19. Other marks include a monogram or the initials of the firm; a crown device was sometimes used.

Star Pottery *Posail Park, Glasgow, Scotland, UK*
Johnstone Wardlaw were manufacturers of earthenwares and stonewares 1880–1907. This impressed or printed mark was used.

Star Pottery Works *Elmendort, Texas, USA*
Ernest Richter established a stoneware pottery in Elmendorf, Bexar County, Texas, in 1888. He sold it in 1905 to Newton, Weller and Wagner. Their firm became the Star Pottery Works in 1909 and continued until 1915. White, Bristol glazed stoneware was manufactured, as well as an unusual type of stoneware and cast-iron patented churn.

Crescents

Hanau *Nr Frankfurt-am-Main, Germany*
See p180. This painted mark was used on tin-glazed earthenwares in the 17th and 18thC.

Bow China Works *Stratford, London, UK*
See p31. Imitating a mark used at Worcester, this crescent mark appears heavily painted in underglaze blue, and was used on figures and wares c1760–76.

Worcester Porcelains *Hereford and Worcester, UK*
See p33. The crescent mark was taken from a device in the arms of the city of Worcester. The mark (above) was used by Dr Wall's factory from c1755–90. The open painted crescent appears on blue and white hand-painted porcelains. It can also be printed and open or printed and hatched over. The mark (below) was used during the Flight period (1783–92). The open painted crescent continued to be used, but was generally smaller and less grey.

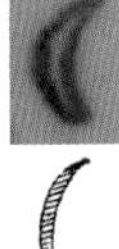

Lowestoft *Suffolk, UK*
The Lowestoft factory (c1757–99) had no formal trademark and many of their bone-ash porcelains are unmarked. However, a number of pieces carry hand-painted versions of other factory marks such as the crescents seen here.

Pinxton Works *Pinxton, Derbyshire, UK*
See p138. The mark of a crescent and a star was used occasionally c1799–1806.

Tessa Fuchs *London, UK*
A producer of Studio-type ceramics from 1961, Tessa Fuchs used this painted, crescent-like symbol. The mark also appears with her name.

W. Goebel *Oeslau, Bavaria, Germany*
Formerly the Oeslau and Wilhelmsfeld porcelain factory founded in 1871, the factory was taken over by W. Goebel from 1879. Ornaments in porcelain, fine earthenware and terracotta were produced. This is one of the marks used.

William Hulme *Gobridge, Staffordshire, UK*
Manufacturers of earthenwares 1948–54, this firm operated from the Argyle Works. This printed mark was used, and also appears without the words 'Imperial Porcelain'.

Crosses

Crosses are often used on ceramics as subsidiary marks, mostly identifying a workman or painter. The major blue and white porcelain factories Bow, Bristol, Worcester, Lowestoft and Liverpool all used scratched or painted crosses.

Lowestoft *Suffolk, UK*
Established in 1757 Lowestoft manufactured a phosphatic soft-paste formula similar to Bow. The main output was Chinese-style blue and white, at least until c1770 when enamel colours were also used and some fine quality painting appears. The factory closed c1802, but produced very little in its last years. There was no factory mark (although they 'borrowed' the crescent mark of Worcester and the crossed swords of Meissen) but did inscribe some of their wares with workman's marks, especially on the inside of the footrim. As well as numerals and letters the cross shown here was also used.

Bristol *Avon, UK*
See p71. The Bristol cross marks which are mostly painted in a pale blue enamel, appear from 1770 until the closure of Champion's factory in 1781. Sometimes the marks are used together with a number or very rarely a date.

Moustiers *Basses Alpes, France*
See p101. A painted cross mark was used on faïence made at Moustiers c1710–40.

Fulda *Hesse, Germany*
See p57. The cross was used as a factory mark on hard-paste porcelain from c1765–80.

Emile Samson *Paris, France*
Emile Samson (1837–1913) was probably the most famous maker of porcelain reproductions, especially of Meissen and Sèvres, although his factory also made imitations of faience. As well as using crossed batons recalling the Meissen crossed swords, Samson employed pseudo-Chinese seal marks and other devices. However, on copies of European porcelains and enamels the factory used an entwined 'S' mark resembling a cross, as here.

Helen Walters *Stroud Green, Hornsey, London, UK*
This potter made Studio-type pottery from 1945. She also used an incised cross and dots mark on pottery made for Doulton 1945–53.

E. T. Leaper *Newlyn, Nr Penzance, Cornwall, UK*
Hand-made pottery was produced from 1954. This mark loosely resembles that of Bernard Leach.

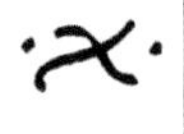

Francesco Xanto Avelli da Rovigo
Urbino, Italy
See p58. Although he signed many of his pieces with a full or an abbreviated signature mark, a considerable body of works by this potter is marked merely with the words 'fabula', 'nota' or 'istoria', or simply with a character similar to a lazy, cursive 'y', or in his late work of c1540–42, with an 'x' similar to the example shown.

Cafaggiolo *Nr Florence, Tuscany, Italy*
One of the most important maiolica workshops in Cafaggiolo was run by the Fattorini family. The mark shown here which dates from a signed piece of 1514 is very close to that of William Cookworthy's mark on Plymouth porcelain (1768–70), in that it looks like the combined numerals '2' and '4', the alchemist's symbol for tin.

William Marshall *St Ives, Cornwall, UK*
William Marshall worked in the pottery of Bernard Leach from 1954. His incised device involves a series of four connected diagonal crosses flanked by dots. His mark should be accompanied by the official Leach pottery mark. Two examples appear here.

Padua *Italy*
The manufacture of lead-glazed pottery and maiolica has been recorded from the 15thC. In the former category are sgraffiato wares echoing the technique of Chinese Cizhou type of stonewares of the Song and Yuan dynasties. Also of note are the 17thC maiolica dishes and wares based on Isnik pottery. The painted mark shown is a rare but typical example.

Carlo Norway *London, UK*
Studio-type pottery and ceramic sculptures and figures were produced 1920–35. This incised key-like cross mark was used.

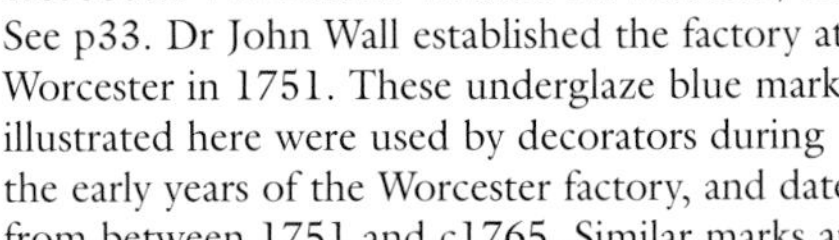

Worcester Porcelains *Hereford and Worcester, UK*
See p33. Dr John Wall established the factory at Worcester in 1751. These underglaze blue marks illustrated here were used by decorators during the early years of the Worcester factory, and date from between 1751 and c1765. Similar marks are found on other early porcelains.

Casa Pirota *Faenza, Emilia, Italy*

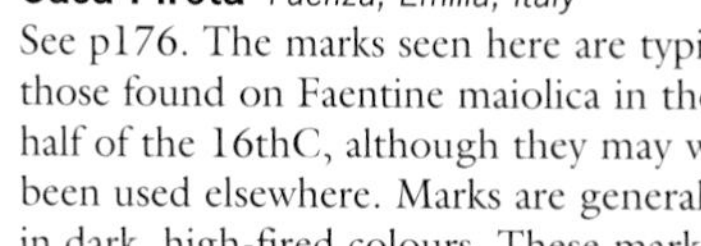

See p176. The marks seen here are typical of those found on Faentine maiolica in the first half of the 16thC, although they may well have been used elsewhere. Marks are generally painted in dark, high-fired colours. These marks have been attributed to the so-called 'Casa Pirota' workshop whose existence is now in doubt.

Prinknash Benedictines
Prinknash Abbey, Gloucestershire, UK
Earthenwares were made here from 1945. This printed or impressed mark appears.

Arrows

Pinxton Works *Derbyshire, UK*
See p138. Factory marks are rare on Pinxton wares – this is one used.

Bow China Works *Stratford, London, UK*
See p31. These incised marks are from the early period of the factory c1750. An incised anchor mark has also been recorded, but this is very rare.

St Petersburg *Russia*
See p39. The Russian Imperial factory was founded in 1744 to produce hard-paste porcelain for the court. The early period up to c1765 was strongly influenced by Meissen and after this date by Sèvres and Paris porcelain. Among the more successful lines was the series of Russian peasants modelled at the turn of the 18thC. The incised or impressed mark of the arrow and circle was sometimes used.

Thomas Plowman *Stalham, Norfolk, UK*
Thomas Plowman founded the Clay Brook Pottery in 1958 and produced Studio-type wares. This impressed mark was used.

Minton *Stoke, Staffordshire, UK*
See p174. The arrow and dots mark (above) appeared on early parian ware figures c1845–50. The painted 'ermine' mark (below) indicates a special soft glaze. This mark, which may appear with or without the letter 'M', was occasionally used as the factory mark during the 1850s.

ARROWS

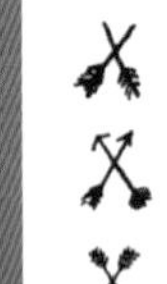

Pouyat, Russinger, Russinger-Pouyat
Rue de la Roquette, Paris, France
The crossed arrows were used by the above concerns in their Paris factories, probably from the late 18th and first half of the 19thC, on hard-paste porcelains. The marks are usually painted in underglaze blue. Similar marks of crossed arrows, crossed tridents or even torches were used in Paris from c1770 to c1840 by a number of concerns at La Courtille, rue Fontaine-au-Roy (or Basse Courtille), and Faubourg du Temple.

Porzellanfabrik Kalk
Eisenberg, Thuringia, Germany
These manufacturers of hard-paste porcelain patterned coffee and tablewares from 1899 used a number of variations of this printed mark.

Ernst Teichert *Meissen, Saxony, Germany*
Ernst Teichert manufactured general pottery, much transfer-printed in blue, with Meissen-style designs from 1884 onwards. The word 'Meissen' usually appears in the marks. Do not confuse with hard-paste porcelain produced at the original Meissen factory which was never marked with the word.

Denver China and Pottery Company
Denver, Colorado, USA
See p54. This mark was also used. Marks usually feature the name 'Denver'.

Henry Mills *Hanley, Staffordshire, UK*
A manufacturer of earthenware from c1892, Henry Mills used this printed mark.

Ridgways *Shelton, Hanley, Staffordshire, UK*
See p212. The printed trademark (above) was registered in 1880. Later versions after c1912 (below) feature the words 'Stoke-on-Trent'.

Birds

Derlwyn Pottery *Betws-y-Coed, Gwynedd, Wales, UK*
Studio-type pottery was made by Ms Campion and Ms Pritchard at the Derlwyn Pottery from 1959, with this incised or painted swallow mark, the place name, and often with the initial of the potter.

Van der Straeten *Linton, Nr Cambridge, UK*
This pottery produced individual Studio-type earthenwares from 1948, with this printed or impressed mark.

Cybis Porcelains *Trenton, New Jersey, USA*
This company (active 1942–present) was founded by Polish artist Boleslaw Cybis. From 1942 to 1949 they made tea and coffee pots moulded with porcelain lace, ribbons and flowers. The company also produced brightly coloured figurines with a bisque finish. Their early work was religious in nature, but their current production includes storybook characters, circus subjects and famous women. These marks appear.

Elenor Whittall *London, UK*
This potter made Studio-type stonewares from 1944 (and porcelains from 1958). She used this impressed owl device that was originally made up from the initials 'E. E. W.'

George Wade & Son Ltd *Burslem, Staffordshire, UK*
Based at the Manchester Pottery from 1922, this firm made earthenwares. This printed owl trademark was used from c1947.

Carlton Ware Ltd *Stoke, Staffordshire, UK*
See p116. This style of mark was used by both Wiltshaw & Robinson 1890–1957 and Carlton Ware Ltd from 1957.

New England Pottery Company
East Boston, Massachusetts, USA
See p192. This mark was one used by this firm.

Crooksville China Company
Crooksville, Ohio, USA
The company (active 1902–late 1950s) made dinnerware, toilet sets and kitchenware decorated with quaint decals. Their best dinnerware line was called Stinthal China, which appears without any Crooksville designation.

Toni Raymond Pottery *Torquay, Devon, UK*
This pottery made earthenwares, tablewares and figures from 1961 and is known for its floral-decorated storage jars. This impressed or printed mark was used.

Watcombe Pottery Co *St Mary Church, Devon, UK*
Earthenwares, terracotta, ornamental wares, busts, figures and other items were produced by this firm c1867–1901. Founded by G. T. Allen, the company was formed to sell terracotta clay found on his property. Many decorative wares were produced that are similar to Wedgwood's jasper ware; busts and ornamental items were also made. Notable are vases with floral decoration which is either pressed, printed or painted. Other items include services, medallions, ewers, candlesticks and flower stands. As well as an impressed name mark, this printed mark featuring a woodpecker was used 1875–1901.

John Fisher *Rowlands Gill, Tyne and Wear, UK*
Studio-type pottery was made here from 1950. This is the personal mark of John Fisher which appears from 1950; he also used an incised or painted monogram mark.

Oxshott Pottery *Oxshott, Surrey, UK*
This wren seal mark was used by Rosemary Wren from 1945. The word 'Oxshott' appears underneath the mark from 1950.

Swan Hill Pottery *South Amboy, New Jersey, USA*
Several owners and a number of potters operated this pottery (1849–89) making earthenware, Rockingham, yellow ware and some white ware for table, kitchen and toilet purposes. Charles Fish owned the pottery for the longest single period; the potters included James Carr, Thomas Locker, Charles Coxon, John L. Rue, and others The business was reorganized in 1889 as the South Amboy Pottery Company, which made, bought and sold pottery. This raised mark was used

Arnhem *Holland*
Faïence was produced here from 1755 to 1773. This mark was used.

Ulysse Cantagalli *Florence, Tuscany, Italy*
From 1878 Cantagalli made maiolica reproductions of early Urbino, Faenza, Gubbio, Deruta and Della Robbia wares. The cockerel appears in various forms, such as the examples seen here. This mark may also appear in a very abstract form.

E. Brain & Co Ltd *Fenton, Staffordshire, UK*
Based at the Foley China Works, this company produced porcelain 1903–63. This printed mark appears c1905. The name 'Foley China' was used in many different marks.

The Hague *Holland*
Hard-paste porcelain was made at this factory founded in 1775, and directed by Anton Leichner from Vienna until his death in 1781. The factory continued until 1790. Notable wares feature floral decoration and monochrome purple designs. Marks including those shown here were used, based on the city coat-of-arms.

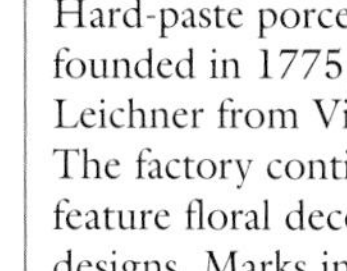

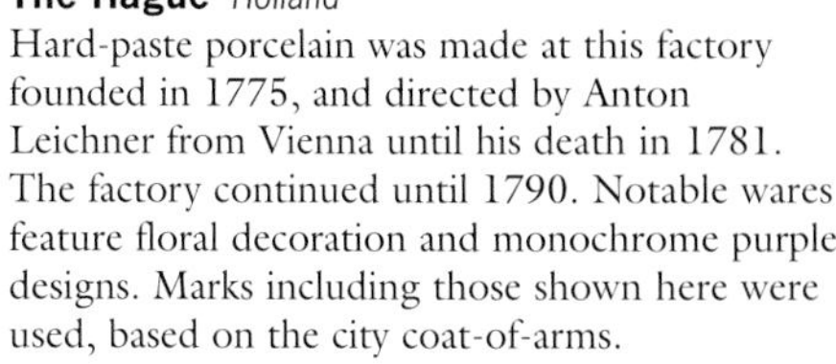

Rozenburg *Holland*
Active 1883–1916, the Rozenburg Pottery initially concentrated on simple earthenwares. However, in the late 1880s and 1890s, the firm led a revival of Dutch ceramics, and its eggshell earthenware is now regarded as some of the finest ever made. Wares were influenced by both Art Nouveau and Japanese art. The mark seen here was used before 1900; after this date it appears beneath a crown.

Holkham Pottery Ltd *Holkham, Norfolk, UK*
Formerly Holkham Studio Pottery (1951–61), this company produced earthenwares from 1961. This printed or impressed mark was used by both firms.

Parrott & Co (Ltd) *Burslem, Staffordshire, UK*
Operating from c1921, this firm made earthenwares at the Albert Street Pottery. This parrot mark was registered in 1921, with a slightly different mark appearing after c1935.

Herculaneum Pottery *Liverpool, Mersey, UK*
See p210. Printed or impressed Liver bird marks were used by the Herculaneum Pottery in various forms c1833–36.

Samuel Barker & Son *Swinton, Yorkshire, UK*
Based at the Don Pottery which was purchased by Samuel Barker in 1834. The company became known as Samuel Barker & Son in 1851 and continued until 1893. Fine earthenwares were made. Creamware, caneware, redware and porcelain were also produced. This rare mark appears c1850.

Berlin *Prussia, Germany*
See p37. This blue-printed factory mark was used at Berlin 1844–47, with a similar mark 1849–70.

Chesapeake Pottery/D. F. Haynes and Son *Baltimore, Maryland, USA*
See p215. A number of marks were used featuring a monogram, initials ('C. C. P'. stood for 'Chesapeake Pottery'; 'H. B. H.' stood for 'Haynes & Bennett'), or the company name.

William Adams & Sons (Potters) Ltd *Tunstall and Stoke, Staffordshire, UK*
See p204. This mark appears on blue printed earthenwares 1804–40.

William Henry Goss (Ltd) *Stoke, Staffordshire, UK*
From 1858 Willam Henry Goss produced parian, porcelain and terracotta. He specialized in ornaments made from jewelled porcelain, such as scent bottles and items of jewellery including brooches. Fine porcelain wares were also made. This printed mark was used from c1862 with 'England' added from 1891. The company was taken over by Cauldon Potteries Ltd in c1934 and retitled Goss China Ltd.

F. Grosvenor (& Son) *Glasgow, Scotland, UK*
From c1869 to 1926 this firm made stonewares and earthenwares. This printed eagle trademark was registered by Frederick Grosvenor in 1879 and was used until 1926.

Enoch Wood & Sons *Burslem, Staffordshire, UK*
Originally established as Enoch Wood, who had been an apprentice under Wedgwood c1784, this pottery operated from the Fountain Works and other addresses in Burslem. Wood was in partnership with James Cauldwell 1795–1818, before the title of the firm changed again to Enoch Wood & Sons and continued until 1846. Fine earthenwares of all types were made. Impressed marks such as this were used 1818–46.

Coxon and Company, Empire Pottery *Trenton, New Jersey, USA*
Charles Coxon and J. F Thompson established this pottery (active 1863–84) to make cream-coloured ware and white granite. Coxon died in

1868, but the pottery was continued by his widow and four sons. They made souvenirs for the 1876 Centennial Exhibition. In 1884, the company was sold to Alpaugh and Magowan.

Goodwin Pottery/Goodwin Brothers
East Liverpool, Ohio, USA
The Goodwin family had several potteries in East Liverpool and Trenton, New Jersey, from 1844. This pottery (1876–1912) was organized to make white ware in several variations, including pearl-white, cream-coloured, ironstone and semi-porcelain; some was decorated.

Thomas Lawrence (Longton) Ltd
Longton, Staffordshire, UK
Based at the Falcon Works 1897–1957 and the Sylvan Works from 1957, this company made earthenwares from 1892. This mark appears from 1944. Others with the name Falcon Ware were also used.

Animals

J. Leofold *Paris, France*
This porcelain manufacturer uses this mark.

Fürstenberg *Brunswick, Germany*
See p35. This mark of a small jumping horse was impressed or incised on busts and reliefs at the end of the 18thC. A letter may appear under the mark and refers to the modeller.

Cassel *Hesse-Nassau, Germany*
Porcelain was made at the faïence factory at Cassel 1766–88 with the mark (above). Note the double tail on this Hessian lion. Earthenwares were produced 1771–1862 with the impressed mark (below).

Frankenthal *Palatinate, Germany*
This lion mark from the arms of the Palatinate was used at Frankenthal c1756–59.

Hudson & Middleton *Longton, Staffordshire, UK*
See p188. This mark was formerly used by W. Hudson (from c1936), and was continued by Hudson & Middleton.

International Pottery/Burgess & Campbell

Trenton, New Jersey, USA

See p223. This mark was among those used by this firm.

Pickard China *Chicago and Antioch, Illinois, USA*

Founded by Wilder Pickard as a ceramic-decorating studio in 1894, the company had a reputation for fine hand-painted and elaborate gold-etched decorations. In 1930 they began to experiment with making their own wares, which they introduced to the market in 1938. Today Pickard makes chinaware for the US embassies around the world.

Wade, Heath & Co (Ltd) *Burslem, Staffordshire, UK*

Based at the High Street Works (1927–38) and the Royal Victoria Pottery (from 1938), this firm (formerly Wade & Co 1887–1927) made earthenwares. This is one of the marks used from c1927. A similar mark with the words 'Wade Heath' above the lion was used from c1934.

Homer Laughlin China Company

East Liverpool, Ohio, and Newell, West Virginia, USA

This mark was among those used. A wide variety of marks appear; most incorporate the name of the company.

(W.) Baker & Co (Ltd) *Fenton, Staffordshire, UK*

See p223. This mark was used c1928–30. A number of different marks was used, most of them incorporate the company name.

Paul Revere Pottery/Saturday Evening Girls

Boston and Brighton, Massachusetts, USA

See p68. This mark, an incised impression of Paul Revere on a horse, was one of those used by this group. The mark appears with a dark background as here, and also with a light background.

George Hobson *Burslem, Staffordshire, UK*

Formerly Charles Hobson (1865–80), and G. & J. Hobson (1883–1901), this firm produced earthenwares 1901–23. Operating at the Albert Pottery (later the Sneyd Pottery), the firm produced services and other items in many types of earthenware. This printed or impressed mark was used 1901–23.

Edward Marshall Boehm Inc

Trenton, New Jersey, USA

This company (active 1950–present) specializes in elaborate porcelain figures of birds, animals and flowers, some of the larger pieces being used as gifts of state by the President of the United States. Boehm was one of the world's most renowned sculptors and a keen conservationalist, and this interest is reflected in his work. Boehm died in 1969, and since then his wife has expanded the business. These are some of the marks that appear. Most marks feature a horse's head, together with the name of the firm.

E. Hughes & Co *Fenton, Staffordshire, UK*

See p178. This printed mark was used from c1908–12. A globe device was used on wares produced after c1912.

Thomas Hughes & Son Ltd

Burslem, Staffordshire, UK

Thomas Hughes took over his grandfather's firm in 1895. The business was first based at the Waterloo Road Works (c1860–76), then at the Top Bridge Works (c1872–94), before moving to the Unicorn Pottery in 1895. A unicorn mark was used from 1930, with this version appearing 1935–37. The firm continued until 1957.

Hollinshead & Kirkham (Ltd)

Tunstall, Staffordshire, UK

See p189. This printed mark was used on earthenwares 1900–24.

Taylor & Kent (Ltd) *Longton, Staffordshire, UK*

See p162. One of the principal printed marks, this example appears from c1939. The firm's initials or name appear on their marks.

Wedgwood & Co (Ltd) *Tunstall, Staffordshire, UK*

See p216. The printed trademark (top) was used; the words 'trade mark' indicate a date after the Act of 1862. The mark (centre) is a new version of the earlier unicorn mark, and was used from c1908. The mark (below) appears from c1956. Occasionally only the trade name or pattern name appears with the mark, such as 'Wacol' or 'Wacolware' or 'Royal Tunstall'. These trade names appear on wares made after c1950.

William Adams & Sons (Potters) Ltd
Tunstall and Stoke, Staffordshire, UK
See p204. This printed mark was first introduced in 1879. The word 'England' was added after 1891.

George Wade & Son Ltd *Burslem, Staffordshire, UK*
See p245. Based at the Manchester Pottery from 1922. This mark was used on earthenwares from c1936.

Donald Brindley Pottery Ltd
Longton, Staffordshire, UK
Based at Chelston Street, this pottery produced earthenware figures and other items from 1961. This printed or impressed mark appears.

Buffalo Pottery Company/Buffalo China Inc
Buffalo, New York, USA
Founded by the Larkin Soap Company in 1901 to make tableware for the company's premium-purchase plan, which supplied porcelain in exchange for purchase certificates collected by the consumer, the firm made a wide variety of transfer-printed and decal decorated earthenware including a line called 'Deldare', decorated with traditional English scenes, printed and filled on a contrasting background. Today's production is largely for the food service industry. These marks appear.

A. Lamm *Dresden, Germany*
This porcelain decorating studio was founded in 1887. As well as the Meissen style, pieces were decorated in the style of Copenhagen. The studio produced very high quality painting.

Franz Junkersdorf *Dresden, Germany*
See p224. This mark appears on porcelains made in the style of Dresden, Meissen and Vienna.

Alfred (and Isaac) Baguley *Swinton, Yorkshire, UK*
Isaac Baguley (formerly employed at the Derby China Works) took over part of the discontinued Rockingham Works in c1842, where he decorated and sold white wares. After his death in c1855, the business was carried on by his son Alfred until 1865, and then at Mexborough c1865–91. Among other techniques, the Baguleys used chocolate or bown Rockingham-style glazes on

services, tea and coffee pots, drinking horns and jugs. White stonewares, cane wares, and green-glazed earthenwares were also made. This printed mark appears 1842–65: the wording may vary.

Rockingham Works *Swinton, Yorkshire, UK*
The Rockingham Works were established c1745, and continued under various owners until 1842. Thomas Bingley was the principal proprietor in 1778, with John and William Brameld as his partners. At this time good quality brown, yellow, white, and blue and white wares were produced. From 1787 to 1800 a type of brown or Rockingham ware was made. The body was covered in a characteristic streaky brown glaze. This style was copied extensively by many other manufacturers. In 1813, the sons of John and William Brameld took over the firm, and increased the quality of the production and the range of wares produced. Due to financial difficulties the Works closed in 1842. The griffin mark in red was used when porcelain was introduced c1826–30 (top); on some rare examples the crest appears with no wording. Later versions of the griffin mark after 1830 (centre) were printed in puce with the words 'Royal Rock(ingham) Works' and/or 'China Manufacturers to the King' c1830–42. Rare examples of the mark (below) appear with 'China Manufacturers to the Queen'; these were probably decorated by Alfred Baguley after 1842.

Bwthyn Pottery *Barmouth, Wales, UK*
This pottery, situated on the coast, produced Studio-type wares from 1956. This mark was used, and may appear printed or impressed.

H. M. Williamson & Sons *Longton, Staffordshire, UK*
Based at the Bridge Pottery, this firm produced porcelain c1879–1941. Many marks were used, including this one from c1908.

Onondaga Pottery *Syracuse, New York, USA*
See p168. Several different marks were used by this firm: most feature the name 'Syracuse China'.

Vodrey Pottery Company *East Liverpool, Ohio, USA*
This is one of the marks used by this firm. It appears in many forms, and may feature 'Semi-porcelain' rather than 'Vodrey China'.

Roblin Pottery *San Francisco, California, USA*
Linna Irelan worked with Alexander W. Robertson to create exquisite small vases 1898–1906. He threw the pots, and she decorated them with a variety of matt and coloured finishes. The mark below includes the figure of a bear, the symbol for California. An incised spider and web mark may also be found. The pottery was destroyed in the San Francisco great earthquake and fire of 1906.

Lavender Groves *Chelsea, London, UK*
See p126. This incised or painted mark appears from 1952.

Barker Pottery Co *Chesterfield, Derbyshire, UK*
Operating 1887–1957, this pottery produced stonewares. This mark was used 1928–57.

Belleek Pottery *Co Fermanagh, Northern Ireland, UK*
The Belleek Works were established in1863 by David McBirney and Robert Williams Armstrong. High quality, ultra-thin porcelain was produced. Notable are ornamental items in marine-type forms with iridescent glazes. Services and wares of all types were also produced. Also made was parian, ordinary white china and white granite ware. The standard trade mark (above) was used 1863–91. The second version (below), with the addition of 'Co. Fermanagh' and 'Ireland', is still used.

S. W. Dean *Burslem, Staffordshire, UK*
This firm produced earthenwares at the Newport Pottery 1904–10, before becoming Deans (1910) Ltd (1910–19). This mark was used 1904–10; other marks occur with the firm's title in full.

Arij de Milde *Delft, Holland*
Red stoneware was produced at Delft from c1675 to the 18thC. Arij de Milde was active in Delft 1680–1708. This was one of the marks used.

T. & R. Boote (Ltd) *Burslem, Staffordshire, UK*
See p222. This printed mark was used 1890–1906. Others usually have the company name or initials.

William Bailey & Sons *Longton, Staffordshire, UK*
Earthenwares were made by this firm at the Gordon Pottery 1912–14 with this printed mark

New Devon Pottery Ltd *Newton Abbot, Devon, UK*
This pottery on the coast of Devon produced earthenwares from 1957 with this printed mark.

Chelsea Keramic Art Works/Dedham Pottery *Chelsea and Dedham, Massachusetts, USA*
These marks were used by the Dedham Pottery. Their rabbit pattern tablewares (designed by Joseph Linden Smith) became one of their best-known styles and was adopted as a trademark. The word 'Registered' may appear under the mark below.

Mousehole Pottery *Mousehole, Cornwall, UK*
Studio-type pottery was produced by Mr & Mrs Picard from 1953. This impressed seal or printed mark appears from 1953.

John Tams (& Son) (Ltd) *Longton, Staffordshire, UK*
From 1875, John Tams manufactured earthenwares at the Crown Pottery, specializing in the production of government measures, jugs and mugs. This mark was used from c1952.

Robinson & Leadbeater (Ltd)
Stoke, Staffordshire, UK
This firm produced high quality parian at several works in Stoke 1864–1924, including figures, groups, busts, centrepieces, caskets, jugs and other items. This printed mark appears c1905–24.

Cromer Pottery *Aylmerton, Nr Norwich, Norfolk, UK*
Earthenwares were produced by this pottery, owned by Rosemary Middleton, from 1952. This impressed crab mark was used.

Cincinnati Art Pottery *Cincinnati, Ohio, USA*
See p52. Marks are usually impressed, but decorators' monograms may also appear, generally incised.

W. T. Copeland (& Sons Ltd)
Stoke, Staffordshire, UK
Formerly Spode (c1784–1833) and Copeland & Garrett (1833–47), this firm has operated since 1847. Porcelain, parian and earthenwares of all types were produced with many different types of decoration. Many innovations were made, including the development of an 'Ivory body'. This mark appears on earthenwares 1867–90.

Fish

Nyon *Nr Geneva, Switzerland*
See p192. Although the form of the Nyon mark does vary, these are typical examples. The mark appears in underglaze blue.

Adolf Hamman *Dresden, Germany*
This porcelain-decorating studio began in 1866. Pieces were decorated in the Dresden, Meissen and Viennese styles. This mark was used.

Pescetto *Savona, Liguria, Italy*
This potter was active in Savona in the late 17thC. This is an example of his marks.

Lille *France*
A soft-paste porcelain factory existed here during the first half of the 18thC. In 1784 Leperre-Durot, under the protection of the Dauphin, founded a hard-paste porcelain factory. The factory was called 'Manufacture Royale de Monseigneur le Dauphin' and the dolphin was used as the mark. Wares were made in the Parisian style. Production continued until 1817.

Dennis Edward Lucas *Hastings, East Sussex, UK*
This potter made Studio-type wares in Hastings from 1956. This incised mark was used from 1956; the words 'Hastings Pottery' may be added on wares from 1963.

Merrimac Ceramic Company/Merrimac Pottery Company
Newburyport, Massachusetts, USA
T. S. Nickerson founded Merrimac Ceramic Company in 1897 to make drainage pipe, florists' crockery and tiles. In 1902, when the business was reorganized as Merrimac Pottery, he made domestic ornamental wares and then decorative garden pottery. The ornamental wares were covered with dark dull or metallic glazes of several different colours. The most famous line was Etruscan, which copied moulded Roman Arretine ware seen in the Museum of Fine Arts, Boston. The factory continued until 1908. These marks were used.

Carter, Stabler & Adams (Ltd) *Poole, Dorset, UK*
See p116. After 1921, Carter & Co became Carter, Stabler & Adams (Ltd), better known as the famous Poole Pottery. The firm was retitled Poole Pottery Ltd from February 1963. Many printed marks in the style of this example, appear from 1950–51; the redrawn version seen here was used from 1956. Another version appears on oven tablewares produced from c1961. A more conventional-style dolphin appears as a special printed mark on individual Studio-type wares from 1963.

Plants, Flowers and Trees

De Roos *Delft, Holland*
See p43. The marks (above and centre) were among those used by this factory (The Rose), during the early 18thC. The mark (below) was registered by proprietor Dirck van der Does in 1764. Van der Does continued as proprietor until 1779, when the factory was run by Hendrick Janszoon.

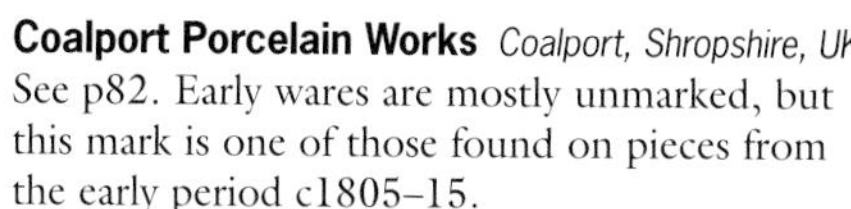

Coalport Porcelain Works *Coalport, Shropshire, UK*
See p82. Early wares are mostly unmarked, but this mark is one of those found on pieces from the early period c1805–15.

William De Morgan *London, UK*
See p120. This Sand's End address mark appears on wares produced after 1888 when the factory relocated to Fulham.

Shaw & Copestake *Longton, Staffordshire, UK*
Earthenwares were produced by this firm 1901–82. Early wares were probably unmarked. This mark appears c1925–36.

Adderley Floral China *Longton, Staffordshire, UK*
A branch of Ridgway Potteries Ltd, this pottery produced bone china figures and ornaments. This printed mark was used from 1945.

Dresden Floral Porcelain Co Ltd
Longton, Staffordshire, UK
This firm produced porcelain figures and floral wares with this printed mark 1945–56.

Grueby Faience Company/Grueby Pottery/Grueby Faience and Tile Company
Boston, Massachusetts, USA
Founded to make glazed brick and architectural tile in 1894, the company added an art pottery line during the late 1890s, producing vases with low-relief floral decoration made with rolled fillets of clay, and covered with a medium green flowing matt glaze that was sometimes accented with yellow, ochre, rose or white. The art pottery was discontinued in 1910, but tiles were made until 1920, when the firm was purchased by the C. Pardee Works of Perth Amboy, New Jersey. This characteristic mark was used, together with other name marks.

Doulton & Co (Ltd) *Lambeth, London, UK*
See p121. This printed or impressed mark was used on Persian-style wares made by Doulton c1920–28.

Lorenz Reichel *Schirnding, Bavaria, Germany*
See p222. This mark was used on porcelain services from 1902. 'Schirnding' or 'Sch' also appears.

Empire Porcelain Co Ltd *Stoke, Staffordshire, UK*
See p208. This printed or impressed mark was used from late 1940s to 1950s, and usually include month and year numbers and date of manufacture.

Britannia China Company
Longton, Staffordshire, UK
See p79. This printed mark was used on porcelains 1900–04. Other fully-named marks were used 1904–06.

Crown China Crafts Ltd *Stoke, Staffordshire, U*
Porcelain and earthenware floral wares were made by this firm at the Crown Works 1946–58. This printed mark was used. The full name of the firm appears.

Selb-Plössberg *Bavaria, Germany*
The porcelain factory at Selb-Plössberg (formerly Selb-Bahnhof) was founded by Rosenthal of Selb in 1867. Output included table and coffee services, vases, bowls, figures, lamps, candelabra and table decorations. This mark was used.

Co-operative Wholesale Society Ltd
Longton, Staffordshire, UK
See p224. This printed mark was one of those used in the 1950s and early 1960s.

Longton Pottery Co Ltd *Longton, Staffordshire, UK*
Earthenwares were made by this firm at the Bluebell Works 1946–55. This printed mark is typical of those used.

New Jersey Pottery Company
Trenton, New Jersey, USA
This pottery (active 1869–83) made cream-coloured white granite ware, plain and decorated. During the 1880 Presidential campaign, they made plates with portraits of the candidates. In 1883, the name was changed to the Union Pottery.

Pope-Gosser China Company
Coshocton, Ohio, USA
Organized by C. F Gosser from 1902, the company first made an ornamental line in a high quality translucent, highly vitrified body, but quickly changed to another form of tableware with decal decoration as its mainstay. One of the most popular patterns, made from 1935, was 'Rosepoint'. During its early years the company won a couple of awards at world's fairs. It became part of American China Corp, a co-operative of eight companies that dissolved in 1932. Pope-Gosser reorganized and continued in operation afterwards until 1958. Marks used feature the company name.

Taylor, Smith and Taylor *East Liverpool, Ohio (with a plant in Chester, West Virginia), USA*
See p105. This mark was among many used.

J. Dimmock & Co *Hanley, Staffordshire, UK*
See p206. This printed mark was one of those used c1878–1904.

Thomas Till & Son(s) *Burslem, Staffordshire, UK*
Formerly Barker, Sutton & Till (1834–43), this firm produced earthenwares at the Stych Pottery c1850–1928. Good quality earthenware services and other useful items were made with coloured bodies. They also made stoneware, jet glazed ware, terracotta, and enamelled and lustrewares. This mark was one of those used c1861.

Wedgwood & Co (Ltd) *Tunstall, Staffordshire, UK*
See p216. 'Asiatic Pheasants' was one of Wedgwood & Co's most successful printed designs and was extensively copied by other manufacturers. This mark appears from c1925.

Grossbreitenbach *Thuringia, Germany*
A factory was founded here in 1778 by Anton Friedrich Wilhelm Ernst von Hopfgarten. He sold the concern to Gotthelf Greiner, the owner of the Limbach porcelain factory in 1882. Porcelain decorated with underglaze blue was made. This clover-leaf mark was used from 1778, but after 1788 it was also used by Limbach and Ilmenau. Pieces bearing this mark after 1788 cannot be attributed definitely to Grossbreitenbach.

Ilmenau *Thuringia, Germany*
See p179. This mark has been attributed to Ilmenau while the factory was leased to Gotthelf Greiner 1788–92.

Sevenoaks Pottery Ltd *Sevenoaks, Kent*
Owned by Gordon Plahn (see p102), this pottery operated between 1958 and 1961 producing Studio-type wares. This impressed seal-type mark was used.

Karlsbader Kaolin-Industry-Gesellschaft
Merkelsgrün, Bohemia, Czech Republic
This company began in 1881, at first producing utuility ware, and later electro-porcelain. This mark is one of those used. Others also feature the clover leaf.

Carrigaline Pottery Ltd *Carrigaline, Co Cork, Eire*
Earthenwares are produced by this firm that was founded in 1928. This mark appears.

A. Bourne Claverdon *London, UK*
Operated by Alice Buxton Winnicott, this pottery operated c1947–50 making Studio-type wares. This impressed or printed mark was used.

Wade (Ulster) Ltd
Portadown, Co Armagh, Northern Ireland, UK
See p192. Many marks featuring clover were used by this firm on die-pressed wares c1955. The letter below is the potter's mark.

Cook Pottery Company *Trenton, New Jersey, USA*
See p218. 'Mellor & Co' was often incorporated into this company's marks, because F. G. Mellor was one of the original founders.

Robert Stewart (Robert Stewart Ceramics Ltd)
Paisley, Strathclyde, Scotland, UK
From 1960 this firm made earthenwares such as covered jars. This mark appears.

J. Glatz *Villingen, Baden, Germany*
This firm produced 'Majolika' wares from 1870. This mark was used.

Beddgelert Pottery *Beddgelert, Wales, UK*
Operated by Mrs A. Davey and Mrs P. Hancock, this pottery was established in 1962, producing Studio-type earthenwares. This mark was used.

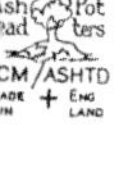

Ashtead Potters Ltd *Ashtead, Surrey, UK*
Earthenwares were produced 1926–36 at the Victoria Works in Ashstead, with this printed mark.

Arequipa Potteries *Fairfax, California, USA*
A pottery was started in 1911 by tuberculosis patients recuperating in this northern California village, who produced ware under the direction of Frederick Hurten Rhead. Albert L. Solon replaced Rhead in 1913. The output consisted primarily of vases, covered jars, jardinières and tiles, in a variety of finishes, some of which were very high quality. The factory closed c1918.

Orange Tree Pottery
Rainton Gate, North Yorkshire, UK
Studio-type wares were made by this company (owned by Mrs Alethea Short) from 1952, with this impressed or printed mark.

G. L. Ashworth & Bros (Ltd)
Hanley, Staffordshire, UK
See p204. This printed mark was used on Mason's Patent Ironstone China from 1957.

Hewitt & Leadbeater *Longton, Staffordshire, UK*
Based at the Willow Pottery, this firm produced porcelain and parian 1907–19. The company became Hewitt Brothers in 1919 and continued until c1926. This printed mark was used 1907–26.

Campbellfield Pottery Co (Ltd)
Springburn, Glasgow, Scotland, UK
This firm was established at 60 Rochester St in the 1870s and from c1884 moved to Flemington St in Springburn. Earthenwares were made until 1905. A thistle mark was used in various forms; the printed example seen here appears c1884–1905.

A. W. Buchan & Co (Ltd)
Portobello, Nr Edinburgh, Scotland, UK
The Portobello Pottery was established in 1770. It was carried on by Murray & Buchan from 1867 and by A. W. Buchan & Co from c1877. Stonewares were produced, with output including bottles, jars, jugs, spirit bottles and other items. From 1949 the printed trade name of the firm was a thistle as seen here.

Robert Heron (& Son)
Sinclairstown, Strathclyde, Scotland, UK
This firm was located at the Gallatown Pottery from 1850, with the address changing to the Fife Pottery from 1884. They produced earthenwares, Rockingham ware and 'Wemyss' ware. This printed mark appears 1920–29.

J. E. Heath Ltd *Burslem, Staffordshire, UK*
Earthenwares such as hotel wares were made by this firm at the Albert Potteries from 1951. This printed mark was one of those used.

Western Stoneware Company
Monmouth, Illinois, USA
The Western Stoneware Company was an extremely large firm created by the merger of many successful stoneware potteries in the Midwest from 1906. The Monmouth Pottery Co, Weir Pottery Co, Macomb Stoneware Co, Macomb Pottery, Whitehall Pottery Co, Fort Dodge Pottery Co and the Clinton Pottery all combined to produce utilitarian stoneware. Their mark is most frequently found on crocks, jugs, and preserve jars. The maple leaf appears in a number of marks used by the firm; this may feature the name of the firm, or 'Monmouth, USA'.

Fine Arts Porcelain Ltd *Charlton, London, UK*
Between 1948 and 1952 this company made earthenwares with this printed mark.

Buildings

Tournai *Belgium*
See p231. This early mark was used at the porcelain factory 1751–96 and may appear in blue, gold, crimson or other colours.

La Tour d'Aigues *Vaucluse, France*
Baron de Bruni established a faïence factory in La Tour d'Aigues in the mid-18thC. Bruni made an application to produce porcelain in 1773. This marks apppears on a faïence dish.

Edward Bingham *Castle Hedingham, Essex, UK*
Edward W. Bingham established his pottery in 1864, and produced earthenwares decorated with applied relief motifs and coloured glazes. As well as English wares, the pottery also made copies of German stoneware, Palissy ware, and Greek and Roman pottery. His son sold the business in 1901, after which the company became Essex Art Pottery. This applied castle mark above a scroll was used 1864–1901.

John Maddock & Sons (Ltd)
Burslem, Staffordshire, UK
Originally established in c1830 and known under a number of titles, John Maddock & Sons (Ltd) produced earthenwares and ironstone from 1855. This mark was used before 1855.

C. T. Maling & Sons (Ltd)
Newcastle-upon-Tyne, Tyne and Wear, UK
See p175. This printed mark and other variations were used 1890–1963.

New Hall Pottery Co Ltd *Hanley, Staffordshire, UK*
Formerly Plant & Gilmore, this firm based at the New Hall Works made earthenwares 1899–1956. This printed mark was used c1930–51. A similar mark appears 1951–56 in black on a white ground.

Old Hall Earthenware Co Ltd
Hanley, Staffordshire, UK
Based at the Old Hall Works in Hanley, which was built in 1770. Job Meigh started a business there that was subsequently operated by his son and his grandson (Charles Meigh). In 1861 the company became known as the Old Earthenware

BUILDINGS

Company Ltd, and after 1886 as the Old Hall Porcelain Co Ltd. It made all types of earthenware, as well as stoneware, jet ware and parian. Output comprised services of all kinds, in particular toilet services, water bottles, tea kettles, spill vases, figures, busts and other ornaments. This printed trademark was registered in 1884, and was continued by the Old Hall Porcelain Co Ltd after 1886. The word 'England' was added between c1891 and c1902, when the factory closed.

Sibley Pottery (Ltd) *Wareham, Dorset, UK*
This pottery produced earthenwares and stonewares 1922–62. This impressed mark was used 1946–53.

Slack & Brownlow *Tonbridge, Kent, UK*
Operating between c1928 and 1934, this company produced ornamental earthenwares with this printed or impressed mark.

J. Green & Co (or & Sons) *London, UK*
A London-based retailers. Porcelains distributed by this firm 1834–42 occur with this printed mark featuring St Paul's Cathedral.

T. G. Green & Co (Ltd)
Church Gresley, Derbyshire, UK
See p224. The mark (top) was first registered in 1888; the mark (bottom) represents a typical printed mark of the 1930s. As well as marks featuring a church device in a variety of forms, others feature pattern names.

William De Morgan *London, UK*
See p120. This mark relates to the period 1882–88 when De Morgan's studio was based at Merton Abbey. Marks from this period include the name.

Clignancourt *Paris, France*
Pierre Deruelle founded a porcelain factory known as Fabrique de Monsieur in 1771, and was given the protection of the brother of Louis XV. Continued by his son-in-law, the factory operated until c1798. High quality porcelain was produced, decorated by skilled artists from Vienna and Sèvres. Before 1784, factories other than Sèvres were forbidden from using gilding or polychrome decoration. This mark appears in gold or red.

Lovatt & Lovatt *Langley Mill, Nottinghamshire, UK*
Formerly Calvert & Lovatt, this factory was founded in 1895 producing stonewares and earthenwares. The name of the firm changed to Lovatt's Potteries Ltd in 1931, and was bought by J. Bourne & Son in 1959 but continued under the same name. This trademark was used c1931–62, with a revised version appearing after c1962.

Milland Pottery *Liphook, Hampshire, UK*
Run by Mr and Mrs Hawkins, this pottery made earthenwares from 1948. This printed or impressed mark appears.

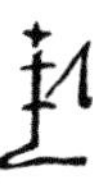

Levantino Family *Savona, Liguria, Italy*
This mark, which is believed to represent one of the beacon lights in the harbour at Genoa, has been ascribed to the Levantino family of Albissola in the late 17th and early 18thC, but has also been claimed for the town of Genoa itself.

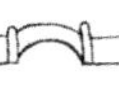

Leonard Acton *Bramber, West Sussex, UK*
Hand-made pottery and items such as animals were made by this potter from 1945. Pieces were marked with this incised outline of a bridge, sometimes accompanied by the initials 'L.A.'

Bancroft & Bennett *Burslem, Staffordshire, UK*
This firm made earthenwares, based at Newcastle Street 1946–50. This printed mark was used.

Paden City Pottery *Nr Sisterville, West Virginia, USA*
This large pottery (active 1914–63) made a variety of high quality semi-porcelain dinnerware with decal decoration that mimicked a broad style of hand painting. They also produced baking ware.

Morley Fox & Co Ltd *Fenton, Staffordshire, UK*
See p197. This mark used by Morley Fox & Co Ltd from 1938 was also used by the firm's successor William Morley & Co Ltd 1944–57.

Boats

Ann Stannard *Potbridge, Odiham, Hampshire, UK*
Studio-type pottery was produced by Ann Stannard and Marigold Austin from 1959. This basic painted mark appears.

A. E. Gray & Co Ltd *Stoke, Staffordshire, UK*
Based at the Glebe Works in Hanley c1913–33 and at Whieldon Road in Stoke 1934–61, this pottery operated 1912–61 producing earthenwares. A. E. Gray was formerly a ceramic decorator. The printed mark (above) was used 1912–30; the mark (below) was used 1934–61, and may feature the words 'England' or 'Made in England'. From 1961 this firm was known as Portmeirion Potteries Ltd.

W. T. Copeland (& Sons Ltd)
Stoke, Staffordshire, UK
See p255. This printed mark was used c1894–1910. A variety of name marks and devices were used around this time.

William Alsager Adderley (& Co)
Longton, Staffordshire, UK
See p204. This printed trademark was used 1876–1905 (and by its predecessor at the Daisy Bank Works, Hulse & Adderley 1869–75). It was also used by the firm's successor Adderleys Ltd 1906–26.

W. H. Grindley & Co (Ltd)
Tunstall, Staffordshire, UK
See p209. This printed mark appears c1936–54. Slight variations do occur.

Karl Nennzoff *Altenkunstadt, Germany*
This factory was originally established in 1933 to produce artistic porcelain. This mark and other variations occur.

F. & R. Pratt & Co (Ltd) *Fenton, Staffordshire, UK*
The Fenton Potteries were operated by F. & R. Pratt & Co from the beginning of the 19thC, producing earthenware services, and functional and ornamental items. Specialities were terracotta and a particular type of underglaze multicolour printing. Etruscan-style Wares were also made. In the 1920s the firm was taken over by the Cauldon Potteries Ltd. This early mark was used: the absence of '& Co.' indicates a date before 1840.

Furnivals (Ltd) *Cobridge, Staffordshire, UK*
See p227. This mark was used c1905–13. In 1913 the style of the firm changed to Furnivals (1913) Ltd; a similar mark was used from 1913.

Greenock Pottery *Greenock, Scotland, UK*
Established by James Stevenson in the early 19thC, this firm produced Staffordshire-type earthenwares c1820–60. This mark has been attributed to James Stevenson & Co of the Greenock Pottery, but is usually associated with Andrew Stevenson of Staffordshire.

Viking Pottery Co *Cobridge, Staffordshire, UK*
Formerly the Viking Tile Co, this firm operated 1950–64. This printed mark was one of those used.

Pots

Geoffrey Maund *Croydon, Surrey, UK*
See p89. This printed or impressed mark was used from c1961.

C. P. Sutcliffe & Co Ltd
Higher Broughton, Greater Manchester, UK
Between c1885 and 1901 this firm produced tiles bearing this printed or impressed mark.

Henry Kennedy & Sons (Ltd)
Glasgow, Scotland, UK
The Barrowfield Potteries were established by Henry Kennedy in 1866, and produced glass-lined stonewares including bottles and jars. The firm continued until 1929. This trademark was used from 1866.

William Ault *Swadlincote, Staffordshire, UK*
Born in 1841, William Ault established a pottery at Swadlincote in 1887. He produced glaze effects and impasto paintings assisted by his two daughters. Several forms made at the pottery were designed by Christopher Dresser. After 1923 the firm became Ault & Tunnicliffe (1923–37) and then Ault Potteries Ltd from 1937.

John Shaw & Sons (Longton) Ltd
Longton, Staffordshire, UK
Formerly J. Shaw & Sons, this pottery operated 1931–63. This mark was used from c1949.

Bailey Potteries Ltd *Fenton, Staffordshire, UK*
This firm produced earthenwares 1935–40. Several printed marks were used such as this.

Blue John Pottery Ltd *Hanley, Staffordshire, UK*
See p114. This printed mark was used 1947–49; a similar mark featuring a single pot and the words 'Made in England', was used from 1949.

Edwin M. Knowles China Company
East Liverpool, Ohio, USA
This pottery (active 1900–63) produced high-quality table and toilet wares in semi-porcelain and ironstone with good printed or decal decorations. The first pottery plant was in Chester, West Virginia; in 1913 they moved to Newell, West Virginia. Offices remained in East Liverpool until 1931. Knowles was the son of Isaac M. Knowles of Knowles, Taylor & Knowles (see p186)

Sterling Pottery Ltd *Fenton, Staffordshire, UK*
Formerly Sterling Pottery Co, this firm produced earthenwares 1947–53. This mark was used.

Jugtown Pottery *Jugtown, North Carolina, USA*
Established by Jacques (d1947) and Juliana Busbee in 1921 to revive the potter's art in North Carolina, the Jugtown Pottery has specialized in table and decorative ware. Traditional North Carolina shapes and glazes, were supplemented with simple forms and transmutational glazes adapted from Asian ceramics. Notable glazes are an orange glaze, and a brown glaze called 'Tobacco Spit'. This impressed mark is used. The pottery has subsequently been operated by other firms.

Holmes & Son *Longton, Staffordshire, UK*
Earthenwares were made by this firm 1898–1903 at the Clayton Pottery. This printed mark was used.

Wearside Pottery Co
Millfield, Sunderland, Tyne and Wear, UK
Previously known as the Sunderland Pottery Co Ltd, this firm made earthenwares and utility wares 1928–57 with this printed or impressed mark.

Wedgwood & Co (Ltd) *Tunstall, Staffordshire, UK*
See p216. This printed mark was used from c1951. The trade name 'Wacol' also appears in other marks.

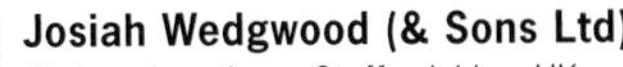

Josiah Wedgwood (& Sons Ltd)
Various locations, Staffordshire, UK
See p146. The printed mark (above) was used on porcelain from c1878, with the word 'England' added after 1891. The mark (centre) was used from c1900 onwards on Wedgwood porcelain; note the addition of three stars under the vase, which do not appear on the previous mark. The mark (below) is the version that was used by Wedgwood from 1962; the pattern name may also appear below the mark on some examples.

D.& J. Henderson/American Pottery Company *Jersey City, New Jersey, USA*
See p129. This mark was one of those used by this firm.

Wood & Son(s) (Ltd) *Burslem, Staffordshire, UK*
See p216. This mark was used from c1917. A similar later version, with a description of the type of ware underneath, was used from c1960.

Arij de Milde *Delft, Holland*
See p254. This mark was also used by this potter c1680–1708.

Figures

Bates Elliot & Co *Burslem, Staffordshire, UK*
Founded 1870, this pottery produced earthenwares, porcelain and other wares at the Dale Hall Works. In 1875 the company became Bates Walker & Co. This staple trademark was used and was continued by the firm's successors, including Gildea & Walker (1881–85) and James Gildea (1885–88).

Pisgah Forest Pottery/Stephen Pottery
Pisgah Forest, North Carolina, USA
Walter Stephen began making pottery in 1901, and started a new venture in Pisgah Forest in 1926. Vases, tea wares, candlesticks and bowls were decorated with scenes of covered wagons, buffalo hunts etc or with overall Persian blue or silvery blue crystalline glazes. The company name was Stephen Pottery for a few years in the 1940s. The factory continues today. A few pieces are incised with the names 'Pisgah Forest' or 'Stephen'.

Sèvres *France*
See p82. This mark was used on paste invented by the great ceramicist Théodore Deck who was director of the factory 1887–91. It appears in relief or printed in underglaze brown.

Fulper Pottery *Flemington, New Jersey, USA*
See p124. This mark also appears. The date 1805 seen on this mark was used by the factory as a starting date although this is not universally agreed.

A. E. Hull Pottery *Crooksville, Ohio, USA*
Organized by Addis E. Hull from 1905, the company has made stoneware vessels and much relief-moulded white kitchen ware, including covered storage jars (called cereal sets), tea and coffee sets, candlesticks, florists' crockery, bowls, jugs, biscuit jars, smoking sets and some ornamental wares such as figures and vases. The firm was reorganized in 1952 after a disastrous fire. This mark appears in many forms, such as impressed marks or paper labels. Several written marks featuring the name 'Hull' were also used.

Pearson & Co *Chesterfield, Derbyshire, UK*
Established c1805, this company made stonewares and earthenwares. This impressed or printed mark was used from 1880. The name changed c1925 to Pearson & Co (Chesterfield Ltd). This mark has also been used as a trademark since 1945 with the addition of the words 'Pearsons of Chesterfield' and 'Made in England'.

Britannia Pottery Co Ltd *Glasgow, Scotland, UK*
Operating 1920–35, formerly known as Cochran & Fleming (1896–1920), this firm made earthenwares marked with the figure of Britannia 1920–35. The mark may also feature the initials 'B. P. Co. Ltd.' and 'Made in Scotland'.

Dudson, Wilcox & Till Ltd *Hanley, Staffordshire, UK*
Earthenwares were made by this firm 1902–26 at the Britannic Works, with a printed or impressed Britannia mark such as this example.

Samuel Johnson Ltd *Burslem, Staffordshire, UK*
Based at the Hill Pottery (later the Britannia Pottery), this firm operated between 1887 and 1931. This printed mark was used c1916–31.

Powell, Bishop & Stonier *Hanley, Staffordshire, UK*
From 1878, this company (previously Powell & Bishop), produced a wide range of products at various locations in Hanley, including earthenware (Stafford Street Works), white granite (Church Works) and porcelain (Waterloo Works). Notable was their 'Oriental Ivory' or cream-coloured ware. This mark was used by Powell, Bishop & Stonier 1878–91, and their successors Bishop & Stonier 1891–1939, sometimes with the word 'Bisto' underneath.

Crown Staffordshire Porcelain Co Ltd
Fenton, Staffordshire, UK
See p207. This printed mark was used from 1930. Other examples were used for special patterns on wares, all featuring the words 'Crown Staffordshire'.

Biltons (1912) Ltd *Stoke, Staffordshire, UK*
See p114. This printed mark was used from 1912. Other marks feature the name of the firm without a device.

Lonhuda Pottery Company *Steubenville, Ohio, USA*
See p97. This mark was used. This mark of a Native American head may also appear as a silhouette.

Globes

Edwin Bennett Pottery *Baltimore, Maryland, USA*
See p113. Most of the marks used by this firm feature the name 'Bennett' or the initials 'E. B.' Decorator marks, usually in the form of monograms, may also appear.

George Clews & Co (Ltd) *Tunstall, Staffordshire, UK*
Operating 1906–61, this pottery produced earthenwares at the Brownhills Pottery. A globe mark was used by the firm from 1906, with this example appearing from 1935.

Globe Pottery Co Ltd
Cobridge and Shelton, Staffordshire, UK
Established in 1914, this pottery produced earthenwares at Shelton from c1934. This printed mark was used from 1917. Some marks feature a figure holding the globe.

Thomas Goode & Co Ltd *London, UK*
See p209. The mark seen here was also used by this firm of retailers.

Grimwades Ltd *Stoke, Staffordshire, UK*
See p215. A number of globe marks were used from 1906, with this example appearing from c1930. Other globe marks may appear beneath a crown, and may feature a sash and pattern name.

W. H. Grindley & Co (Ltd) *Tunstall, Staffordshire, UK*
See p209. This printed mark was used from 1925, but globe marks in various forms were used from c1880. These earlier marks may feature a ship above the globe.

James Kent (Ltd) *Longton, Staffordshire, UK*
Porcelain and earthenwares were produced by this firm at the Old Foley Pottery from 1897. Several printed marks were used, including some featuring a globe. These first appeared in c1910; this example is from c1950.

Locke & Co *Worcester, Hereford and Worcester, UK*
Porcelain was produced here 1896–1914, before this company based at the Shrub Hill Works was taken over by the Worcester Royal Porcelain Co Ltd. This printed mark was used c1898–1902. A similar mark was used after 1902, with the word 'Ltd' added to the style.

Alfred Meakin (Ltd) *Tunstall, Staffordshire, UK*
See p211. This globe-type mark was used c1875–97. After 1897 'Ltd' was added to the style of the firm.

Minton *Stoke, Staffordshire, UK*
See p174. The standard printed globe trademark first appeared in c1863. This example was used c1863–72. A revised version with a crown, and the letter 'S' added to the company name was used from c1873, with 'England' added below from 1891. 'Made in England' appears c1902–11. From c1912 the mark featured a wreath.

Moore (Bros) *Longton, Staffordshire, UK*
See p157. This printed mark was used from c1880, with 'England' added from c1891. An earlier mark features 'Moore' printed or impressed.

J. Mortlock/Mortlock Ltd *London, UK*
This leading firm of 19thC retailers was established in 1746 and stopped trading in c1930. This printed trademark was first registered in 1877. Marks used by this firm often also include the name of the manufacturer.

Wheeling Pottery Company/Wheeling Potteries Company *Wheeling, West Virginia, USA*
This company (active 1879–1910) was organized to produce plain and decorated white granite table and toilet wares. In 1889, several potteries were consolidated under the Wheeling Potteries Company, each making a different type of ware including utilitarian pottery, semi-porcelain, sanitary ware and art ware, including highly-decorated faïence. A large concern, by 1904 the firm was employing about 1,200 people. The company was reorganized as the Wheeling Sanitary Manufacturing Company in 1910. Many different marks were used, including a number of variations of the globe mark seen here.

Thomas Till & Son(s) *Burslem, Staffordshire, UK*
See p259. Many forms of globe mark were used by this firm, including this example which appeared from c1919. Other feature the name 'Thos. Till & Sons' or 'Till & Sons'.

Arthur Wood & Son (Longport) Ltd
Longport, Staffordshire, UK
Established in 1928, this firm produced earthenwares at the Bradwell Works. Several globe marks appear, including this one from c1934.

William Brownfield (& Son(s))
Cobridge, Staffordshire, UK
This company produced earthenware 1850–91, with porcelain after 1871. It later became Brownfields Guild Pottery Society Ltd (1891–98) and Brownfields Pottery Ltd (c1898–1900). This printed mark was used 1871–91. A similar double globe mark was used 1891–1900.

Clementson Bros (Ltd) *Hanley, Staffordshire, UK*
See p206. This printed double globe mark appears 1901–13. The marks used by this firm all feature the name 'Clementson Bros', with the addition of 'Ltd' after 1910.

David Chapman & Sons *Longton, Staffordshire, UK*
Based at the Atlas Works from 1889, this pottery produced porcelain. This printed mark was used with or without the word 'Longton' underneath. A similar mark was used by this firm's successor the Atlas China Co Ltd 1906–10, with the words 'Atlas China'.

Hawley Bros (Ltd) *Rotherham, South Yorkshire, UK*
Established in 1868, this firm made earthenwares. This trademark was registered in 1898 and is printed on wares. The same mark was continued by the Northfield Pottery Co until c1919.

Bells

J. & M. P. Bell & Co (Ltd) *Glasgow, Scotland, UK*
This firm established the Glasgow Pottery in 1842, making high quality white and printed earthenware. Later, porcelain, white and pearl granite ware and decorated sanitary ware were also made. A bell mark appeared from 1881, and may appear within a garter mark. The factory continued until 1928.

Belle Vue Pottery *Hull, Humberside, UK*
This factory was started c1802 by two potters named Smith from Hull and Job Ridgway of Shelton. In 1826 the works were taken by William Bell who produced cream, white, blue-printed, and green-glazed wares principally for export until 1841. This mark was used c1826–41 and may also appear without the factory name.

Wings

Red Wing Stoneware *Red Wing, Minnesota, USA*
See p139. This mark was one of those used.

Powell & Bishop *Hanley, Staffordshire, UK*
Previously Livesley Powell & Co, this firm was known under this title 1867–78, before becoming Powell, Bishop & Stonier (see p271). This caduceus was registered as a trademark in 1876. A similar mark was also used by their successors, Bishop & Stonier (Ltd) (1891–1939), and may feature 'Bisto' or 'Bishop England'.

Winkle & Wood *Hanley, Staffordshire, UK*
Operating 1885–90, this pottery used this printed mark. The firm subsequently became F. Winkle & Co (1890–1931).

R. H. & S. L. Plant (Ltd) *Longton, Staffordshire, UK*
Formerly R. H. Plant (1881–98), this firm was based at the Tuscan Works, producing a wide range of porcelain. The trade name 'Tuscan' was incorporated into many marks from c1907.

Villeroy & Boch *Septfontaines, Luxembourg*
This firm was originally started c1766 by three brothers Jean-François, Dominique and Pierre-Joseph Boch. Jean-François became sole proprietor in 1795. White and cream-coloured earthenwares were made usually with blue painted or printed Chinese-style landscapes. Plaques were made from 1784. In 1836, the Boch family merged with the Villeroy family who founded the factories at Frauenberg (1760), Wallerfangen (1789) and Schramberg (1820), and they went on to establish a works at Mettlach in Germany in 1842. This mark appears at Septfontaines and Mettlach.

Miscellaneous

Chantilly *Oise, France*
See p200. This mark usually appears in red enamel and occasionally black for the early period, underglaze blue and sometimes crimson for the later period. Other colours occasionally occur.

Hornsea Pottery Co Ltd *Hornsea, Humberside, UK*
Based at the Edenfield Works, this pottery produced earthenwares from c1951. This printed mark was used from 1951.

Joseph Bourne & Son Ltd *Denby, Derbyshire, UK*
The works at Denby were started in 1809 by a Mr Jager. In 1812 Joseph Bourne, son of potter William Bourne, took over and made stoneware items such as bottles, for which he won a medal in 1851. Footwarmers, pestles and mortars, pie moulds and medical appliances were also made. The trade name Denby appears in many marks, including thisone from c1895.

Thomas Lawrence (Longton) Ltd
Longton, Staffordshire, UK
Based at the Falcon Works (1897–1957) and the Sylvan Works (from 1957), this pottery produced earthenwares from 1892. It was originally established at Trent Bridge Pottery in Stoke. Early wares were unmarked. This printed or impressed mark appears from 1947. Other marks feature the tradename Falcon Ware.

J. H. Baum *Wellsville, Ohio, USA*
Baum (active 1880–97) made white granite and cream-coloured earthenware table and toilet wares.

Het Bijltje *Delft, Holland*
This factory ('The Hatchet') was first recorded as owned by B. van Houten and Jacob Wemmertz Hoppesteyn. Justus Brouwer, proprietor 1739–75, registered this mark in 1764.

Cafaggiolo *Nr Florence, Tuscany, Italy*
See p105. This trident mark has been attributed to Cafaggiolo.

J. B. Owens Pottery Company *Zanesville, Ohio, USA*
Owens (active 1896–1907) built and operated several potteries during his life, but this one featured art wares that were designed, made and decorated by leading potters, chemists and decorators. Overall the work was derivative, with many references to the pottery produced at Rookwood (see p102), but Owens' ware won gold medals in at least one international fair.

Basing Farm Pottery *Ashington, West Sussex, UK*
See p33. This seal-type mark was used at this pottery from 1962.

The Royal Factory *Copenhagen, Denmark*
See p213. The 'wave mark' (above) was adopted by the factory in 1775, and appears in underglaze blue. The vertical wave mark (below) is found on figures.

Leslie G. Davie *Rye, East Sussex, UK*
Located at The Needles Studio, this potter made Studio-type ware 1954–62. This Needles mark was used; major pieces were signed and dated.

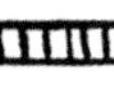

Josiah Spode *Stoke, Staffordshire, UK*
See p233. This workman's mark appears on some early porcelains c1790–1805. A similar mark also appears on Coalport porcelains from c1810 to 1820.

Alpha Potteries *Sidcup, Kent, UK*
See p111. This incised mark was used 1954–58. This symbol was also used in an impressed seal-mark 1954–58.

Roger Fry *London, UK*
Tin-glazed earthenwares were made at the Omega Workshops c1913–19. This impressed or incised mark appears.

Chelsea Pottery *London, UK*
Earthenwares were produced at this pottery from 1952. This impressed or incised Chelsea Pottery mark appears, sometimes with the words 'Chelsea Pottery. Hand Made in England'.

Saint-Cloud *Seine-et-Oise, France*
See p70. This 'sun-face' mark appears, always blue in colour.

Girolamo Salomini *Savona, Liguria, Italy*
This potter and his family were active in Savona in the 17th and 18thC. This mark has been attributed to Salomini.

Tooth & Co *Woodville, Derbyshire, UK*
See p93. This trademark was registered by Tooth & Co in 1884. The word 'England' was added after 1891. 'Made in England' appears on 20thC examples.

A. B. Jones & Sons (Ltd) *Longton, Staffordshire, UK*
Based at the Grafton Works and other addresses, this firm made general ceramics 1900–72. Many marks were used, including this one that appears from c1913. The company became Royal Grafton Bone China Ltd.

Ott and Brewer/Etruria Pottery
Trenton, New Jersey, USA
See p159. This mark was also used, and features both the company name and the name 'Trenton'.

Staffordshire-type Marks

Detail of Crown Staffordshire mark, 1930s

Royal Arms

The British Royal Arms have been the basis for many printed or impressed marks used by several 19th- and 20th-century British, and some overseas manufacturers.

For British makers, the form of this mark can act as a guide to dating: those engraved after 1837 feature the quartered shield (see below right), but pre-1837 arms have an extra shield (inescutcheon) in the centre (see below left). From 1801 to 1814 the inescutcheon is capped; 1814–37 the inescutcheon is crowned.

For the factories and makers below, the Royal Arms appear with the following wording:

A.C.CO.
Akron China Company *Akron, Ohio, USA*
See p77. These initials appear on their coat-of-arms, with the words 'Extra Quality Ironstone China Warranted'.

A.C.CO.
American Crockery Company *Trenton, New Jersey, USA*
The pottery (active 1876–99) made white granite table and toilet ware with printed decoration. These initials were used, together with 'Iron Stone China'.

ADAMS/TUNSTALL/ENGLAND
William Adams & Sons (Potters) Ltd
Tunstall and Stoke, Staffordshire, UK
See p204. This mark WAS used 1890–1914. 'Tunstall' was added after 1896.

W. & T. ADAMS
William & Thomas Adams *Tunstall, Staffordshire, UK*
Based at Greenfields, this firm (1866–92) produced earthenware. This name mark appears with the Royal Arms. Other emblems were used with the name in full.

SAML. ALCOCK & CO.
Samuel Alcock & Co *Cobridge and Burslem, Staffordshire, UK*
Active c1828–59, based first in Cobridge (c1828–53), and at the Hill Pottery, Burslem (c1830–59). Wares included porcelain, parian and fine earthenwares. Noted for fine and durable semi-porcelain. Sometimes used a version of the Royal Arms with the name of the firm or initials below.

A. & M.
Alpaugh and Magowan *Trenton, New Jersey, USA*
The Empire Pottery was purchased by Alpaugh and Magowan (active 1884–92) from Coxon & Company (see p248) and made thin porcelain dinner, tea and toilet wares and decorated white granite wares. In 1892, they became part of the Trenton Potteries Company (see p72).

AP (IN MONOGRAM)
Anchor Pottery *Trenton, New Jersey, USA*
See p228. This firm also used a coat-of-arms with an 'AP' monogram, and the words 'Iron Stone China Warranted'.

ASHWORTH
G. L. Ashworth & Bros (Ltd) *Hanley, Staffordshire, UK*
See p204. The Royal Arms were used on earthenwares from 1862 usually with the name 'Ashworth'.

B.B./BURFORD BROS
Burford Brothers *East Liverpool, Ohio, USA*
See p173. These initials and the firm name appears on the mark together with 'Iron Stone China' and 'Warranted'.

BIRKS BROS. & SEDDON
Birks Brothers & Seddon *Cobridge, Staffordshire*
This firm made ironstone wares 1877–86; the mark features their name.

BROWN-WESTHEAD, MOORE & CO
Brown-Westhead, Moore & Co *Hanley, Staffordshire, UK*
See p165. This printed mark was used from 1890. Slight variations of the wording occur.

HENRY BURGESS
Henry Burgess *Burslem, Staffordshire, UK*
Formerly T. & R. Boote, this firm was active 1864–92, producing earthenwares. The Royal Arms were used, with the name or initials of the firm below.

CLEMENTSON BROS.
Clementson Bro. (Ltd) *Hanley, Staffordshire, UK*
See p206. This mark was used 1867–80.

R. COCHRAN & CO
R. Cochran & Co *Glasgow, Scotland, UK*
Based at the Verreville Pottery (and the Britannia Pottery to 1896), this firm was active 1846–1918. Earthenwares, stonewares and porcelain (until 1846) were produced. The Royal Arms was one of the marks used.

COCHRAN & FLEMING

Cochran & Fleming *Glasgow, Scotland, UK*

Based at the Britannia Pottery in St Rollox established by Robert Cochran in 1857 and run by him until 1896, this firm was established by Alexander Cochran (son of Robert) and James Fleming in 1896. All types of earthenware were made for the home and export markets. In 1920 the firm became the Britannia Pottery Co.

COCKSON & SEDDON

Cockson & Seddon *Cobridge, Staffordshire, UK*

Known by this name 1875–77, this firm became Birk Bros & Seddon. A printed Royal Arms mark was used.

C.P.CO. (IN MONOGRAM)

Cook Pottery Company *Trenton, New Jersey, USA*

See p218. The Royal Arms were used with 'CPCo' monogram in the centre of the shield, and may also feature the name 'Mellor & Co' after F. G. Mellor, one of the original founders.

C.P.CO. (IN MONOGRAM)

Crown Pottery Company *Evansville, Indiana, USA*

See p212. This mark was used with the words 'Iron Stone China Warranted'.

D.D./DALE AND DAVIS

Dale and Davis *Trenton, New Jersey, USA*

Based at the Prospect Hill Pottery 1880–94, making decorated semi-porcelain and white granite table and toilet wares. Isaac Davis had previously had his business and had also worked for John Moses at the Glasgow Pottery (see p186). His souvenirs of the 1876 Centennial Exhibition with views of the buildings are attractive.

DRESDEN

Dresden Pottery Works *East Liverpool, Ohio, USA*

Originally Brunt, Bloor, Martin and Co, Dresden Pottery Works (active 1875–1927) became part of the Potter's Co-operative Co in 1882 under H. A. McNicol. The Dresden Pottery Co owned the works in its last two years, making award-winning white granite table and toilet wares, cuspidors, toys and hotel ware in 1876. The nature of the body improved over the years and decal decorations were added, but the character remained much the same.

E.L.P. CO.

East Liverpool Pottery Company *East Liverpool, Ohio, USA*

See p87. These initials appear with 'Ironstone China'.

ELSMORE & FORSTER

Elsmore & Forster *Tunstall, Staffordshire, UK*

Earthenwares, parian and other wares were made 1853–71. Variations of the Royal Arms mark appear with the firm on a ribbon below. They became Elsmore & Son (1872–87).

EC. & CO.

Ford, Challinor & Co/Ford and Challinor
Tunstall, Staffordshire, UK

Earthenwares were made at the Lion Works 1865–80. These initials appear with the Royal Arms and a number of other marks 1865–80.

T. FURNIVAL & SONS

Thomas Furnival & Sons *Cobridge, Staffordshire, UK*

See p227. Known by this title 1871–90, the firm used a Royal Arms mark with the name of the firm c1881–90. Variations do occur.

HB

Henry Burgess *Burslem, Staffordshire, UK*

See p280. The firm's initials also appear with the Royal Arms.

H. & D.

Hallam & Day *Longton, Staffordshire, UK*

Formerly Hallam & Johnson, this firm produced earthenwares 1880–85 at the Mount Pleasant Works. These initials appear with the Royal Arms and other marks.

C. & W.K. HARVEY

C. & W. K. Harvey *Longton, Staffordshire, UK*

Based in Longton, this firm produced earthenwares, porcelain and other wares 1835–53 The Royal Arms with initials and name was used.

JC (IN MONOGRAM)

New York City Pottery *New York, New York, USA*

See p136. This monogram appears within the mark with 'Trade Mark' and 'Stone China'.

J.& T.F

Jacob & Thomas Furnival *Hanley, Staffordshire, UK*

Based at Miles Bank, this firm produced earthenwares c1843. In c1844 they became Thomas Furnival & Co. These initials occur with the Royal Arms.

JOHNSON BROS

Johnson Bros (Hanley) Ltd *Hanley, Staffordshire, UK*

See p210. The Royal Arms was used with 'Johnson Bros.'

J.R. & CO.

John Ridgway (& Co) *Hanley, Staffordshire, UK*
Formerly J. & W. Ridgway (1814–c1830), John Ridgway ran the Cauldon Place Works until 1855, when it became J. Ridgway, Bates & Co and then Brown-Westhead, Moore & Co 1858–61. Fine quality porcelains and earthenwares were produced, including a 'Stone China' body. Many variations of the Royal Arms occur, with or without the initials 'J. R.' or 'J. R. & Co', or the name of the firm in full.

JAMES KENT

James Kent (Ltd) *Longton, Staffordshire, UK*
See p272. The Royal Arms mark was used, also featuring 'Royal Semi China' above the mark, 1897–1915.

L.B.B. & CO.

L. B. Beerbower *Elizabeth, New Jersey, USA*
See p239. A coat-of-arms was used with these initials and 'Warranted Stone China'.

JOHN MATTHEWS/LATE PHILLIPS

John Matthews *Weston-Super-Mare, Avon, UK*
Formerly C. Phillips, this firm made terracotta and other wares 1870–88. An impressed Royal Arms mark with this factory name was used. The firm later became C. G. Warne.

ALFRED MEAKIN LTD.

Alfred Meakin (Ltd) *Tunstall, Staffordshire, UK*
See p211. A Royal Arms mark was used from c1897. Early versions occur without 'Ltd.'

CHARLES MEAKIN

Charles Meakin *Hanley, Staffordshire, UK*
Based at the Eastwood Pottery (previously at Burslem 1870–82), this firm made earthenwares 1883–89. A printed Royal Arms mark was used 1870–89; 'Hanley' was added 1883–89.

H. MEAKIN

Henry Meakin *Cobridge, Staffordshire, UK*
Earthenwares were made at the Abbey Pottery 1873–76. Many printed marks with this name were used including the Royal Arms. Other 'H. Meakins' were operating in Staffordshire during this period.

J. & G. MEAKIN

J. & G. Meakin *Hanley, Staffordshire, UK*
The Royal Arms were used in many of this firm's marks. The word 'England' was added from c1890.

MEIGH'S CHINA

Charles Meigh & Son *Hanley, Staffordshire, UK*

Based at the Old Hall Pottery, (formerly C. Meigh, Son & Pankhurst 1850–51) this firm produced earthenwares 1851–61 including white and blue-printed wares, stoneware, jetware and parian. Several marks including the Royal Arms occur with the name Meigh, Meigh's or C. Meigh & Son. The firm became Old Hall Earthenware Co Ltd in 1861 (see p263).

MELLOR & CO.

Cook Pottery Company *Trenton, New Jersey, USA*

See p218. The designation Mellor & Co was frequently used by the Cook Pottery Company.

MELLOR TAYLOR & CO.

Mellor, Taylor & Co *Burslem, Staffordshire, UK*

See p211. A printed or impressed Royal Arms mark was one of those used 1880–1904.

MORLEY & ASHWORTH

Morley & Ashworth *Hanley, Staffordshire, UK*

Formerly F. Morley & Co (see p211). Operating 1859–62, this firm made earthenwares, ironstones and other wares. It became G. L. Ashworth & Bros 1862–1968 (see p204).

P. & CO. LTD.

Pounty & Co. (Ltd) *Bristol, Avon, UK*

See p115. A printed Royal Arms mark was used from c1889 with these initials and 'Bristol Semi Porcelain'.

PARAGON

Paragon China (Co) Ltd *Longton, Staffordshire, UK*

Fomerly the Star China Co (1900–19), this firm made porcelain at the Atlas Works, Longton from 1920. 'Paragon' appears on a number of Royal Arms marks. The same mark was also used by the Star China Co. The firm was taken over by T. C. Wild & Sons Ltd. in 1960 but continued under the same title.

J. L. PASMANTIER AND SONS

Sterling China Company *East Liverpool, Ohio, USA*

See p147. A coat-of-arms with the name under was used.

PINDER BOURNE & CO.

Pinder, Bourne & Co *Burslem, Staffordshire, UK*

See p234. The Royal Arms was used by Pinder, Bourne & Co 1862–82. 'Burslem Staffordshire' appears beneath the Royal Arms.

P.P.COY. L.
Plymouth Pottery Co *Plymouth, Devon, UK*
Active 1856–63, this firm produced blue-printed earthenwares. These initials appear with the Royal Arms. It is important to note that other firms existed with the same initials, and could have used this mark.

F. PRIMAVESI
F. Primavesi (& Son) *Cardiff and Swansea, Wales, UK*
This firm of retailers operated c1850–1915. The mark includes the words '& Son' after c1860.

R. & M./RIDGWAY & MORLEY
Ridgway & Morley *Hanley, Staffordshire, UK*
This firm produced earthenwares at the Broad Street Works in Shelton 1842–44. Many marks occur including the Royal Arms with this name or initials.

RIDGWAYS, BEDFORD WORKS
Ridgways (Bedford Works) Ltd *Hanley, Staffordshire, UK*
See p212. The firm operated under this title 1920–52. One of the marks used was the Royal Arms.

ROYAL BAYREUTH/BAVARIA
Porzellanfabrik Tettau *Tettau, Franconia, Germany*
See p45. This factory used a version of the Royal Arms with the initial 'T' on a shield in the centre.

ROYAL IRONSTONE CHINA/WARRANTED
East End Pottery Company *East Liverpool, Ohio, USA*
This pottery (active 1894–1908) made white granite and semi-porcelain dinner and toilet ware. They were part of the East Liverpool Potteries Co 1900–03, but by 1905 it was operating independently as East End China Co. The name was changed to Trenle China Co in 1909.

ROYAL IRONSTONE CHINA/WARRANTED/ STAR DEVICE
Wheeling Pottery Company/Wheeling Potteries Company *Wheeling, West Virginia, USA*
See p273. This mark was one of those used.

R. & T.
Jersey City Pottery *Jersey City, New Jersey, USA*
See p129. This mark with the initials of the proprietors.

S.A.& CO.
Samuel Alcock & Co *Cobridge and Burslem, Staffordshire, UK*
See p279. These initials were used.

S.P. CO.
Steubenville Pottery Company *Steubenville, Ohio, USA*
See p194. These initials appear within a coat-of-arms. Another arms mark was used with 'Royal Ironstone China Warranted'.

STONE CHINA
Hicks, Meigh & Johnson *Shelton, Staffordshire, UK*
See p203. Both this firm and its predecessor, Hicks & Meigh, used a Royal Arms mark and 'Stone China' only, and a number printed below. The pattern name may also appear. The mark used by Hicks & Meigh (c1806–22) was more detailed than that used by Hicks, Meigh & Johnson (1822–35). On wares made by Hicks & Meigh, the mark varies in size and on large pieces may be over 3in (7.6cm).

SWINNERTONS
Swinnerton's Ltd *Hanley, Staffordshire, UK*
Earthenwares were produced here 1906–70. Many marks were used including the Royal Arms.

T.P.C. CO.
Dresden Pottery Works *East Liverpool, Ohio, USA*
See p281. These initials were used in the mark.

TURNER'S
G. W. Turner & Sons *Tunstall, Staffordshire, UK*
Formerly Turner & Tomkinson (see p73), earthenwares were made by this firm 1873–95. A Royal Arms printed mark was used 1891–95.

U.P.CO. IN MONOGRAM
Union Co-operative Pottery Company/Union Potteries Company *East Liverpool, Ohio, USA*
See p107. This mark was one of those used.

A.J. WILKINSON LTD.
Arthur J. Wilkinson (Ltd) *Burslem, Staffordshire, UK*
See p216. Royal Arms were used. 'Ltd' does not appear before c1896. 'Royal Ironstone China' was also used.

W.M.CO.
Willets Manufacturing Company *Trenton, New Jersey, USA*
See p108. This mark appears.

WOOD & SONS LTD.
Wood & Son(s) (Ltd) *Burslem, Staffordshire, UK*
See p216. The Royal Arms was one of the marks used by this firm, and appears from c1910.

WOOD, SON & CO.

Wood, Son & Co *Cobridge, Staffordshire, UK*
Earthenwares and ironstones were produced 1869–79, when it became known as W. E. Cartlidge. This name mark appears below the Royal Arms.

WYS

William Young & Sons/William Young's Sons
Trenton, New Jersey, USA
Based at the Excelsior Pottery Works, this firm (1857–79) made white household crockery as well as porcelain hardware trimmings. A few porcelain pitchers were made with ivy in relief overall. When William Young retired in 1870, his sons continued the pottery, eventually selling the works to the Willets Manufacturing Company.

Garter Marks

Garter marks appear with or without a crown, and many variations occur in the 19thC on pieces made in Britain, France and Europe. A firm's initials or name may occur in the centre or in the border of the mark.

GEBRUDER BENEDIKT/MAYERHÖFEN

Benedikt Brothers *Meierhöfen, Bohemia, Czech Republic*
See p238. This mark was used.

C. & H.

Cockson & Harding *Shelton, Staffordshire, UK*
Based at the New Hall Works in Shelton, this company produced earthenwares 1856–62, before becoming known as W. & J. Harding. A garter featuring the pattern name and the firm's initials is a typical example.

A.B. DANIELL & SON

A. B. & R. P. Daniel *London, UK*
Known under a variety of different names, this firm of retailers operated c1825–1917. Wares were made for the firm by Coalport and others. A garter mark was used, and features the name and the address of the firm.

DERBY

Derby Porcelain Works *Derbyshire, UK*

See p161. Garter marks were used by workmen and artists at the King Street Works, c1849–61. These are distinguished by the words 'Derby' and 'Late Bloor'.

F. & C.

Ford, Challinor & Co/Ford and Challinor
Tunstall, Staffordshire, UK

See p282. A garter mark featuring the initials F. & C. or F. C. was one of those used 1865–80.

F. & R.

Ford & Riley *Burslem, Staffordshire, UK*

See p190. The garter mark was one of those used 1882–93.

H. & B.

Heath & Blackhurst/Heath, Blackhurst & Co
Burslem, Staffordshire, UK

Earthenwares produced 1859–77 with many different marks with these initials. A garter-shaped mark was favoured.

CHARLES HOBSON

Charles Hobson (& Son) *Burslem, Staffordshire, UK*

This firm produced earthenwares 1865–80. The name of the firm appears in full on a garter-shaped mark on a design registered in 1883.

K. & B.

Knapper & Blackhurst
Tunstall and Burslem, Staffordshire, UK

This firm produced earthenwares at the Boston Works 1867–71, and at Dale Hall 1883–88. These initials may have been used by other manufacturers.

W. & R. MEIGH

W. & R. Meigh *Stoke, Staffordshire, UK*

This firm produced earthenwares at the Bridge Bank Works 1894–99. They then changed to F. Hancock & Co. A printed garter-shaped mark was used 1894–99.

M. & CO. (IN MONOGRAM)

Minton *Stoke, Staffordshire, UK*

See p174. A garter-shaped mark was used c1841–73 while known as Minton & Co. Many other marks were used.

P. B. & CO.

Pinder, Bourne & Co *Burslem, Staffordshire, UK*

See p234. A garter-shaped mark was used by this firm.

S.B. & S.
Samuel Barker & Son *Swinton, Yorkshire, UK*
Earthenwares were produced by this firm at the Don Pottery 1834–93. A garter mark surrounding a lion occurs c1851–93, and may also include the name 'Don Pottery'; '& Son' or '& S ' appears on all marks from 1851.

T.I. & J.E.
Thomas, Isaac & James Emberton *Tunstall, Staffordshire, UK*
Based at the Highgate Pottery, this firm produced earthenwares 1869–82. A printed garter-shaped mark was used with the initials shown above.

T.M. & S.
Thomas Maddock & Sons *Trenton, New Jersey, USA*
Thomas Maddock had an interest in Astbury and Maddock which preceded this company and made only sanitary ware. Maddock and Sons, 1882–1929, added white earthenware tableware. A third Maddock pottery, John Maddock and Sons, made only sanitary ware.

T.N. & CO.
Thomas Nicholson & Co *Castleford, Yorkshire, UK*
Earthenwares were produced c1854–71. A garter-shaped mark was one of those used, with these initials.

T.R. & CO
T. Rathbone & Co *Tunstall, Staffordshire, UK*
See p188. A crowned garter-shaped mark was used from c1898. These initials were also used earlier by Thomas Rathbone & Co of Portobello, Scotland.

T.T.CO. (IN MONOGRAM)
Taylor, Tunnicliffe & Co *Hanley, Staffordshire, UK*
See p162. Garter-type marks and other marks featuring this monogram were used c1875–98.

T.W. & S.
Thomas Wood & Sons *Burslem, Staffordshire, UK*
Earthenwares were made by this firm at the Queen Street Pottery 1896–97. These initials were found on many marks, including garter-type examples.

VICTORIA
Blakeney Art Pottery *Stoke, Staffordshire, UK*
This pottery, run by M. J. Bailey and S. K. Bailey, made earthenwares from 1968. Output included 'Flow Blue Victoria' printed ware, Staffordshire figures and floral art containers. A printed backstamp with this name was used.

Staffordshire Knot Marks

Many 19thC British printed marks are based on the Staffordshire knot. The mark appears often with the maker's initials or names inside the segments of the knot.

The firms detailed below used the knot mark as one of their principal devices, although their names and initials may also appear within other marks. The title of the firm is preceded by the wording that appears on the mark.

AJM
Arthur J. Mountford *Burslem, Staffordshire, UK*
From 1897 to 1901 earthenwares were made by this potter at the Salisbury works bearing this printed mark.

B & CO.
Bodley & Co *Burslem, Staffordshire, UK*
Based at the Scotia Pottery in 1865, this company produced earthenwares with these initials.

B&H
Bodley & Harrold *Burslem, Staffordshire, UK*
Also based at the Scotia Pottery (see above) 1863–65.

BSA
Burslem School of Art *Burslem, Staffordshire, UK*
Pottery figures, groups and similar wares were made 1935–41, marked with initials and sometimes the instructor (William Ruscoe), or a pupil, and the date.

E.B. & CO.
E. Brain & Co Ltd *Fenton, Staffordshire, UK*
See p247. A printed Staffordshire knot mark with the date 1850 and 'Foley China' was used from 1903.

G&B
Goodwin & Bullock *Longton, Staffordshire, UK*
Based at the Dresden Works 1852–58 (and 1858 at High Street, Longton) this firm produced porcelain.

GFB
George Frederick Bowers (& Co) *Tunstall, Staffordshire, UK*
Porcelain and earthenware was made 1842–68 at the Brownhills Works. These initials appear inside the knot.

H.A. & CO.

H. Aynsley & Co (Ltd) *Longton, Staffordshire, UK*
This firm, active from 1873 at the Commerce Works, produced lustre, Egyptian Black, turquoise and painted ware, and stoneware mortars. The name and initials of the firm appear in many marks, including the Staffordshire knot mark. 'Ltd' was added in 1932. Late marks include the name in full.

HC CO.

Hanley China Co *Hanley, Staffordshire, UK*
Formerly Hanley Porcelain Co (see below), this firm made porcelain at Burton Place 1899–1901. A crowned knot mark was used.

HJW

H. J. Wood (Ltd) *Burslem, Staffordshire, UK*
Established in 1884, this firm first made jet and Rockingham glazed earthenware, and later general earthenwares. The rope mark was used from c1884 with these initials.

HPCO.

Hanley Porcelain Co *Hanley, Staffordshire, UK*
Formerly Thomas Bevington, this company made porcelain 1892–99. A Staffordshire knot was used with these initials.

KENT

William Kent Porcelain (Ltd) *Burslem, Staffordshire, UK*
Earthenwares were made by this firm 1944–62 (electrical porcelain continued to be made after this date). The name 'Kent' appears with 'Staffordshire Ware' on the mark.

KPH

Kensington Pottery Ltd *Hanley and Burslem, Staffordshire, UK*
Based at the Kensington Works in Hanley (c1922–37), and Trubsham Cross, Burslem (from c1937), this company produced earthenwares. These initials appear with 'Kensington Ware' and 'England' from c1922.

NEW BRIDGE POTTERY

Edward F. Bodley & Son *Longport, Staffordshire, UK*
Formerly E. F. Bodley & Co (see p292), this firm moved to the New Bridge Pottery in Longport 1881–98. A printed mark with this name was used.

NEW WHARF POTTERY

New Wharf Pottery Co *Burslem, Staffordshire, UK*
Active 1878–94, this firm produced earthenwares.
A crowned knot mark was used c1890–94.

PHILLIPS

George Phillips *Longport, Staffordshire, UK*

A producer of earthenwares 1834–48, this firm used a number of marks with the name Phillips or G. Phillips. The Staffordshire knot appears with the name and 'Longport'.

RHP

R. H. Plant & Co *Longton, Staffordshire, UK*

Porcelain and stone china ware were made at the Carlisle Works 1881–98, including tea and breakfast sets and fancy goods. A crowned and winged printed knot mark was used.

R.H. & S.L.P.

R. H. & S. L. Plant (Ltd) *Longton, Staffordshire, UK*

Formerly R. H. Plant & Co (see above and p275), a crowned and winged printed knot mark used from c1898.

R&S

Robinson & Son *Longton, Staffordshire, UK*

Porcelain was produced by this firm at the Foley China Works 1881–1903. A printed trade mark incorporated the Staffordshire knot mark with 'Established 1850'. This firm subsequently became E. Brain & Co (see p247).

RSR

Ridgway, Sparks & Ridgway *Hanley, Staffordshire, UK*

Based at the Bedford Works in Shelton, this firm produced earthenwares 1873–79. These initials appear in many marks including the Staffordshire knot.

S&B

Smith & Binnall *Tunstall, Staffordshire, UK*

Formerly Rathbone, Smith & Co (1883–97), this firm produced earthenwares 1897–1900. It later became the Soho Pottery. The firm used a printed knot mark.

SCOTIA POTTERY

Edward F. Bodley & Co *Burslem, Staffordshire, UK*

Established at the Scotia Pottery 1862, this firm produced earthenwares together with Bodley & Co (see p290) until 1881. This printed mark was one of those used. It was also used by Bodley & Harrold, based at the Scotia Pottery 1863–65.

T.A. & SG.

T. A. & S. Green *Fenton, Staffordshire, UK*

Formerly M. Green & Co, it was T. A. & S. Green 1876–89. From 1889 it was the Crown Staffordshire Porcelain Co. These initials appear within a crowned knot mark.

T.G.

Thomas Green *Fenton, Staffordshire, UK*

Formerly Green & Richards (1833–47), Thomas Green operated this company, based at the Minerva Works, until his death in 1859 when it became M. Green & Co (1859–76). Good quality porcelain sevices of all types, toy sets, jugs, mugs, feeders and other items were produced in both porcelain and earthenware. A printed crowned knot mark together with these initials was used 1847–59.

TT

Thomas Twyford *Hanley, Staffordshire, UK*

Based at the Bath Street Works and Cliffe Vale Potteries from c1888, this firm made sanitary earthenwares 1860–98. These initials appear on the mark 1860–98. The firm was known as Twyfords Ltd from 1898.

JOHN WARDLE & CO.

John Wardle & Co *Mexborough, Yorkshire, UK*

Based at the Denaby Pottery, this firm operated 1866–70 making earthenwares, printed creamwares and other items. The knot mark appears with this name mark and 'Near Rotherham Denaby Pottery'.

WB

William Brownfield (& Son(s)) *Cobridge, Staffordshire, UK*

See p273. These initials appear with a knot mark.

WPCO

Wellington Pottery Co *Hanley, Staffordshire, UK*

Formerly Bednall & Heath (1879–99), this firm produced earthenwares at the Wellington Pottery 1899–1901. It subsequently became W. H. Lockitt (1901–19) (see p181).

WW/DENABY POTTERY

Wilkinson & Wardle *Mexborough, Yorkshire, UK*

This firm made earthenwares at the Denaby Pottery 1864–66. Printed or impressed marks feature these initials, or the full title of the firm. From 1866 the firm became John Wardle & Co (see above).

WW & CO.

W. Wood & Co *Burslem, Staffordshire, UK*

Based at the Albert Street Works 1873–1932, this firm made earthenwares, door furniture and other wares. A printed knot mark was used 1880–1915 with these initials; a crowned mark was used 1915–32.

Name & Initial Marks

Some pottery and porcelain producers use marks that feature just their name or initials, and do not have a particular illustrated form. Others use a wide range of marks that are characterized either by distinguishing names and initials, or trademarks. These may be stencilled, incised, impressed, printed or painted.

In this section, the name or initial marks used are featured written in the way that they would appear on the mark (together with possible variations).

Detail of Royal Winton, 1930s

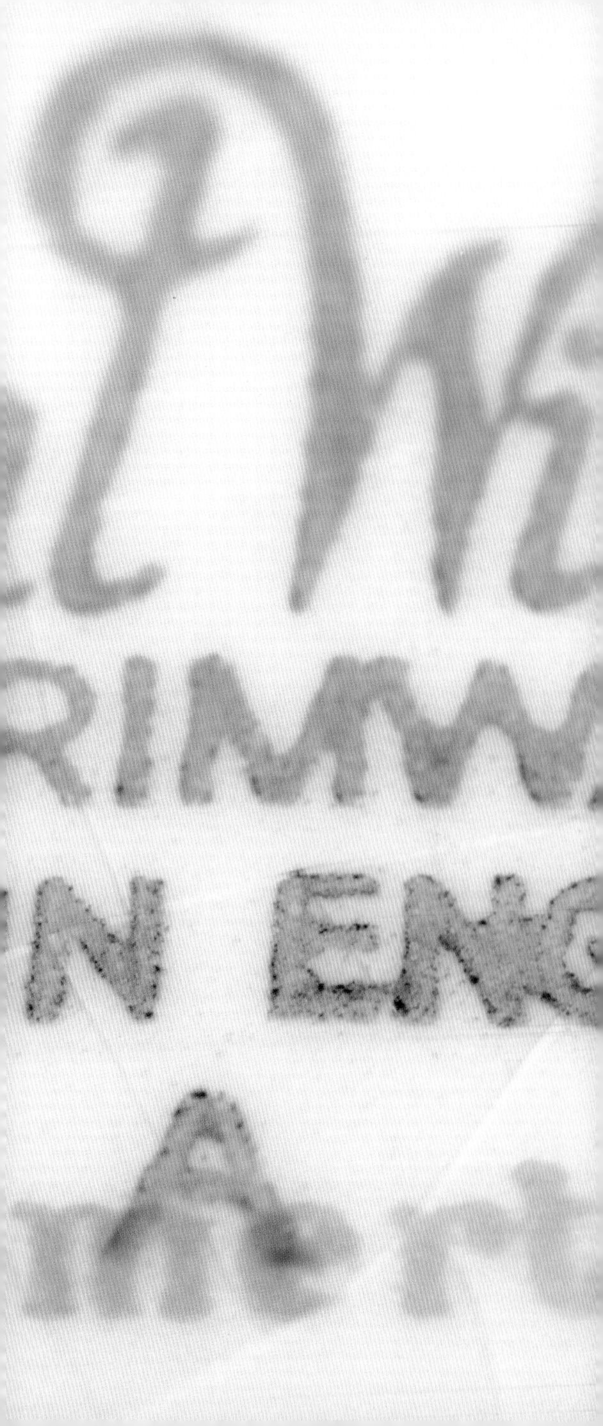

In this section, name and initial marks appear alphabetically according to the form in which they appear in the mark. Variations of the names used by the same potter or factory may appear in brackets, or on a new line.

ALABAMA POTTERY CO./FT. PAYNE, ALA.
Alabama Pottery Company *Fort Payne, Alabama, USA*
One of the most productive of the Alabama potteries, this firm (active 1890–1910) is recorded at Fort Payne in 1890. Earlier, traditional alkaline-glazed stoneware had been made there by Elizer McPherson 1875–1900, but the Pottery Company focused on Albany slip and Bristol white glazed wares. This stencilled mark appears.

ALDRIDGE
Aldridge & Co *Longton, Staffordshire, UK*
Based at the Normacot Works, this pottery produced earthenwares 1919–49. It was later known as Aldridge Pottery Co (Longton) Ltd. Name marks are impressed.

AMERICAN LIMOGES
Limoges China Company *Sebring, Ohio, USA*
This pottery produced a large quantity of semi-porcelain dinnerware with decal patterns from 1900. In 1920 the daily output was 45,000 pieces. It closed in 1955. A variety of devices are used with the pattern names, but the name 'Limoges' is usually present, sometimes with 'American Limoges' and 'Lincoln China Co.'

ARABIA
O/Y Arabia A/B *Helsinki, Finland*
Founded in 1874, this company produced domestic earthware and porcelain. Style was influenced by a Belgian teacher of ceramics, A. W. Finch, who taught in Finland 1897–1902. In 1948 the firm was taken over and renamed Wärtsilä-koncernen A/B Arabia.

ARCADIAN (CHINA)
Arkinstall & Sons (Ltd) *Stoke, Staffordshire, UK*
Based at the Trent Bridge Pottery, and subsequently at the Arcadian Works 1904–24, this company produced porcelain before it was taken over by Robinson & Leadbeater in 1908.

D.L . (H.R.) ATCHESON/ ANNAPOLIS, IA/IND.
Atcheson Pottery *Annapolis, Indiana, USA*
Three potters from Ohio, David L. Atcheson, David Huggins, and Jacob Bennage, established a stoneware manufactory at Annapolis, Parke County, Indiana, in 1841.

The Atcheson family remained involved through various partnerships until at least 1904, when Bristol white glazed wares were being made. During the early years storage jars and jugs were produced in salt-glazed stoneware.

AVON

Avon Pottery *Cincinnati, Ohio, USA*
Founded by Karl Langenbeck, this pottery (active 1886–88) used yellow Ohio clay or a white body to make a variety of art wares with glossy coloured glazes, some taking advantage of the clarity of the glaze to show white decorations beneath the glaze or to be subtly shaded from bottom to top. This incised mark appears. This pottery and mark should not be confused with the Avon Faïence Company that was located in Wheeling, West Virginia, and made slip-decorated art wares in 1902 and 1903.

R & J BADDELEY

Ralph & John Baddeley *Shelton, Staffordshire, UK*
These potters produced earthenwares 1750–95 using this impressed mark.

T. (THOS) BADDELEY/HANLEY

Thomas Baddeley *Hanley, Staffordshire, UK*
An engraver active 1800–34 at various addresses in Hanley. He used these signature marks on pieces that featured his engravings. Pieces may also be dated.

W. BADDELEY

William Baddeley *Longton, Staffordshire, UK*
Worked at the Drury Court Works in Longton c1864–75. Pieces feature this impressed mark.

(C. J. C.) BAILEY/FULHAM (POTTERY LONDON)

C. J. C. Bailey (or Bailey & Co) *Fulham Pottery, London, UK*
See p79. Several incised or impressed marks were used by this firm, many of which incorporated the above names.

BAKER BEVANS & IRWIN

Baker, Bevans & Irwin *Swansea, Wales, UK*
Based at the Glamorgan Pottery, this firm produced earthenwares c1813–38. This name mark appears.

BAKEWELL BROS. LTD.

Bakewell Bros Ltd *Hanley, Staffordshire, UK*
Based at the Britannia Works, this pottery was active 1927–43. Many marks feature the factory name. The name of the body 'Royal Vitreous' may also be added. The addition of 'Stoke-on-Trent' indicates a date after 1931.

COPYRIGHT BALL BROS./SUNDERLAND

Ball Brothers, Sunderland *Tyne and Wear, UK*

The Deptford Pottery in Sunderland was founded in 1857 by William Ball for the manufacture of flowerpots. In 1863, he began to make 'Sunderland ware' for the domestic market. Output also included flower vases and seed boxes. The firm was known as Ball Brothers 1884–1918. Most pieces are unmarked, but this mark does appear.

O.L. & A.K. (A.K.) BALLARD/BURLINGTON, VT.

Ballard Brothers *Burlington, Vermont, USA*

Three brothers, Alfred K., Orrin L. and Hiram N. Ballard, bought out a stoneware manufactory in Burlington, Vermont, in 1856. The city was an important ceramics centre from c1806. After 1867, Alfred was sole proprietor until 1875 when the pottery was sold to F. Woodworth. Wares made by the Ballard Brothers include Rockingham hound-handled pitchers, flasks and washbowl and pitcher sets as well as blue-decorated, salt-glazed stoneware.

BARKER

John, Richard and William Barker *Longton, Staffordshire, UK*

These three brothers, based at Lane End, produced earthenwares, basaltes and similar wares in the late 18th and early 19thC. This name mark has been found.

BARRATTS OF STAFFORDSHIRE

Barratts of Staffordshire Ltd *Burslem, Staffordshire, UK*

See p207. This name mark was incorporated into many of the marks used by this firm from 1945.

BATCHELDER/LOS ANGELES

Batchelder Tile Company *Pasadena and Los Angeles, USA*

Tiles were first made in Batchelder's backyard workshop in Pasadena from 1909. The business moved into a small factory in 1912 and in 1920 to larger facilities in Los Angeles. Relief-moulded tiles, fountains, door frames and mantels as well as special-order architectural pieces were made. Although the tiles were not glazed, they were coloured with slips rubbed onto the surface. The company failed in 1932 during the Great Depression. The mark appears in a mould on the back of the tiles after 1916.

BATES WALKER & CO.

Bates Walker & Co *Burslem, Staffordshire, UK*

Based at the Dale Hall Works, this firm operated 1875–78 producing earthenwares, jasper-type wares and porcelain. Formerly Bates, Elliot & Co (see p269), the firm became Bates, Gildea & Walker 1878–81.

B. B. & I.

Baker, Bevans & Irwin *Swansea, Wales, UK*

See p297. A number of marks were used by this firm incorporating these initials.

BEAVER FALLS, ART TILE CO. LTD./BEAVER FALLS PA.

Beaver Falls Art Tile Company *Beaver Falls, Pennsylvania, USA*

Chemist Francis W. Walker organized the company (active 1886–1927) to make plain and relief-moulded tiles with brilliant coloured glazes that showed little or no crazing over time. This made them suitable for use in parlour stoves. Although popular designs were made, heads and full figures were a speciality of this pottery in the late 19thC. Sculptor Isaac Broome worked for them in the 1890s. Marks are frequently moulded into the backs of the tiles.

BEECH & HANCOCK

Beech & Hancock *Tunstall, Staffordshire, UK*

Based at the Church Bank Works (c1857–6l) and the Swan Bank Pottery (c1862–76), this firm made ceramic wares for the domestic market in 'sponged', painted, gilded, enamelled and lustred styles. High quality stonewares and blackwares were also produced. This name appears in many printed marks. The initials 'B. & H.' may also appear.

S. BELL

Samuel and Solomon Bell *Strasburg, Virginia, USA*

Peter Bell came from Maryland to Winchester, Virginia, in 1824, where he manufactured redware and later stoneware. Samuel and Solomon were his sons, and they founded their own pottery in Strasburg (1833–82). Decorated earthenwares and decorated salt-glazed stonewares were made. This impressed mark was used.

BELLEEK/CO. FERMANAGH

Belleek Pottery *Co Fermanagh, Northern Ireland, UK*

See p254. This impressed or relief mark was used 1863–90.

BELPER (& DENBY)/BOURNES POTTERIES, DERBYSHIRE

Belper Pottery *Nr Derby, Derbyshire, UK*

Brownwares were produced towards the end of the 18thC. From 1800, the pottery was taken over by William Bourne who continued the production of salt-glazed blacking, ink, ginger-beer and spirit bottles. In 1812 his son Joseph moved to the Denby Pottery and the two works carried on until 1834 when the Belper Pottery closed, and the concern was entirely transferred to Denby.

BEVINGTON & CO./SWANSEA
Bevington & Co *Swansea, Wales, UK*
Operating 1817–21, this firm produced creamwares and porcelain. Pieces occasionally feature this impressed name mark. The firm subsequently became known as T. & J. Bevington.

B. G. & W.
Bates, Gildea & Walker *Burslem, Staffordshire, UK*
See p298. This firm was active 1878–81 using these initials. The firm later became Gildea & Walker (see p269).

B. H. & CO.
Beech, Hancock & Co *Burslem, Staffordshire, UK*
This firm produced earthenwares at the Swan Bank Pottery in Burslem 1851–55. After 1857 the firm relocated to Tunstall, and was known as Beech & Hancock (see p299). These distinguishing initials appear.

B. M. & CO./SARACEN POTTERY
Bailey Murray & Co *Glasgow, Scotland, UK*
The Saracen Pottery was established in 1875 by Bailey, Murray & Brammer at Possil Park The firm produced Rockingham ware, cane-coloured, Egyptian black jet and mazarine blue ware on a large scale. Output mainly comprised teapots, jugs and other domestic items. From c1884–1900 the firm became the Saracen Pottery Co.

BOSTON
Jonathan Fenton & Charles Carpenter
Boston and Charlestown, Massachusetts, USA
A stoneware manufactory was established in Boston in 1793 by Jonathan Fenton and Charles Carpenter. Exceptional work was produced by the partners in two different styles: salt-glazed with stamped and blue decorated birds, fish, etc. and wares dipped top and bottom in an iron-brown glaze. They marked their wares 'BOSTON' with letters of the same size. After dissolving the partnership in 1796, Carpenter returned to Massachusetts in 1801 to start a stoneware pottery in Charlestown. Dipped wares similar to those made earlier were produced, marked 'Boston' (two sizes of letters) and, later, 'Charlestown,' until Carpenter died in 1827.

BRAMELD
Rockingham Works *Swinton, Yorkshire, UK*
See p253. This name appears in several of the marks used 1806–42. Various crosses or stars may appear after the name 'Brameld'.

C.W. BRAUN/BUFFALO N.Y.

Charles W. Braun *Buffalo, New York, USA*

Charles W. Braun, a Prussian potter, bought the Heiser family pottery in Buffalo in 1857 and produced blue-decorated stoneware until 1896. Bird designs, frequently as good as those on Rochester and Utica wares, were popular.

BRENTLEIGH WARE

Howard Pottery Co (Ltd) *Shelton, Staffordshire, UK*

This trade name was incorporated in marks from 1925.

(JAS.) BROADHURST

James Broadhurst & Sons Ltd

Fenton and Longton, Staffordshire, UK

Established c1862, the firm was based at the Crown Pottery, Longton until 1870. Here James Broadhurst made gold and silver lustrewares. In 1870 they moved to the Portland Pottery at Fenton. In 1897 '& Sons' was added to the mark with 'Ltd.' from c1922. The full name appears from 1957.

JOHN BURGER (J. BURGER JR., BURGER & LANG)/ROCHESTER, N.Y.

John Burger *Rochester, New York, USA*

See p115. These impressed name marks were used.

B. W. & B.

Batkin, Walker & Broadhurst *Lane End, Staffordshire, UK*

This firm produced earthenwares, stone china and other wares 1840–45. These initials appear in printed marks of differing design; the pattern name may also appear.

A. CADMUS/CONGRESS POTTERY/SOUTH AMBOY N.J.

Abraham Cadmus/Congress Pottery

South Amboy, New Jersey, USA

This pottery (active 1849–54) made Rockingham and yellow ware in table and kitchen forms and is especially known for his pitchers, one of which has a fire brigade marching around the sides. The mark was impressed.

CANONSBURG POTTERY CO./CANONSBURG, PA./USA

Canonsburg Pottery/Canonsburg China Company

Canonsburg, Pennsylvania, USA

This pottery (active 1901–78) made large quantities of semi-porcelain dinner and toilet sets and sets of odd dishes decorated with decals. Later it made ceramic inserts for electric slow cookers (crock pots). This mark appears with many pattern and shape names.

CAMBRIA (CAMBRIAN POTTERY)
Swansea Pottery *Swansea, Wales, UK*
See p333. These impressed or printed marks appear in many forms c1783–c1810.

CATALINA POTTERY
Gladding, McBean and Company, *California, USA*
Although known for its ceramic architectural products, this company also owned several important potteries for domestic items, including Tropico Pottery from 1923, which made tiles, garden ware and vases; Catalina Pottery from 1937, which made table ware; and Franciscan Ware, an earthenware line that the company developed in 1934 to make dinner and ornamental wares. The company was acquired by Wedgwood from Interpace Corporation in 1979 and in 1985 the factory was closed and production of Franciscan moved to England. This mark appears printed and on sticker labels.

B. G. & C. (L. & B. C.) CHACE/SOMERSET
Somerset Potters' Works
Somerset, Massachusetts, USA
The potter Asa Chace made redware in Somerset, Massachusetts by 1768. In 1847 his grandsons, Leonard, Benjamin G., and Clark opened the Somerset Potters' Works which continued until 1882. Some salt-glazed, cobalt-blue brush-decorated examples may be found.

CHAMBERS, LLANELLY
Chambers & Co *Llanelly, Wales, UK*
This firm was owned by William Chambers c1839–54, who founded the South Wales Pottery (see p332).

CHARLESTOWN
Jonathan Fenton & Charles Carpenter
Boston and Charlestown, Massachusetts, USA
See p300. This impressed mark appears on later wares.

C. J. M. & CO.
Charles James Mason & Co
Lane Delph, Staffordshire, UK
See p210. This firm operated under his style 1829–45. These initials are found in a number of marks.

N. CLARK (JR.)/ATHENS (N.Y.) (N. CLARK & CO., LYONS, N.Y.)
Nathan Clark Pottery *Athens, New York, USA*
See p116. These impressed marks were used.

G. COCKER

George Cocker *Various addresses, UK*

A figure modeller trained at the Derby Works, George Cocker modelled for various firms and also independently. Figures and groups in unglazed porcelain or parian occur with his incised signature. The periods of his work are: Derby 1808–c1817 and 1821–40; Coalport 1817–19; Worcester 1819–21; London c1840–50; Mintons c1850–60.

COPELAND & GARRETT

Copeland & Garrett *Stoke, Staffordshire, UK*

Formerly Spode (see p233), this firm operated 1833–47. Porcelain, earthenwares and parian were produced with several marks that included the factory name. The firm later became W. T. Copeland (see p255).

W. & E. CORN

W. & E. Corn *Burslem and Longport, Staffordshire, UK*

Producers of earthenwares 1864–1904. Pieces are rarely marked before 1900; this name mark appears in different printed marks 1900–04.

COWDEN & WILCOX (EH. COWDEN)/HARRISBURG, PA.

Cowden & Wilcox *Harrisburg, Pennsylvania, USA*

An important Pennsylvania stoneware pottery started in 1860 at Harrisburg by John Wallace Cowden and Isaac J. Wilcox. After 1867, John's son Frederick joined the firm and remained after his father's death in 1872 and Wilcox's retirement in 1885. In 1896, J. W. Cowden joined his father Frederick, and the company ran until 1915. Excellent decorated stoneware was made, and designs included the man-in-the-moon, ducks, eagles, and boats.

C.P.CO.

Crown Pottery Company *Evansville, Indiana, USA*

This pottery (active 1891–c.1955) made decorated ironstone and semi-porcelain wares. Later their ware was sold in the white, but their business declined due to lack of expansion. These initials appear with the pattern name.

CROWN DUCAL

A. G. Richardson & Co. Ltd *Cobridge, Staffordshire, UK*

See p207. This trade name was used in several different marks used by this firm.

CROWNFORD

Ford & Sons (Ltd) *Burslem, Staffordshire, UK*

See p306. This trade name was used from the 1930s.

PAUL CUSHMAN

Paul Cushman *Albany, New York, USA*

Paul Cushman established Albany's best known stoneware manufactory c1807 on Lion (Lyon) Street (later Washington Street) 'half a mile west of Albany gaol', an address that is incorporated into some marks. A variety of utilitarian forms, often decorated with incised designs and cobalt blue were produced until Cushman's death in 1833. They are popular with today's collectors and highly valued.

AUGUSTE DELAHERCHE

Auguste Delaherche *Various locations, France*

Born in 1857, this potter worked at the Ecole des Arts Décoratifs, Paris (1877, 1879–83), and was director of the L. Pilleux factory in Goincourt (1883–86) making ceramic architectural decoration. He ran his own pottery at Armentières 1894–1904 and was awarded a gold medal at the Paris World Exhibition of 1889. His name mark appeared in a circle; his initials were also used with a number of devices.

DILLWYN (& CO.)/SWANSEA
DILLWYN'S ETRUSCAN WARE

Dillwyn & Co *Swansea, Wales, UK*

See p333. This firm operated the Cambrian Works, Swansea c1811–17 and c1824–50. 'Dillwyn & Co' appeared in impressed or printed marks of various forms c1811–17. 'Dillwyn' or 'Dillwyn, Swansea' was used c1824–50. The printed mark 'Dillwyn's Etruscan Ware' appears c1847–50.

DIXON (AUSTIN, PHILLIPS) & CO.

Sunderland or 'Garrison' Pottery

Sunderland, Tyne and Wear, UK

See p322. 'Dixon & Co' appears on marks c1813–19 ; 'Dixon, Austin & Co' c1812–40; 'Dixon, Austin, Phillips & Co' c1827–40; 'Dixon, Phillips & Co' c1840–65.

DUCHESS

A. T. Finney & Sons (Ltd) *Longton, Staffordshire, UK*

See p208. Many marks feature the trade name 'Duchess'.

(J.) DUDSON

James Dudson *Hanley, Staffordshire, UK*

Based at the Hope Street Works from 1838, James Dudson operated a pottery until his death in 1882, when it was carried on by his son. Ornamental porcelain, stonewares, Wedgwood-type jasper wares, mosaic wares, flowerpots and candlesticks were produced. Many designs were registered. 'Dudson' appears on wares 1838–88; 'J. Dudson' 1888–98. From 1898 the firm became Dudson Bros Ltd.

DUNN, DUNLAP & CO.

Van Scholk & Dunn/Dunn, Dunlap & Co

Matawan, New Jersey, USA

Founded by Josiah Van Scholk in 1802, the pottery made salt-glazed stoneware utilitarian vessels, many with small flowers drawn in blue. They also made drape-moulded redware pie plates. Although these latter are not marked, a number of jigger moulds for plates of this shape survive from the 1860s and 1870s that were incised 'DD&Co' (Dunn, Dunlap & Co) by their potter William Lowe. The factory continued until c1875.

J. DUNTZE/MANUFACT/R/N. HAVEN, CT.

John Duntze *New Haven, Connecticut, USA*

A stoneware manufactory owned and operated by Absalom Stedman 1825–33. It was taken over in 1833 by the potter John Duntze, who ran this East Water Street Works until 1852. Fine, ovoid salt-glazed stoneware was produced, occasionally decorated in manganese brown.

EAST LAKE POTTERY/BRIDGETON, N.J.

East Lake Pottery *Bridgeton, New Jersey, USA*

George F. Hamlyn (active c1885–c1910) advertised in 1889 as a manufacturer and dealer in stoneware, earthenware, Rockingham and terracotta. However, only redware has been found with his mark.The mark appears impressed.

EASTWOOD

William Baddeley *Hanley, Staffordshire, UK*

William Baddeley produced Wedgwood-type earthenwares and basaltes at Eastwood, Hanley c1802–22. His mark was 'Eastwood'. The word 'East' may sometimes be indistinct and can be mistaken for 'Wedgwood': collectors must be wary of this. Another potter named William Baddeley worked at Longton c1864–75, producing terracotta and similar wares (see p297).

B(ARNABAS) EDMANDS (EDMANDS & CO.)/CHARLESTOWN

Edmands & Co *Charlestown, Massachusetts, USA*

See p121. These impressed marks were used.

D.J. (I.) EVANS & CO.

D.J. Evans & Co *Swansea, Wales, UK*

Formerly known as Evans & Glasson (see p306), this firm operated the Cambrian Works from 1862 until its closure in c1870. The name marks above were used c1862–70.

EVANS & GLASSON/SWANSEA
Evans & Glasson *Swansea, Wales, UK*
David Evans ran the Cambrian Works at Swansea (see p333) in this style c1850–62. He produced blue and white and agate earthenwares, mainly for Wales, Ireland, the south-west of England and Chile. Production ceased c1870.

F. & SONS (LTD.)
Ford & Sons (Ltd) *Burslem, Staffordshire, UK*
Based in Newcastle Street, Burslem, this company operated as Ford & Sons c1893–1938, then became Ford & Sons (Crownford) Ltd. 'F. & Sons' was used in many marks 1893–1938. 'Ltd' may occur after 1908.

FERRYBRIDGE
Tomlinson & Co *Ferrybridge Pottery, Yorkshire*
See p335. This mark (the 'D' is sometimes reversed) was used from 1804.

FRANCISCAN WARE/MADE IN CALIFORNIA U.S.A.
Gladding, McBean and Company *California, USA*
See p302. This printed mark was used. A number of variations were used.

FRANKOMA
Frankoma Pottery *Sapulpa, Oklahoma, USA*
Founded and operated by the Frank family from 1936, this pottery has made earthenware dinnerware in a variety of patterns (such as Mayan-Aztec, a line introduced in the 1940s), as well as Christmas plates, sculptured wares, souvenir items, florists' crockery and novelties as commissioned. State plates in a variety of colours were also produced. Marks are usually printed. The name 'Frankoma' appears in the mark, sometimes with pattern name; stickers are also used; descriptions and marks are sometimes moulded into the backs or bottoms of souvenir items.

FRAUENFELTER CHINA (USA)
Frauenfelter China Company *Zanesville, Ohio, USA*
Charles Frauenfelter started making restaurant and kitchenware in the pottery that had been producing chemical china. He further refined the product and began making stylish shapes on a cream-coloured vitreous body. The firm continued until 1939. The marks are printed.

G. & C. J. M.
G. M. & C. J. Mason *Lane Delph, Staffordshire, UK*
See p210. Marks incorporating the initials of George Miles and Charles James Mason occur before 1829.

JOHN GEDDES/VERREVILLE POTTERY

John Geddes (& Son) *Glasgow, Scotland, UK*

This firm was based at the Verreville Pottery, which was originally built for a glass-house in 1777. It was sold in 1806 to John Geddes on the understanding that he was not to produce crown or bottle glass. He produced flint glass, and after 1820 earthenwares. Geddes worked with various partners, including Robert Alexander Kidston after 1827. In 1838 the works was passed to Kidston, who began to make porcelain as well as glass and earthenware. Figures, porcelain basketwork and flowers were produced by skilled craftsmen who had previously worked at Derby and Coalport. Kidston and his partners carried on the concern until 1846, when it became Robert Cochran & Co, producing only earthenwares and white granite wares. Robert Cochran died in 1869 and the firm was taken over by his son, continuing until 1918. The mark above was used c1806–24; '& Son' was added 1824–27.

W.S. GEORGE

W. S. George Pottery Company *East Palestine, Ohio, USA*

Although this was called the Continental China Company 1904–09, W. S. George had controlling interest in the operation which was set up in the old factory of the East Palestine Pottery Company (1884–1904). Like its predecessors, the W. S. George Pottery Company made white and decorated ware, including semi-porcelain dinner and toilet ware. The firm continued until 1960. Many marks appear with pattern names arranged in circles, lines, wreaths or other devices, but all include 'W. S. George'.

GIBSON & SONS (LTD.), GIBSONS

Gibson & Sons (Ltd) *Burslem, Staffordshire, UK*

See p197. Many marks were used by this firm. 'Gibsons' mainly appears in marks used after c1940.

GLASGOW POTTERY CO./TRENTON N.J.

Glasgow Pottery *Trenton, New Jersey, USA*

See p186. This printed mark was used.

GLOBE POTTERY CO. LTD.

Globe Pottery Co Ltd *Cobridge and Shelton, Staffordshire, UK*

See p271. This name mark was incorporated into a large number of marks used by this firm.

GOODWIN'S HOTEL CHINA

Goodwin Pottery/Goodwin Brothers

East Liverpool, Ohio, USA

See p249. This printed mark was used.

GORHAM/EST.1881/FINE CHINA/FLINTRIDGE/USA
Gorham Company *Providence, Rhode Island, USA*
This company, known for many generations for its high quality silver products (from 1831), expanded during the late 1960s and early 1970s by buying selected manufacturers, including the Flintridge China Company, Pasadena, making dinnerware since 1945. Gorham/Flintridge produced fine porcelain tableware in shapes and patterns to compete with Lenox China. Indeed, Lenox bought the Gorham Company in 1991. This printed mark appears.

GRAFTON CHINA
A. B. Jones & Sons (Ltd) *Longton, Staffordshire, UK*
See p165. This trade name was used in marks.

G. (GEO) GRAINGER/WORCESTER
George Grainger (& Co)
Worcester, Hereford and Worcester, UK
See below and p166. Many painted or printed marks include this name mark. After c1850 '& Co' was added.

GRAINGER LEE & CO./WORCESTER
Grainger, Lee & Co *Worcester, Hereford and Worcester, UK*
A porcelain works was established by Thomas Grainger in 1801. He went into partnership with a skilled painter, and the company became Grainger, Wood & Co. In 1812 he went into partnership with his brother-in-law, and the style changed to Grainger & Lee. After Lee retired from the business, it was carried on by Thomas Grainger until 1839, when he was succeeded by his son George, and the firm became G. Grainger & Co. Early wares feature this written mark; printed marks also occur in many forms.

GRAINGER WOOD & CO./
WORCESTER/WARRANTED
Grainger, Wood & Co *Worcester, Hereford and Worcester, UK*
See above. This company produced porcelains c1801–12. Most examples are unmarked, but some written marks similar to the one above were used.

GREATBATCH
William Greatbatch *Fenton, Staffordshire, UK*
Potter and modeller, William Greatbatch was apprentice to Thomas Whieldon. He was associated with Josiah Wedgwood from c1760, and modelled relief designs on salt-glazed and green-glazed ware. His name appears on some wares with transfer prints coloured by hand in the 1770–80 period. Later printed creamwares may bear the name on the print.

B. GREEN/PHILAD:
Branch Green *Philadelphia, Pennsylvania, USA*
Branch Green was a stoneware potter in Troy, New York, in 1799 and moved to New Jersey by 1805. In 1809 he moved his factory to Philadelphia at '2nd above Germantown Road.' He produced jugs, pitchers, jars, butter tubs and milk pots. Many of the jugs were intended for liquor distillers or retail spirits merchants as they are stamped 'Wine', 'Rum', etc. He operated until 1827.

GREENWOOD CHINA/TRENTON, N.J.
Greenwood Pottery Company *Trenton, New Jersey, USA*
See p220. This impressed name mark was used.

GRINDLEY HOTEL WARE
Grindley Hotel Ware Co Ltd *Tunstall, Staffordshire, UK*
Established in 1908, this company made earthenwares.

W.H. GRINDLEY & CO.
W. H. Grindley & Co (Ltd) *Tunstall, Staffordshire, UK*
See p209. This name was incorporated into many marks.

GROSVENOR CHINA
Jackson & Gosling *Longton, Staffordshire, UK*
Founded c1866 at King Street, Fenton, this firm was based at the Grosvenor Works in Longton from c1909. It operated under various owners 1866–1961. Porcelain services were produced for the home and export markets.

(W. H.) HACKWOOD
William Hackwood *Hanley, Staffordshire, UK*
This potter produced earthenwares at the Eastwood Pottery 1827–43. The impressed name 'Hackwood' is found. The firm later became William Hackwood & Son.

HAIDINGER
Gebrüder Haidinger *Elbogen (Locket n.O), Czech Republic*
The Haidinger Brothers founded a porcelain factory in 1815 with the support of Niedermayer, director of the Vienna Porcelain Works 1805–27. Initially greyish-white porcelain was made. Output later improved, and pieces were taken to Sèvres in 1836. The last of the Haidinger Brothers died in 1870 and in 1873 the factory was sold to Springer & Oppenheimer.

HALL
Samuel Hall, Hanley *Staffordshire, UK*
This potter produced earthenwares c1841–56. The name 'Hall' appears on some rare earthenware figures which

were attributed to John and Ralph Hall (see below). However, directories do not list them as producers of figures, while Samuel Hall is listed as such.

I. HALL (& SONS)
John Hall (& Sons) *Burslem, Staffordshire, UK*
Active as a potter 1814–32, John Hall was in partnership with Ralph Hall 1802–22. In 1822 he took over the Stych Pottery in Burslem and continued until 1832. The mark 'I. Hall' appears in many marks 1814–22; 'I. Hall & Sons' was used c1822–32 and may be impressed or printed.

R. HALL (& SON, & CO.)
Ralph Hall & Co (& Son) *Tunstall, Staffordshire, UK*
Ralph Hall owned the Swan Bank Works c1822–48 and produced earthenwares. He had been in partnership with John Hall at the Stych Pottery in Burslem 1802–22, and in Tunstall 1811–22 (see above). His name was found in several printed marks: 'R. Hall' appears 1822–41; 'R. Hall & Son' was used on American subject prints c1836; 'R. Hall & Co.' was used in several printed marks 1841–49.

HAMMERSLEY & CO.
Hammersley & Co *Longton, Staffordshire, UK*
Based at the Alsager Pottery, this firm produced porcelain 1887–1932 before becoming Hammersley & Co (Longton) Ltd. The factory name appears in many marks.

HAMPSHIRE POTTERY
Hampshire Pottery Company/James S. Taft & Company
Keene, New Hampshire, USA
See p62. This printed mark appears in a double circle.

GEO.F HAMLYN/EAST LAKE POTTERY/BRIDGETON, N.J.
East Lake Pottery *Bridgeton, New Jersey, USA*
See p305. The mark is impressed.

(T.)HARLEY
Thomas Harley *Lane End, Staffordshire, UK*
Thomas Harley produced earthenware services, jugs etc c1802–08. His name mark appears impressed on fine lustre decorated jugs, and printed or written in letters.

(T.) HARRINGTON/LYONS (N.Y.)
Thompson Harrington *Lyons, New York, USA*
In 1852, Thompson Harrington took over the Lyons, New York pottery that George G. Williams had run for Nathan Clark & Co. Harrington, too, had specialized in

utilitarian salt-glazed stoneware. However, his marked wares are prized by collectors for their cobalt-blue trailed lions, horses and sunbursts with human faces at the centre. He also produced brown Albany slip-glazed stoneware. The firm closed in 1872. These impressed marks appear.

HARTLEY, GREENS & CO./LEEDS POTTERY

Hartley, Greens & Co *Leeds, West Yorkshire, UK*

This firm was based at the Leeds Pottery from c1781, producing creamwares for export until it became bankrupt in 1820. This name mark appears in many forms.

HAVILAND (& CO.)

David Haviland *Limoges, France*

An important porcelain factory was founded here in 1842, producing porcelain wares and decorating pieces from other factories. David Haviland's sons Charles and Théodore took over in 1879. A subsidiary firm at Auteuil (1873–85) produced wares decorated in the Impressionist style. Haviland also used Tang shell motifs from c1870. A number of marks feature the name above.

HAWLEY BROS. (LTD.)

Hawley Bros (Ltd) *Rotherham, South Yorkshire, UK*

In 1855, the Northfield Pottery in Rotherham was bought by George Hawley who produced earthenwares. After his death the business was continued by his son William and his two brothers, and was called W. & G. Hawley and then Hawley Bros until 1903 when it became Northfield Hawley Pottery Co Ltd. This name mark was used; 'Ltd' appears on some marks from 1897.

THEODORE HAVILAND

Théodore Haviland *Limoges, France*

See above. Théodore Haviland founded his own porcelain factory in 1893, producing table services and luxury ware. Renowned artists were employed by him as decorators. His name appears in many marks.

H.B.

Hawley Bros (Ltd) *Rotherham, South Yorkshire, UK*

See above. A printed mark featuring these intertwined initials was used 1868–98.

H. & C.

Hope & Carter *Burslem, Staffordshire, UK*

Based at Fountain Place, this company produced earthenwares 1862–80. G. L. Ashworth & Bros took over c1880. These initials are found, often with the pattern name.

H. D./DUBLIN

Henri Delamain *Dublin, Eire*

The Belgian Henri Delamain made pottery in Dublin from 1752, although a delftware pottery had been in existence from 1735. Wares are characterized by bright blue or manganese purple decoration, usually comprising elaborate scroll borders around landscape paintings. Most wares are unmarked, but monogram 'HD' is known with 'Dublin'.

HEREND

Moritz Farkashazy-Fischer *Herend, Hungary*

A porcelain factory was founded here in 1839 by Moritz Farkashazy-Fischer with the help of Prince Esterhazy. Many of the items made were replacements for pieces from famous collections; these were made to such a high standard that only the marks gave them away. Polychrome decoration was used that required items to be fired up to three times. Quality of later pieces was variable. The place name 'Herend' is incorporated into numerous marks.

HOLLAND & GREEN

Holland & Green *Longton, Staffordshire, UK*

This firm produced earthenwares, ironstones and other wares at the Stafford Street Works 1853–82. Toilet services of high quality were made in rich colours with elaborate gilding.

S. HOLLINS

Samuel Hollins *Shelton, Staffordshire, UK*

Samuel Hollins made fine redware teapots and other items, basaltes and other Wedgwood-type wares at Vale Pleasant c1774–1813. He was also a partner in the New Hall China Works until his death in 1820. His name appears impressed.

HONITON (LACE ART) POTTERY (CO.)

Honiton Art Potteries Ltd *Honiton, Devon, UK*

Established in 1881, this company which operated under various titles and owners, produced earthenwares. Early wares were usually unmarked. 'The Honiton Lace Art Pottery Co' appears as a printed or impressed mark and was registered in 1915. 'Honiton Pottery Devon' appears as a printed, moulded or impressed mark from 1947.

F M. (F D.) HONORÉ

F. M. Honoré *Boulevard St. Antoine, Paris, France*

A porcelain factory was established by F. M. Honoré in 1785. In 1812 his sons Edward and Théodore joined him. They then joined Dagoty and opened a new factory, and the name changed to 'Dagoty et Honoré'. The partnership ended in 1820 and the factories were divided.

HOWE & CLARK/ATHENS
Nathan Clark Pottery *Athens, New York, USA*
See p116. This impressed mark was used.

HÜTTL
Theodor Hüttl *Budapest, Hungary*
A factory was founded by Theodor Hüttl in 1852, initially for porcelain painting but later full production began. Work was mainly commission-based. Hüttl died in 1910, and the firm was continued by his sons.

I. I.
John Ifield *Wrotham, Kent, UK*
The above initials occur on examples of Wrotham earthenware, with dated examples from 1674 and 1676. The initial 'I' was often used instead of 'J'.

IMPERIAL (PORCELAIN)
Wedgwood & Co (Ltd) *Tunstall, Staffordshire, UK*
See p216. This trade name appears from c1906.

I. M. & S.
John Meir & Son *Tunstall, Staffordshire, UK*
See p314. These initials also refer to this firm.

INTERNATIONAL CHINA/TRENTON, N.J.
International Pottery/Burgess & Campbell
Trenton, New Jersey, USA
See p223. This printed mark was used.

IROQUOIS CASUAL CHINA BY RUSSEL WRIGHT
Iroquois China Company *Syracuse, New York, USA*
Semi-porcelain tableware was made. From 1939, the new owner made only hotel ware. In 1946, the company started three new dinnerware lines, including 'Casual China' by designer Russel Wright, and 'Impromptu' and 'Informal' designed by Bob Seibel. By c1960, the company only made the three dinnerware lines. The factory continued until 1969. This printed mark appears.

JACKSON & GOSLING
Jackson & Gosling *Longton, Staffordshire, UK*
See p309. This name mark was used in many marks.

J. B.
James Beech *Tunstall and Burslem, Staffordshire, UK*
This firm operated at the Swan Bank Potteries in Burslem and Tunstall 1877–89. These initials appear with the printed mark of a swan, often with the pattern name.

J. B. & S. (SON)

James Beech & Son *Longton, Staffordshire, UK*
Producers of porcelain 1860–98, this firm should not be confused with James Beech (see previous page). Several printed marks include the initials above, including a crowned Staffordshire knot mark (with the word 'England' 1891–98). These initials were also used by James Broadhurst & Sons Ltd (see p301) 1870–1922. 'Ltd' was added from 1922.

J. (F.) & C. W.

James & Charles Wileman *Longton, Staffordshire, UK*
Based at the Foley China Works, this firm (formerly Henry Wileman) produced earthenwares 1864–69. These distinguishing initials were found in several printed marks.

J. F. W.

James F. Wileman *Longton, Staffordshire, UK*
The firm James & Charles Wileman (see above) was continued by James F. Wileman 1869–92. His name or initial mark appears on printed marks of differing design.

J. M. & S.

Job Meigh (& Son) *Hanley, Staffordshire, UK*
See p318. These initials appear c1812–34, but usually relate to J. Meir & Son, based at the Greengates Pottery in Tunstall 1837–97. Originally John Meir (c1812–36) this firm made earthenware services, and the initials appear in many different marks.

J. T. (& S.)

John Tams (& Son) (Ltd) *Longton, Staffordshire, UK*
Based at the Crown Pottery from c1875, this firm made Government measures, jugs and mugs. The initials 'J. T.' appear 1878–90, and may also appear as a monogram within a garter, crown and wreath mark. 'J. T. & S.' appears c1903–12 when the company was John Tams & Son. After 1912, the firm became John Tams Ltd.

J. & W. R.

John & William Ridgway *Shelton, Staffordshire, UK*
Originally Job Ridgway & Sons (see p324), this firm used a variety of marks that featured the distinguishing initials seen here.

K. E. & K.

Knight Elkin & Knight *Fenton, Staffordshire, UK*
Also listed as Knight, Elkin & Co, this firm succeeded Elkin, Knight & Bridgwood after 1840. After Elkin retired in 1846 the name changed to J. K. Knight.

KELSBORO' WARE

Longton New Art Pottery Co Ltd *Longton, Staffordshire, UK*
Based at the Gordon Pottery, this company produced earthenwares 1932–65. Variations of the mark occur, but all include the tradename 'Kelsboro'.

KISHERE (POTTERY)/MORTLAKE (SURREY)

Joseph Kishere *Mortlake, London, UK*
Stonewares were made by Joseph Kishere at the Mortlake Pottery c1800–43. Impressed marks appear in a number of forms, including those above. William Kishere succeeded his father.

KIRKHAM (S)

Kirkham's Ltd *Stoke, Staffordshire, UK*
Operating between 1946 and 1961, this company produced earthenwares with a variety of marks that feature this name.

J. K. KNIGHT

John, King, Knight *Fenton, Staffordshire, UK*
See p314. This name mark was used 1846–53, before the firm became Knight & Wileman. The name 'Foley' sometimes appears with these marks.

KNOWLES

Matthew Knowles & Son *Brampton, Derbyshire, UK*
The Welshpool and Payne Potteries came into the hands of Matthew Knowles in 1835. He was later joined by his son, and the style of the firm changed to Matthew Knowles & Son. All types of brown and stonewares were made for export to Australia, Russia, Africa and Jamaica, as well as for the domestic market. The output included good quality stoneware spirit bottles, kegs and barrels, ginger beer bottles made in both stoneware and brown ware, jam jars, stew and sauce pots, bowls, colanders, tobacco jars, jugs and a wide variety of other items. Notable were high quality water filters, and finely-coloured Chesterfield ware. The firm closed in 1911.

KORZEC

Prince Iwan Czartorsky *Korzec, Poland*
A porcelain factory was founded here by Prince Iwan Czartorsky, and was active 1790–97. The factory was burned down in 1798 and production transferred to Gorodnitza. In 1803, Mérault from Sèvres managed the factory, and some very beautiful pieces were produced. The name 'Korzec' appears in many marks used by the factory.

K.T. & K./CHINA

Knowles, Taylor and Knowles *East Liverpool, Ohio, USA*

See p186. This is one of the marks used.

KUZNECOVS (/LATVIJA)

T. J. Kusnetzoff *Various locations, Europe*

T. J. Kusnetzoff was one of a family of porcelain factory owners that ran large, successful companies throughout the 19thC and early 20thC, producing utility wares. A number of marks are used; some feature the name as above, on others the name appears in Cyrillic script.

LAMSON & SWASEY/PORTLAND, ME.

Lamson & Swasey *Portland, Maine, USA*

In 1875, an earthenware pottery was opened by Rufus Lamson and Eben Swasey at Portland, Maine but soon the Portland Pottery Works began to make salt-glazed utilitarian stoneware, sometimes decorated in blue. After Lamson left in 1883, Swasey took on L. Frank Jones until Lamson's return in 1886. The firm continued until c1905. Many examples are half dipped in Albany slip producing a distinctive glaze contrast. This impressed mark was used.

LANCASTER SADLAND LTD.

Lancaster & Sadland Ltd *Hanley, Staffordshire, UK*

Formerly Lancaster & Sons (Ltd) (see p167), this name appears in several marks of differing design from 1944.

J. LOCKETT & CO.

J. Lockett & Co *Lane End, Staffordshire, UK*

This firm produced earthenwares at King Street, Lane End c1812–89, at Longton 1882–1960, and from 1960 at Burslem. Impressed or printed marks appear with the name in full as seen above.

J. LOCKETT & SONS

J. Lockett & Sons *Longton, Staffordshire, UK*

This firm produced earthenwares 1828–35 with this impressed mark. The firm later became John & Thomas Lockett.

L. S.

Lancaster & Sons (Ltd) *Hanley, Staffordshire, UK*

See p167. These initials were used in many marks 1900–06; '& Sons' or '& S' was added from 1906.

MCCOY (USA)

Nelson McCoy Pottery *Roseville, Ohio, USA*

This pottery (1910-present) made stoneware churns, butter jars, crocks and drainage tiles when it was first organized, but for many years has manufactured a variety of novelty consumer items, including biscuit jars, planters, and florists' crockery. Today it is owned by the Mount Clemens Pottery Company, Michigan but still operates under its original name. Note that it should not be confused with J. W. McCoy Pottery, Roseville, Ohio, which made florists' crockery in the style of Rookwood, 1899–1911.) 'McCoy' and 'McCoy USA' are the most usual name marks; sometimes the 'M' and 'c' overlap.

J. MCCULLY/TRENTON
Joseph McCully Pottery *Trenton, New Jersey, USA*
Joseph McCully and his nephew made and marked slip-decorated redware plates, platters and jars c1800–52. This name mark is impressed in an oval.

MALING
Maling (various Christian names)
Sunderland, Tyne and Wear, UK
William Maling established the North Hylton or Hylton Pottery in 1762 for his sons Christopher and John. John's son Robert joined the business in 1797, and the firm continued until 1815 when a new factory was built at Ouseburn, Newcastle. Early wares are unmarked, but an impressed name mark was occasionally used c1800–15. This mark was also used at the Ouseburn Pottery by Robert Maling c1817–59. In 1859, Robert's son Christopher became the owner of the firm. The style changed to C. T. Maling, and he built the Ford Potteries in Newcastle. The firm continued there until 1963 (see p175). He used the 'Maling' name mark c1859–90.

J. MANTELL/PENN YAN
James Mantell *Penn Yan, New York, USA*
This pottery was operated near the village of Penn Yan before 1830 by the Campbell family but by 1855 James Mantell, who had been born in England and worked as a potter at Lyons, New York, owned the factory, first with Shem Thomas, and later alone. The business was successful and many well-decorated examples survive. Shem Thomas went on to operate his own stoneware kiln at Harrisburg, Pennsylvania in 1856 and also worked at the Cowden & Wilcox Pottery until his death in 1871. This impressed mark appears.

MAW (& CO.)
Maw & Co (Ltd) *Broseley, Shropshire, UK*
Originally established at Worcester in 1850, this firm produced plain, geometric, mosaic and ordinary encaustic

tiles. The concern was moved to the Benthall Works at Broseley in 1852. A great deal of experimentation was carried out, and many different decorative techniques were used. Notable were tesserae (small pieces of pottery) for mosaic work decorated with rich enamels, embossed tiles, sgraffiato decorated tiles, 'slip painting', and *pâte-sur-pâte.* Art pottery was produced from c1875, which comprised a variety of majolica wares. The firm continued until c1970.

T. J. & J. MAYER

Thomas, John & Joseph Mayer *Burslem, Staffordshire, UK*
This firm was based at the Dale Hall Works 1843–55, became Mayer Bros & Elliot and then Mayer & Elliot (see p65). The firm's wares were shown at the 1851, 1853 and 1855 Exhibitions, and their range of general ceramics were highly regarded, particularly their moulded parian ware. The title 'Mayer Bros' was also used.

MAYER CHINA/BEAVER FALLS, PA.

Mayer China Company/Mayer Potteries Company
Syracuse, New York, USA
See p236. This printed mark was used in the 20thC.

C J MEADERS/CLEVELAND, GA.

Cheever and Q. Lanier Meaders *White County, Georgia, USA*
Cheever Meaders (1887–1967) took over the management and production of the original family pottery in 1920 and continued to make traditional alkaline-glazed stoneware for local use. His wife, Arie, developed a line of decorated tablewares and inspired her husband to produce some original forms of his own. Their son, Q. Lanier Meaders, eventually joined in the family business in 1967, and he is best known for the humorous face-jugs he fashions in stoneware. The business continued until 1989. The name 'Lanier Meaders' also appears incised in script.

MEIGH

Job Meigh (& Son) *Hanley, Staffordshire, UK*
Based at the Old Hall Pottery, this firm produced earthenwares c1805–34 (& Son from c1812). This impressed name mark was used 1805–34. The firm later became Charles Meigh, and this name appears on wares 1835–49. The firm became C. Meigh, Son & Pankhurst in 1849, and the Charles Meigh & Son in 1850 (see p284).

MELBAR WARE

Barlows (Longton) Ltd *Longton, Staffordshire, UK*
Based at the Melbourne Works, this company produced earthenwares 1920–52. This trade name mark appears.

MERCER POTTERY/TRENTON N.J.
Mercer Pottery Company *Trenton, New Jersey, USA*
Established by James Moses in 1868, this large pottery specialized in decorated semi-porcelain table, toilet wares and druggists' wares. Mercer shared the business with the International Pottery Company (see p223) organized in 1879, and the New York City Pottery (see p186); the three potteries also shared for a time a mark with two shields differentiated only by the name that appears below. The trade name 'Mercer China' also appears in a number of marks.The Mercer Pottery Company continued until 1900.

MIDDLESBORO POTTERY (CO.)
Middlesbrough Pottery Co *North Yorkshire, UK*
See p171. The name 'Middlesboro Pottery' or 'Middlesboro Pottery Co' appeared in impressed or printed marks c1834–44, and may feature an anchor device. 'Middlesboro Pottery' was also used by its successor, the Middlesbrough Earthenware Co 1844–52, again with an anchor device.

MIDWINTER
W. R. Midwinter (Ltd) *Burslem, Staffordshire, UK*
See p211. This name mark appears in many different marks.

C. J. (W. F.) MILLER/VICKSBURG, MISS.
C. J. and W. F. Miller *Vicksburg, Mississippi, USA*
C. J. Miller established his stoneware pottery along the Mississippi River at Vicksburg in 1890 and produced white Bristol glazed wares until his son, W. F. Miller, took over the pottery in 1910. Made jugs, crocks and jars until at least 1930. These stencilled marks appear.

MONMOUTH/POTTERY CO./MONMOUTH, ILL.
Monmouth Pottery Company *Monmouth, Illinois, USA*
A major commercial stoneware factory was erected at Monmouth, Illinois in 1893 by William Hanna, a banker, and associates, to take advantage of rich and extensive local deposits of stoneware clays. The factory had an annual production of over six million gallons of pottery when, in 1906, it merged with the Western Stoneware Company. Bristol and Albany slip-glazed wares are often found, and blue sponge-decorated pitchers, crocks etc are avidly collected. This mark in raised letters appears.

MOORE (BROS.)
Moore (Bros) *Longton, Staffordshire, UK*
See p157. 'Moore' printed or impressed, was used c1868–75; 'Moore Bros' appears 1872–1905. 'Moore Bothers England' was used 1891–1905.

MORLEY WARE
William Morley & Co Ltd *Fenton, Staffordshire, UK*
See p197. This trade name appears in marks used by both Morley Fox & Co Ltd and William Morley & Co.

MORRISON & CARR
New York City Pottery *New York, New York, USA*
See p186. This mark appears impressed in an oval.

NANTGARW
Nantgarw China Works *Glamorgan, Wales, UK*
This works was opened by William Billingsley of Derby in 1813. Following an inspection of the premises and the production by Mr Dillwyn of the Cambrian Pottery, Billingsley and his partner Samuel Walker were persuaded to move to Swansea. After two years Billingsley and Walker returned to Nantgarw where they produced high quality porcelain for about four years before production ended. Notable is a service presented to the Prince of Wales (later George IV). This impressed, painted or stencilled name mark was used; sometimes the initials 'C. W.' for 'China Works' are also included.

NASHVILLE POTTERY
Nashville Pottery Co *Nashville, Tennessee, USA*
In 1888, William McLee and C. C. Laitenberger started a stoneware pottery at Nashville, producing a fine Albany slip-glazed utilitarian ware. The pottery continued until 1900; in the 1901 Nashville City Directory, the factory is listed as 'vacant.' This impressed mark was used.

NEALE (& CO.)
(James) Neale & Co *Hanley, Staffordshire, UK*
See p154. This name mark was used in many forms; '& Co' was added c1778–86. Their predecessors, Neale & Palmer, marked their wares with their name c1769–78.

N(ORTH) STAFFORDSHIRE POTTERY CO. LTD.
North Staffordshire Pottery Co Ltd
Cobridge and Hanley, Staffordshire, UK
This firm produced earthenwares 1940–52 before being taken over by Ridgway Potteries Ltd. Their registered trademark was a rock emerging from water, and the slogan 'Strong As The Rock'. It was continued by Ridgways.

E. & L. P. (J. & E.) NORTON/BENNINGTON, VT.
Edward & Luman P. Norton *Bennington, Vermont, USA*
The most prolific of the stoneware potteries of Bennington, Vermont was run by Edward and Luman

Preston Norton, after the death of Julius Norton who, with his cousin Edward, had managed the factory since 1850. Wares dating from their partnership include some of the finest and most elaborate cobalt-blue trailed lions, deer, eagles etc found on American stoneware. While under Edward and Luman's partnership, decorated wares continued to be made, though not as imaginative. They did, however, make fancy Rockingham pottery forms, including hound-handled pitchers, teapots, and spittoons. This firm closed in 1881. These impressed marks appear.

F. B. NORTON (& CO., SONS, & SONS)/ WORCESTER, MASS.

Frank B. Norton *Worcester, Massachusetts, USA*
In 1858 Frank B. Norton of the Bennington, Vermont family of potters and Frederick Hancock opened a successful stoneware manufactory at Worcester, Massachusetts. Norton's sons entered the pottery business in 1868, and Hancock left the business in 1877. A highly popular, blue-decorated and salt-glazed stoneware was produced using some of the slip-trailed designs introduced at Bennington. He continued until 1894.

O. P. CO/CHINA (IMPERIAL)

Onondaga Pottery *Syracuse, New York, USA*
See p168. This printed mark was used.

O.P. CO./SYRACUSE/CHINA

Syracuse China Company *Syracuse, New York, USA*
Although this company was not officially created until 1966, the trade name 'Syracuse China' had been used since 1897 on an individual product line made by the Onondaga Pottery Company (see 168). The line created in the 19thC was a vitreous china dinnerware line. Today, Syracuse specializes in high-quality hotel and institutional ware. This mark was printed on wares pre-1966.

PALISSY

Albert E. Jones (Longton) Ltd *Longton, Staffordshire, UK*
Formerly A. B. Jones & Sons (Ltd) (see p165), this name mark was used both by this firm 1905–46 and its successor Palissy Pottery Ltd 1946–89.

PATTERSON & CO.

Patterson & Co *Newcastle-upon-Tyne, Tyne and Wear, UK*
This firm was based at the Sheriff Hill Pottery from c1830. They made white wares, mainly for export to Scandinavia. In 1904 the Sheriff's Hill Pottery Co was formed. Many printed or impressed marks include this name.

APSLEY PELLATT & CO.

Apsley Pellatt (& Co Ltd) *London, UK*

The name of this firm of ceramics and glass retailers (established in c1789) appears on some marks, mainly during the second half of the 19thC or early 20thC.

PENN YAN

James Mantell *Penn Yan, New York, USA*

See p317. This impressed mark was used.

J. PHILLIPS/SUNDERLAND POTTERY
PHILLIPS & CO.

Sunderland or 'Garrison' Pottery

Sunderland, Tyne and Wear, UK

Established by John Phillips c1807, this works was run by Dixon, Austin, Phillips & Co producing white and Queen's ware with all types of decoration. The works closed in c1865. The mark above was used c1807–12. Phillips & Co appears c1813–19.

PHOENIX/FACTORY/ED SC

Phoenix Factory *Shaw's Creek, South Carolina, USA*

In 1840 Collin Rhodes and Robert Mathis established the Phoenix Factory pottery, which made probably the most elaborate and decorative southern stonewares. Thomas Chandler is credited with the development of the brown and white slip-decorated alkaline-glazed pieces made there, although Rhodes maintained this style of decoration after Chandler left in 1845 and Mathis withdrew in 1846. The factory closed in 1853. This impressed mark was used.

PORT DUNDAS/GLASGOW POTTERY

Port Dundas Pottery Co Ltd *Glasgow, Scotland, UK*

These works produced stoneware c1816, and operated under many owners until 1845 when they were taken over by James Miller who traded as James Miller & Co and then the Port Dundas Pottery Co. Output included chemical vessels, apparatus of various types and later water pipes. Stoneware beer, ink and spirit bottles and other items with a cream-coloured glaze were also produced. This firm helped the development of the steam-driven potter's wheel. The firm continued until 1932.

PRAG

K. L. Kriegel and others *Prag, Bohemia, Czech Republic*

Originally a stoneware factory founded by the Kunerle brothers in 1793, the factory produced porcelain in 1837 when K. L. Kriegel became the director. Kriegel and K. Wolf became leaseholders 1837–41. Kriegel and E.

Hoffman Von Hoffmansthal became the owners in 1882. Attractive porcelain figures dominated the production. The name 'Prag' is incorporated into many marks, including 'Prag-Smichow', the mark used 1854–94.

PRATT

William Pratt *Lane Delph, Staffordshire, UK*

In c1780 William Pratt founded a factory producing lead-glazed earthenware, coloured and moulded figures, jugs and other wares. The works were taken over by his eldest son Felix in 1810. Later the ware was copied by local potters. In the mid-19thC the Pratt family also produced ware decorated with polychrome transfer prints, such as the well-known pot lids. The impressed name 'Pratt' occasionally appears, but it is difficult to determine which member of the family employed this mark.

PRICE (BROS.)

Price Brothers *Burslem, Staffordshire, UK*

Established in 1896, this firm produced earthenware initially at the Crown Works. This name mark was used 1896–1903 and by its successors, Price Bros (Burslem) Ltd (1903–61) and Price & Kensington Potteries Ltd at Longport (from 1962).

S. (H.) PURDY/OHIO

Solomon and Henry Purdy *Mogadore, Ohio, USA*

Solomon Purdy established a stoneware pottery in Zanesville in 1812. He moved to Akron in 1828 and later to Mogadore. His early ovoid shapes in cobalt-blue, brush-decorated salt-glazed stoneware are among the more highly sought-after. In 1840, Solomon's son, Henry Purdy, took over management of the shop and continued in business until 1850. These impressed marks were used.

QUEEN ANNE

Shore & Coggins *Longton, Staffordshire, UK*

See p329. This name was one of those used from c1949.

ERIC RAVILIOUS

Eric Ravilious, *Staffordshire, UK*

Utility wares were designed by Eric Ravilious for Wedgwood during the late 1930s. Alphabet nurseryware was designed in 1937; another well-known design is the zodiac series. Most designs were not executed until the 1950s. Some were reissued in the late 1980s due to popular demand, but these lack the characteristic signs of wear of the originals. Wares are signed in a small rectangular panel 'designed by Eric Ravilious', and carry an imprinted Wedgwood mark.

HENRY REMMEY/MANUFACTORY/PHILADELPHIA
Remmey Manufactory *Philadelphia, Pennsylvania, USA*
Henry H. Remmey, the son of potter John Remmey of Manhattan, New York, purchased c1827 an existing stoneware factory in Philadelphia. After 1859 his son, Richard C. Remmey, ran the company. Some fine decorated 'afterhours' and gift pieces are known, but the main production was simply decorated with leaves in cobalt blue.

J. REMMEY/MANHATTAN WELLS/NEW YORK
John Remmey Snr, Jnr and III *Manhattan, New York, USA*
The first John Remmey operated a stoneware factory on Pottbaker's Hill in southern Manhattan from c1735. After his father's death in 1762, John Remmey Jnr continued until his death in 1792. By then, he had been joined by his two sons, John III and Henry. The pottery adjoined the water works, and this explains the use of 'Manhattan Wells, New York' to identify their location on their marked pots. Infrequently, blue incised floral decoration was added to the utilitarian wares. The concern continued until 1820.

C. RHODES MAKER
Phoenix Factory *Shaw's Creek, South Carolina, USA*
See p322. This slip-trailed mark was used by Collin Rhodes.

G. RICHARD& C.
Giulio Richard *Milan, Italy*
A factory was founded here in 1833 by Luigi Tinelli and produced porcelain and faïence. Copies of Wedgwood wares were made but feature the mark of this factory. Luigi's brother Carlo took over the business and went into partnership with Giulio Richard from Turin in 1841. Richard became the sole owner in 1870, and in 1896 his company amalgamated with Ginori of Doccia.

RIDGWAY (& SONS)
Job Ridgway & Sons *Shelton, Staffordshire, UK*
Job Ridgway originally established a firm at Cauldon Place c1802, having formerly been in partnership with his brother George at the Bell Works (c1782–1802). Job took his sons into partnership in c1808. Job died in 1814, and the firm became John & William Ridgway until c1830 when John Ridgway took over the firm (see p283).

RIDGWAYS
Ridgways *Shelton, Hanley, Staffordshire, UK*
See p212. This name mark appears in the wide range of marks used by this firm 1879–1920, and its successor Ridgways (Bedford Works) Ltd 1920–52.

S. RISLEY/NORWICH

Sidney Risley *Norwich, Connecticut, USA*

A stoneware pottery was established c1836 in Norwich, Connecticut by Sidney Risley. He had been a potter in East Hartford but opened the shop after the Armstrong & Wentworth pottery closed. Risley died in 1875 and his son, George S. Risley, ran the business until he was killed in an explosion in 1881. Some Rockingham ware was made as well as utilitarian stoneware. This impressed mark appears.

R. M. (& S)

Ralph Malkin (& Sons) *Fenton, Staffordshire, UK*

Based at the Park Works in Fenton, this firm made the earthenwares 1863–92. The name of the firm changed to Ralph Malkin & Sons in 1882. These initials are found in many printed marks, often with the pattern name.

W. ROBERTS/BINGHAMTON, N.Y.

William Roberts *Binghamton, New York, USA*

William Roberts was born in Llanfachreth, North Wales in 1818 and arrived in the USA in 1827. By 1848 he was operating a Binghamton pottery with his father-in-law, Noah White, of Utica, New York. Cobalt-blue slip-trailed wares may be found, dating from the later years of the pottery's production. The concern continued until 1888.

ROGERS

John & George Rogers *Longport, Staffordshire, UK*

These brothers owned the Dale Hall Pottery from c1784, and produced tableware. Notable are their light blue Willow pattern services. Their early mark was 'Rogers' impressed or printed. After the death of George, the firm continued as John Rogers & Son until c1836: the name 'Rogers' was also used up to this time.

(J.) ROSE

Coalport Porcelain Works *Coalport, Shropshire, UK*

See p82. The founder of the Coalport Works, John Rose's name mark appears in various forms on many pieces.

ROSLYN CHINA

Reid & Co *Longton, Staffordshire, UK*

See p211. This trade name was continued by this firm's successor Roslyn China 1946–63.

ROYAL ART POTTERY/ENGLAND

Clough's Royal Art Pottery *Longton, Staffordshire, UK*

Formerly Alfred Clough Ltd (Royal Art Pottery), this company produced earthenwares from 1961. This name mark appears above a crown device, with the word 'England' appearing underneath. The same mark was used by the firm's predecessor 1951–61.

ROYAL BARUM WARE
C. H. Brannam Ltd *Barnstaple, Devon, UK*
See p220. This trade name appears on 20thC marks.

ROYAL BOURBON WARE
New Pearl Pottery Co Ltd *Hanley, Staffordshire, UK*
Based at the Brook Street Potteries, this firm (formerly Pearl Pottery Co Ltd) operated 1936–41. It was closed during WWII, and the factory was sold in 1947. This trade name was used.

ROYAL BRADWELL
Arthur Wood & Son (Longport) Ltd
Longport, Staffordshire, UK
Formerly Arthur Wood (1904–28), this firm was based at the Bradwell Works from 1928 producing earthenwares.

ROYAL CHELSEA
New Chelsea Porcelain Co (Ltd) *Longton, Staffordshire, UK*
See p228. This trade name was used c1919–61.

ROYAL CHINA
E. Hughes & Co *Fenton, Staffordshire, UK*
See p178. This trade name appears in a number of marks.

ROYAL (CHINA)/SEBRING, OHIO
Royal China Company *Sebring, Ohio, USA*
This pottery made semi-porcelain tableware and vitreous hotel ware with printed or decal decoration 1934 to c1985. In 1969, it was purchased by the Jeannette Corporation. The mark above usually appears with the pattern name.

ROYAL CROWN POTTERY
Trentham Bone China Ltd *Longton, Staffordshire, UK*
Based at the Royal Crown Pottery, this firm produced porcelain 1952–57. This name mark appears.

ROYAL GRAFTON
A. B. Jones & Sons (Ltd) *Longton, Staffordshire, UK*
See p165. The trade name 'Royal Grafton' was used from c1949 and later became Royal Grafton Bone China Ltd.

ROYAL HARVEY
Gibson & Sons (Ltd) *Burslem, Staffordshire, UK*
See p197. This trade name was used c1950–55.

ROYAL LANCASTRIAN
Pilkington's Tile & Pottery Co Ltd *Manchester, UK*
See p193. The impressed 'P' mark of the Pilkington Factory sometimes includes the words 'Royal Lancastrian'. Some wares bear only these words, c1914–38. 'England' was added c1920; 'Made in England' appears c1920–38.

ROYAL LEIGHTON WARE
Leighton Pottery *Burslem, Staffordshire, UK*
See p224. This trade name was used c1946–54.

ROYAL MAYFAIR
Chapmans Longton Ltd *Longton, Staffordshire, UK*
See p214. This trade name appears in some marks 1938–41.

ROYAL NORFOLK
Norfolk Pottery Co Ltd *Shelton, Staffordshire, UK*
See p213. This trade name appears in marks from 1958.

ROYAL PRINCE
Hall Bros (Longton) Ltd *Longton, Staffordshire, UK*
From 1947 this firm produced porcelain figures, vases and other wares at the Radnor Works. This trade name appears in marks 1947–51.

ROYAL STAFFORD CHINA
Thomas Poole *Longton, Staffordshire, UK*
See p203. This trade name was used in many of the marks used by this firm 1912–52. The firm became Thomas Poole (Longton) Ltd in c1925. In 1948 it merged with Gladstone China Ltd and after 1952 continued as Royal Stafford China.

ROYAL STANDARD
Chapmans Longton Ltd *Longton, Staffordshire, UK*
See p214. This trade name was used on marks from c1930.

ROYAL STUART
Stevenson, Spencer & Co Ltd *Longton, Staffordshire, UK*
Porcelain was produced by this firm 1948–60 (after 1960 the firm became a distributor only). This was one of the trade names used from c1951.

ROYAL TORQUAY POTTERY
Royal Aller Vale & Watcombe Pottery Co
Torquay, Devon, UK
Formerly Aller Vale Art Potteries (1887–1901), this firm produced earthenwares c1901–62. This impressed or printed name mark was used by this firm c1901 onwards.

ROYAL TUDOR WARE
Barker Bros *Lane End, Staffordshire, UK*
See p205. This trade name was incorporated into a number of marks from c1937.

ROYAL TUNSTALL
Wedgwood & Co (Ltd) *Tunstall, Staffordshire, UK*
See p216. This trade name was used from c1957.

ROYAL VALE/ROYAL VITRIFIED
Ridgway Potteries Ltd *Hanley, Staffordshire, UK*
See p212. 'Royal Vale' was one of several different trade names used. The trade name 'Royal Vitrified' was used c1905–20 while this firm was operating under the name of Ridgways.

ROYAL WATCOMBE
Royal Aller Vale & Watcombe Pottery Co
Torquay, Devon, UK
See p327. This name mark was used c1958–62.

ROYAL WINTON
Grimwades Ltd *Stoke, Staffordshire, UK*
See p215. This trade name appears in many marks c1910.

ROYAL WORCESTER
Worcester Porcelains *Hereford and Worcester, UK*
See p33. This company became the Worcester Royal Porcelain Co Ltd in 1862. Several marks feature this name.

R.R.P.CO./ROSEVILLE, O./USA
Ransbottom Brothers Pottery Company/Robinson-Ransbottom *Roseville, Ohio, USA*
This is one of the few US companies to make stoneware products profitably throughout the 20thC. Since its foundation in 1900, the pottery has produced poultry feeders, flowerpots and garden crockery such as bird baths, jardinières, vases, urns and strawberry jars. Jars, jugs, bowls, milkpans and cuspidors (a globular spittoon with a wide flaring rim or a high, funnel-shaped mouth) were also made early, and kitchenware was added later. The Robinson Clay Products Company bought the pottery in 1920 and renamed it Robinson-Ransbottom. This mark appears in many variations.

RYE
Rye Pottery *Rye, East Sussex, UK*
See p183. The name 'Rye' appears in many of the marks used by this firm c1869–1939 and from 1947.

SALEM

Salem China Company *Salem, Ohio, USA*

This pottery made ironstone and earthenware from 1898, before developing a line of dinnerware heavily decorated with brilliant decals in a wide variety of patterns. Since 1967, the firm has been a distributor of Japanese and English wares made with the Salem China backstamp. The name 'Salem' appears within a variety of marks.

SALON CHINA

Salt & Nixon (Ltd) *Longton, Staffordshire, UK*

Based at the Gordon Pottery and the Jubilee Works from 1910, this firm produced porcelain 1901–34. This trade name appears on many of their marks.

SATTERLEE & MORY/FORT EDWARD

New York Stoneware Company *Fort Edward, New York, USA*

See p136. This impressed mark was used.

S. B. & CO.

Thomas Sharpe (Sharpe Brothers & Co)

Burton-on-Trent, Staffordshire, UK

See p330. These initial marks appear in many forms c1838–95. 'Ltd' was added from 1895.

S. & C.

Shore & Coggins *Longton, Staffordshire, UK*

See p161. This firm operated under this style 1911–66 producing porcelain. These initials appear on many marks.

SCHERZER

Zeh Scherzer & Co *Rehau, Bavaria, Germany*

Founded in 1880, this company produced porcelain coffee and tea services and gift items. Between 1924 and 1926 the company owned the Elsterwerke, Mühlhausen. This name was incorporated into some of the factory marks used by the firm.

A.(NTHONY) SCOTT (& SONS)

Southwick Pottery *Sunderland, Tyne and Wear, UK*

The Southwick Pottery was built in 1788 by Anthony Scott, and run by various members of the family until c1897. They produced white, coloured and brown earthenwares. The style of the firm changed many times, and the marks used were as follows: 'A. Scott & Co' (c1800–29); 'Anthony Scott & Sons' (c1829–38); 'Scott Brothers & Co' (c1838–54); A. Scott (c1854–72 and c1882–97); 'A. Scott & Son' (c1872–82). These marks should not be confused with Scott Bros of Portobello (see p330).

SCOTT BROS. (P.B.)

Scott Brothers *Portobello, Edinburgh, Scotland, UK*

This firm operated c1786–96 producing earthenwares. Marks are impressed.

SEBRING/SEBRING POTTERY COMPANY

Sebring Pottery Company

East Liverpool and Sebring, Ohio, USA

The company began production in East Liverpool in 1887, and moved to Sebring in 1898 when the town was founded to support the several potteries being created by the Sebring brothers. It first made white granite dinner and tea sets and later changed to semi-porcelain dinner ware and hotel ware with decal decorations. 'Ivory Porcelain' was introduced in 1923. It continued until 1934. These names appear in many marks that incorporate pattern names.

SEWELL (& DONKIN, & CO.)

St Anthony's Pottery

Newcastle-upon-Tyne, Tyne and Wear, UK

See p333. The impressed or printed name 'Sewell' appears 1804–c1828; 'Sewell & Donkin' was used 1828–52; 'Sewell & Co' appears 1852–78.

(T.) SHARPE

Thomas Sharpe (Sharpe Brothers & Co)

Burton-on-Trent, Staffordshire, UK

The Swadlincote Works were established by Thomas Sharpe in 1821, and operated by him until his death in 1838. The firm was then continued by his brothers, and became Sharpe Bros & Co. Production included Derbyshire ironstone, cane (yellow) ware, drab ware, Rockingham, mottled ware and black lustreware. All types of domestic wares were produced, including speciality wares such as Toby jugs. After 1895 output mainly comprised sanitary wares. Various combinations of Sharpe's name appear.

A.(NTHONY) SHAW

Anthony Shaw (& Co) (& Son)

Tunstall and Burslem, Staffordshire, UK

Founded c1851, this firm made wares principally for the American export markets, including white granite ware and cream-coloured ware for the US and printed, lustred and painted wares for South America. This name appears in many printed or impressed marks of differing design; the Royal Arms is often used. '& Son' was added to the style and marks c1882–98; '& Co' was substituted for '& Son' from c1898. The firm was taken over by A. J. Wilkinson Ltd c1900.

SHAWNEE/USA

Shawnee Pottery Company *Zanesville, Ohio, USA*

Named after an Indian arrowhead found on the property during construction, the pottery (1937–61) specialized in inexpensive colourful florists' crockery and novelty table and kitchen ware. As an example, for the Corn King pattern all forms were based on the shape and texture of an ear of corn including the husks. Marks and paper labels include the name 'Shawnee, USA' along with pattern names.

SHELLEY

Wileman & Co *Longton, Staffordshire, UK*

See p314. This pottery produced porcelain 1892–1925. This trade name was used from c1911. The firm became Shelley Potteries Ltd in c1925 (Royal Albert Ltd from 1967), and marks in various forms were used.

SHENANGO CHINA

Shenango Pottery Company *New Castle, Pennsylvania, USA*

Formed in 1901, this company made semi-porcelain dinner and toilet sets. They made porcelain 1936–58 for the Theodore Haviland Company of Limoges, France, under the style 'Haviland, New York' as well as vitreous dinner and hotel ware. By 1951, Shenango fully owned the fine porcelain company Castleton China, known for its 'Museum' shape designed by Eva Zeisel and for the service made for the White House during Lyndon Johnson's time (1963–69). Today, Shenango continues to make high-grade hotel and institutional ware.

SHORTHOSE (& HEATH)

Shorthose & Heath (John Shorthose)

Hanley, Staffordshire, UK

Based in Hanley c1795–1815 the company produced cream-coloured services, white and printed goods, black basaltes and other wares. John Shorthose worked there from c1807–23 making good quality lustrewares, often with white relief patterns. His pieces are occasionally marked.

JOHN SIMPSON

John Simpson *Burslem, Staffordshire, UK*

This potter made slip-decorated earthenwares in the early 18thC. This name occurs. Three potters of this name were on Wedgwood's list of Burslem potters c1710–15.

RALPH SIMPSON

Ralph Simpson *Staffordshire, UK*

Ralph Simpson (1651–1724), made slip-decorated earthenwares similar to those made by the Tofts (see p335).

WILLIAM SIMPSON

William Simpson *Staffordshire, UK*

This name appears on a slip-decorated posset pot dated 1685, and also appears in contemporary records in various Staffordshire centres during this period.

SIMPSONS (POTTERS) LTD.

Simpsons (Potters) Ltd *Cobridge, Staffordshire, UK*

Formerly the Soho Pottery Ltd (see p214), this firm produced earthenwares at the Elder Works from 1944. This name appears in their marks which also feature a number of different trade names.

S. M.

Samuel Malkin *Burslem, Staffordshire, UK*

This potter produced slip-decorated earthenwares during the early 18thC. Some pieces include these initials within the designs; one example is signed in full. Dated examples range between 1712 and 1734.

W.J. SMITH/BRIDGETON, N.J.

Cohansey Street Pottery *Bridgeton, New Jersey, USA*

William J. Smith (active 1865–95) made brown glazed redware in kitchen forms, such as pie plates and handled jars as well as whimsies or what were called image toys, especially of birds. This mark was incised in script.

SOHO POTTERY (LTD.)

Soho Pottery (Ltd) *Tunstall and Cobridge, Staffordshire, UK*

See p214. This name appears in the wide variety of marks.

SOMERSET POTTERS WORKS

Somerset Potters' Works, *Somerset, Massachusetts, USA*

See p302. This impressed mark was used.

SOUTH WALES POTTERY

South Wales Pottery *Llanelly, Wales, UK*

This pottery was established by William Chambers in 1839 and was operated by him until 1854. He produced white and cream-coloured, edged, painted and printed ware. Other types of wares include parian, figures and enamelled wares. From 1850 white granite and underglaze printed wares were produced for sale in the US. Coombs and Holland took over in 1854 but the partnership ended in 1858, and Holland continued alone until 1869 when he was joined by D. Guest. In 1877 the firm changed to Guest & Duesbury and purchased the copper-engraved plates from many other Welsh potteries. The firm continued until c1927. This name mark is one of those used c1839–58.

SPODE

Josiah Spode *Stoke, Staffordshire, UK*

See p233. This impressed, painted or printed name mark was used in many of Josiah Spode's marks. The name has also been incorporated into the marks of his successor, W. T. Copeland (& Sons Ltd) (see p255).

ST. ANTHONY'S

St Anthony's Pottery *Newcastle-upon-Tyne, Tyne and Wear, UK*

One of the oldest potteries in the area, St Anthony's Pottery was established c1780. It was bought by Mr. Sewell c1803 and then became Sewell & Donkin (1828–52) and Sewell & Co (1852–78). Production mainly comprised cream-coloured, printed and blue-painted wares. Several forms of mark were used, including this one 1780–1820.

STANGL

Stangl Pottery Company *Trenton, New Jersey, USA*

After the Fulper Pottery of Flemington, New Jersey (see p124), suffered a devastating fire in 1929, the pottery's manager J. M. Stangl took over and concentrated production in their Trenton factory, making novelty finishes on casual dinnerware. Sgraffiato decorations through white slip on red earthenware were produced in many popular patterns. They also produced a line of colourful bird figurines in earthenware that is extremely popular today. The Stangl trade name was sold to Pfaltzgraff (see p195) in 1978. Marks appear printed and on paper labels; the name appears often with the pattern name.

STEUBENVILLE (CHINA)

Steubenville Pottery Company *Steubenville, Ohio, USA*

See p194. Later marks usually feature the mark above, along with the pattern names.

SWANSEA

Swansea Pottery *Swansea, Wales, UK*

A works had existed here since at least the middle of the 18thC, originally built to produce copper, but it was later converted into a pottery. Bought by Messrs Coles & Haynes in 1783, the works were enlarged by George Haynes after the death of Coles in 1800 and named the Cambrian Pottery. Earthenwares were made at first, but later a refined cream-coloured ware was produced, together with an opaque porcelain and other types of wares. Lewis Dillwyn took over in 1802, and he employed talented painters, including William Young. High quality porcelain was produced for Dillwyn after 1814 by William Billingsley and Samuel Walker, but these men were dismissed after it transpired that they had illegally left their positions at the Worcester Porcelain Works. T. & J. Bevington took over the works in 1817, but they returned to Lewis Dillwyn in 1824, and were subsequently operated by his son from 1840. Notable are imitations of Wedgwood's Etruscan wares, known as 'Dillwyn's Etruscan Ware', made from c1847. In c1851 the works were taken over by David Evans. The works closed c1870, and the engraved copper plates were sold to the South Wales Pottery, Llanelly.

E. SWASEY & CO./PORTLAND, ME.
Lamson & Swasey *Portland, Maine, USA*
See p316. This impressed mark was used.

SYRACUSE/CHINA/U.S.A.
Syracuse China Company *Syracuse, New York, USA*
See p321. This modern mark appears printed in several different ways.

J. S. TAFT (& CO.)/KEENE, N.H.
J. S. Taft & Co *Keene, New Hampshire, USA*
James Scholly Taft and his uncle, James Burnap, purchased a wooden-ware factory in Keene in 1871 and converted it to the production of earthenware. Stoneware was quickly added to their output, and in 1874 the company bought another factory for redware production. The company continued until 1898.

WILLIAM TALOR (TALLOR)
William Talor (or Tallor) *Burslem, Staffordshire, UK*
This name appears on rare slip-decorated earthenwares; one features the date 1700. Another is known, marked with the name 'William Tallor'.

TAMS
John Tams (& Son) (Ltd) *Longton, Staffordshire, UK*
See p314. The name 'Tams' or 'Tams Ware' appears in a number of different marks from c1930; others include the words 'Tams England'.

D. G. THOMPSON/MORGANTOWN
David Greenland Thompson *Morgantown, West Virginia, USA*
John Wood Thompson purchased a redware pottery at Morgantown in 1827 and produced both redware and stoneware until his retirement in 1853. The firm passed to three sons, including David Greenland Thompson who managed it until he died in 1890. Blue-decorated brushed and stencilled designs may be found along with impressed designs. This impressed mark appears.

J. THOMPSON

Joseph Thompson *Ashby de la Zouch, Leicestershire, UK*
Based at the Hartshorne or Wooden Box Pottery, this firm was first operated by Joseph Thompson who founded the works in 1818. He was succeeded by his sons Richard and Willoughby, and the title of the firm changed to Thompson Brothers from 1856. Derby ironstone, brown, cane, buff, and yellow ironstone ware, blackware, Rockingham, terracotta and sanitary goods were produced. White wares, porcelain and other decorated items were also made by Thompson Brothers. Holland & Thompson continued the firm until it closed in 1882.

J. T. (& SONS)/ANNFIELD (GLASGOW)

John Thomson (& Sons) *Glasgow, Scotland, UK*
This firm was based at the Annfield Pottery c1816–84, and produced ceramics for the home and export markets. The works closed c1884. Many different marks were used: 'J. T.' with or without 'Annfield' was used c1816–65. '& Sons' was added from c1866, and 'Glasgow' may also appear.

JAMES (RALPH, THOMAS) TOFT

James, Ralph, Thomas Toft *Hanley, Staffordshire, UK*
Three brothers, James (b1673), Ralph (b1638) and Thomas (b1689), produced slip-decorated earthenwares, some of which bear their names. Thomas Toft's work is most frequently marked; over 30 signed examples are recorded.

TOMLINSON & CO.

Tomlinson & Co *Ferrybridge Pottery, Yorkshire, UK*
Ferrybridge Pottery was established by William Tomlinson and partners in 1792 and the firm was known as William Tomlinson & Co until 1796. Ralph Wedgwood joined the business and the name changed to Tomlinson, Foster, Wedgwood & Co. Ralph was the eldest son of Thomas Wedgwood of Etruria (cousin and partner of Josiah Wedgwood). This partnership was dissolved c1800 and the company once again became known as Tomlinson & Co until 1834 when it changed to Tomlinson, Plowes & Co. In 1804 the name of the works was changed from the Knottingley Pottery to the Ferrybridge Pottery. William Tomlinson's son Edward continued the works until 1826. Wares were principally cream, cane and greenwares; blackwares and fine white earthenwares were also produced. Shortly afterwards, the works were taken over by James Reed and Benjamin Taylor who began production of porcelain. After 1856 the works were owned by Lewis Wolf and later by his sons. Subsequent owners include Poulson Bros (1897–1919) and T. Brown & Sons (Ltd).

TRENT

Trent Tile Company *Trenton, New Jersey, USA*

Isaac Broome was the first modeller for the company, active 1882–1938, specializing in heads and figures. English modeller William W. Gallimore followed Broome. The firm made tiles mostly covered in glossy coloured glazes. In 1938, the company went into receivership and was purchased by Wenczel Tile Company and continued until 1994. 'Trent' appears impressed or raised on the back of tiles.

TROPICO

Gladding, McBean and Company

Various locations, California, USA

See p302. This mark appears raised on tiles.

TUSCAN CHINA

R. H. & S. L. Plant (Ltd) *Longton, Staffordshire, UK*

See p275. This trade name appears on many marks.

UHL POTTERY WORKS/EVANSVILLE, IND.

Uhl Pottery Works *Evansville and Huntingburg, Indiana, USA*

One of the best-known of the Indiana potteries is the Uhl Pottery Works of Evansville, founded in 1854 by German potters, August and Louis Uhl. In 1891 the pottery moved to Huntingburg and continued in production into the 20thC. Utilitarian forms comprised the bulk of their production, but later decorative vases, piggy banks, and planters were made in bright enamel glazes.

UNWIN

Joseph Unwin (& Co) *Longton, Staffordshire, UK*

Formerly Poole & Unwin (1871–76), based at the Cornhill Works in Longton, this firm produced earthenwares, figures and other wares 1877–1926. This moulded name mark appears within a diamond-shaped outline. '& Co' was added to the firm's title in 1891.

U. H. P. CO. (LTD.)/ENGLAND

Upper Hanley Pottery Co (Ltd)

Hanley and Cobridge, Staffordshire, UK

Based in Hanley (c1895–1902) and Brownfield's Works in Cobridge (c1902–10), this pottery produced earthenwares 1895–1910. The initial mark 'U. H. P. & Co' appears in various forms 1895–1900; 'Ltd' was added from c1900.

VAN SCHOIK & DUNN

Van Schoik & Dunn/Dunn, Dunlap & Co

Matawan, New Jersey, USA

See p305. This impressed mark was used.

VERNON/CALIFORNIA
VERNONWARE/MADE IN U.S.A.
Vernon Kilns/Vernon Potteries *Vernon, California, USA*
This pottery (active 1928–58) produced earthenware dinnerware, including many designs by the well-known illustrator Rockwell Kent. Metlox Potteries, which owned it 1958–1960, continued to make some Vernon Kilns patterns. Marks sometimes include the pattern name.

VODREY DUBLIN POTTERY
Vodrey's Pottery *Dublin, Eire*
Pottery was produced c1873–85 with this impressed mark.

VOLKMAR (& CORY)
Volkmar Pottery
Various locations, New York and New Jersey, USA
Charles Volkmar trained as an artist in Paris and studied pottery decoration at the Haviland factory. He worked as a potter in Greenpoint, New York, then moved to Tremont. By 1888 he was working in Menlo Park, New Jersey, making tiles. He returned to Brooklyn in 1893 and made items with blue decoration. For a few months in 1896 he made blue-decorated plaques with Kate Cory, and later a line of vases with matt glazes or painted landscapes. In 1903, he founded Volkmar Kilns, Charles Volkmar & Son with Leon in Metuchen, New Jersey making a variety of effects until 1911. Many marks appear, incised or in relief.

WARWICK CHINA
Warwick China Company *Wheeling, West Virginia, USA*
See p231. This printed mark was used.

W.& C.
Walker & Carter *Longton, Staffordshire, UK*
Based at Longton 1866–72 and at Stoke 1872–89, this firm (formerly Walker, Bateman & Co) produced earthenwares. These initials appear in many marks, some of which include an anchor (1866–89).

WEDGWOOD & CO.
Tomlinson, Foster, Wedgwood & Co
Ferrybridge Pottery, Yorkshire, UK
See p335. This impressed mark was used c1796–1801.

WEIR POTTERY CO.
THE WEIR PAT' MAR 1ST 1892
Weir Pottery Company *Monmouth, Illinois, USA*
Alhough it was operated as an independent stoneware pottery for only a short time (1899–1905), the Weir

Pottery Company of Monmouth, Illinois, left an enormous legacy of signed and marked wares. Founded in 1899 by local banker William S. Weir, the pottery produced 500,000 moulded stoneware pitchers, mugs, steins, vases etc as premiums for the Sleepy Eye Milling Co of Minnesota; these featured a bust portrait of the Sioux Indian Chief, 'Old Sleepy Eye'. The company also made the patented Weir Stone Fruit Jars. Marks are impressed.

WELLER (POTTERY)
Weller Pottery/S.A. Weller Company
Fultonham and Zanesville, Ohio, USA
See p236. This impressed or incised mark was used.

WELLSVILLE CHINA
Wellsville China Company *Wellsville, Ohio, USA*
The company purchased the abandoned Pioneer Pottery Company works and by 1912 was producing semi-porcelain dinner and toilet wares, tea sets, cuspidors and other accessories and speciality items. Vitreous hotel ware was added in 1933. Controlling interest passed to Sterling China (see p147) in 1959, and the factory was closed in 1969. Many marks appear, featuring the pattern name and 'Wellsville China', sometimes appearing as 'W. C. Co.'

W. H. & S.
William Hackwood & Son *Shelton, Staffordshire, UK*
Formerly William Hackwood (see p309). This firm took over the New Hall Works in 1842. William Hackwood died in 1849 and the firm was continued by his son Thomas. They made various types of earthenware, mainly for the Continental markets. These initials are incorporated into many marks, often with the name of the pattern.

THE WHEELING (STONE CHINA) POTTERY CO.
Wheeling Pottery Company/Wheeling Potteries Company
Wheeling, West Virginia, USA
See p273. This printed mark was used.

A. O. WHITTEMORE/HAVANA, N.Y.
Albert O. Whittemore *Havana, New York, USA*
Albert O. Whittemore built a stoneware pottery in Havana, New York in 1863 and operated it as the Schuyler Stoneware Works until 1893. Some of the elaborate blue-decorated wares produced there rank among New York's finest and most imaginative. Whittemore had originally been a maker of beaver hats in New York City, but also established a farm and iron foundry in Havana.
This impressed mark appears.

WILSON

David Wilson (& Sons) *Hanley, Staffordshire, UK*

This potter and later his sons (from 1815) produced earthenwares and china, particularly lustred wares c1802–18. This mark was also used by David Wilson's father, Robert Wilson 1795–1801 (see p150).

ARTHUR WOOD (& SON)

Arthur Wood & Son (Longport) Ltd

Longport, Staffordshire, UK

See p326. This name features in many of the marks used. On some moulded wares the name 'Wood' only appears.

R(A). WOOD

Ralph Wood *Burslem, Staffordshire, UK*

Ralph Wood (1715–72) and his son (1748–95) were potters at the Hill factory in Burslem, and produced finely-modelled earthenware figures and other wares. Marked wares mainly comprise figures, reliefs and Toby jugs.

M. WOODRUFF/CORTLAND, N.Y.

Madison Woodruff *Cortland, New York, USA*

This potter had been associated with several earlier potteries in Homer and Cortland, New York in the Finger Lakes region before purchasing the Thomas Chollar Pottery in 1849. Floral-decorated utilitarian stoneware was made at various kilns in Cortland until his death in 1885.

W. S. & CO. (STAFFORD POTTERY)

William Smith (& Co) *Stockton-on-Tees, UK*

The Stafford Pottery was established by William Smith for the manufacture of brownware in 1825. Earthenware was added to the production soon afterwards. The style changed to William Smith & Co in 1926, and then to G. Skinner & Co (c1855–70), and subsequently Skinner & Walker (1870–c1880). Production mainly comprised 'Queen's Ware', a fine, white earthenware, and a fine brownware, much of which was exported to Europe. In 1848, an injunction was granted preventing this firm using the name 'Wedgewood & Co' or 'Wedgewood' in their marks, which they had been doing illegally.

ZSOLNAY/PECS

Zsolnay *Pêcs, Hungary*

Established in 1862, this firm produced Islamic-inspired pierced wares until the 1890s, and later vases with organic forms and iridescent glazes. All pieces are marked, and feature a mark showing the five towers of Pêcs.

Chinese & Japanese Marks

The first marks on Chinese ceramics probably date from the Warring States period (480–221BC), but these potters' marks, in the form of inscriptions, are rarely found. Only the porcelains made at Jingdezhen have been marked consistently, from the Ming Dynasty onwards. The reign marks of the Emperors of the Ming (1368–1643) and Qing (1644–1916) Dynasties are featured in this section.

The majority of Japanese ceramics are usually less than 150 years old. Within this phase, output was dominated by two types of ware: Satsuma and its related earthenware genre, and the so-called Kutani eggshell porcelains.

Detail of Noritake mark, c1920

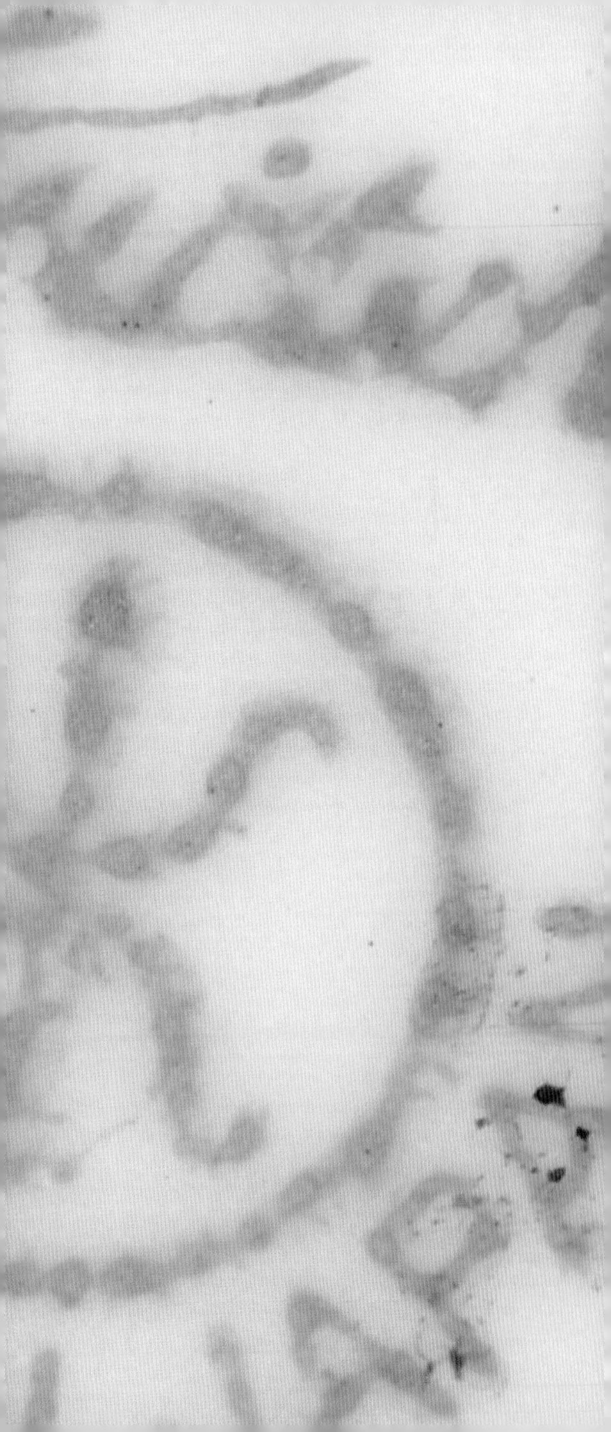

CHINESE MARKS

MING DYNASTY 1368–1643

Apart from Jingdezhen porcelain, few Chinese ceramics are marked. The earliest marks probably date from the Warring States Period (480–221 BC), but these are of the greatest rarity, and are not generally encountered outside museums. Cizhou and Ding wares are occasionally inscribed, but again these are exceptional. The systematic marking of porcelain only began in the early 15thC using six character marks, although four character marks were also employed. Most marked pieces from Jingdezhen are retrospective using reign marks from earlier and respected reigns. The marks of emperors Xuande (1426–35), Chenghua (1465–87), Kangxi (1662–1722), Yongzheng (1723–35) and Qianlong (1736–95) are commonly used on much later wares and therefore should be treated with the greatest caution: always seek expert advice.

Some marks used include commendations or are well-wishing symbols, although these generally are only used from the late Ming onwards. Until the early 18thC marks were written under the glaze in cobalt blue, or much more rarely were incised beneath the glaze. Late in the reign of Kangxi, some Imperial pieces were enamelled on top of the glaze, although the vast majority continued to be written in underglaze cobalt blue. At the turn of the 18thC overglaze iron-red was used increasingly on non-export-type porcelain.

Other marks on Chinese porcelain from the late Ming period onwards include animals, flowers and objects. The hare or the rabbit appears late in the 16thC, followed by the crane or heron. During the Kangxi period (1662–1722), the *lingzhi* or sacred fungus was introduced together with a lotus head, the artemesia leaf, and the *ding* (a bronze vessel form). These marks were sometimes used on 19thC copies of Kangxi porcelain.

A Xuande dice bowl, 1426–35

Ming Reign Marks

永樂年製

大明宣德年製

Yongle and Xuande, 1403–24, 1426–35

The earliest underglaze blue marks of Yongle and Xuande appear on Imperial-quality monochrome and blue and white wares. The porcelain from the early period is varied in form, but almost all have characteristically thick glazes saturated with bubbles which give a blurred appearance to the underlying blue designs and marks. The mainly floral patterns are confidently but carefully painted.

大明成化年製

Chenghua, 1465–8

Chenghua porcelain is delicately painted with perceptibly less vigour and a more open look to the scrolling foliage. This reign is noted for the so-called 'Palace bowls' and the ultra-refined *doucai* or polychrome enamelled porcelains that feature red, yellow, brown and green overglaze enamels within an underglaze blue outline.

大明弘治年製

Hongzhi, 1488–1505

Porcelain made during the Hongzhi dynasty, while maintaining the colourful styles developed in the latter part of the 15thC became increasingly stylized and weaker towards the end of the reign.

大明正德年製

Zhengde, 1506–21

Zhengde is arguably the last classic Ming reign, with some pieces recalling the high standards of the previous century, but generally becoming either too crowded or too stylized. The reign is notable for pieces inscribed in Arabic or Persian, and intended for the Imperial household. Wares include brush rests, censers and dishes. It was during this reign that the first Western European traders, the Portuguese, made a landfall in China.

大明嘉靖年製

Jiajing, 1522–66

The reign of Jiajing is noteworthy for the introduction of a brilliant purplish-blue and a greater use of figure subjects. This emperor followed the religion of Daoism, and symbols such as the pine tree (representing longevity), the *lingzhi* and the crane were used. Also from this period, Chinese porcelains appear with Western symbols, letters and armorials.

大明隆慶年製

Longqing, 1567–72

The wares made during the short reign of Longqing cannot, without reign marks, be distinguished from porcelain made in the dynasties that preceded or followed, and has attracted the attention of copyists in the 19th and 20thC.

大明萬曆年製

Wanli, 1573–1619

During the reign of Wanli the export trade in porcelain grew enormously to the detriment of quality. Mass production is evident on most pieces, the poor quality of the clay, improper refinement of the materials leaving pinholes and large dark blemishes on the surface, and the use of simple, repetitive decoration. This latter type was known as 'kraak porselein', and formed the backbone of the export market until 1657. There are no reign marks on this type of ware, but animal marks do occasionally appear.

大明天啟年製

Tianqi, 1621–27

Also a relatively short reign, the Tianqi period produced an interesting group of wares made for the Japanese market. Mainly in blue and white, but sometimes in *wucai* colours, this type of porcelain falls into two different categories. The first is an informal type, painted with figures, landscapes or vegetation and is rarely marked. These simple wares were often used in the Japanese tea ceremony. The second type of wares, known as *Shonzui*, are more meticulously made and often feature tight, geometric patterns. Wares from this period may also have rims dressed in an iron-brown glaze to prevent chipping.

崇禎年製

Chongzhen, 1628–43

This reign is noted for the so-called Transitional wares (porcelain made during the overlapping Ming and Qing dynasties). These heavily-potted wares are often quite brilliantly painted in a lustrous cobalt blue and show a break from the repetitious kraak porselein-type. A few pieces are inscribed with cyclical reign marks, but as in the previous reign there are few conventionally marked specimens from this turbulent period of Chinese history.

QING DYNASTY 1644–1916

The early years of the Qing dynasty were marked by internal strife which had a devastating effect on production at Jingdezhen. It was not until well into the reign of Kangxi (1662–1722) that normal production was resumed. In 1683 with the appointment of Zang Ying Xuan as director of the Imperial kilns, Chinese porcelain enters a long period in which some of the most refined and beautiful objects were made. This brilliant era ends with the retirement of the last great director Tang Yin c1752.

During the Kangxi period there were a considerable number of innovations and revivals. For example the Ming *wucai* palette in which underglaze blue is combined with overglaze enamels, including red, green, manganese brown and yellow, was abandoned in favour of the *famille verte* colour scheme in which a bright overglaze blue replaces the darker underglaze cobalt. Towards the end of the reign *famille verte* too was superseded by another palette, namely *famille rose* which uses colours saturated in white, creating an opaque and pastel effect, and which also introduces rose-pink for the first time. As well as these developments, a number of new monochromes appeared, such as an apple green, a fine turquoise and the copper-derived peach-bloom glaze, tea dust and robin's egg.

In addition, there was the revival of underglaze copper-red painting which had fallen into disuse during the Ming dynasty. Export porcelain from this period was carried out by private kilns and while the designs are somewhat stiff by comparison with the earlier Transitional wares, they are invariably well made and thinly-potted using a clean white porcelain and economically-applied glaze. It was in this reign that the practise of putting reign marks on export ware became common. The marks most often encountered were those of the much-admired Chenghua period (1465–87). In fact, contemporary Kangxi reign marks are ironically quite rare on export porcelain. Other marks include the lotus flower, the *ding* and the artemesia leaf.

Yongzheng (1723–35) was a period synonymous with the greatest refinement in all Chinese porcelain, and it is important for collectors to be aware that there are a great number of later copies of its wares.

The Qianlong reign continued to observe the traditional values laid down by his immediate predecessors, at least for a while. In the second half of his reign there are signs of a predilection for over elaboration, which continued throughout the later Qing period.

Qing reign marks

清順年製

Shunzhi, 1644–61

The first emperor of the Qing or Manchu dynasty. The wares of this period are quite varied, whether in blue and white or in the polychrome *wucai* palette, and are essentially a continuation of the Transitional tradition. Generally, there is a subtle move away from the more academic treatment of figurative and floral subjects of the High Transitional into the casually drawn and somewhat stiffer style of Kangxi. The very few marked specimens of this period are marked in conventional script.

大清康熙年製

Kangxi, 1662–1722

This is the first of the three most important reigns of the Qing dynasty. In terms of export material the majority of wares are blue and white, the minority *famille verte* (see p345). Monochromes both for export or for the domestic market include new and revived colours. In the latter category are a copper-derived glaze termed *sang-de-boeuf* and another known as peach-bloom. Other colours include lavender blue and a flecked darkish cobalt – *bleu soufflé*. Towards the end of this long reign, enamels saturated in white first appear. This pastel palette is known as *famille rose* and while a rose-pink is part of the scheme it often by no means dominates the other colours. For a time *famille verte* and *famille rose* overlap but by about 1730 the earlier green family has virtually disappeared.

The reign mark of Kangxi is relatively rare on non-Imperial pieces; the most frequently used mark in this period is an 'ancestral' Chenghua. Official seal-script marks are of the utmost rarity and should be treated with great suspicion.

Yongzheng, 1723–35

This relatively short reign is generally regarded as probably the best in terms of ceramic refinement although there is no clear change technically or stylistically between this reign and the early years of the following Qianlong (1736-95). By comparison between this and the preceding Kangxi there is a tendency towards a more intimate scale in graphic subjects. In addition, this period is noted for a strong classicising movement with a considerable number of pieces recalling the great monochrome stonewares of the Song and the early Ming blue and white and sacrificial red porcelains. It is during this reign that we see reign marks executed both in official and seal script.

大清乾隆年製

Qianlong, 1736–95
Considered to be the last classic reign of the Qing dynasty, this period saw enormous changes. There is generally a sense of over-elaboration and decadence in the second half of the 18thC. Robin's egg and tea dust are just two of the more popular colours of this period, but as well as blue and white, *famille rose* porcelains are predominant.

嘉慶年製

Jiaqing, 1796–1821
From the early 19thC onwards forms and decoration found in Chinese porcelain are usually based on styles from previous dynasties. Some very fine pieces were produced as well as the usual types of export wares.

LATER QING DYNASTIES

As noted above, the later Qing dynasties did not produce wares in new or inidividual styles. The marks of these dynasties and their corresponding dates are shown below.

大清道光年製

Daoguang
(1821–50)

大清咸豐年製

Xianfeng
(1851–61)

大清同治年製

Tongxi
(1862–73)

大清光緒年製

Guangxu
(1874–1908)

大清宣統年製

Xuantung
(1909–12)

洪憲年製

Hongxian
(1916)

JAPANESE MARKS

Marks on early Japanese porcelain are relatively scarce until the late 17th century. The manufacturers of pottery and porcelain during the Edo period never used their own Imperial reign marks although they did borrow Chinese marks. Usually they are poor copies of the more celebrated Ming emperors, such as Xuande (1426–35), Chenghua (1465–87) or Jiajing (1522–66). Sometimes they are garbled, as in the celebrated Van Frytom series at Burghley House. Other marks seen on such early porcelains are usually single seal type characters set within a square frame, and may include the symbols for happiness *fuku* or gold *kin*, prosperity or some such auspicious character. Edo porcelain does not carry Japanese imperial marks.

Decorative wares, from the Meiji period (1868–1911), are frequently marked. They are inscribed with several characters that usually denote the place of manufacture such as Kaga, Satsuma or Hizen. Those destined for the foreign market are repetitious and clichéd: idealized landscapes, geisha and natural subjects. Such wares, particularly Kutani (Kaga) are often inscribed with a multiplicity of casually drawn characters in black or red. Eggshell teawares are by far the most numerous category but do not often bear marks. To employ a popular barometer the BBC's *Antiques Roadshow* experts will, during a programme, handle more Japanese ceramics of this type and period than almost any other type of imported ceramic.

Among the more interesting types of later ceramics are those from the Noritake factory which abandoned the aforementioned meretricious styles in favour of the contemporary Art Deco. International designers, including Frank Lloyd Wright, contributed to some of the most sophisticated patterns. These wares are marked with the distinctive circular device and are much sought after by modern collectors.

Some accomplished studio-type wares were made by individuals or small workshops in the early 20th century. These are almost invariably marked with the potter's or decorator's signature.

Pattern on the foot of a Nabeshima saucer dish, c1700.

A Selection of Japanese Marks

Underglaze cobalt blue seal mark *fuku* (= happiness). Many versions of the *fuku* mark appear on Japanese porcelain, especially during the Edo period. This example is the 'running' *fuku* mark because of its more dynamic calligraphic structure. It seems to be applied almost exclusively to the more refined porcelains made in Arita in the 18th century, including some attributed to the Kakiemon kiln. All pieces bearing this device will usually have three stilt marks (ie the small crater-like blemishes left when the kiln supports are broken off after firing). These blisters are typical of early Arita ware.

Underglaze blue *kin* (= gold) mark. Such marks seem mostly to be employed on the better quality blue and white Arita porcelain made in the late 17th or early 18th century. A feature of almost all in this category is the iron-brown dressing on the rim and the unglazed welt from the kiln support.

An underglaze blue seal mark *fuku*. Probably the most common mark on all of Japanese porcelain, although unlike this underglaze blue 17th-century version, the majority will be in overglaze enamels, usually black or red and from the Meiji period.

Underglaze mark of Hirado. This denotes a late manufacture as early Hirado wares, from about 1750 to 1850, are unmarked. This porcelain is among the finest in terms of purity of body and glaze from Hizen province.

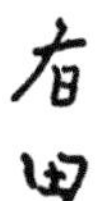

A typical Hizen manufacturer's mark. In the latter half of the 19th century there was a proliferation of porcelain factories producing elaborately decorated wares for export – Hichozan Shimpo and Fukugawa are among the most prominent.

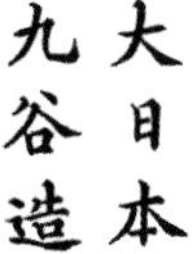

Among the largest producers of exportware, Kutani specialized in eggshell porcelain, mainly tea services or vases painted in a limited palette of black and red with gilt highlights with predictable Japanese subjects: riverside landscapes, geisha strolling among blossoming trees. The marks are usually painted in red or black.

Additional Information

This section contains: details of fakes and copies, appendices providing further information on Patent Office Registration marks, year marks and cyphers found on wares made at Derby, Minton, Sèvres, Worcester and Wedgwood, and a list of decorator marks used by painters, gilders and potters at Sèvres. There is also a detailed glossary.

Detail of Crown Derby mark, c1800

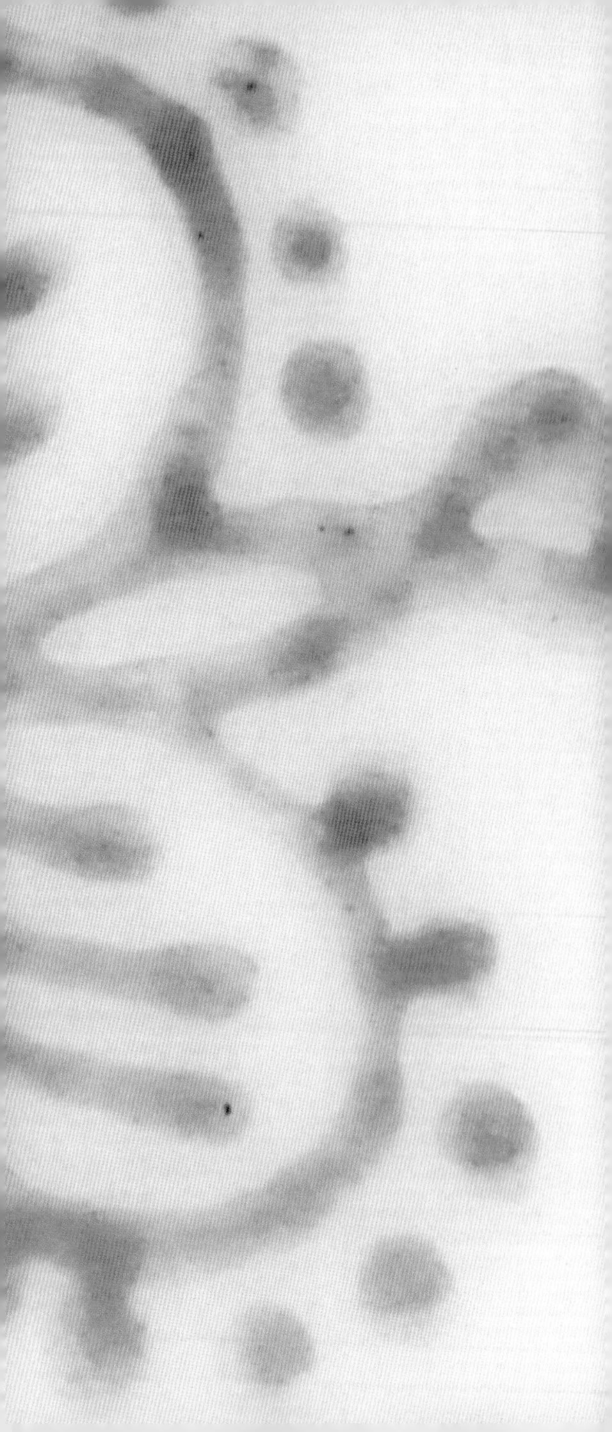

FAKES & COPIES

China & Japan

Chinese reign marks have always been a problematical issue. Until the turn of the 15thC, the six or, more rarely, four-character reign marks appeared almost exclusively on Imperial porcelains. However, in the 16thC Chinese potters began to copy earlier reign marks.

In the 16thC, the most frequently copied marks were those of Xuande (1426–35) and Chenghua (1465–87). A famous example is a bowl dated 1541, made for Pedro de Faria, the Portuguese governor of Goa. The base carries the six-character mark of Xuande who died over 100 years before the bowl was made. The calligraphy of the genuine marks is distinctive when compared to the more casually drawn versions that appear on faked examples.

Copyists in the 17thC used the Xuande mark, and also the mark of Jiajing (1522–66). Chenghua was also used, and became increasingly popular during the reign of Kangxi (1662–1722). Jang Qi Jing, the superintendent of the Imperial kilns, banned the use of the reign mark from 1677–80, perhaps because of the implied disrespect if the mark appeared on lower quality porcelains. We do not know how strictly this ban was enforced but it is clear that as well as using old reign marks, the potters of Jingdezhen used symbols such as the artemisia leaf, the lotus or the *ding* (a bronze tripod vessel). The practice of marking with symbols was probably abandoned later in the reign of Kangxi but was revived in the latter half of the 19thC.

It was during the reign of Kangxi that the reproduction of classic wares of the Song and Ming dynasties became popular, a trend which continued to the end of the dynasty, early in the 20thC. Many of these pieces bear deceptively good copies of the reign marks of their original period. A thorough knowledge of the material and, where applicable, an understanding of the brushwork, is important.

This trend continued through the 18thC and, while some of the copies are marked with early marks, the majority carry contemporary reign marks. Unfortunately even these pieces were themselves copied in the 19thC and 20thC, and particularly today.

During the reigns of Yongzheng (1723–35) and Qianlong (1736–95) a number of marks were written in seal script as opposed to the conventional script used on early Qing and Ming porcelains. The characters in this formalized script appear within a square seal. Most marks were painted in underglaze blue, but from the reign of Kangxi a few pieces are marked in overglaze enamels. Towards the end of the 18thC, many pieces are marked in iron-red, a tradition that was carried on into the 20thC.

In the 19thC, large numbers of Imperial or Chinese porcelains in 18thC style were made at Jingdezhen. Some of these pieces bore contemporary reign marks, but many more were made with the marks of Kangxi, Yongzheng and Qianlong. These copies are very deceptive, and some have even fooled experts. Before buying pieces of Chinese porcelain, it is absolutely essential to spend as much time as possible studying the material and the reign marks, and it would also be helpful to seek the advice of a specialist.

Marks on Japanese ceramics are often more problematical than those on Chinese porcelain. Marks of famous potters were copied almost as a matter of course, especially with regard to stoneware. They borrowed the more celebrated Chinese reign marks of the Ming dynasty particularly during the early 18th century. Stoneware types associated with the tea ceremony were especially prone to fraud and should be treated with circumspection.

Italy

From the middle of the 19thC, a number of factories and individuals began to make their own versions of Rennaisance-style maiolica, and also some extremely deceptive forgeries. The factory of Ginori at Doccia near Florence, produced convincing pastiches of 16thC maiolica of which there is an interesting example in the Wallace Collection. Other centres included Pesaro, Gubbio, Gualdo Tadino and Florence. In Pesaro, Ferruccio Mengaroni (1875–1925) produced some outstanding forgeries of early maiolica. Ulisse and Guiseppe Cantagalli, who established a factory in Florence in 1878, produced large numbers of reproductions of Hispano-Moresque, Turkish (Isnik) pottery as well as Renaissance maiolica. The factory mark is a singing cockerel.

19thC copies can be detected by the neat and smooth rims and carefully finished footrims. Early maiolica is often slightly irregular with rims of variable thickness and profile. The glaze on the original can be patchy or uneven, with a bubbled surface and zones of stronger colour. 19thC copies are covered in even, creamy or greyish glazes giving a mechanical look. In old maiolica studios, flatware was fired in stacks, each piece supported on a triangular arrangement of ceramic stilts which left blemishes on the upper surface. Therefore all but the uppermost dish in a stack would show these weals. Late pieces do not have such stilt marks. The types of colours used can also help to distinguish between the genuine article and a copy, and later examples exhibit a tendency towards over-elaboration.

France

Earthenwares

Among the earliest wares in France to be copied or faked are the elaborate, lead-glazed wares produced by Bernard Palissy and his followers towards the end of the 16thC. There are two distinct types: first, large dishes, with lizards, serpents, frogs and other reptiles modelled in high-relief among ferns and foliage; second, shallow, circular or oval dishes moulded in low-relief with figure subjects, mainly of classical inspiration. These types of wares were widely copied in the 19thC in response to a demand for 'historical' wares. For example, the Portuguese Mafra factory at Caldas da Rainha made considerable quantities of 'Palissy' type pottery. These crude versions usually feature a factory mark. French copies by Charles Avisseau or George Pull are more difficult to distinguish, but the later copies are painted in slightly harsher, acid colours, whereas Palissy used warmer earthy tones. In addition, the modelling on later versions is more cluttered and less spontaneous than the originals.

Faïence

The great days of French faïence ended with the development of porcelain and more importantly creamware (*faïence fine*) in the latter half of the 18thC. One type of faïence that is still found is low quality ware made for tourists. In Normandy, Brittany and other parts of northern France, these items are to be found in almost every town and resort. Modern pieces are invariably marked with the initials or name of the pottery, and its location. With the notable exception of the leading faïence factories such as Strasburg, Niderviller or Marseilles, few 18thC factories marked their wares as extensively marks were usually confined to initials or a simple device. Place names such as Rouen or Lille (with the date 1767) are found on modern copies and forgeries. Deliberate copies have been made of faïence from Strasburg, Sceaux, Nevers and Marseilles. In particular, pieces from Marseilles were copied extensively in the late 19th and early 20thC. Perhaps the most commonly faked mark is the 'VP' monogram of the Veuve Perrin factory.

Porcelain

French porcelains have been extensively faked, especially pieces from the Vincennes-Sèvres factory. It is safe to say that over 95 per cent of pieces bearing the interlaced 'L's of Sèvres are later hard-paste copies of high-rococo originals. It is essential to study the way in which Sèvres enamellers inscribed their wares in the l8thC. Familiarity with the Sèvres porcelain in the greatest public collections in France, the USA and the UK is also a requirement. In addition, a knowledge of the date letters on Sèvres is useful (for further details of date letters, see p363). For example, the date letter 'B' (for 1754) found on a piece of porcelain with a rose-pink ground must be a fake, as the colour was only introduced in 1757. Most fakes tend to carry fairly early (and therefore more desirable) date letters.

At the time of the French Revolution there was a considerable body of undecorated Sèvres porcelain stockpiled at the factory. After the Revolution this was sold off and much of it enamelled in the old style. This group presents some problems as it is perfectly genuine 18thC porcelain, with the decoration added later. The combined result is a forgery, and can be difficult to identify. There were also concerns in England which specialized in reproducing soft-paste Sèvres porcelain, such as John Randall whose work was exceptional. Soft-paste copies are much rarer than French hard-paste copies. Hard-paste porcelain was only made from 1768 onwards; pieces in this material with earlier date letters are fakes.

Other French factories were also copied or faked but these are relatively uncommon. The Samson factory produced hard-paste copies of St Cloud, Mennecy and Chantilly softpaste porcelains. Most have the Samson entwined 'S' mark as well as the original factory mark.

Germany

Stoneware

The classic stonewares of Cologne, Frechen, Raeren, Westerwald, Siegburg and Kreussen have all been copied, particularly in the latter half of the 19thC. The copies of Frechen or Cologne stonewares are generally fairly mechanical-looking, compared to the uneven, irregularly glazed originals.

Copies of Raeren wares by Hubert Schiffer, active in the late 19thC, although made in the traditional manner, are too neatly finished to deceive, and most are impressed with the manufacturer's 'HS' monogram.

Westerwald blue and white stonewares are still made today, but modern pieces are invariably marked. Many of the Historismus pieces from the 19thC are often large and over-elaborate compared to the humbler wares of the 17th and 18thC. Whatever the size or shape, all the copies are tightly and stiffly decorated, with perfectly flat bases; early Westerwald bases tend to be slightly concave. In many cases the dense, blackish cobalt blue of the originals, is replaced by a bright-blue with a sticky appearance. In the late 19thC the Merkelbach factory made some good quality pieces, However, most have the impressed name or initials on the base.

Copies of Siegburg wares made by Peter Lowenich and others in the last quarter of the 19thC can be exceptionally difficult to attribute because they are made in the same manner and with the same moulded designs as the 16thC originals. In general the copies appear too well-made.

Finally, the enamelled stonewares of Kreussen made in the 17th and early 18thC were also faked. These include the *waltzenkrug* (a short, cylindrical tankard) and the *schraubflasche* (a flask with rounded sides). There are many copies of this group and these are usually neatly potted, but decorated in a stiff and over-zealous manner using 19thC enamels which tend to be slightly duller in colour than those used earlier.

Porcelain

This category has always been attractive to the copyist and forger. Meissen was the target of almost every other factory, at least in terms of imitation of its style in the middle of the 18thC. However, the distinctive palette of Meissen eluded them all as did its superlative modelling. While it is easy to distinguish Meissen from other German hard-paste factories in the 18thC, it is not so easy to separate early from late Meissen, particularly on small objects such as snuff boxes where there is little undecorated surface to help. In these cases one has to rely on the quality of the decoration alone, the appraisal of which is beyond most except the experienced expert. The best copies of Meissen were made by the Samson factory (established in 1854) but while the modelling and the colouring are of high standard the pure white paste of this French factory is totally different from the flecky greyish paste of Meissen.

The Meissen crossed-swords mark is, together with the interlaced 'L's of Sèvres, the most copied symbol in all of western porcelain. Few copies have the sureness of the original. The mark was copied not only in Germany but in France and England.

Other German factories, such as Fulda, Furstenberg and Ludwigsburg, were copied in the 19thC and a thorough knowledge of the different pastes and enamels is essential before venturing into this particular area of collecting.

Faïence

Most fakes in this category appear to be of the more expensive enamelled wares, although relatively few are encountered.

Holland

Delftware

Delft became the most important tin-glazed earthenware centre in the middle of the 17thC. At first the emphasis was on Chinese-style blue and white wares although by the early 18thC, polychrome decorated pieces became popular. While many factories closed towards the end of the 18thC (the competition from English creamware and less expensive porcelain administering the death-blow) a few continued in the 19thC making tourist-type wares in the manner of earlier Delftware. These late copies and pastiches are not difficult to spot, but a few with well known factory marks, such the 'PAK' monogram of the De Griesche A (The Greek A) factory, are deceptive. This category includes frequently collected Delftware animals and figures.

Britain

Almost every category of British ceramics – Staffordshire slipware, English delftware, Astbury, Wheildon, Wedgwood, Worcester, Chelsea and Lowestoft, and even the humble Staffordshire 'flatback' – has been forged or copied.

The 19thC in Britain was a period of deliberate recreation of past styles in all areas of the decorative arts, including ceramics. Spode, Coalport, Minton, Wedgwood and other major manufacturers produced wares in the current styles: neo-rococo, neo-Gothic and the Aesthetic Movement. At the same time, however, there was interest in genuine old pottery and porcelain from a growing group of collectors. The period from about 1880 until c1930 probably marks the most prolific activitity of fakers in Britain, not only in the field of ceramics but also in furniture, arms and armour, bronzes, glass and in the printed book.

Slipware

Slipware enjoyed a continuing tradition from the 17thC until well into the 19thC. Pieces made by the great Staffordshire potters, Thomas Toft, William Tallor (or Talor) and Ralph Simpson were eagerly sought by collectors. A number of signed and dated pieces by this group of potters were well known, and the high prices paid for their dishes and vessels encouraged potters to make some very deceptive copies, which they then inscribed with the names of these celebrated figures. Many pieces subsequently passed into some of the most notable collections, some no doubt remaining undetected to this day.

Delftware

Delftware fakes are another intriguing group. Whereas there are a great number of forgeries of French faïence there are relatively few of English delftware. This may be explained by the continuous production of French tin-glazed pottery into the 20thC: the basic skills are therefore still available, making it possible to achieve a passable copy. In Britain the manufacture of tin-glazed earthenware virtually ceased in the early 19thC, and the necessary skills were lost.

In the late 19th and early 20thC a number of fakes began to appear on the market in London. They were genuine 17thC wine bottles that had originally been covered in an undecorated, plain white glaze, a fairly common practice in the latter half of the 17thC. Just as with Staffordshire slipware, there was great demand at the turn of the 19thC for 17thC ceramics, especially pieces bearing a date and/or a name. In order to gain from this apparent shortfall, a group of forgers inscribed these 'white' pieces with 17thC dates. This meant that the piece had to be refired – a difficult task, particularly with material such as delftware. A number were irretrievably damaged: the globules of moisture trapped within the absorbent clay under the glaze exploded through the surface of the glaze during firing. Several of these pieces still exist. The more successfully fired wares can still be identified by the unconvincing hand in which the dates and inscriptions are written.

Astbury, Whieldon and Wedgwood

These wares have also been forged, and of special interest are the celebrated 'Pew groups' which can fetch large sums of money. In the 1920s and '30s a few of these Pew groups (so-called because the figures are seated on pews) appeared on the market featuring the names of Staffordshire's most famous potters. As the models were clearly all made by the same person they did not fool experts for long. However, while Pew groups with names like Astbury, Whieldon or Wedgwood should arouse the gravest suspicion, unnamed examples cannot neccessarily be dismissed as fakes.

Other Staffordshire wares

Fakes of other Staffordshire pottery include agate ware and early Wedgwood-Whieldon cauliflower ware, but perhaps most surprising are Victorian flat-back figures and cottages. Within the past 30 years there has been a spate of fakes of this type, not only of collectable figures but also cottages and money boxes.

Porcelain

In terms of porcelain, the British factories that have received the most attention from the faker are Chelsea and Worcester, although forgeries of Lowestoft, Longton Hall, Bow and Derby are also known. The majority of copies of Chelsea and Worcester soft-paste that are encountered are made from French hard-paste porcelain, mainly produced by the Samson factory, and are slightly greenish or bluish in tone. Copies of Chelsea almost invariably feature the gold anchor mark, which tends to be a fraction larger than the original. Many other European factories employed the gold anchor, and it is the most commonly faked English mark. These late 19thC copies are decorated in harsh blues and reds, unlike the softer, more irregular colours of the 18thC.

The Samson factory also made copies of Worcester, with panels of exotic birds or flowers: most of these have either the crescent or the seal mark of Worcester. The greenish, glassy glaze of Samson, is quite distinct from the duller, more greyish surface of genuine Worcester porcelain.

Another group of fakes were made in Torquay, c1945. Produced by a husband and wife team, they are made from a convincingly primitive and fissured material. However, their figures and wares of Chelsea, Derby and Longton Hall are poorly cast, modelled and decorated compared to the originals. In their day they duped many experts until A. J. B. Kiddell of Sotheby's, London, proved them to be forgeries. Fortunately this latter type of fake is extremely rare.

USA

The domestic ceramics industry developed slowly in the USA, but by the 18thC a cottage industry had developed and a distinctive style of slip-decorated redware was being made in several parts of New England. It was made until the early 20thC, and is now widely reproduced.

Bennington in Vermont became a potting centre at the end of the 18thC. The stonewares that were produced set standards that were widely copied, particularly throughout New England, until the beginning of the 20thC. American stonewares are distinguishable from European by their larger size and relatively thick potting. Other Bennington Potteries, including the United States Pottery, produced lustrous brown 'Rockingham' wares and also American porcelain, particularly figures. Very little Bennington pottery is marked, but impressed trade names or monograms may appear. It should also be noted that the ware is widely reproduced.

APPENDICES

Patent Office Registration Marks

One of the most useful marks for identifying and dating British ceramics is the diamond-shaped Patent Office Registration Mark that appeared on pieces made from 1842 to 1883. Registration began in 1839, following the Copyright of Design Act, but the insignia was used from 1842. Ceramics belong to class IV.

The months for both periods:

A	December	**D**	September	**H**	April	**M**	June
B	October	**E**	May	**I**	July	**R**	August
C/O	January	**G**	February	**K**	November	**W**	March

The index to year letters 1842–67:

A	1845	**J**	1854	**S**	1849
B	1858	**K**	1857	**T**	1867
C	1844	**L**	1856	**U**	1848
D	1852	**M**	1859	**V**	1850
E	1855	**N**	1864	**W**	1865
F	1847	**O**	1862	**X**	1842
G	1863	**P**	1851	**Y**	1853
H	1843	**Q**	1866	**Z**	1860
I	1846	**R**	1861		

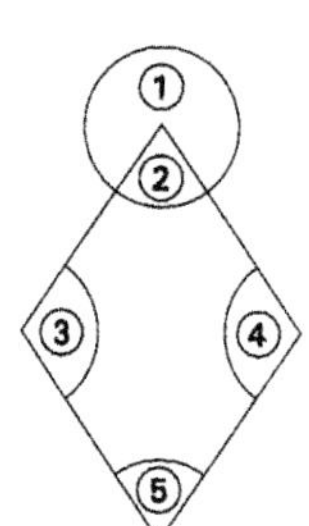

1: class 2: year 3: month
4: day 5: parcel number

The index to year letters 1868–83:

A	1871	**K**	1883
C	1870	**L**	1882
D	1878	**P**	1877
E	1881	**S**	1875
F	1873	**U**	1874
H	1869	**V**	1876
I	1872	**X**	1868
J	1880	**Y**	1879

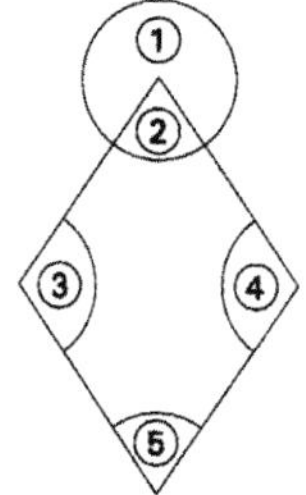

1: class 2: day 3: parcel number
4: year 5: month

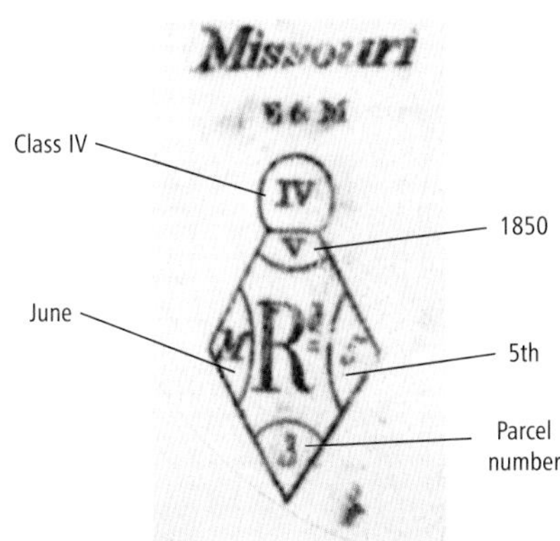

From 1884 consecutive numbers only were used, prefixed in most cases by 'Rd' or 'Rd No.' A guide to the year of manufacture according to the number featured is given below:

1	**1884**
19754	**1885**
40480	**1886**
64520	**1887**
90483	**1888**
116648	**1889**
141273	**1890**
163767	**1891**
185713	**1892**
205240	**1893**
224720	**1894**
246975	**1895**
268393	**1896**
291241	**1897**
311658	**1898**
331707	**1899**
368154	**1901**
385500	**1902***
402500	**1903***
420000	**1904***
447000	**1905***
471000	**1906***
494000	**1907***
519000	**1908***
550000	**1909***

*approximate only

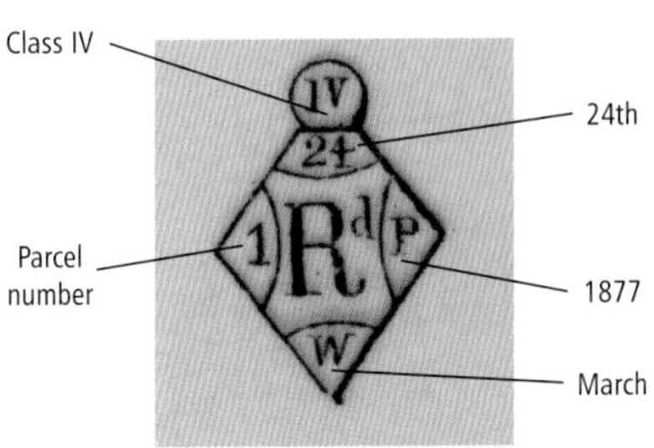

Derby

From 1882 the Derby Porcelain Works has used year cyphers which appear below the marks shown.

This mark was used c1878–90 at the time the company was known as the Derby Crown Porcelain Co Ltd.

Used from 1890 when the company name changed to Royal Crown Derby Porcelain Co Ltd, this mark also includes the word 'England' from 1891, and 'Made in England' from c1920.

1882	1883	1884	1885	1886	1887	1888
1889	1890	1891	1892	1893	1894	1895
1896	1897	1898	1899	1900	1901	1902
1903	1904	1905	1906	1907	1908	1909
1910	1911	1912	1913	1914	1915	1916
1917	1918	1919	1920	1921	1922	1923
1924	1925	1926	1927	1928	1929	1930
1931	1932	1933	1934	1935	1936	1937
I	II	III	IV	V	VI	VII
1938	1939	1940	1941	1942	1943	1944
VIII	IX	X	XI	XII	XIII	XIV
1945	1946	1947	1948	1949	1950	1951
XV	XVI	XVII	XVIII	XIX	XX	XXI
1952	1953	1954	1955	1956	1957	1958

Minton

From 1842, Minton included year cyphers in the marks impressed on their pieces.

J	January	**A**	April	**H**	July	**O**	October
F	February	**E**	May	**Y**	August	**N**	November
M	March	**I**	June	**S**	September	**D**	December

1842	1843	1844	1845	1846	1847	1848	1849
1850	1851	1852	1853	1854	1855	1856	1857
1858	1859	1860	1861	1862	1863	1864	1865
1866	1867	1868	1869	1870	1871	1872	1873
1874	1875	1876	1877	1878	1879	1880	1881
1882	1883	1884	1885	1886	1887	1888	1889
1890	1891	1892	1893	1894	1895	1896	1897
1898	1899	1900	1901	1902	1903	1904	1905
1906	1907	1908	1909	1910	1911	1912	1913
1914	1915	1916	1917	1918	1919	1920	1921
1922	1923	1924	1925	1926	1927	1928	1929
1930	1931	1932	1933	1934	1935	1936	1937
1938	1939	1940	1941	1942			

From 1943 this system was discontinued and replaced by figures corresponding to the year of production preceded by a number allocated to the maker of the piece.

Sèvres

Date letters were used at Sèvres 1753–93 to show the year of manufacture. The letter appeared within or alongside the interlaced 'L' mark. Letters that appear below the mark are usually those of the painter, gilder or potter.

Year marks 1753-93

A	1753	**L**	1764	**X**	1775	**II**	1786
B	1754	**M**	1765	**Y**	1776	**JJ**	1787
C	1755	**N**	1766	**Z**	1777	**KK**	1788
D	1756	**O**	1767	**AA**	1778	**LL**	1789
E	1757	**P**	1768	**BB**	1779	**MM**	1790
F	1758	**Q**	1769	**CC**	1780	**NN**	1791
G	1759	**R**	1770	**DD**	1781	**OO**	1792
H	1760	**S**	1771	**EE**	1782	**PP**	1793
I	1761	**T**	1772	**FF**	1783		
J	1762	**U**	1773	**GG**	1784		
K	1763	**V**	1774	**HH**	1785		

Marks of painters, gilders and potters at Sèvres

These are alphabetical by initial or monogram, and then by device or other mark. Potters are marked with an asterisk.

A	**Auvillain*** 1877–after 1900
A A A.	**Asselin, Charles-éloi** 1765–1804
A	**Lapierre, Auguste*** 1833–43
A	**Richard, Auguste** 1811–48
A	**Archelais, Jules** 1865–1902
AB	**Blanchard, Alexandre** 1878–1901
A.B.	**Brachard jeune, Alexandre*** 1784–92, 1795–99, 1802–27
AB	**Barré, Louis-Désiré** 1846–81
AB	**Bonnuit, Achille-Louis** 1858–62, 1865–94
AB	**Boullemier, Antoine-Gabriel** 1802–42
AB	**Belet, Adolphe** 1881–82
AB	**Briffaut, Alphonse-Théodore-Jean** 1848–90
AC	**Cieutat, Alphonse*** 1894–1928
AC	**Coursaget** 1881–86
AD	**David, François-Alexandre** 1844–81
AD	**Dumain, Alphonse*** 1884–1928
A.D	**Ducluzeau, Mme Marie-Adélaïde** 1818–48
AD	**Dammouse, Pierre-Adolphe*** 1852–80
AD	**David, François-Alexandre** 1844–81
AD	**Dubois, Alexandre*** 1896–1915
AF	**Fournier, Anatole** 1878–1926

Ligué, Denis 1881–1911

Allard, Jean-Baptiste* 1832–41

Lacour, Armand* 1895–1911

Longuet, Alexandre* 1840–76

Meyer, Alfred 1858–71

Moriot, François-Adolphe 1843–44

Percheron, Alexandre* 1827–64

Poupart, Antoine-Achille 1815–48

Apoil, Charles-Alexis 1851–64

Belet, Émile 1876–1900

Bouvrain, Antoine-Louis 1826–48

Boulanger père 1754–84

Barré 1773–74, 1776–78

Baldisseroni, Shiridani 1860–79

Barrat l'oncle 1769–1791

Brachard aîné, Jean-Charles-Nicolas* 1782–1824, or one of the Bougons 1754–1812

Boitel, Charles-Marie-Pierre 1797–1822

Baudouin père 1750–1800

Boullemier fils, Hilaire-François 1817–55

Béranger, Antoine 1807–46

Boullemier fils, Hilaire-François 1817–55

Bulidon 1763–92

Bono, Etienne-Henri* 1754–81

Boquet, Louis-Honoré* 1815–60

Buteux, Théodore 1786–1822

Bailly père 1753–67

Bourdois* 1773–74

Couturier, Claude 1762–75

Castel 1772–97

Barriat, Charles 1848–83

Constans, Charles-Louis 1803–40

Cabau, Eugène-Charles 1847–85

Constantin, Abraham 1813–48

Develly, Jean-Charles 1813–48

Desnoyers-Chapponet aîné 1788-1804, 1810–28

Chabry fils, Etienne-Jean 1765–87

Lucas, Charles 1878–1910

Delahaye, Charles-François-Jules* 1818–52

Commelin, Michel-Gabriel 1768–1802

cn **Chanou jeune, Henri-Florentin*** 1746–79, 1785

C.P **Capronnier, François** 1812–19

cp **Chappus aîné, Antoine-Joseph*** 1761–87

CR **Robert, Charles*** 1889–1930

CV **Villion, Charles*** 1894–1941

D **Doré, Pierre** 1829–65

D **Delatre cadet*** 1754–58

D.D.. D.. **Dusolle** 1768–74

D **Tardy, Claude-Antoine** 1755–95

da **Danet père*** 1759-after 1780

DE **Drouet, Ernest-Emile** 1878–1920

DF **Delafosse, Denis** 1804–15

D.F. **Davignon, Jean-François** 1807–15

DG **Derichweiler, Jean-Charles-Gérard** 1855–84

D.G. **Drouet, Gilbert** 1785–1825

D.G. **Godin, Mme Catherine** 1806–28

Dh **Deutsch** 1803–19

D.I **Didier père** 1787–1825, or fils, **Charles- Antoine** 1819–48

DJ **Devicq, Jules*** 1881–1928

D^{ll}B **Boullemier, Mlle Virginie** 1814–42

D.P. **Depérais, Claude-Antoine** 1794–1822

DR **Drand** 1764–75, 1780

DT **Dutanda, Dutenda, Nicolas** 1765–1802

D **Doat, Taxile** 1879–1905

D.y **Durosey, Charles-Christian-Marie** 1802–30

E **Latache, Etienne** 1867–79

E. **Ouint, Edouard*** 1888–93

E.A **Apoil, Mme Suzanne-Estelle** 1865–92

B **Bulot, Eugène-Alexandre** 1855–83

E.D. **Drouet, Ernest-Emile** 1878–1920

EdeM **Mauisson, Mlle de** 1862–70

E **Escallier, Mme Eléonore** 1874–88

EF **Fromant, Eugène** 1855–85

EG **Guillemain, Ambroise-Ernest-Louis** 1864–85

H **Hallion, Eugène** 1870, 1872–74, 1876–93

EL **Leroy, Eugène-éléonor** 1855–91

M **Moriot, Mlle Elise** 1881–86

P **Porchon** 1880–84

ER **Richard, Eugène** 1833–72

Réjoux, Emile-Bernard 1858–93

Simard, Eugène 1880–1908

Humbert, Jules-Eugène 1851–70

Falconet, Etienne-Maurice* 1757–66

Fallot 1773-1790

Fernex, Jean-Baptiste de* c1756

Fontaine, Jean-Joseph 1825–57

Lévé, Félix 1777–1800

Pfeiffer 1771–1800

Boullemier, François-Antoine 1806–38

Barbin, François-Hubert 1815–49

Courcy, Alexandre-Frédéric de 1865–86

Charrin, Mlle Fanny 1814–26

Ficquenet, Charles 1864–81

Fischbag, Charles* 1834–50

Goupil, Frédéric 1859–78

Hallion, François 1865–95

Mérigot, Maximilien-Ferdinand 1845–72, 1879–84

Paillet, Fernand 1879–88, 1893

Régnier, Joseph-Ferdinand* 1826–30, 1836–70

Vaubertrand, François 1822–48

Fumez 1777–1804

Genest, Jean-Baptiste-Étienne 1752–89

Godin, François-Aimé* 1813–48

Boterel, Georges* 1888–1933

Derichweiller, Jean-Charles-Gérard 1855–84

Gérard, Claude-Charles 1771–1824

Georget, Jean 1801–23

Lebarque, Georges* 1895–1916

Gébleux, Léonard 1883–1928

Gobert, Alfred-Thompson 1849–91

Robert, Mme Louise 1835–40

Grémont jeune 1769–75, 1778–81

Ganeau, Pierre-Louis 1813–31

Vignol, Gustave 1881–1909

Houry, Pierre 1752–55

Laroche, de 1759–1802

Hericourt c1755

Renard, Henri c1881

Huard, Pierre 1811–46

Mark	Painter
he	**Héricourt jeune** 1770–73, 1776–77
HF	**Faraguet, Mme** 1857–79
H. H.	**Laserre, Henri*** 1886–1931
HP.	**Prévost aîné** 1754–93, or le second 1757–97
HR	**Robert, Henri*** 1889–1933
HS	**Sill** 1881–87
HT	**Trager, Henri** 1870–1909
HU	**Uhlrich, Henri** 1879–1925
hy	**Huny** (doubtful mark) 1785–1800, 1810
IC	**Chanou, Jean-Baptiste*** 1779–1825
J. J	**Jubin** 1772–75
J.A	**André, Jules** 1840–69
Ja	**Jacob-Ber, Moïse** 1814–48
JA	**Archelais, Jules** 1865–1902
JB	**Boileau fils aîné*** 1773–81
J.C	**Célos, Jules-François** 1865–95
J.T.	**Trager, Jules** 1847, 1854–73
jc.	**Chappuis jeune** 1772–77
JD.	**Chanou, Mme Mère** 1779–1800
JE E	**Jardel, Bernard-Louis-Emile** 1886–1913
E E	**Julienne, Alexis-Etienne** 1837–49
JR, Jh.R, JhR	**Richard, Nicolas-Joseph** 1833–72
jh.	**Henrion aîné** 1770–84
JL	**Lambert, Henri-Lucien** 1859–99
JR	**Régnier, Hyacinthe*** 1825–63
J.	**Legay, Jules-Eugène*** 1861–95
JL	**Liance fits aîné*** 1769–1810
J.G	**Gély, Léopold-Jules-Joseph*** 1851–89
j.n.	**Chauveaux fils** 1771–83
JQ	**Jaquotot or Jacquotot Mme Marie-Victoire** 1801–42
JR	**Risbourg, Julien*** 1895–1925
JR	**Roger, Thomas-Jules*** 1852–86
jt	**Thévenet fits** 1752–58
KK	**Dodin, Charles-Nicolas** 1754–1802
L	**Le Cat*** 1872–after 1900
L	**Lévé, Denis** 1754–1805
L	**Lecterc, Auguste*** 1897–1911
L.	**Couturier** entered 1783
B	**Blanchard, Louis-Etienne-Frédéric** 1848–80
B	**Belet, Louis** 1878–1913

Mark	Painter
LB	**Le Bel jeune** 1773–93
LB	**Le Bel, Nicolas-Antoine** 1804–45
LC	**Charpentier, Louis-Joseph** 1852, 1854–79
Le	**Le Bel aîné, Jean-Etienne** 1766–75
LG	**Le Guay, Etienne-Charles** 1778–81, 1783–85, 1808–40
LG	**Guéneau, Louis*** 1885–1924
LG L.G.	**Le Guay père, Etienne-Henri** 1748–49, 1751–96
LG	**Le Grand, Louis-Antoine** 1776–1817
lg	**Langle, Pierre-Jean-Victor-Amable** 1837–45
L.G.cé	**Langlacé, Jean-Baptiste-Gabriel** 1807–44
Li	**Liance, Antoine-Mathieu*** 1754–77
LL LL	**Lécot** 1773–1802
LM	**Mirey** 1788–92
LM	**Mimard, Louis** 1884–1928
P	**Peluché, Léon** 1881–1928
LP	**Parpette jeune, Mlle Louise** 1794–98, 1801–17
LR	**Laroche, de** 1759–1802
LR	**Le Riche, Josse-François-Joseph*** 1757–1801
M	**Moiron** 1790–91
M	**Moyez, Jean-Louis** 1818–48
M	**Michel, Ambroise** 1772–80
M	**Morin, Jean-Louis** 1754–87
M	**Massy** 1779–1803
MA	**Mascret, Achille** 1838–46
Mas	**Mascret, Jean*** 1810–48
MB	**Bunel, Mme Marie-Barbe** 1778–1816
MC	**Micaud, Pierre-Louis** 1795–1834
ME MA	**Maugendre*** 1879–1887
ML	**Mascret, Louis*** 1825–64
m.P	**Moyez, Pierre*** 1827–48
MR	**Morin, Charles-Raphaël** 1805–12
MR	**Moreau, Denis-Joseph** 1807–15
MS	**Solon, Marc*** 1857–71
MV	**Morin** 1880–after 1900
N	**Aloncle, François** 1758–81
NB	**Bestault, Nestor*** 1889–1929
ng.	**Nicquet** 1764–92
O	**Ouint, Emmanuel*** 1877–89
o.ch	**Ouint, Charles** 1879–86, 1889–90

Oger, Jacques-Jean* 1784–1800, 1802–21

Milet, Optat 1862–79

Pine or Pline, François-Bernard-Louis 1854–70 or later

Perrottin or Perottin 1760–93 or later

Parpette, Philippe 1755–57, 1773–1806

Avisse, Alexandre-Pau 1848–84

Boucot, Philippe 1785–91

Pihan, Charles 1879–1928

Fachard, Pierre* 1899–1934

Philippine aîné 1778–91, 1802–25

Philippine cadet, François 1783–91, 1801–39

Pithou jeune 1760–95

Pierre jeune, Jean-Jacques 1763–1800

Knip, Mme de Courcelles 1808–09, 1817–26

Pierre aîné 1759–75

Parpette aîné, Mlle 1788–98

Perrenot aîné 1804-1809, 1813–15

Robert, Pierre 1813–32

Petit aîné, Nicolas 1756–1806

Pithou aîné 1757–90

Riton, Pierre 1821–60

Sioux aîné 1752–91

Richard, Nicolas-Joseph 1833–70 or later

Robert, Jean-François 1806–34, 1836–43

Richard, Pierre 1815–48

Girard 1772–1817

Maqueret, Mme 1796–98, 1817–20

Robert, Jean-François 1806–43

Rémy, Charles 1886–97, 1901–28

Roussel 1758–74

Riocreux, Denis-Desiré 1807–28

Riocreux, Isidore 1846–49

Samson, Léon* 1897–1918

Méreaud aîné, Pierre-Antoine 1754–91

Sandoz, Alphonse* 1881–1920

Chanou, Mlle Sophie, Mme Binet 1779–98

Noualhier, Mme Sophie 1777–95

Sieffert, Louis-Eugène 1881–87, 1894–98

Schradre 1773–75, 1780–86

Sinsson or Sisson, Jacques 1795–1846

Sinsson or Sisson, Louis 1830–47

Sinsson or Sisson, Pierre 1818–48

Swebach, Jacques-Jose (called Fontaine) 1803–14

Binet 1750–75

Troyon, Jean-Marie-Dominique 1801–17

Tardy, Claude-Antoine 1755–95

Latache, Étienne 1870–79

Fragonard, Théophile 1839–69

Letourneur* 1756–62

Trager, Louis 1888–1934

Tristan, Etienne-Joseph 1837–71, 1879–1882

Villion, Paul* 1886–1934

Vandé, Pierre-Jean-Baptiste 1779–1824

Vandé père 1753–79

Gérard, Mme née Vautrin 1781–1802

Vavasseur aîné 1753–70

Weydinger père 1757–1807

Weydinger second fils, Joseph 1778—1804, 1807–08, 1811, 1816–24

Hileken 1769–74

Hilken (?) Before 1800

Weydinger troisième fils, Pierre 1781–92, 1796–1816

Walter c1867–70

Micaud, Jacques-François 1757–1810

Grison 1749–71

Catrice 1757–74

Rocher, Alexandre 1758–59

Fouré 1749, 1754–62

Bouillat père, Edmé-François 1758–1810

Bouillat fils, F. 1800–11

Joyau 1766–75

Roisset, Pierre-Joseph 1753–95

Choisy, Apprien-Julien de 1770–1812

Martinet, Émile-Victor 1847–78

Le Guay, Pierre-André 1772–1818

Anthaume, Jean-Jacques 1752–58

Aubert aîné 1754–58

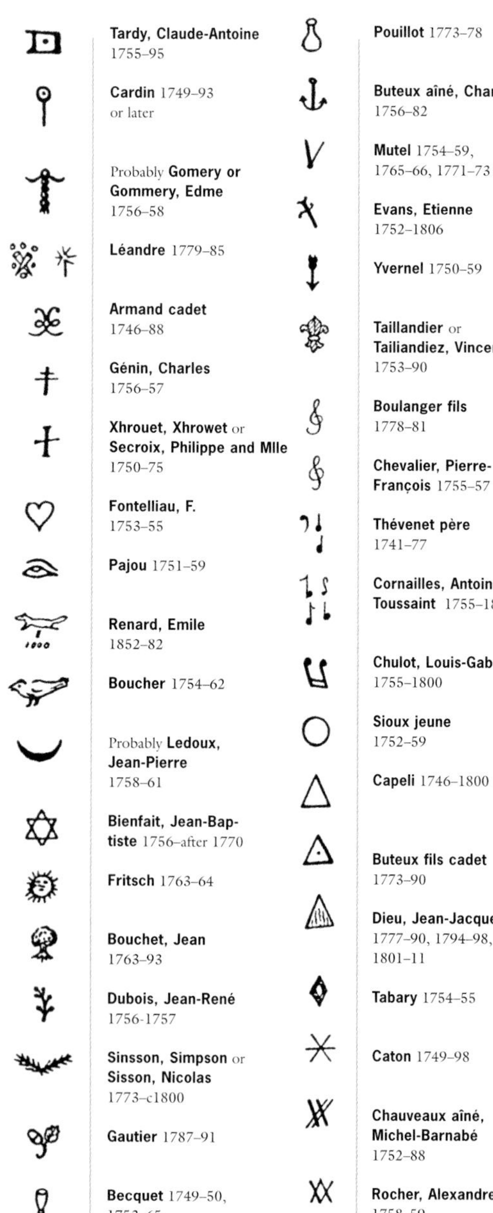

Tardy, Claude-Antoine 1755–95

Cardin 1749–93 or later

Probably **Gomery or Gommery, Edme** 1756–58

Léandre 1779–85

Armand cadet 1746–88

Génin, Charles 1756–57

Xhrouet, Xhrowet or **Secroix, Philippe and Mlle** 1750–75

Fontelliau, F. 1753–55

Pajou 1751–59

Renard, Emile 1852–82

Boucher 1754–62

Probably **Ledoux, Jean-Pierre** 1758–61

Bienfait, Jean-Baptiste 1756–after 1770

Fritsch 1763–64

Bouchet, Jean 1763–93

Dubois, Jean-René 1756-1757

Sinsson, Simpson or **Sisson, Nicolas** 1773–c1800

Gautier 1787–91

Becquet 1749–50, 1753–65

Pouillot 1773–78

Buteux aîné, Charles 1756–82

Mutel 1754–59, 1765–66, 1771–73

Evans, Etienne 1752–1806

Yvernel 1750–59

Taillandier or **Tailiandiez, Vincent** 1753–90

Boulanger fils 1778–81

Chevalier, Pierre-François 1755–57

Thévenet père 1741–77

Cornailles, Antoine-Toussaint 1755–1800

Chulot, Louis-Gabriel 1755–1800

Sioux jeune 1752–59

Capeli 1746–1800

Buteux fils cadet 1773–90

Dieu, Jean-Jacques 1777–90, 1794–98, 1801–11

Tabary 1754–55

Caton 1749–98

Chauveaux aîné, Michel-Barnabé 1752–88

Rocher, Alexandre 1758–59

Bardet 1751–58

Fontaine, Jacques 1752–75, 1778–1807

Noël, Guillaume 1755–1804

Raux aîné 1766–79

Sioux aîné 1752–91

Tandart jeune, Charles 1756-1760 or **Tandart, Jean-Baptiste** 1754–1803

Théodore 1765–71 or later

Viellard aîné 1752–90

Mongenot 1754–64

Carrié or Carrier 1752–57

Bertrand 1757–74

Bertrand 1750–1800

Buteux fils aîné, Charles-Nicolas 1763–1801

Méreaud jeune, Charles-Louis 1756–79

Vincent jeune 1753–1806

Barré, Louis Désiré 1846–81

Bieuville or Bienville (Bieauville?), Horace 1879–1925

Brécy, Paul* or Henry* 1881–after 1900

Courcy, Alexandre-Frédéric de 1865–86

Fournier, Anatole 1878–1926

Gély, Léopold-Jules-Joseph 1851–88

Goupil, Frédéric 1859–78

Meyer, Alfred 1858–71

Richard, François 1832–75

Richard, Emile 1867–1900

Roussel, Paul-Marie 1850–71

Sandoz, Alphonse 1881–after 1900

Schilt, Louis-Pierre 1818–55

Wedgwood

From 1860, as well as their usual name mark, the Wedgwood factory began to use a system of date marking using three impressed letters. The first denotes the month, the second is a potter's mark, and the third indicates the year of manufacture. The system went through three year mark cycles until 1907 when the system was amended so that the first letter indicated the cycle of year marks in use.

Monthly marks 1860–64

J	January	**A**	April	**V**	July	**O**	October
F	February	**Y**	May	**W**	August	**N**	November
M	March	**T**	June	**S**	September	**D**	December

Monthly marks 1865–1907

J	January	**A**	April	**L**	July	**O**	October
F	February	**M**	May	**W**	August	**N**	November
R	March	**T**	June	**S**	September	**D**	December

First cycle of year marks

O	1860	**R**	1863	**U**	1866	**X**	1869
P	1861	**S**	1864	**V**	1867	**Y**	1870
Q	1862	**T**	1865	**W**	1868	**Z**	1871

Second cycle of year marks

A	1872	**H**	1879	**O**	1886	**V**	1893
B	1873	**I**	1880	**P**	1887	**W**	1894
C	1874	**J**	1881	**Q**	1888	**X**	1895
D	1875	**K**	1882	**R**	1889	**Y**	1896
E	1876	**L**	1883	**S**	1890	**Z**	1897
F	1877	**M**	1884	**T**	1891		
G	1878	**N**	1885	**U**	1892		

Third cycle of year marks

A	1898	**H**	1905	**O**	1912	**V**	1919
B	1899	**I**	1906	**P**	1913	**W**	1920
C	1900	**J**	1907	**Q**	1914	**X**	1921
D	1901	**K**	1908	**R**	1915	**Y**	1922
E	1902	**L**	1909	**S**	1916	**Z**	1923
F	1903	**M**	1910	**T**	1917		
G	1904	**N**	1911	**U**	1918		

Fourth cycle of year marks

A	1924	**C**	1926	**E**	1928
B	1925	**D**	1927	**F**	1929

After 1929 the last two years of the date appear in full.

Worcester

In 1862, the Worcester Porcelain Works became known as Royal Worcester. From 1867 a system of dating by year letters was used together with the standard printed mark.

1867–90

A	1867	**H**	1873	**P**	1879	**W**	1885
B	1868	**I**	1874	**R**	1880	**X**	1886
C	1869	**K**	1875	**S**	1881	**Y**	1887
D	1870	**L**	1876	**T**	1882	**Z**	1888
E	1871	**M**	1877	**U**	1883	**O**	1889
G	1872	**N**	1878	**V**	1884	**a**	1890

From 1891 'Royal Worcester England' was added round the standard mark. From 1892 a dot was added for each year.

1892 one dot added above 'Royal'
1893 two dots, one either side of 'Royal Worcester England'
1894 three dots
1895 four clots
1896 five dots

From 1915 there were 24 dots, some placed below the main mark.

1916 dot replaced by a star below the mark
1917 one dot added to star
1918 two dots added to star

From 1927 there were 11 dots with the star.

1928 dots and star replaced by a small square
1929 small diamond
1930 division sign
1931 two inter-linked circles
1932 three inter-linked circles
1933 one dot added to three circles
1934 two dots added to three circles

From 1941 there were nine dots. Between 1941 and 1948 there were no changes made in year marks.

1949 'V' placed under mark
1950 'W' placed under mark
1951 one dot added to 'W'
1952 two dots added to 'W'
1953 three dots added to 'W'
1954 four clots added to 'W'
1955 five dots added to 'W'
1956 'W' is replaced by 'R', clots are added until
1963 13 dots appear with the circled 'R' device

From 1963 all new patterns feature the year in full.

GLOSSARY

Acid gilding Decorative patterns are etched into porcelain with hydrofluoric acid, then gilded and brushed.

Agate ware A type of pottery revived by Staffordshire potters in the mid-18thC made to resemble agate by the partial blending of different coloured clays.

Alafia An Arabic word for benediction or blessing, used symbolically by Moorish potters in early Hispano-Moresque lustreware.

Albarello A drug jar originating in Persia in the 12thC but adopted in Europe from the 15thC. A variation is the so-called 'dumb-bell' form popular in northern Italy, especially in the Veneto.

Alla porcellana Literally 'in the style of Chinese blue and white porcelain'. A type of scrolling foliage derived from Ming wares used on Italian maiolica in 15th and 16thC.

American Belleek A late-19thC American version of the thinly-potted wares originally made at the Irish Belleek factory.

Applied moulding Relief decoration made separately and applied later.

Arcanist One who possesses a porcelain formula – from arcanum, the Latin for mystery.

Arita Where most early Japanese porcelain was made from c1610, including Imari, blue and white, Kakiemon, and Nabeshima.

Armorial wares Wares decorated with coats-of-arms or crests, either transfer-printed or painted. Usually refers to Chinese porcelain bearing European coats-of-arms, produced from 16thC.

Artificial porcelain Another term for soft-paste porcelain.

A tulipano A pattern devised at the Doccia factory, depicting formal sprays of Oriental flowers.

Baluster In ceramics, a term employed to describe a shape of a vase or other vessel with the profile of an elongated pear or teardrop.

Baroque A vigorous decorative style that grew out of the Renaissance, characterized by lively figures and symmetrical ornament. Meissen's porcelain of the early 18thC is the most notable.

Basaltes A fine black stoneware developed by Josiah Wedgwood in the 1760s.

Basketweave A relief pattern resembling woven willow twigs (oziers) used on borders by most European factories in the 1730s.

Bat-printing A type of transfer printing used by early 19thC Staffordshire firms. The design was transferred from engraved plates to a glazed surfaces via slabs of glue or gelatin (bats).

Bellarmine A Rhenish stoneware vessel of bulbous form with a narrow neck on which is stamped the bearded face associated later with Cardinal Roberto Bellarmino, a stern anti-Protestant. These vessels were made over a long period from the15th to the early 19thC.

Berettino A style of decoration initially associated with Faenza from the 1520s on but was later adopted by north Italian potteries, particularly Venice. The object is entirely covered in pale or dark blue tin-glaze which is then painted in white and other colours.

Bianco-di-Faenza A type of maiolica developed in the mid-16thC at Faenza. It is covered in a thick milk-white glaze, and is usually cursorily decorated in a restricted palette of ochre and blue termed *compendiario.*

Bianco-sopra-bianco Literally 'white-on-white'. A type of maiolica and other later tin-glazed wares (eg Bristol), painted in white enamel on an off-white or bluish ground, resulting in an effect similar to lacework.

Birnkrug A Dutch or German earthenware and stoneware pear-shaped jug or mug, produced in the 17thC, and later adopted by the early porcelain factories.

Biscuit Unglazed porcelain or earthenware fired once only. The term also refers to white porcelain (especially figures) that has been left unglazed and undecorated.

Blackware A type of ancient Chinese ceramics similar to greenware but with more iron in the formula.

Blanc de Chine A translucent white Chinese porcelain, unpainted and with a thick glaze, made at kilns in Dehua in the Fukien province from the Ming dynasty and often copied in Europe.

Bleu celeste A sky-blue ground colour developed by Jean Hellot at Vincennes in 1752.

Bleu-du-Roi Also *bleu nouveau.* A rich blue enamel used as a ground colour at Sèvres.

Bleu lapis An intense cobalt blue ground of almost purplish tone, introduced at Vincennes in 1749.

Bleu persan French adaptation of *berettino* decoration, popular in the late 17thC at Nevers and copied at Rouen, and also in England.

Blue and white The term for any white porcelain decorated in cobalt blue.

Blue scale A decorative pattern of blue overlapping fish scales. Also termed 'imbrication'.

Bocage Densely-encrusted flowering tree stumps supporting a group or used as a backdrop.

Body The material from which pottery or porcelain is made (although paste is more often used for porcelain). Also refers to the main part of a piece.

Bonbonnière A small box or covered bowl for sweetmeats, often in novelty form.

Bone ash Burnt, crushed animal bone that is added to soft-paste mixture to fuse the ingredients.

Bone china A porcelain recipe consisting of petuntse, kaolin and dried bone, supposedly invented by Josiah Spode II c1794. It became the mainstay of the English porcelain industry from c1820.

Botanical wares Wares decorated with painted flowers, generally copied from prints or engravings.

Brocade Decorative patterns derived from textiles, using repeated geometric motifs, abstract designs, or reserves enclosing animal, figural or floral subjects set against a contrasting (usually floral) ground.

Cachepot An ornamental container for flower pots. A smaller form of jardinière.

Camaieu Painted decoration in different tones of one colour. See also *grisaille*.

Campana vase An inverted, bell-shaped vase sometimes with a handle on each of the shoulders.

Caneware A pale straw-coloured stoneware developed in Staffordshire in the late 18thC and used by many factories including Davenport, Spode and Wedgwood.

Canton porcelain The term for wares produced and enamelled in Canton province for export to the West. Usually heavily decorated with reserves of figures, flowers, birds and butterflies on a complex ground of green, pink and gold scrolling foliage.

Cartouche A decorative motif in the form of a scroll of paper with rolled ends, bearing a picture, motif or monogram. Also used to describe a frame, usually oval, decorated with scrollwork. See also **vignette**.

Cash pattern A Chinese repeat pattern based on the design of Chinese coins with a square central hole. Also known as coin pattern.

Caudle cup In England the term generally refers to a bulbous cup used for caudle, a spicy, usually milk-based, porridge.

Celadon Green-glazed stoneware so-named after a character in a French play who wore pale green ribbons. Originally made in China during the Song dynasty (960–1279), it remained popular into the Ming dynasty. It was also produced in Korea, Thailand and later in Japan.

Chiaroscuro The term for decorative use of contrasting shade and light.

China A general term for porcelain derived from the 'China wares' imported into Europe from the 16thC.

In 19thC England it came to mean almost any porcelain-type ceramic.

Chinese export porcelain Chinese hard-paste porcelain made from the 16thC to suit European tastes.

Chinese Imari Chinese copies or pastiches of Japanese Imari wares, made largely for export from c1700. The decoration involves Japanese brocade designs and the typical Imari palette of dark underglaze blue, iron-red and gilt, with no spur marks.

Chinoiserie The European fashion for Chinese decoration and motifs, influential in the decorative arts in the 17th and 18thC.

***Ciselé* gilding** Thickly-applied gilding with patterns tooled in to increase the decorative effect.

Clobbering The Dutch term for over-printing blue and white Oriental porcelain in coloured enamels with designs rarely compatible with the original theme.

Cloud pattern An incised or painted scrolled design, often of square form, on Chinese porcelain.

Cobalt blue A pigment used in blue and white decoration.

Colloidal gold A form of gold solution, used in gilding.

Comb pattern A pattern, often painted in underglaze blue, that looks as if it has been made with a toothed comb. Found mainly on Nabeshima porcelain.

Commedia dell'Arte Traditional Italian comedy, with characters extemporising on a general theme. Characters were modelled in porcelain by Meissen, Nymphenburg and others.

Compendiario A form of decoration found on Faentine maiolica, painted in a restricted palette of blue and yellow ochre, generally with a sketchy design. Popular from about the middle of the 16thC and copied elsewhere.

Crabstock The form taken by a handle or spout on 18thC English pottery. It is based on the knotty contours of a pruned crab-apple tree.

Crackle A network of fine cracks introduced as decoration into the glazing of some Chinese Song dynasty porcelain and copies.

Craze Tiny, undesirable surface cracks caused by shrinking in the glaze, or other technical defects.

Creamware Finely potted leadglazed earthenware covered in a cream-coloured glaze, developed over a long period in the 18thC, but brought to refinement by Wedgwood in the 1760s.

Decal decoration Lithographic transfer printing, also known as decalomania in the USA.

Delft Tin-glazed earthenware. Technique introduced to the Netherlands by Italian potters probably towards the end of the 15thC. The town of Delft only became prominent from about 1650 onwards.

Delftware Tin-glazed earthenware made in England (called faïence in Germany, France and Scandinavia). When capitalized as Delftware, it refers to the same type of wares made in the Netherlands.

Deutsche Blumen Painted flowers, single or in bunches, used as decoration in the mid-18thC. The style is derived from botanical wood-block prints.

Diaper A pattern of repeated diamonds or other geometrical shapes on Chinese porcelain.

Ding Yao A type of porcelain made in China during the 10thC Song dynasty, with a creamy-white body and an orange translucence.

Documentary piece Wares that bear evidence indicating the origin of the piece, such as the signature of the decorator or modeller, or an armorial mark.

Doucai A form of decoration using overglaze enamels (red, yellow, brown, green and black) within an underglaze blue outline. First used in 15thC China.

Dry edge An unglazed area around the base of some early Derby figures.

Earthenware Non-vitreous pottery that is not stoneware. See also **tin glaze**.

Encaustic decoration Painting with colours mixed with wax and fused to the body of the ware by heat.

Enghalskrug A type of jug with a bulbous, egg-shaped body surmounted by a tall, narrow neck. It was popular for about 100 years from mid-17thC in Germany and Holland.

Faïence see **Delftware**

Famille jaune A type of *famille verte*, with a yellow ground.

Famille noire A variant of the 17thC and 18thC Chinese *famille verte* palette, with reserves set against a black background.

Famille rose A palette dominated by opaque rose pink enamel.

Famille verte A type of 17th and 18thC Chinese decoration largely based on brilliant green enamels. Much copied on European earthenware and some porcelain.

Fan-shaped or scroll-shaped reserves Reserves in the form of Oriental scrolls, often fan-shaped, bearing writing or printing.

Fazackerley A palette associated with Liverpool delftware from about 1750, and which includes a soft sage-green, manganese-brown, pale blue, yellow and red.

Feldspar A rock-forming mineral used to make hard-paste porcelain. A variant of bone china, Feldspar china was made from c1820.

Fire cracks The term for the splitting in the body that can appear after firing. Usually regarded as acceptable.

Firing The process of baking ceramics in a kiln. Temperatures range from 800°C (1472°F) for earthenware to 1450°C (2642°F) for some hard-paste porcelain and stoneware.

Flambé glaze A Chinese glaze made from reduced copper, dating from the Song dynasty. It is usually deep crimson, flecked with blue or purple, and often faintly crackled. It was used on 18thC Chinese porcelain and copied in Europe.

Flatbacks Mainly Staffordshire pottery figures and groups made from about 1840 until early in the 20thC. As the name implies, the backs are almost flat and undecorated as they were principally intended for the mantelpiece.

Flatware Flat or shallow wares such as plates, dishes and saucers.

Fluting A pattern of concave grooves repeated in vertical parallel lines. The inverse of gadroon.

Footrim A projecting circular base on the underside of a plate or pessel.

Frit The powdered glass added to fine white clay to make a type of soft-paste porcelain.

Fritware A silicous clay-bodied ware developed in Persia in the 12thC and used extensively throughout the Islamic world.

Gadroon Decorative edging consisting of a series of convex, vertical or spiralling curves.

Galletto A decorative pattern of red and gold Chinese cockerels, devised at the Doccia factory.

Garniture de cheminée A set of three or more contrasting vases, intended for mantelpiece display.

Gilding The application of gold leaf or gold mixed with honey or mercury. See also **acid gilding,** ***giselé*** **gilding** and **gloss-gilding**.

Glaze A glassy coating painted, dusted or sprayed onto the surface of porcelain and stoneware which becomes smooth and shiny after firing. The body then becomes non-porous.

'Green' Term for unfired ware.

Gloss-gilding The gilding of porcelain using gold in solution.

Graniteware A type of ironstone with a speckled appearance, designed to imitate granite.

Greenware High-fired Chinese ceramics with a green-cloured glaze, dating from the late Han dynasty (25–220 AD).

Grisaille Painted decoration using a mainly black and grey palette and resembling a print.

Grotesque A fantastical type of ornament originally based on the wall decoration of the underground ruins (grotte) of Nero's Golden House in Rome rediscovered in about 1480.

Ground The base or background colour on a body, to which decoration and gilding are applied.

Guilloche A neo-classical pattern of twisting hands, spirals, double spirals or linked chains.

Hans Sloane wares Porcelain with a botanical theme produced at the Chelsea factory 1752–57.

Hard-paste porcelain The technical term for porcelain made according to the Chinese formula combining kaolin and petuntse.

Hausmaler The German term for an independent painter or workshop specializing in the decoration of blanks, especially from Meissen.

'Heaping and piling' Accidental concentrations of cobalt blue that appear on 14thC and 15thC Chinese blue and white porcelain.

Hirado A type of Japanese blue and white porcelain made on Kyushu from the 18thC. The wares have a distinctive, milky-white body, a velvet-like glaze and superlative pictorial decoration.

Hispano-Moresque ware A highly important and influential group of lustred pottery, made in Spain from the 13thC onwards. The main centres were at Malaga and Manises, near Valencia.

Historismus A trend in late 19thC European decorative arts which involved the reproduction of many classical and traditional forms and styles, often in an elaborate way.

Hongs Warehouses in China by European traders, and used for storing goods for export.

Hookah or **narghili** A type of Middle-Eastern smoking pipe. See also **kendi**.

Huashi Literally 'slippery stone'. The Chinese term for a type of soft-paste porcelain most often used for small, finely decorated pieces.

Imari A type of Japanese porcelain made in the Arita district in the 17th and 18thC and exported from the port of Imari. Features dense brocade patterns and a palette of underglaze blue, iron-red and gilding.

Imperial wares Wares produced in China at least as early as the Northern Song dynasty (980–1127) intended for the home market.

Impressed Indented marks and hallmarks, as opposed to incised.

Incised Scratched into the surface of a piece. Used of marks and decoration.

Indianische Blumen German term for floral decoration on Meissen porcelain derived from Kakiemon styles. Generally 1720–40.

'In the white' or blanks Undecorated porcelain wares.

Istoriato A style of painting on Italian maiolica from the 16thC. The artist uses the dish or vessel as a canvas on which to represent some narrative subject derived from biblical, allegorical, mythological or genre sources, usually via an engraving. The most important centres were Urbino, Castel Durante and Faenza.

Japonaise or Japanesque The term for European designs c1862–1900 inspired by Japanese decoration.

Jardinière See **cachepot**.

Jasper ware A highly-refined white-bodied stoneware used by Josiah Wedgwood from about 1775. Jasper can be stained blue, green, yellow or claret. Copied by many other makers.

Jewelled decoration A decorative method whereby drops of translucent enamel are applied over gold or silver foil, in imitation of precious gems.

Kakiemon A much-copied decorative style introduced by the Kakiemon family in the Arita district of Japan during the 17thC. Typically, sparse and asymmetrical decoration in a vivid palette on a dead-white *nigoshide* ground.

Kaolin A fine white china clay used to make true porcelain.

Kendi The Persian word for a globular-bodied drinking vessel with a short spout, made during the 15th and 16thC in China for export to the Middle East. See also **hookah**.

Kinrande The term for a Japanese pattern of gilt on a red ground that originated in mid-16thC China and was much copied in Japan.

Knop Literally, the bud of a flower. Refers to the decorative knobs on teapot and vase covers.

Kraak-porselein The Dutch term for late Ming Chinese blue and white porcelain that was mass produced for export to Europe. Also, the segmented patterns which typically decorated the borders of this type of flatware.

Kutani A type of Japanese porcelain, allegedly made at Kutani in Kaga province in the early 17thC although most, if not all, was made in Arita in a so-called Kutani style. The style was revived in the 19thC as *ao-Kutani* (green Kutani).

Kwaart A thin clear lead-glaze applied over already decorated Dutch delftware to intensify the colours and create a shinier finish. It is equivalent to *coperta* in Italy.

Kylin A dragon-headed beast with the body and limbs of a deer and a lion's tail. In Chinese mythology it is a symbol of goodness. Also known as a *chilin* or *qilin*.

Kyoto A centre of porcelain-making in 19thC Japan.

Lambrequins Late baroque French ornament resembling delicate lacework or tracery generally pendant from borders. Very popular with Rouen potters (and at St Cloud) at the end of the 17th and beginning of the 18thC. It is mainly done in cobalt blue but sometimes heightened with red.

Laub und bandelwerk Literally 'leaf and strapwork'. The German term for baroque cartouches that surround a pictorial reserve.

Lead glaze A clear glaze composed of silicous sand, salt, soda, potash and a lead component such as litharge (lead monoxide).

Leys jars A type of large rounded wine-jar with shoulder handles.

Lingzhi A fungus symbolizing longevity; a common 16thC Chinese decorative motif.

Li shui A type of Song dynasty celadon wares.

Lithophane A kind of thin, low relief pictorial plaque that reveals a chiaroscuro effect when held up to the light.

Lustre A type of decoration using metallic oxides to produce lustrous surface effects. For example, silver gives a soft golden yellow while copper appears a ruby red colour. These oxides were applied to a fired glazed piece and re-fired at a lower temperature in a reduction kiln. A successful firing would leave a deposit of virtually pure metal on the surface creating the desired lustre. The technique was probably borrowed by Mesopotamian potters from Egyptian glass makers in the 9thC. From then on it was used on Persian, Syrian and Egyptian pottery as well as in post-medieval Spain and Renaissance Italy. The technique was revived by European potters in the latter half of the 19thC.

Luting Joining two or more elements in a ceramic object by means of a semi-liquid clay or slip 'glue'.

Maiolica Tin-glazed earthenware produced in Italy from 15th to 18thC. Although tin-glazed ware was made on the peninsula from the 11th or 12thC, it was not truly developed until the Renaissance.

Majolica Developed by Thomas Minton in the middle of the 19thC. It is usually a heavily-potted, complex, moulded type of lead glazes, including spinach green, dark cobalt blue, brown, ochre, often surprisingly in combination with opaque pastel colours such as turquoise and pink. A number of other factories in England, France, Sweden and America subsequently produced this type of ware.

Mandarin pattern A mainly red and purple decoration of figures within complicated diaper borders, often found on Chinese export porcelain mid-18th to early 19thC.

Manganese Mineral used to make purple brown pigments.

Mannerist style A complex and articulate manifestation of the late Renaissance. Employing twisted, exaggerated and bizarre forms often entrapped by strapwork and grotesques, it was highly influential in the decorative arts for almost a century beginning in the 1520s.

Mason's Patent Ironstone China A type of fine porcellaneous stoneware introduced in England in 1813 by Charles James Mason of Lane Delph in Staffordshire. A similar type of ware was later made by many other manufacturers.

Mazarin blue The English version of Sèvres *gros bleu*, introduced in the late 1750s.

Meiping A high-shouldered, short and narrow-necked Chinese baluster vase, designed to hold a single flower spray.

Millefleurs The French term for a type of dense floral decoration.

Mon A Japanese insignia.

Monochrome Decoration executed in one colour.

Mount A decorative metal attachment for porcelain.

Muffle The chamber inside a kiln that prevents wares from being damaged by flames during firing.

Nabeshima wares Arita wares made from the mid-17thC at Okawachi. Palettes consist of blue and white, coloured enamels or celadon.

Neo-classical A decorative style, based on a revival of Etruscan, Greek, Egyptian or Roman ornament.

Nigoshide The dead-white body and colourless glaze used for the best quality Kakiemon porcelain.

Oeil de perdrix Literally, 'eye of a partridge'; a pattern of dotted circles in enamel or gilding, used at Sèvres and copied by artists at Meissen.

Onion pattern A popular decorative pattern in blue underglaze employed at Meissen and other Continental factories.

Ormolu A gilded, brass-like alloy of copper, zinc and tin, used for mounts on fine furniture and other decoration.

Overglaze The term for any porcelain decoration painted in enamels or transfer-printed on top of a fired glaze.

Ozier See **basketweave**.

Palette The range of colours used in the decoration of a piece, or favoured by a factory or decorator. Also includes gilding.

Parian A semi-matt biscuit porcelain made from feldspar and china clay. Originally called 'statuary porcelain', it became known as 'parian' because of its similarity to the white marble from the Greek island of Paros.

Paste The mixture of ingredients from which porcelain is made.

Pâte-sur-pâte A kind of porcelain decoration involving low-relief designs carved in slip and applied in layers to a contrasting body.

Peach bloom A glaze derived from copper, ranging in hue from red to green. First seen in Chinese wares of the Kangxi period.

Pearlware A fine earthenware, similar to creamware but with a decided blue tint to the glaze. Developed by Wedgwood in c1779, and soon adopted by all the major potters in England and Wales.

Petit-feu Low-fired enamel colours developed in Germany towards the end of the 17thC and in France in the late 1740s.

Petuntse or **'china stone'** A fusible, feldspathic bonding mineral used to make hard-paste porcelain.

Pierced decoration A method of decoration whereby a pattern is cut out of the body with a knife prior to firing.

Plasticity A term to describe the pliability of a china clay.

Polychrome Decoration executed in more than two colours.

Porcelain A translucent white ceramic body fired at a high temperature. The formula can be either hard-paste or soft-paste.

Powder-blue A mottled blue ground achieved by blowing dry pigment through gauze.

Porcellaneous A piece with some of the ingredients or features of porcelain but which is not necessarily translucent.

Pratt ware Essentially a creamware decorated in high-fired colours including ochre, yellow, green, brown and blue. Made widely throughout Britain in the early 19thC.

Press-moulding The moulding of figures or applied ornament achieved by pressing clay into an absorbent mould.

Privilege The granting of a privilege by Royal decree guaranteed monopolistic rights to a potter for a limited number of years. An example is the privilege obtained by Nicholas Poirel at Rouen in 1644 and then transferred to Edmé Poterat. This gave Poterat and his family the right to produce faïence in the city for the next 50 years. The loss of this monopoly in 1694 allowed other potters to establish their own factories in competition with the Poterat family.

Puce A purple red colour formed from manganese oxide.

Punch'ong A type of greyish coarse celadon stoneware, usually coated in slip, made in South Korea in the 15th and 16thC.

Putti Decorative motifs of small, naked, male cherub-like figures.

Quatrefoil A shape or design incorporating four foils, or lobes.

Queen's Ware The name given to Josiah Wedgwood's creamware after it had found favour with Queen Charlotte. Subsequently this type of ware was extensively copied.

Raku ware An individually modelled type of earthenware made in Japan for the Tea Ceremony from the late 16thC up to the present day.

Reign marks Marks applied to some Chinese porcelains to denote the emperor during whose reign a piece was made. In many cases, however, marks were 'borrowed' by later potters from earlier, important reigns to add importance to their wares.

Reserve A self-contained blank area within a pattern reserved for other decoration.

Robin's egg glaze A pale blue speckled glaze developed in China during the 18thC.

Rockingham ware Pottery with a brown glaze, often mottled with yellow. Made in Britain and the USA.

Rococo A decorative European style that evolved in the early 18thC from the baroque. Typically featured asymmetric ornament and flamboyant scrollwork.

Rose Pompadour A dealer's term for the rich, deep pink glaze used by Sèvres as a ground colour c1757–64. Named after Louise XV's famous mistress, Madame du Pompadour.

Saltglaze A thin, glassy non-porous glaze applied to some stoneware by throwing salt into the kiln at the height of firing. The surface is faintly dimpled like the surface of an orange.

Sang-de-boeuf Literally, 'ox-blood'. A bright red glaze, toning to darker areas, first used during the Qing dynasty in China.

Satsuma A major Japanese port famed from the 16thC for its crackle-glazed earthenware with bright enamel and gilt decoration.

Schnelle A tall tankard with tapered sides made in the Rhineland, especially at Siegburg, from the 1550s up to c1600.

Schwarzlot A type of linear painting in black developed in Germany.

Scroll-feet A type of base that incorporates a scroll motif, either in shape or in decoration.

Seladon fond Meissen's sea-green ground used to decorate wares in the 1730s. See also **celadon**.

Semi-porcelain A term coined in the 19thC and used by ceramics manufacturers to cover hybrid wares similar to ironstone china.

Sgraffiato (or sgraffito) The term for patterns incised into the slip surface of a piece exposing the contrasting body underneath.

Shoki-Imari 'Early Imari' wares.

Shonzui A type of high quality 17thC Ming export porcelain made for the Japanese market and often decorated with brocade patterns and diapers.

Shu fu Opaque white porcelain with a matt, blue-tinged glaze, made at Jingdezhen in Yuan dynasty China and incised with the characters 'shu fu', meaning 'Privy Council'.

Sleeve vase A long, thin cylindrical vase.

Slip A mixture of clay and water used for decorating ceramic bodies and for slip-casting and sprigging.

Soapstone or soaprock A type of steatite used instead of kaolin in soft-paste porcelain from 1750.

Soft-paste or artificial porcelain A porcelain formula made from a mixture of kaolin and powdered glass (frit), soapstone or bone ash. See also **hard-paste porcelain**.

Sprigged wares The term for wares decorated with small, low-relief moulding applied with slip.

Stilt marks or spar marks Small defects on the base or foot rim, made by the supporting stilts (or cockspurs) used during firing.

Stone china A type of fine, porcellaneous stoneware first developed by John Turner of Lane End, Staffordshire c1800 and originally called Turner's Stoneware. Josiah Spode subsequently named the formula 'Stone China'. It is hard and compact, and sometimes slightly translucent. Many firms then began to produce this type of ware.

Stoneware Ceramic ware made from clay, and sand or flint, fired at a higher temperature to earthenware (c1350°C), making it durable and non-porous. Pieces are often saltglazed or left unglazed and can be almost as translucent as porcelain.

Swag A decorative motif of looped flowers or foliage.

Thrown wares Hollow wares shaped on a pottery wheel.

Thumbpieces The angled attachment to the upper part of a cup, mug or jug handle.

Tin-glaze An opaque glassy white glaze made from tin oxide; commonly used on earthenware bodies such as delftware, faïence and maiolica.

Toby Jug A tankard in the form of a seated toper clutching a mug of foaming ale. It first appeared in Staffordshire in about 1760. The hat is detachable and forms the lid.

Transfer-printing A decorative technique whereby a design can be mass produced by transferring it from an inked engraving onto paper, and then to a ceramic body.

Transitional porcelain The term for porcelain that was produced in Jingdezhen, China, in the declining years of the Ming and the early Qing dynasty.

Trek The Dutch word for the fine outlining, mainly on blue and white wares, mostly done in dark manganese. It is especially noticeable on wares painted in the so-called 'Transitional' style in the latter half of the 17thC.

Trompe l'oeil Pictorial decoration intended to deceive the eye.

Underglaze A coloured sheath or pattern applied to biscuit porcelain before glazing and firing.

Vert pomme A mid-green enamel ground introduced at Sèvres c1757.

Vignette An area of design or a picture that merges into the surrounding area.

Violette A violet enamel ground introduced at Sèvres in 1757.

Violeteers A vessel intended to hold herbs or petals.

Vitrifiable colours Coloured enamels that become fixed and glassy when fired.

Wall pocket An 18thC pottery flat-backed vase with small holes for suspension against a wall for the purpose of holding flowers.

Waster A deformed or damaged pot rejected by the factory.

Wreathing Spiral throwing marks following the contours of a vessel.

Wucai A five coloured Chinese palette developed in the Ming dynasty; contains underglaze cobalt blue, iron-red, turquoise, yellow and green enamels, usually with black outlines.

Yingquing One of the earliest forms of Chinese porcelain, often with carved or moulded designs.

GENERAL INDEX

C

N

S

T

U